ECOS

Ecos

CONNECTING WITH THE ECOLOGICAL SELF

Don Pierce

Heartwood Path

Contact:
Heartwood Path
info@heartwoodpath.com
805-689-7042
www.heartwoodpath.com

ISBN/SKU: 979-8-9857352-4-6
EISBN: 979-9857352-5-3

To my second parents, Fred and Agnes Pierce.

Contents

Read This First

Although anyone may find the practices, challenges, and understandings in this book to be useful it is made available with the understanding that neither the author nor the publisher are engaged in presenting specific medical, psychological, emotional, sexual, or spiritual advice. Nor is anything in this book intended to be a diagnosis, prescription, recommendation, or cure for any specific kind of medical, psychological, emotional, sexual, or spiritual problem. Each person has unique needs and this book cannot take these individual differences into account. Each reader is encouraged to engage in a program of treatment, prevention, and cure only in consultation with a licensed, qualified physician, therapist, or other competent professional.

Introduction

ECOS: CONNECTING WITH THE ECOLOGICAL SELF

Wholeness, indispensable in the maintenance of life, is complete in the More-Than-Individual Self. This entity, also known as the Ecological Self, is everyone's individual selves plus everyone's relations to all other beings, both big and small. It is both individual and communal. It is everything, every being, the totality too vast to see or fathom.

Without participating in this section of the Heartwood Path, or engaging in some other holistic personal growth program, you will not be able to make significant progress towards a satisfying present and a magnificent future. Although not mandatory, if you have not read the first three books in this series, you may find it helpful to purchase and read them at this time. **Kosmos** gives you the overview of the Heartwood Path and important background information. **Logos** keeps you from swimming upstream in life by presenting pertinent and important universal principles. **Egos** will help you identify and protect the important gifts that you bring to the world. This book, **Ecos**, helps you make that all important connection to the Ecological Self and, in the process, improves your relationships, makes you happy, and regenerates the natural environment. **Ecos** helps you expand your sense of self, and widen your relationships to discover how your relationships allow you to attain a more complete maturity. Until an awareness of the More-Than-Individual Self is achieved, all plans for world betterment will be sabotaged by the limited perspectives of those involved.

If you prefer to forge ahead, without going back to previous books, you can always go to www.heartwoodpath.com and press the link for one-on-one guidance. This service makes going down the Heartwood Path even more enjoyable and productive.

We are honored that you are about to bring these gifts to the world with the help of the Heartwood Path. Proceed by moving to the next learning station, a waypoint we call "Integration."

1

Integration

CONNECT WITH NATURE

We all live in the world. Although we can think of ourselves as individuals we do not and cannot live our lives in isolation.

As shown in the previous Heartwood Path book, everyone is unique and everyone brings different gifts to the world that are based on their own wonderful peculiarities. In addition to this state of specialness for every being, people included, there is an unavoidable state of being in a relationship with the whole.

You are, therefore, a life form, an actual creature with an inner self, and a person with a unique essence, spirit, and nature. But you are also a being that requires relationships beyond your individual reality to survive and to flourish.

The last book—**Egos**—was about your individual being, which we have been calling your "individual self." This book—**Ecos**—is about your "Interbeing"—your requisite relationships with beings, little and large, that together with your individual self makeup what we have been calling the "Greater Self."

All being, which means all reality, all life, and all actuality, is experienced as being in the world. We arise, happen, materialize, and ensue as creatures imbedded into the natural and cultural fabric of the world. While existing in relationship with other beings has become a literary cliche, getting a hold on one's place in the world is actually a considerable undertaking and the topic of this book.

Developing an extended Self that includes nature is the job we have to perform if we are to become, like Thoreau, Einstein, and Lincoln: humorous, realistically oriented, spontaneous, democratic in our views, and have the other highly regarded characteristics Abraham Maslow called the healthy, self-actualized person (Borden, 2014, pp. 101-103). Maslow's term "the actualized self" has to do with one's desire for self-fulfillment, the actualizing of one's potential. Of course, when one is able to see more, include more into one's perspective, and include more into one's frame of reference, one is able to expand one's potential and be more likely to achieve more, to actualize a potential that is broadened by a wider perspective, and to possibly actualize a better world for oneself and others.

We have to see the whole thing to protect the whole thing. Without an expanded perspective we cannot do much good beyond our limited view. Richard J. Borden writes: "Ecological awareness expands the context of life; it also enlarges who we are as a person" (2014, p. 250). The development of such awareness is the purpose of this book.

Some of what you read here will, at first, probably strike you as being either outright false, or, at best, merely a flowery metaphor. When you face intellectual conflicts, discomforts, and contradictions pay close attention. You will be on the verge of learning something important. Do not expect much analysis, but be ready for synthesis; for, as Jung says: "Analysis kills, synthesis brings to life" (Borden, 2014, p. 293).

Everything I say in this series of books is both true and partial. When you find the metaphors here and there do not gloss over them.

"Everything is metaphor," says Wolfgang von Goethe (1749-1832), "You cannot think without metaphors" (Borden, 2014, p. 272).

After progressing through the previous two books you may now be feeling that the Heartwood Path is a long unfolding blossom of information. I assure you that the current chapter is essential to the purpose of finding the place where happiness and sustainability meet.

The length of the Heartwood Path route is required in the interest of addressing a vital but difficult topic in a way that is both accurate and understandable.

Had we ended the Heartwood Path at the end of the last course we would not have presented information necessary for your success in these complex and troubling times. With each new batch of politicians arriving on the scene, hard-won environmental safeguards seem tenuous, at best. And happiness seems fleeting. Like the previous Heartwood Path books, this tack is another important step towards rectifying such problems.

A personal example will illustrate the relationship between achieving environmental stays of execution and the happiness of one person who cares. I, for example, was initially thrilled as a child to see my beloved Current and Jack's Fork rivers be designated as the nation's first scenic riverways. And the night we celebrated the vote to stop the dam on the Meramec River was the happiest evening of my professional environmental career. Unfortunately, my happiness over the achievement of "protective" recreational status for all three rivers was short-lived. Float these rivers on a weekend in the summer and you will see why I now believe we ought to have also been working on the psychological development of the river users, and why I sometimes think that park designation is an elaborate and unintentional way to destroy a natural area. That said, our problems today are worse than hearing disturbing cuss words where the pleasant laughing sounds of belted kingfishers once prevailed.

It has become painfully obvious that our global problems are greater than our typical collection of solutions. There seems to be no end to issues much more serious than the conversion of once tranquil gravel bars into rowdy beer "gardens." Disappointments over local protective measures are not the only threats to our happiness. Wars, terrorism, pollution, species loss, poverty, and many other international issues are robbing us of our happiness and the sustainability of the environment.

It may not seem like we are living in the best of times right now. Often solutions fall short. As romantic as it sounds, we cannot go back to the pastoral days of yore. This book will give you what is necessary to ensure that simpler pleasures and better days lie in your future.

Yes, better days lie ahead for those who follow the Heartwood Path! But not without facing some hard-to-accept facts, and not without being willing to make some significant changes.

Of all the changes that would be useful, two may, at first, seem like odd bedfellows. These often unlinked proposed changes will be revealed in this book to be both related and of paramount importance in the quest for a magnificent future.

To correct problems one has to first identify the issues. So, here they are: The first is a shortcoming of the environmental movement: environmentalists such as myself have been largely treating nature as a separate object when we ought to have been treating it as a fellow subject. This failure will be discussed at the next stop, Waypoint 4.2. The second issue is a shortcoming in most people's sense of Self: most of us develop our individual selves without also developing our Universal Selves. This failure will be discussed at Waypoint 4.3. After examining the problem within the environmental movement and the problem with most people's psycho-spiritual development, the balance of your time in this leg of the Heartwood Path will be spent participating in ways to put necessary related changes into effect, solutions that will lead you closer to that venerable place we call "Gladandgreen Junction."

To Gladandgreen Junction...

HumaNatureConnect Activity

Start-up Protocol

If this is not a day when you prefer to spend time in nature without an agenda, do the Heartwood Path Start-up Protocol found in the Appendix.

Setting Yourself On A Course To Gladandgreen Junction

This is a four-part activity:

First. Write down down a brief personal story from your past that relates to how you feel about the following statements:

"In convincing us that the world is composed of distinct subjects and objects (Descartes) insulated us from concern with the world and made it next to impossible for us to regard the world as anything but a storehouse of material" (Evernden, 1993, p. 54).

"The division of the world into subject and object is trivial. The world is an ingredient of consciousness" (Evernden, 1993, p. 58).

Second. In two or three sentences, describe how you would feel if you were to change the common phrase "I think, therefore I am." to "I care, therefore I am."

Third. To care actively in a way that leads to Gladandgreen Junction, practice "Awakened Doing." Begin by making a special kind of "To Do" list every day. At the beginning of your planning process each day do not just focus on listing mundane tasks that you want to achieve. Instead, first determine how you want to feel during the day or at the end of the day. Then, develop your "To Do" list in a way that it will most likely bring about your preferred feelings. Some days you may wish to feel calm, for example. Other days you may wish to feel accomplished. You are engaging in "Awakened Doing" when you allow your desired feelings to inform and set your activities for the day. Use the following format as you include on your "To Do" list action items that will make you glad and action items that will further the goal of environmental sustainability. Only after you have listed such action items do you make a list of mundane chores such as purchasing milk or washing the car.

Fourth. Answer the following questions: Can you tell whether stocks of ground waters, fishes, soils, and forests are dwindling? Can you detect increasing accumulations of pollutants and wastes? Can you agree that capital, energy materials, and labor are increasingly being devoted to exploitation of deeper, more distant, and more dispersed resources? Do you know that capital, energy, materials, and labor is being diverted to defend or gain access to resources that are concentrated in a few remaining places (such as Alaska or the Middle East)? Have you noticed a trend toward the deterioration of physical capital of long-lived infrastructure such as roads and bridges? Have you noticed increased debate or a reduction in investments in health care and housing to meet consumption needs and desires or to pay for debts? Have you noticed an increase in the debate over resources or pollution control? Have you noticed reduced social solidarity? Have you noticed increased hoarding? Have you ever noticed a greater gap between the "haves" and the "have-nots"? Although some of these questions may be answered in the affirmative for reasons other than human society overshooting its ecological limits, it takes absurd levels of rationalization to conclude that most of the problems listed above do not stem from ecological impropriety at the hands of humans.

Follow-up Protocol

For best results, write down your impressions of this activity in your journal using the Heartwood Path Follow-up Protocol found in the Appendix. Afterwards, consider sharing your interpretations with others.

Heartwood Path Axioms

Key Assertions From Waypoint 4.1

4.1.1.

It has become painfully obvious that our global problems are greater than our typical collection of solutions.

4.1.2.

To correct problems one has to first identify the issues.

4.1.3.

The first issue is a shortcoming of the environmental movement: environmentalists such as myself have been largely treating nature as a separate object when we ought to have been treating it as a fellow subject.

4.1.4.

The second issue is a shortcoming in most people's sense of self: most of us develop our individual selves without also developing our Universal Selves.

4.1.5.

Getting a hold on one's place in the world is a considerable undertaking.

4.1.6.

It has become painfully obvious that our global problems are greater than our typical collection of solutions.

Nocturnal Pilgrimage 4.1

For best results, write down your impressions of each night's dreams in your journal using the Heartwood Path Dreaming Time

Protocols found in the Appendix. Afterwards, consider sharing your Dream Tending with others.

Your progress down the Heartwood Path continues after the sun goes down. Soon after you fall asleep your dreamtime adventure will begin. Though to the novice it seems otherwise, your dreams are not separate from your waking life. As we shall see, dreams and your waking life are interconnected. We are greatly enriched when we notice these connections. They are practical gifts. The dialogue between the inner and outer worlds yields personal wisdom to anyone who follows the Heartwood Path.

The first noticing of the interconnection between dreams and waking life is often one's witnessing of coincidences between what one dreams and what one experiences in the real world. Dreams are often wisdom coming from the land.

The wisdom rides to us on our feelings, sensations, images, emotions, and natural senses. In whatever form they come, they will be fraught with meaning.

Paying attention to the apparent coincidences between dream events and waking events can be protective, informative, nurturing, guiding, or healing. They also often inform us of disturbances in the land or in the psyche.

"Considering the human earth relationship through the lens of dreams provides an approach to the global ecological crisis grounded in human subjectivity and evolutionary psychology . . . In the soft womb of the psyche lay the seeds of all creation. We enter that fertile darkness each night as we dream" (Chalquist, 2010, p. 187).

"Dreaming sleep," writes Karen Jaenke, "is an evolutionary function that allows an animal to upgrade its strategies for survival by integrating the recent experience of the individual with the total behavioral repertoire of all species encoded into the brain" (Chalquist, 2010, p. 190). Anthony Stephens writes that our "dreams nightly put us in touch with the wisdom of the 2 million year-old human being who exists as a living potential within the collective unconscious of us all" (Chalquist, 2010, p. 190). Jaenke points to three types of Earth Dreams, each illustrating "the process of restoring humans to a participatory relationship with the earth":

1. Earth Communing Dreams, which "reveal the necessity of re-covering psychic and somatic kinship with the earth;"
2. Earth Destruction Dreams, which "ask the dreamer to bear wit-ness to elemental destruction through the earth-body connec-tion;" and
3. Earth Healing Dreams, which "show the human-earth relation-ship is healed through balancing opposites found in the psyche and in nature" (Chalquist, 2010, p. 187).

As you continue to do the HumaNatureConnect Activities in this course:

1. look for Earth Communing Dreams that mirror, mother, and mend "the isolated and wounded soul" and "generate in the dreamer deep feelings of kinship between person and place;"
2. look for Earth Destruction Dreams that show unspeakable horror but also encouraged us the grieve and, thereby, open out hearts to earth kinship; and
3. look for Earth Healing Dreams that portray the balancing of opposing forces: "sky and earth, spirit and matter, fire and water, light and dark, solar and lunar, upper and lower, ascent and decent, masculine and feminine, North and South, hot and cold" (Chalquist, 2010, p. 200). Think of these dreams of opposite forces as testimonials to the ancient wisdom that recognizes the balancing of opposites as "a deep and abiding principle that secretly permeates all of life" and allows for the healing of the earth.

Set an intention for your next dream. Sleep, dream, and, as you tend to your dreams, look for examples of Earth Dreams.

More will be said about the importance of Dream Tending in the next waypoint, called "The Problem Of The Objectivization Of Nature," which also has a great methodology for helping you get more out of your outdoor experiences. I will also there begin to share some of my pertinent impressions about the usefulness of lucid dreams and what the Characters in them, many non-human, have taught me about being happy in a beautiful, biologically diverse, and sustainable world.

2

The Problem Of The Objectivization Of Nature

STOP TREATING NATURAL BEINGS AS IF THEY HAD NO SENTIENCE

The environmental movement is not reaching it potential because, like its opponents, it treats nature like an object. The way it often fails to recognize that ecological systems are more than materials governed by mathematical equations is one example of how this objectivization occurs. As if they need to be as credible as academic ecologists, environmentalists use mostly objective facts to gain public support. Since its inception, with a few exceptions, there has been practically no "sensuous intuiting of natural harmonies" (Evernden, 1993, p. 5). Like their opponents (the Industrialists), environmentalists see nature as a collection of objects, measurable through the use of numbers, when they ought to be feeling nature's unity in process as a universe of fellow subjects.

Environmentalists are on target when they herald that nature's wholes are greater than the sum of its parts. Without the guidance that comes from experiencing nature's rhythms, environmentalists turn to scientists (who focus mostly on the parts and the Realm of Exteriority—the behaviors and system of natural beings) for authoritative support.

Armed with such supposed legitimacy, we environmentalists too often feel that it is better to temper our emotional outbursts. We also feel that it is better to hide our mystical attachments to the balance of nature. But what is gained in public acceptance or the complicity of agreement is lost by not embracing the perversity of truth.

Often the eartHearts' sentiments about how they feel about the plight of nature are discomforting to others. If we should happen to alarm anyone (God, forbid!), it is typically felt that we better be armed with cold, objective facts. But something else is needed for the eartHeart's arsenal.

Does anyone really believe that detailed inventories and benefit-cost ratios are all that can be said about a natural being in its natural place? Such determinations are fodder for federally-required environmental impact statements which, more often than not, give the appearance of protecting the environment but actually serve the purposes of the developers. The subjectivity used by eartHearts is almost never included. What about someone's private act of love for a natural place?

All acts are facts. If something occurs it is part of reality. All events have certainty and actuality. If they don't they may not have occurred. But if you experience an occurrence, such as the attainment of guidance from your encounter with an attractive natural being, your experiencing of that occurrence is a fact. As you proceed down the Heartwood Path, do not allow anyone to persuade you that your experience of an occurrence you witnessed is not a fact.

The objective facts in the form of data from resource managers often demonstrate that conserving natural resources is good for securing our Standard Of Living—the indicator of the availability of stuff, from snow peas to snowmobiles. Subjective facts yielded by impassioned testimonials, inspired rhetoric, and emotional prose speak better than data regarding how fellow natural beings secure an excellent life. As a way to assess our collective environmental situation, the Quality of

Life indicator addresses the non-stuff, the immeasurable aspects of life, such as acts of experiencing open space, associations, and loved ones.

Like the Industrialist, the Environmentalist often resorts to the use of scientific data to justify that nature is for something. This approach is expedient and it is accepted by the public, at large. But, since Environmentalists and Industrialists differ over the uses of nature, a different approach may be in order. EartHearts realize that turning natural beings into mere objects is counter-productive. The objectivization of nature, eartHearts argue, does nothing to persuade society of the significance of the non-human and of the value experienced by a person in the presence of natural beings.

The values that EartHearts espouse are typically not objective. These values are not held as external to the eartHeart's own mind. For this reason, they rarely express, for example, monetary evaluations.

Instead, when speaking of nature, eartHearts focus on the subjective; that is, the value of nature in terms of the eartHearts' own opinions, tastes, and feelings. Doing so enables eartHearts to refrain from considering natural beings as mere resources devoted solely to human use. It gives them a more complete understanding of the ways nature gives them greater information; valued guidance; and physical, mental and emotional healing.

An eartHeart's sanction does not come from just science, nor from just mathematics; but it does come from the authority of her own subjective experiences. Remember, all acts are facts.

By using her fifty-four natural senses and focusing on her own impressions, the eartHeart bucks the trend towards a reliance on science alone. Her preference in this regard is actually a prudent choice. As Neil Evernden says, referencing William Blake: "The rise in science coincides with a drastic diminution in human perception, and contrary to common belief, in human understanding as well" (1993, p. 32).

Jungian therapist and author Ann Ulanov adds credence to our subjective linkage of personal growth, environmental sustainability, and personal happiness when she says that the . . .

"loving of life and life's sources is a stirring, from the bottom up, not to be denied. The inward journey to 'maintain a subjective wholeness and enlarge oneself—like the best of jazz,' mirrors reality . . . and . . . aims at happiness" (Borden, 2014, p. 292).

To increase their understanding, to add to their happiness, and to further the goal of environmental sustainability, eartHearts refrain from making nature into an object and support instead the making of bonds with natural beings that are regarded as fellow subjects. Eart-Hearts teach others that nature is not merely an expendable resource, nor an object with no sentience. Nature, revealed through bridges of awareness that span from mind to fellow subject, is, for the eartHeart, a partner for the all-important formation of impressions that result in both happiness for the perceiver and sustainability for the natural world. These results occur most easily to the perceiver who has over-come the problem associated with having a shallow or immature level of development, the topic of the next waypoint.

To Address The Problem Of The Objectivization Of Nature...

HumaNatureConnect Activity

Start-up Protocol

If this is not a day when you prefer to spend time in nature with-out an agenda, do the Heartwood Path Start-up Protocol found in the Appendix.

Correcting The Objectivization Of Nature

Write down how you feel about anyone or all of the following statements:

"One does not really experience the boundary of the self as the epidermis of the body, but rather as a gradient of involvement in the world" (Evernden, 1993, p. 64).

"Each secretly hears his own name called whenever he hears any region of being named with which he is vitally involved" (Evernden, 1993, p. 64).

"Appropriate ethical limits can only arise within a new Ethos, a new paradigm for understanding what we and other beings are. And an understanding of ourselves and others is the fundamental task of thinking" (Evernden, 1993, p. 69).

Describe what it feels like to have a territory.

Follow-up Protocol

For best results, write down your impressions of this activity in your journal using the Heartwood Path Follow-up Protocol found in the Appendix. Afterwards, consider sharing your interpretations with others.

Heartwood Path Axioms

Key Assertions From Waypoint 4.2

4.2.1.

Stop treating natural beings as if they had no sentience.

4.2.2.

Like their opponents (the Industrialists), environmentalists see nature's patterns as an object, measurable through the use of

numbers, when they ought to be feeling nature's unity in process as a universe of fellow subjects.

4.2.3.

Environmentalists are on target when they herald that nature's wholes are greater than the sum of its parts.

4.2.4.

All true acts are facts.

Nocturnal Pilgrimage 4.2

For best results, write down your impressions of each night's dreams in your journal using the Heartwood Path Dreaming Time Protocols found in the Appendix. Afterwards, consider sharing your Dream Tending with others.

As day turns to night, reflect on today's message and your time communing with nature. Incubate (call forth) a dream of your choosing, perhaps an Earth Dream. Be confident in the importance of Dream Tending to your progress towards Gladandgreen Junction. And learn a nifty additional method that will help you with tomorrow's nature communing. But first, some more about dreams.

Writes Karen Jaenke:

"If humans are to bring forth a new relationship to the Earth, its seeds will be in dreaming . . . Dispelling the illusion of separateness, our dreams pull back the veil, revealing the hidden fields of energies into which our lives are cast . . . Dreams restore connection to what is essential" (Chalquist, 2010, p. 188).

Make sure your journal is next to your bed so you can obtain the benefits of your dreams.

Pertinent And Instructive Gems From My Dream Tending Journal

I dreamt that Perky,

my pet parakeet,

whom I loved dearly,

was not real.

But I still loved him anyway.

And he appreciated that.

Lesson Learned: It is not the physicality of my bird, or of myself, or of my admired Natural Beings that is paramount. It is rather the psychic reality, and not the impossible independent physical reality of one's bird, of one's Self, and of one's admired Natural Beings, that counts. Whether in the field or in one's dreams, it is the Image, the impression, the articulated imagination that is the main common refrain of this series of courses, that comes closest to what is leading one to be happy in a beautiful and sustainable environment, and, most importantly, that is the consciously observed reality we experience and live. We are not really attracted to things but to the Images we and the things co-create. We make these Images on the bridge of awareness that connects ourselves to other fellow subjects, each with their own sensitivities and volition.

Look over the following information for a way to obtain more benefits from tomorrow's nature experience. We will begin with a four-part process which is a good addition to our Start-up Protocol for the Heartwood Path Activities. Use what we shall call "Integral Immersion" to help you attune your body to non-rational sensing modalities and, in so doing, help you to better commune with nature.

In addition to engaging in "Integral Immersion," you have two very good options if you are experiencing uncertainty or otherwise having difficulty in your pilgrimage down the Heartwood Path. First, go back over the pertinent information. Second, at any time, receive one-on-one guidance. This second option is free to buyers of the printed courses. If you have not purchased the printed versions of the courses, you may still purchase guidance separately. Obtain Guidance whenever you have a question or need assistance. It is afford-able, easy, and very helpful. We look forward to hearing from you. If no help is needed now, enjoy getting rid of your inappropriate mental projections by moving on to the first of four introductions to "Integral Immersion."

Integral Immersion, Part One:

Minimizing Inappropriate Mental Projections

To determine how well your nature communing is lifting your emotional discomforts (which take away from your sense of happiness), it is first necessary to focus on yourself, not your chosen attractive natural being. Find and face an attractive natural being but do not yet seek its consent to participate in a HumaNatureConnect Activity. Focusing your attention on your own self, pay particular attention to any vague discomforts. Invite these feelings forth. Name them. Write them down in your journal. Then, following the Start-up Protocol, do the HumaNatureConnect Activity, as usual, but pay attention to what happens to your discomforts. Wait for a shift within yourself that feels like a pleasant discharge of energy. As you commune with nature for the Activity, periodically re-examine what is happening to your named discomforts until you have cut through your emotional residue, feel a clearer frame of mind, and make way for authentic responses that co-arise in communication with the chosen natural being. For today, practice self-focusing on your named discomforts. In a subsequent step, described in the following waypoint, you will learn a technique used as you shift your attention to include your chosen natural setting.

When you are ready, proceed to the next waypoint: "The Problem Of The Shallow, Unextended Self." What you need for greater happiness and environmental sustainability is really starting to come together.

3

The Problem Of The Shallow, Unextended Self

DEVELOP THE SET OF RELATIONSHIPS THAT MEAN SOMETHING TO YOU

It is best for anyone seeking to make a difference in the world to extend their sense of self into their setting. A self that does not include its setting—its neighborhood, its habitat, or its environment—will be torn from its greater part. Without this extension, one will not feel the pain of others, one will not seek to right injustice perpetrated against others, one will not fully incorporate nature into one's life, and one will not put a check on personal behaviors that are destructive to others.

Freud stated that "in order to prevent it from being torn, the I has to aim itself on objects outside the self" (Evernden, 1993, p. 46). Call it "attachment" or call it "expanding the boundaries of the self," either way, each person has to love another being to remain healthy and to reach their potential. "Ultimately," writes Evernden, "we must all invest ourselves in the world" (1993, p. 46).

For most people, the problem with the development of self is a failure to make the kind of investments in relationships (with other people and with natural beings) that stimulate the broadening of perspective. When this failure occurs widely throughout the population not only do too many people become shallow but the world also fails to be evoked in the best ways possible.

"Our behavior is a function of our experience. We act according to the way we see things. If our experience is destroyed, our behavior will be destructive" (Evernden, 1993, pp. 48-51).

When we fail to make associations with others and, thereby, fail to extend or deepen our sense of Self, we begin to see things only from our own vantage point. This shallow sense of self does not incorporate others into our view. What we do not perceive is beyond our concern. Our experiences are not affected by relationships. Without experiences that demonstrate the sentience of another being, those natural entities considered beyond the self are quite often perceived as objects, beings without sentience or feeling.

It is easier to be destructive to an object than it is to be destructive to a fellow subject with sentence and feelings similar to our own. Multiplied by the vast numbers of people with shallow development, the resulting mass of destruction takes its collective toll on people's happiness and the sustainability of the environment.

To Address The Problem Of Having Shallow, Unextended Self Development...

HumaNatureConnect Activity

Start-up Protocol

If this is not a day when you prefer to spend time in nature without an agenda, do the Heartwood Path Start-up Protocol found in the Appendix.

Deepening And Extending Your Sense Of Self

Write down how you feel about the following statements:

". . . the wilderness defender may remember that it was his experience, not real estate, that prompted his concern" (Evernden, 1993, p. 143).

"As we come to think only with the eyes, so to speak, a different world unfolds, a world which, as it turns out, is much more amenable to manipulation and control than was the older construction from a balance of senses" (Evernden, 1993, p. 84).

Follow-up Protocol

For best results, write down your impressions of this activity in your journal using the Heartwood Path Follow-up Protocol found in the Appendix. Afterwards, consider sharing your interpretations with others.

Heartwood Path Axioms

Key Assertions From Waypoint 4.3

4.3.1.

Develop the set of relationships that mean something to you. It is best for anyone seeking to make a difference in the world to extend their sense of self into their setting.

4.3.2.

For most people, the problem with the development of self is a failure to make the kind of investments in relationships (with

other people and with natural beings) that stimulate the broadening of perspective.

4.3.3.

It is easier to be destructive to an object than it is to be destructive to a fellow subject with sentence and feelings similar to our own.

Nocturnal Pilgrimage 4.3

For best results, write down your impressions of each night's dreams in your journal using the Heartwood Path Dreaming Time Protocols found in the Appendix. Afterwards, consider sharing your Dream Tending with others.

Before sleeping tonight, continue to learn how to get the most from your Heartwood Path communing with nature activities by doing the next part of the Integral Immersion procedure.

Integral Immersion, Part Two:

Observing The Chosen Attractive Natural Being And Its Setting

We will next introduce a method for perceiving a natural being —Goethean Phenomenology—and then a second additional method— Defocalization—for perceiving the setting around a chosen attractive natural being.

Goethean Phenomenology

In the next activity, our chosen method for perceiving the attractive natural being will be Goethean Phenomenology (phenomenology being the study of consciousness and the objects of direct experience). Try this approach here, practice it during the next several activities and, if you like it, use it whenever you like on subsequent nature communing experiences. This additional technique is named after the "German Shakespeare" Wolfgang von Goethe, acclaimed author of the play *Faust*, who is also recognized for his scientific work on morphology and color (in English, "Goethe" is pronounced "Gerta").

Goethean (pronounced "Gertean") Phenomenology . . .

> "requires the element of time be re-introduced by the observer in a specific way because how a phenomenon changes speaks far more directly to its nature than any isolated moment, however detailed. A Goethean observer endeavors to connect with a phenomenon in as wide a variety of contexts as is feasible" (Evernden, 1993, p. 333).

Goethe thought of this process as "an artful empiricism, aesthetically placing the observer within the world of the observed" (p. 333-334). Goethe believed that natural phenomenon "deserve our attention" and called his free-giving of systematic attention "an act of love that allows us to perceive beyond the normal habits of modernist consciousness " (p. 334).

To follow Goethe's methodology openly and directly, perceive a chosen attractive natural being over time. Look for how the being, a fellow subject, changes or adapts to environmental variations. Doing so will build a sensitivity within the soul to gesture, mood, and tone. Paying attention to the being's bearing, style, and movement with enough extended observation will help you to perceive the being's signature. This signature eventually displays aspects of its being which may be hidden. As you build your sensitively to these qualitative gestures you will notice that what you perceive no longer seems to be separate from yourself. What used to be "out there" starts to have the character of sensations and feelings that arise "from within." These sensations and feelings arise as a kind of *language* in the space in between one's mind and the world around us. The result of this activity is the . . .

"development of your powers of subtle observation, and increased sensitivity to relationships between what appear initially to be separate phenomena, and a growing intimacy with your own process of knowing" (Evernden, 1993, p. 340).

Defocalization

As you sit with the attractive natural beings during your Heartwood Path Activities, keep your eyes alert but soften the gaze. Doing so allows you to see peripheral movements. A soft gaze actually helps you to see by refraining from looking so hard. Defocalization, contrary to monocular focus, brings the multiplicity of fluttering movements to your attention.

In addition to softening your gaze, scan your senses, especially your sense of smell and your hearing, but also any of the natural senses, bodily sensations, emotional responses, and spontaneous mental images that may add to your experience. Take good notes of all of your sensing capabilities. Continue this practice in place until you no longer hear the alarm calls of birds or until your senses otherwise tell you that you are welcome to the site.

After learning how to do Part Two of the Integral Immersion practice, prepare yourself for bed by choosing what dream you want to later call forth (or summon, we have been using the word "incubate") and by making sure your dream journal is within easy reach of your bed. To increase the chances that you will have a dream about a particular topic (in other words, to incubate a dream), before bedtime, come up with a single phrase or question encapsulating the topic you wish to dream about. Also formulate any actions you want to carry out in the dream. State the topic of your planned dream over and over. Then, without doing anything else, lie down to go to sleep.

Pertinent And Instructive Gems From My Dream Tending Journal

I dreamt that I died and all of the wisdom of the world, with an authoritative voice like Jesus, told me that my Soul was going to descend back into my body. But, when it did, instead of the expected shadowy Ghost of Myself, what I saw was my imagination returning to me along with my ability to be reflective, to dream, and to have fantasies.

Lesson Learned: Reality, whether it comes from forms in the Realm of Exteriority or from dreams in the Realm of Interiority, is both symbolic and metaphorical. Events, always the manifestation of meaning, do not occur unless they are my own or some other being's experience. They are happenings formed by the ability to interpret with love, intention, and a sense of what is right or wrong. Together with my Soul—which is really my imagination, my dreams, my fantasies, and my reflections—I can determine what is, what could be, and what ought to be.

When you are ready, move to the next waypoint: "The EartHeart's Task." Here you will learn about the importance of making other natural beings into fellow subjects rather than perceiving them as nonsentient objects. You will also receive Parts Three and Four of the extremely useful and important Integral Immersion practice.

4

The EartHeart's Task

MAKE FELLOW SUBJECTS

No human is entirely an individual. Each of us is also all that we see, all that flows into us from a myriad of sources, and all that can be considered part of our integrity. We are the land, the ocean, and the river. We are one with all life.

This oneness arises as mysterious and magical experiences that make us feel more alive. "By inviting in these experiences of interconnectedness" writes Macy and Johnstone, "we can enhance our sense of belonging in to our world. This mode of being widens and deepens our sense of who we are" (2012, p. 86).

This course concerns the compelling need of humans to reincorporate nature into our lives, to integrate our individual sense of self with the Greater Self that includes the Earth, to have direct experiences of nature, to use nature as a tonic for personal healing, and to find ways to make nature experiences lend meaning to our lives.

In order to find such meaning we all need to become clear about who we are. As you will discover in the following activity, who we are is more complicated than you may have previously considered. We often tend to think of ourselves as distinct individuals when, in truth, our sense of identity also "involves a connected self that emerges from our relationships, contexts, and communities" (Macy & Johnstone, 2012, p. 88).

To Make Fellow Subjects...

HumaNatureConnect Activity

Start-up Protocol

If this is not a day when you prefer to spend time in nature without an agenda, do the Heartwood Path Start-up Protocol found in the Appendix.

Describing Who You Are

Imagine describing yourself to someone you do not know. Imagine that this stranger asks: "Would you please tell me who you are?" Write down your first response in your journal. Then imagine being asked the same question again. Attempt to answer it in a different way. You may describe your individual self but also include descriptions of your relationships, contexts, and memberships. Keep answering this question until you have ten different responses about your More-Than-Individual Self.

As you did at the beginning of the last course, put your answers in a sealed envelope. It will be interesting to read your responses after becoming more aware of your unfolding More-Than-Individual self.

Follow-up Protocol

For best results, write down your impressions of this activity in your journal using the Heartwood Path Follow-up Protocol found in the Appendix. Afterwards, consider sharing your interpretations with others.

Heartwood Path Axioms

Key Assertions From Waypoint 4.4

4.4.1.

Make fellow subjects.

4.4.2.

We need to find ways to make nature experiences lend meaning to our lives.

4.4.3.

A dream is a pronouncement of nature.

4.4.4.

No human is entirely an individual. Each of us is also all that we see, all that flows into us from a myriad of sources, and all that can be considered part of our integrity. We are the land, the ocean, and the river. We are one with all life.

Nocturnal Pilgrimage 4.4

For best results, write down your impressions of each night's dreams in your journal using the Heartwood Path Dreaming Time

Protocols found in the Appendix. Afterwards, consider sharing your Dream Tending with others.

Use your quiet, pre-sleep time at night to learn the final two parts of the helpful Integral Immersion practice.

Integral Immersion, Part Three:

Inquiring About Finding Happiness And Sustainability Through Lucid Dreaming

Lucid Dreaming has two key aspects: 1) being aware that you are dreaming and 2) altering your dreams while you are dreaming. A crucial advantage of lucid dreaming is that your dreams are easier to remember for your Dream Tending practice.

Here are some helpful things you may choose to do while you are engaged in lucid dreaming as part of this practice:

1. Focus your dreaming mind on an imagined attractive natural being.
2. Resist further control by maintaining a phenomenalogical attitude by accepting what comes.
3. Suspend your beliefs for the time of your dream.
4. Increase your level of trust.
5. Resist also the temptation to think of your dreams as a story. And
6. Create a way to recall your dreams—a Dream Memory Warehouse—as described below and in the following waypoint.

Dream researcher and author Ryan Hurd says, dreams are "real moments in time that reveal the shared imagination space between the landscape and (one's) embodied presence" (Evernden, 1993, p. 256). "A dream is a happening in space, an articulation of space" writes Jungian analyst and author Robert Bosnak (1986, p.7).

Suggestion 6 above is a tool Bosnak proposes to help you recall your dreams. Bosnak suggests that you store the imaginal bits of your dreams someplace where you can later walk through the memory warehouse and recall more parts of the dream. With Bosnak's suggestion in mind, dream while sleeping, and, upon waking write down the various dream parts and store them in some sort of physical arrangement (of stones or twigs or leaves) at or near an attractive natural object. Then visit this arrangement on another day to recall the parts of your dream. Place within this little constructed warehouse, natural objects that represent the parts of the dream you wish to remember. Use the optimal function you receive by communing with your attractive natural being to help you use the arranged natural objects to:

1. recall the dream,
2. make associations with sub-conscious aspects of yourself,
3. amplify dream images into archetypes, or
4. animate dream images into living beings, as previously discussed.

When you are done with Integral Immersion, Part 3, remove the evidence of your cairn so that others can visit the site in its undisturbed attractiveness. This will allow nature to shine without the distracting blemish of your arrangement.

Integral Immersion, Part 4:

Describing An Attractive Fellow Being As A Subject

In this part of the Integral Immersion practice two important additions to the communing with nature protocol are added: 1) "What Is, What Could Be, and What Ought To Be," and 2) "Gratitude Sent And Received." Together these activities complete the Integral Immersion practice which helps participants with the why's and way's of converting natural objects into fellow subjective beings. The first of these parts makes sure that the participant is perceiving and reacting to the natural being in a way befitting a fellow subject. The second gets participants purposefully interacting about gratitude in an imagined give and take from natural fellows.

What Is, What Could Be, and What Ought To Be

Since the making of natural beings into objects is one key way how we got into our sad state of ecological malaise, we are in this exercise seeking to demonstrate how to buck the trend. When prompted to write down what a natural being is, do not speak objectively. Remember that along the Heartwood Path the focus is not on natural objects any more than it is on purely inner world fantasy.

When answering "what is?" focus on the bridge of awareness between a natural being and your perception of it; in other words, on your awareness of a fellow being. We will not be looking for observations of measurable facts. We will, however, be looking for your opinions, assumptions, interpretations, and beliefs. Another personal example will help you understand this exercise. Ms. Sermos, a popular teacher at Wydown Middle School near St. Louis, Missouri during the Early Nineties, on an overnight camping adventure I was leading for them in southern Illinois, asked me if I knew a way to encourage her students to make more fruitful journal entries. I told her that I did, and I now present what I did for her students for your benefit. During the field trip, she expressed her pleasure at the journal entries she was reading pertaining to our "What Is, What Could Be, and What Ought To Be" exercise. With journals in their packs, the students followed me to a beautiful canyon with a active waterfall, Jackson Falls. For the "what is" portion of the exercise, most students, since I did not tell them to do otherwise, wrote objectively, something like: "grey sandstone canyon two hundred feet wide, twenty-five feet tall, with a waterfall and lots of trees." That is an objective statement, an example of the kind of journal entries we are not looking for from Heartwood Path participants during this exercise. One student, however, spoke subjectively: "The beautiful, pristine canyon, open on one side, looks like it was made from the mold of the crescent moon. I wanted to take a refreshing shower in the waterfall that splashed on moss cover rocks, too delicate to be chairs." That's the kind of subjective, self-reflective "What Is" response we are looking for.

When responding during the "What Could Be" portion of this exercise, let your imagination run wild. Your answer may be about some needed correction, but it need not always be politically correct. Again, that same student's imaginative "What Could Be" response is a valid example: "There could be escalators from the creek to the top of the canyon and a McDonalds overlooking the whole scene."

When answering the "What Ought To Be" question the same eighth grader that imagined the McDonalds at Jackson Falls provided an example of how you may choose to respond. He said: "This place ought to be preserved so students can witness how nature works and learn something about themselves."

This exercise puts the *integral* into the Integral Immersion practice because the questions and answers reflect all four quadrants of the Heartwood Path Four-Leaf Model of Integrity (which is an adaptation of Ken Wilber's Four Quadrants). *If you need a review, go back to Waypoint 2.6: Coherence Chart.*

The "What Is" portion asks the responder to give subjective answers that correspond to the two leafs (or quadrants) in the right side (the top one being about behaviors and the bottom one about physical systems). The "What Could Be" portion is pertinent to the upper left leaf (or quadrant) that has to do with intentions.

The "What Ought To Be" portion corresponds to the lower left leaf (or quadrant) in that it has to do with ethics. For all of your subsequent journal entries, consider maintaining an integral perspective by including: 1) a **qualitative** description regarding you and your subject's behaviors and physical systems; 2) your intentions; and 3) a reflection about ethics. Doing so will make your journal entries much more meaningful.

Gratitude Sent And Received

This last part of our Integral Immersion methodology borrows from *naikan*, a spiritual practice from Japan that helps with self-reflection. To learn to do it properly, rather than merely reading about it, let's break from our typical format and engage in an extra activity right now:

Important Additional Activity:

Naikan

Visit a nearby natural place with pen and paper in hand. Spend some time perceiving a natural being and its surrounding setting, perhaps using methods described previously, or reflect on a distant natural being and it's surrounding setting. Write a love letter to your chosen being and/or setting. In your letter, express your reverence and gratitude. Consider everything that you receive from your natural fellow subjects. Then, imagine what your chosen natural subject might say if it could write a letter of gratitude to you. As usual, write about this activity in your journal.

After trying all parts of the Integral Immersion practice, incubate a dream for tonight's reverie (by mentally or verbally repeating the hoped-for subject of tonight's dream over and over again before falling asleep), sleep, and do your Dream Tending immediately upon waking.

Pertinent And Instructive Gems From My Dream Tending Journal

I dreamt that my carefree frolicking in a natural and clear stream was suddenly interrupted my the presence of a beautiful woman, dressed in a sheer white gown, who told me that species loss and other global environ-

mental problems were not the earth's benign attempt to teach us something
as the old invariably gives way to the new. We were not ready for such a
lesson anyway. She said we are, however, capable of responding to what
was actually happening: Her daughter, the earth, was being raped by
modern culture. Created by man, this culture could be changed by man,

"Get on with it," she said.

And then she said, curiously,

"don't be ashamed."

Lesson Learned: Mother Nature wants each of us to intercede on behalf of the earth. She wants us to avoid empty protests such as "occupations" and public theatre that serve to draw undue negative attention against the protestors. When the seriousness of the protest outshines the corrective suggestion, the recommended change of policy, or the answer to the problem, then the protestors are focusing too much on their own sense of victimization and not enough on what needs to be done to stop the dam, kill the proposed power plant, reject the pipeline, or save the wilderness. She wants us to instead "get on" with such tasks as lobbying for protective laws, watchdogging responsible agencies, and educating people about their buying choices. Having said this, she also knows that there are times when one simply has to show one's outrage vehemently, even when perfect solutions are evasive. She warns that loss of social status, less time for work and family, less time to build up a fortune, and stating stridently what the public is not yet ready to hear—all likely to be embarrassing or shameful—will be the unwanted consequences of citizen action. Sometimes, environmental protest requires the protestors to publicly shed the vanity of being admired. Other times environmental protest requires the protestors to even shed the surety of a so-called "sound position." If you cannot be sound, be unsound. But don't be quiet.

By reading this book, you will see the difficult things that need to be done, things that even your allies will not be ready to accept. You will be vilified when you request that others in your culture amend their planet killing ways. Keep your solutions up front, protest emotionally when no solutions are apparent, and persevere.

When ready, move to the next waypoint: "Becoming Whole." There, you will learn how to connect with the Universal Self and discover three ways to find that enviable place—that role—where your own happiness meets the world's great need.

5

Becoming Whole

CONNECT WITH THE UNIVERSAL SELF

Feeling the pain of the world, reincorporating nature into one's life, and putting a personal check on environmentally destructive behaviors are three ways to interact with your relationships, contexts, and communities. They are also the means we shall use to help you find your More-Than-Individual self and, in so doing, find your own place in the world. In participating in this part of the Heartwood Path, you will discover that one's More-Than-Individual self is actually a wonderful place where one's own deep need (for happiness) intersects with the world's deep need (for sustainability). We shall demonstrate that treating the planet poorly is just as bad for one's own health as it is for the planet's health (Winter and Koger, 2004, p. 122).

Feeling the pain of the world, reincorporating nature into one's life, and putting a personal check on environmentally destructive behaviors—our chosen ways to discover one's More-Than-Individual self—are made easier when one does not either focus on the concrete reality of objects (including natural beings) nor on living in a dream world where everything is considered to be just a figment of one's own imagination. Instead, to find your more complete self, focus on the

AttractiveNaturalBeingImpression, discussed in the previous Heart-wood Path book. The topic of natural attractive being impressions brings us to one of the most important things to remember throughout this book series and in your life:

Do not just focus on the natural objects.

Do not live in a dream world.

Instead, commune with attractive natural beings and blend the actuality of the natural beings and your experiencing of them into an inseparable AttractiveNaturalBeingImpression.

It is not the separate things, nor the separate inner world events that matter here. While on the Heartwood Path, do not contemplate outer world beings as separate objects. It is not the objects but the experiencing of the attractive natural beings that matters, especially when working to identify one's own more complete sense of self.

To An Ecological Self Identity...

HumaNatureConnect Activity

Start-up Protocol

If this is not a day when you prefer to spend time in nature with-out an agenda, do the Heartwood Path Start-up Protocol found in the Appendix.

Building The Focal Point

Practice building the kind of focal point that will be helpful to you in all of your subsequent HumaNatureConnect Activities. To do so, do not focus as we have been doing on the chosen attractive natural beings and do not live in a dream world by focusing solely on your inner world cognitions. Instead, blend in your mind the actuality of the natural beings and your experiencing of them into an inseparable AttractiveNaturalBeingImpression. You cannot do this activity with the being alone. And you cannot do this activity with random inner world feelings and thoughts. No individual being is going to send you guidance on its own accord, without your participation. Your own inner world thoughts may be helpful to you but, in paying attention to them alone, you will not be taking advantage of the amazing intelligence inherent in nature. To correct these short-comings, focus on the experience of perceiving the attractive natural being–an activity that requires both the outer world being and your own inner world impression of it. By building a psychological bridge between an attractive natural being and your own inner world, your thinking can more readily tap into the wisdom of nature.

Follow-up Protocol

For best results, write down your impressions of this activity in your journal using the Heartwood Path Follow-up Protocol found in the Appendix. Afterwards, consider sharing your interpretations with others.

Heartwood Path Axioms

Key Assertions From Waypoint 4.5

4.5.1.

Connect with nature.

4.5.2.

Feeling pain, being in nature, and stopping environmental destruction are three ways to find that place where one's happiness meets the world's need.

4.5.3.

Treating the planet poorly is just as bad for one's own health as it is for the planet's health.

Nocturnal Pilgrimage 4.5

For best results, write down your impressions of each night's dreams in your journal using the Heartwood Path Dreaming Time Protocols found in the Appendix. Afterwards, consider sharing your Dream Tending with others.

Practice conjuring up a dream for tonight's reverie. Incubate your dream for tonight by saying over and over what you want to dream about immediately before you fall asleep. As before, make physical representations of your dream images out of natural objects and place them next to an attractive natural object. When you get a moment, go again to your dream warehouse and attempt to recall your dream, make associations between your dream images and repressed or suppressed aspects of your memory, amplify your dreams by turning your dreams into recurrent symbols or universal images called archetypes, or animate your dream images by having conversations with the natural objects that represent your dream images. Doing these things over and over will help you make sense out of your dreams and possibly glean some guidance from nature through your Dream Tending. In consideration of others, if you are not going to visit your assembled natural objects within a day or so, disassemble them and turn the setting back into its original condition.

Pertinent And Instructive Gems From My Dream Tending Journal

I dreamt that I was a youthful member of a televised troop, like Disney's
Mouseketeers. But instead of singing and dancing in cute little Mickey
Mouse hats, we all marched around the courthouse in front of television
cameras as we carried environmental protest signs. We each wore a t-shirt
with an image of an endangered species that was being threatened by the
County's proposed highway project. Our opponents, standing across the
street, wore construction helmets. They derisively but cleverly called us the
"Head-On Collision Coalition." Our spokeswoman painted in the mind's eye
of the reporter our vision of the future county: rich in biological diversity,
having a public transportation system, and having enough controls on
urban sprawls to make the proposed highway unnecessary. She mentioned
that we planned to secure this future my implanting this vision in the
minds of the members of the public, one person at a time. Recognizing that
we were not stereotypical environmentalists, she asked what she should call
us.

Thinking for a moment, our spokeswoman replied,

"We are Imagineers, eartHeart Imagineers."

Lesson Learned: Image is the primary phenomenon of one's psychic
life. For eartHeart Imagineers the most significant recurring images,
whether in dreams or in natural settings, are of attractive natural
beings. Formed not solely in one's mind nor exclusively in one's
conscious observation, the recurring images pertinent to eartHearts
are formed on the bridge of awareness where one's own sensitivities
and volition merge with the image of the physical materiality of the
attractive natural being—a fellow subject that inspires your image of its

volition, sensitivities, and attractive presence whenever one seeks to have a connection experience with it.

When you are ready, move the next waypoint: "Eco PsychPhys." There, you will find ways to reduce the stress you may feel regarding the plight of the natural environment.

6

Eco PsychPhys

BENEFIT FROM AN UNDERSTANDING OF ENVIRONMENTAL PSYCHOPHYSIOLOGY

This discipline has a lot to do with . . .

Environmental Stressors

An example of an environmental stressor would be you smelling the herbicide your neighbor is spraying to control weeds in her yard. Knowing that she is spraying Round-up—a very poisonous substance— is likely to cause you to have a stress response that will likely have both a physiological and a psychological component. All such stressors activate the sympathetic division of your autonomic nervous system, stimulate the so-called "fight or flight response," increase the heart rate, cause the body to produce a rush of the hormone cortisol which, in turn, suppresses the immune system, leaving one more vulnerable to serious diseases. Eventually your neighbor zaps all her poison ivy and you no longer smell the poison and so your body's parasympathetic division of your autonomic nervous system helps you to return to a relaxed state.

Then you smell the fumes from the city truck spraying herbicides on weeds along the curbs. With the frequent spraying from your neighbor and the spraying of herbicides along the road in front of your house your anxiety has become nearly constant. You now have an increased chance for stroke and heart attack (Winter and Koger, 2004, p. 140). It's still only 8 a.m. Next, you need to get in your car and go to the job that you need because you have the house or apartment, that you have to leave empty all day because you have to work to pay for the mortgage, clothes, car, vet bills, and more. This scenario is now considered to be "normal," but our bodies have not evolved yet to handle the ongoing levels of stress we now experience. There is a so-called "mismatch" between our psychophysiology and the common lifestyles of those living according to the dominant social paradigm (Winter and Koger, 2004, p. 126).

The above scenario may be considered "normal;" but, if you think about it, you might consider it to be "crazy." Many people are reevaluating their lifestyles to examine its affect on themselves and the planet. People often become uneasy about their acceptance of the dominant social paradigm—characterized by acceptance of abundance, progress, growth, prosperity, and faith in science and technology. Such a re-evaluation is often preceded by the noticing of the discrepancy between conflicting ideas and values, sometimes pertaining to the rewards and costs of one's lifestyle. During such a reevaluation an uncomfortable state of tension known as "cognitive dissonance" emerges in which the reviewer notices discrepancies and, due to the discomfort such realizations typically produce, become highly motivated to take the necessary steps to reduce the tension. Such steps may include changing beliefs and behaviors—usually for the sake of maintaining an appearance of consistency (Winter and Koger, 2004, p. 54). You may, for example, feel that your status in the neighborhood warrants you having the belief about the importance of having a totally weed-free yard that is made that way by a toxic chemical. Or, you may say to yourself that, as important as you are, you deserve to have a single-use water bottle rather than to change your behavior regarding the purchasing of drinks in single-use containers. It may take some goading from others for you to recognize that you are controlled by cognitive dissonance at the expense of the natural environment.

Antidotes To The Stress Of Environmental Problems

Sometimes the stress of environmental problems it's so severe one feels the ancient response to either fight or flee. Just as changing beliefs and behaviors are the answers to cognitive dissonance, the answers to what one can do about the serious consequences of the fight or flight response include:

1. Engaging in physical exertion. Exercise allows the parasympathetic system to "provide more complete recovery" (Winter and Koger, 2004, p. 147). Living in cities designed to accommodate automobiles rather than pedestrians and bicyclists makes this remedy more difficult to put into place.
2. Active coping, such as solving problems. There is a psychological payback when one feels environmentally responsible for solving the nagging problem of solid waste by recycling, for example.
3. Optimism. Good things happen. Says the optimist: all the bad things that will happen will be postponed. If you are not an optimist now, maybe someday you will be. It won't count, however, if you get there after you got everything. We all know that if optimism feels good, not to worry . . . you'll get over it. If you get stuck on any branch of the Beanstalk of Spiritual Growth, don't fret . . . daydream while you enjoy the view. When you get down, assume good weather is coming but bring your raincoat.
4. Social connection. Exposure to restorative environments such as places without buildings and cars counters the fight or flight response. Natural places help us get away "from the demands of regular life, find fascinations that are inherently appealing,

offer a refreshing and inspiring sense of vastness, and offer a sense of compatibility with one's "activity preferences." (Winter and Koger, 2004, pp. 149-151). Such exposure to restorative environments offer cyclical solutions—meaning that they are not only good for the person but also good for the place. Experiencing restorative environments "in nature can also help to motivate environmentally responsible behavior such as recycling" (Winter and Koger, 2004, p. 151). And

5. Asking open-ended questions having to do with how you feel about what is happening in the world, as demonstrated in the following activity:

To Questions That Spur Full Responses...

HumaNatureConnect Activity

Start-up Protocol

If this is not a day when you prefer to spend time in nature without an agenda, do the Heartwood Path Start-up Protocol found in the Appendix.

Benefiting From Environmental Psychophysiology Through The Asking Of Open-ended Questions

Ask yourself the following open-ended questions:

1. What do you imagine the world to be like in the future?
2. What are your worst fears about the future?
3. What are the ways you avoid thinking about the future?
4. What are some ways you can use your feelings about the future?

Follow-up Protocol

For best results, write down your impressions of this activity in your journal using the Heartwood Path Follow-up Protocol found in the Appendix. Afterwards, consider sharing your interpretations with others.

Heartwood Path Axioms

Key Assertions From Waypoint 4.6

4.6.1.

All stressors activate the sympathetic division of your autonomic nervous system, give you the so-called "fight or flight response," increase the heart rate, cause your body to produce a rush of the hormone cortisol which, in turn, suppresses your immune system leaving you more vulnerable to serious diseases.

4.6.2.

Our bodies have not evolved yet to handle the ongoing levels of stress we now experience regularly.

4.6.3.

People often become uneasy about their acceptance of the dominant social paradigm—characterized by acceptance of abundance, progress, growth, prosperity, faith in science and technology.

4.6.4.

Answers to what one can do about the serious consequences of the fight or flight response include: engaging in physical exertion, coping by solving problems, optimism, social connection, and asking open-ended questions about what to do about one's plight.

4.6.5.

The dream world is utterly authentic.

Nocturnal Pilgrimage 4.6

For best results, write down your impressions of each night's dreams in your journal using the Heartwood Path Dreaming Time Protocols found in the Appendix. Afterwards, consider sharing your Dream Tending with others.

The next time you fall asleep try moving around in your dream to look at it from various perspectives. Doing so will gradually build up your ability to have the lucid dreams that can give you guidance from nature.

Pertinent And Instructive Gems From My Dream Tending Journal

I dreamt that I was looking at a picture of a little boy who just moved with his mother and brother into the fancy new mansion owned by his new step father but was being scorned by his mother for crying for no apparent reason. The little boy, perhaps a little confused by the sudden changes in his life, was going to be able to have everything he wanted except for his old friends: Davey, Huckleberry, and Flipper. There were no toys in the picture, as these were left behind.

Lesson Learned: The picture in my dream, like all Images, whether they come in dreams or in outdoor activities, are self-referential. You may be fooled at first but, in actuality, they are really about yourself. They are allusions. They call something to mind without mentioning it explicitly. It is impossible to take oneself out of any Image that is perceived. Perceived Images do not need to be verified by anyone else or by any external incident. One way we tend to attempt to validate an image—to give it its ground—is the imagination it takes to make myths—stories we like to live by. Images of demons in dreams can turn into uncouth friends. Little boys, yanked from their past, can be both pathetic and fortunate. Images are too rich, and too full of multiple dimensions, to be made into narrowly-defined signs. Do not collapse your Images of Dream Characters or Natural Beings into a sign with a single meaning. Instead, allow them to remain unfolded as an ever-blossoming, slowly revealing, and complex symbol. And don't pity the little boy, no matter how sad the Image of him appears. Eventually, as the myth goes, he recovered his "Rosebuds," Huckleberry found his way home, Flipper swims just off shore, and Davey, crazy with something, gazes at him through the eyes of the people he now serves. So it's a happy on-going life, after-all!

Consider doing some of your outdoor activities in protected wild areas such as the congressionally designated wilderness areas in National Parks, National Wildlife Refuges, or National Forests. Few places are so stunningly beautiful or so full of attractive natural beings waiting to satisfy your eco-yearnings—the subject of the next waypoint.

To move ahead after practicing moving around in a dream (which you can do at your convenience, day or night) or in a protected wild area, move to the next waypoint: "Eco-yearning." There, you will learn about transcendent experiences.

7

Eco-yearning

SEEK OUT TRANSCENDENT EXPERIENCES THAT LEAD TO A YEARNING TO CARE FOR THE ENVIRONMENT

More than fear, information, or knowledge, it is transcendent experiences—moments of extreme happiness, feelings of lightness and freedom, a sense of harmony with the world, and moments that are totally absorbing and feel important—that cause a person to want to feel an affinity with nature. It is the emotional experience in nature, rather than just the experience of nature, that is proven to be an important factor in motivating people to care for the environment. One way to express your affinity with nature is to mark your concern for it, as described in the following activity:

To Admit Your Pain Regarding Ecocide...

HumaNatureConnect Activity

Start-up Protocol

If this is not a day when you prefer to spend time in nature without an agenda, do the Heartwood Path Start-up Protocol found in the Appendix.

Acknowledging Your Feelings Of Ecological Loss

Determine what is being lost in nature, either locally or globally. Near your chosen natural being or in a special secluded place nearby look for natural beings (stones work well) that represent each of your feelings over lost aspects of nature. With these natural beings build a pile of remembrance—a cairn—wherein each natural being (stone) is a token of your mourning for loss in nature. Consider this cairn as a way for you to acknowledge your feelings of loss and grief. Return to this symbol and add a natural being to it each time you feel grief over what is being lost. Allow the building and visiting of this cairn to serve as a way for you to break up any discounting numbness you may feel over ecological losses. Obviously, this cairn will not "correct" negative feelings nor will it fix ecological problems directly, but that is not its purpose. Your Cairn of Remembrance Over Ecological Losses is, nevertheless, an important task of the Great Work! for it helps you express the validity and significance of your pain for the world. Use the validity and significance of your pain to take steps towards finding solutions. Be sure to disassemble your cairn as soon as you can so that it is not a distraction for others seeking to enjoy the undisturbed outdoor space.

Follow-up Protocol

For best results, write down your impressions of this activity in your journal using the Heartwood Path Follow-up Protocol found in the Appendix. Afterwards, consider sharing your interpretations with others.

Heartwood Path Axioms

Key Assertions From Waypoint 4.7

4.7.1.

More than fear, information, or knowledge, it is transcendent experiences—moments of extreme happiness, feelings of lightness and freedom, a sense of harmony with the world, and moments that are totally absorbing and feel important—that cause a person to want to feel an affinity with nature.

4.7.2.

It is the emotional experience in nature, rather than just the experience of nature, that is proven to be an important factor in motivating people to care for the environment.

4.7.3.

It is helpful to be able to attentively observe the transition from image consciousness to waking consciousness.

Nocturnal Pilgrimage 4.7

For best results, write down your impressions of each night's dreams in your journal using the Heartwood Path Dreaming Time Protocols found in the Appendix. Afterwards, consider sharing your Dream Tending with others.

For good dream tending it is helpful to work on the relationship between your perceptions (impressions) of the dream world and the waking world. As we have done one time before, we will have you address this topic, not by reading, but by doing.

Important Additional Activity:

Dream Or Remembered Images Vs. Waking Images

For this activity, make sure that you can return to the same three attractive natural being twice. To become better acquainted with the differences between dream images and waking images, observe carefully the transition from image consciousness (your awareness of inner world images in the mind's eye) to waking consciousness (your awareness of visual inputs from the outer world). Image consciousness is done by moving through your memory to the natural being of which you have the clearest recollection. Close your eyes and begin to recall all aspects of your most recently chosen attractive natural being and its surroundings. Recall textures, colors, sounds, smells, shapes, anything you can. Write down these recollections in your journal. Without too much delay, go back to that same natural being and, with eyes open, notice the difference between image consciousness (which is often filled with recollections of previous visual images) and waking consciousness (which is the awareness of the collecting of visual inputs in the Now). Repeat this sequence until you are remembering and witnessing at least three natural beings. Pay particular attention to the variations that occur at the moment you make the transition from recalled images (from dreams or from memories while awake) to actual images seen with the eyes in the Now; that is, between image consciousness and waking consciousness. With these teachings in mind, write down your impressions in your journal. Note if any patterns emerge regarding the differences between the way you remember the natural beings and the way they actually present themselves to you in the Now.

Do not bother yourself here with the making of interpretations. Dreams, and the recalled images in them, have the capacity to hold more guidance than you could ever understand at first brush. For now, just practice recording your impressions without shrinking them down into any narrow signs of meaning.

Pertinent And Instructive Gems From My Dream Tending Journal

I dreamt I had a big problem, or maybe it was a host of problems. I was not sure in the dream. I knew I needed the assistance of some powerful helpers. Not knowing what they were for, I had difficulty deciding who or what to summon. Suddenly, I entered a circular room, the Hall of Heroes. On the twelve doors that ringed this great hall there were dimly lit little words, verbiage that did not mean much to me: mentor, lover, magician, caregiver, orphan, creator, child, warrior, creator, mentor, ruler and rebel. Of the twelve labeled doors, three opened up, revealing to me a vibrant, fanciful, bright, clear, personified Image pertaining to the word on the doors. The Image of the Rebel appeared as an angry and resourceful woman who was poised to overcome the status quo. The Image of the Lover displayed the Archetype's devotion, passion and willingness to be sacrificed for her devotee or her devotee's cause. The Image of the Mentor suggested an Archetype that would use her wisdom and experience to prepare others for future trials. The Dream ended before the other doors opened, but it was reassuring just to know where these heroic helpers could be found.

Lesson Learned: The words on the doors fell flat. Just as there are no words in nature so too are there usually no words in dreams. The power of the Natural Being and the power of Dream Characters does not flow from words. It comes from the Images, particularly from very attractive or very unattractive Images. Be in love with the beauty of

Images of Natural Beings, wherever you find them. Being allusions, these beautiful Images of Natural Beings, full of the intelligence of nature, will inform you, heal you, and guide you. When the attractive Images are of archetypes, universal principles—all useful to one's life—will be displayed.

As you do the activity, psychologically reinforce how relaxing the spending of time in nature can be by diminishing or losing any time-obsession that you may have. To do so, put away your watch.

I often lead people on wilderness excursions that involve traveling on a flowing stream. During these outings, if anyone asks me the hour of the day I just say: "River time." If such an answer is not satisfying to you then you probably need more time in nature.

As often as possible, trade working on the clock for living WITH-OUT a clock outdoors. Doing so will be good for you. When hearing "Four o'clock" is less satisfying than hearing "Now, o'nature" you know you are making an important and healthful transition.

For the moments you are with your natural beings in their natural environments, forget about schedules. Do not attend to your calendar until you are back indoors.

Feel how luxurious it can be to experience freedom from time-pressures. When you are ready to proceed, move to the next waypoint: "Quirks To Problems."

There, you will learn how quirks in our cognitive psychology lead to environmental problems.

8

Quirks To Problems

UNDERSTAND HOW QUIRKS IN OUR COGNITIVE PSYCHOLOGY LEAD TO ENVIRONMENTAL PROBLEMS

How we all process information is crucial to how we cause and solve environmental problems. Occasionally we overreact and sometimes we under-react.

Some of the "quirks" in our psychological functioning that lead to environmental problems follow:

1. We are "cognitive misers." We only take in a small amount of the available information—just enough to navigate the situation but sometimes not enough to see and react to environmental problems.

2. We make unfortunate associations. Sometimes the associations we form in our brain are not helpful, such as associating used paper with the trash can rather than with the recycling bin. We tend to pay more attention to visible problems such as litter more than we do to more dangerous invisible problems like ozone

depletion. The notion of "Out of sight, out of mind," therefore, prevents many solutions to environmental problems.

3. We are more apt to seek to protect animals with neotonic faces (baby-like) than we are to seek to protect animals with non-baby-like faces.

4. We are psychologically "wired" to respond to changes and, if the environmental problem does not produce an immediate, noticeable change, we often tend to discount or ignore its importance of issue.

5. We are psychologically predisposed to being motivated by short-term, concentrated benefits rather than by long-term widespread costs (future benefits are considered less attention-worthy than short-term costs). This pervasive limitation in our perceptual capacity makes many environmental measures hard for many people to accept readily.

6. We are easily distracted by irrelevant information, a psychological tendency that allows opponents of environmental measures to put up "smokescreens" (in the form of other provocative news or spreading false perceptions of wrongdoing) as a way to distract the public from seeking meaningful reforms.

7. We have a hard time comprehending very small or very large numbers. This quantitative illiteracy makes it difficult for many people to understand the severity of pollution risks, for example. (Winter and Koger, 2004, 154-174).

8. We tend to limit our sense of self to include only our individual aspect, leaving out our broader, ecological self—a cognitive quirk addressed in the following activity.

Getting to know any psychological quirks that you may have is an important step in learning how you may need to think differently in order to get better results. After looking over the above list, you may find yourself going a little deeper into the information that is available, you may find yourself caring more than you used to about animals that do not have cute faces, you may find yourself recognizing that you are being subjected to "smokescreens" as a way to maintain the un-wanted status quo, or you may begin to start thinking about important longterm consequences. It may take some extra effort to overcome the psychological quirks that are so common amongst people, but working on them can, at best, help to alleviate significant environmental prob-lems and, at least, begin a process that will help you to re-connect with your More-Than-Individual Self. Until this happens a lot more, there is little hope for protecting that which is not considered us; namely, the environment.

To An Admission Of Your Own Inner World Weirdness...

HumaNatureConnect Activity

Start-up Protocol

If this is not a day when you prefer to spend time in nature with-out an agenda, do the Heartwood Path Start-up Protocol found in the Appendix.

Identifying Your Cognitive Quirk Of Obscuring Your Sense Of An Ecological – A Self Imposed Limitation That Leads To Environmental Problems

Write down in your journal your responses to the following statements:

Says Arne Naess:

" . . . the extensive moralizing within the ecological movement has given the public the false impression that they are being asked to make a sacrifice—to show more responsibility, more concern and a nicer moral standard. But all of that would flow naturally and easily if the self were widened and deepened so that protection of nature was felt and perceived as protection of our very selves" (Macy and Johnstone, 2012, p. 86).

Immanuel Kant points out an important distinction for you to consider now:

"We tend to perform moral action out of a sense of duty or obligation. In contrast, we perform beautiful acts when we do what is morally right because it is attractive to us, the action motivated more by desire than duty. When our connected self is well developed, we are more often drawn to beautiful acts. When we lose our sense of felt connectedness, we miss out on this sort of beauty, with tragic consequences" (Macy and Johnstone, 2012, p. 91).

Write down how you relate these statements to your understanding of Natural Attraction Ecology, which identifies the strands in the web of life, indicates that they function according attractions, and maintains that all relationships are held together in the web of life because they are attracted to do so. *For more about Natural Attraction Ecology, return to Waypoint 1.27: Basis and Basics in the Heartwood Path book:* **Kosmos.**

After writing down your responses, imagine what you would say to a stranger who asks: "Who are you?" Write down how, if at all, you define yourself as a "flow of becoming" rather than a "fixed thing with characteristics that can't be changed" (Macy and Johnstone, 2012, p. 93). Describe in your journal what happens through you. Describe how you feel about the notion that your emotions do not arise solely from within your individual self but come from your Ecological Self as well.

Follow-up Protocol

For best results, write down your impressions of this activity in your journal using the Heartwood Path Follow-up Protocol found in the Appendix. Afterwards, consider sharing your interpretations with others.

Heartwood Path Axioms

Key Assertions From Waypoint 4.8

4.8.1.

How we all process information is crucial to how we cause and solve environmental problems.

4.8.2.

We are "cognitive misers," only taking in a small amount of the available information; we make unfortunate associations (such as perceiving used paper as worthless trash rather than as recyclable material); we tend pay more attention to visible problems such as litter than we do to more dangerous invisible problems like ozone depletion; and we are more apt to seek to protect animals with baby-like than we are to seek to protect animals with non-baby-like faces.

4.8.3.

We are psychologically "wired" to respond to changes and, if the environmental problem does not produce an immediate, noticeable change, we often tend to discount or ignore its importance; we are psychologically predisposed to being motivated by short-term, concentrated benefits rather than by long-term widespread costs (future benefits are considered less attention-worthy than short-term costs); and we are easily distracted by irrelevant information, a psychological tendency that allows opponents of environmental measures to put up

"smokescreens" as a way to distract the public from seeking meaningful reforms.

4.8.4.

Our inability to comprehend very large and very small numbers makes it difficult for many people to understand the severity of pollution risks.

4.8.5.

Carefully experience the transition between sleeping and waking.

Nocturnal Pilgrimage 4.8

For best results, write down your impressions of each night's dreams in your journal using the Heartwood Path Dreaming Time Protocols found in the Appendix. Afterwards, consider sharing your Dream Tending with others.

Tonight, before you dream, establish the intention to wake up consciously; that is, according to the following procedure:

1. Really experience the transition between sleeping and waking.
2. If possible, wake up before your alarm goes off.
3. Remain exactly in the position you're in and observe the way sleeping changes to waking.
4. Feel how your body wakes up. Where are the tensions? Keep doing this for a few days without trying to remember any dreams.
5. Just observe the moment of waking, letting all distracting thoughts fade away.

6. Write down your impressions in your journal.

While doing the next outdoor activity, consider leaving your money indoors. You cannot usually spend money in nature. Compare the artificial and symbolic nature of the things you can buy with money to the soothing naturalness of the attractive beings you find outdoors.

When ready, move to the next waypoint: "Quit The Quirks." There, you will learn how eartHearts obtain better information, act on the information, correct reasoning errors, and refuse to leave solutions to the experts.

9

Quit The Quirks

USE THE WAYS TO OVERCOME THE QUIRKS THAT LEAD TO TROUBLE

The first step in overcoming the previously stated psychological tendencies is to recognize that they can deceive us. Three other ways to overcome these quirks in our cognitive functioning include:

1. getting better information and then acting on it,
2. noticing and then correcting the reasoning errors listed in the previous waypoint, and
3. refusing to leave environmental solutions to so-called experts by taking more responsibility upon oneself (Winter and Koger, 2004, pp. 174-175).

We can, with proper motivation, dramatically shift the way we think about the planet. We can recognize our psychological "quirks," make conscious decisions that overcome these tendencies, and encourage ourselves and others to engage in sound environmental behaviors. One of the best ways to so engage is to overcome what has become the most common response to global issues—"powerlessness" (Macy and

Johnstone, 2012, p. 105). In the face of local and global environmental problems the common tendency is to feel helpless, weak, unpersuasive, voiceless, and ineffective. To begin the effort to overcome these types of powerlessness, do the following activity and continue through this series of courses to its end. Along the way you will encounter how to go into action by yourself (the topic of Heartwood Path Course: **Volitos**), how to be effective in a group (the topic of the Heartwood Path Course: **Collectivos**), and how to persevere (the topic of the Heartwood Path Course: **Remeos**).

To Feel More Ardent...

HumaNatureConnect Activity

Start-up Protocol

If this is not a day when you prefer to spend time in nature without an agenda, do the Heartwood Path Start-up Protocol found in the Appendix.

Overcoming The Sense Of Powerlessness

Write down the ways the Great Work! of leading yourself and others to that place where personal happiness meets planetary health can happen through you. When doing so, describe more about what you can give rather than just about what you can gain.

Follow-up Protocol

For best results, write down your impressions of this activity in your journal using the Heartwood Path Follow-up Protocol found in the Appendix. Afterwards, consider sharing your interpretations with others.

Heartwood Path Axioms

Key Assertions From Waypoint 4.9

4.9.1.

Recognize that we can be deceived by our psychological tendencies.

4.9.2.

Three ways to overcome the quirks in our cognitive functioning include: 1) getting better information and then acting on it, 2) noticing and then correcting reasoning errors, and 3) refusing to leave environmental solutions to so-called experts by taking more responsibility upon oneself.

4.9.3.

Work to overcome any sense of powerlessness.

Nocturnal Pilgrimage 4.9

For best results, write down your impressions of each night's dreams in your journal using the Heartwood Path Dreaming Time Protocols found in the Appendix. Afterwards, consider sharing your Dream Tending with others.

Before heading to the next waypoint, sleep and dream. Make dream associations. Look for archetypes in your dreams. Pull out dream images and animate them by turning them into three-dimensional Dream Figures.

Pertinent And Instructive Gems From My Dream Tending Journal

I dreamt I saw a huge tornado moving across the floodplain in my direction. In this swirling storm were both my memories and the various physical subjects of my most recent attention. When the tornado touched ground right before me, it's power ran out and, emerging from the dust, was a lady dressed in ancient warrior garb. I asked her what I could do for her and, although she used no words, she informed me that I would not be able to preserve enough places fast enough to save the earth. When she placed her hands on my temples I knew I had to change the destinies of inscapes and not just landscapes.

Lesson Learned: We cannot afford to wait to make significant changes in the way we treat the Earth. Given the multitude of dire projections, we can no longer wait for a miracle to save us. Time for that has long passed. Besides, you and I and others seeking to protect the planet are the miracle we have been waiting for.

Ours is the generation that needs to choose to protect the last wilderness areas, to keep the air and water clean, to protect all species of wildlife; to save the expansiveness of forests, and to learn to live without such a dependence on petroleum. We no longer have the luxury of leaving the problem of environmental degradation to future generations to solve.

When you move outdoors to do the following activity, consider going to a place that is free from vehicle noise, machinery racket, or other obtrusive artificial annoyances. Note how you feel when you are relatively free of artificial noise.

When ready, move to the next waypoint: "Carry On." There, you will learn of the value of thinking more about sustainability and less about consumption.

10

Carry On

THINK ABOUT SUSTAINABILITY RATHER THAN CONSUMPTION

Sustainability and happiness are the two chief attributes of Gladand-green Junction—the metaphorical destination of the Heartwood Path. In the previous Heartwood Path book, we talked a lot about happiness. Here, we will focus on sustainability.

We live in a world of deep imbalances—too much carbon in the atmosphere, dwindling supplies of drinking water, lost topsoil, and many other disturbing disparities. The plight of the environment is worrisome because we see so many examples of inequities and pollution we fear that we ourselves and, even more upsetting, our children will not have ample opportunities to flourish.

A sustainable ecosystem, according to college professor Peter Senge, "is one that generates a level of health, vitality, and resilience that allows its members to both live and evolve" (Ehrenfeld, 2008, p. xiv.). It is very difficult to achieve sustainability when so many of us are compulsive shoppers, when a minuscule fraction of what we buy is still being used six months later, and when we see ourselves as being apart from nature.

There is no rule that we have to continue to think of the Earth in mostly consumptive and mechanistic ways. Instead, we can, if properly tutored, think about sustainability and ecological systems. We can, if helped by good teachers, expand our time frame for decisions to include consideration for those who, as some joke, have not done a darn thing for us—namely, future generations. We can, if properly instructed, shift our ethics toward an Earth-friendly belief system that benefits the planet, its people, and the economy. We can learn, if properly educated, that all of our actions are causes that affect other people and the planet as a whole. We all need to learn nature's lessons in cause and effect right now.

The environmental crisis is severe and immediate. The average person does not have access to the information or resources needed to avert exposure to toxins and so we commonly end up doing too little too late to protect ourselves.

To The Cognition Of Preservation Instead Of Depletion...

HumaNatureConnect Activity

Start-up Protocol

If this is not a day when you prefer to spend time in nature without an agenda, do the Heartwood Path Start-up Protocol found in the Appendix.

Thinking About Sustainability Rather Than Consumption

Write yourself a letter from Mother Earth. As you do so, do not put much thinking into it. Just let the words come. Here's one way to start: "Dear (insert your name): This is your Earth Mother writing . . ."

Follow-up Protocol

For best results, write down your impressions of this activity in your journal using the Heartwood Path Follow-up Protocol found in the Appendix. Afterwards, consider sharing your interpretations with others.

Heartwood Path Axioms

Key Assertions From Waypoint 4.10

4.10.1.

We can, if properly tutored, think about sustainability and ecological systems.

4.10.2.

We can expand our time frame for decisions to include consideration for future generations.

4.10.3.

We can shift our ethics toward an Earth-friendly belief system that benefits the planet, its people, and the economy.

4.10.4.

The average person does not have access to the information or resources needed to avert exposure to toxins and so we commonly end up doing too little too late to protect ourselves.

4.10.5.

Upon waking, do not change your position, look at your most vivid dream for a moment, with eyes closed, reach for your pen

and paper, write down whatever you can about the dream, always trying to move as little as possible.

Nocturnal Pilgrimage 4.10

For best results, write down your impressions of each night's dreams in your journal using the Heartwood Path Dreaming Time Protocols found in the Appendix. Afterwards, consider sharing your Dream Tending with others.

Ever watch a hunting dog observing its prey? It lies motionless. That is how you can do a better job recalling your dreams. It seems to me that dreams are encoded into the position the body was in during the dream. For this reason, create a quiet Zen-like atmosphere during the motions right after you wake up from sleep. Do not be jolted by a loud alarm. Do not immediately jump out of bed, make coffee, or check your cell phone. These sorts of things will make it very difficult to remember your dreams, possibly because your mind will begin to process your actions rather than recall your dreams. Instead of immediately scurrying around upon waking, do not change your position. Dreams will come to you more easily if you retain the position your body was in during the dream. Since you probably were dreaming in the position your body was in upon waking, do not move as you recall your most recent dreams for a moment. With eyes closed, reach for your pen and paper and write down whatever you can about the dream. Any fragments will be helpful later on. If nothing comes up as you remain motionless for two to three minutes, pause, and then gently assume another position that is common for you during sleep. Again, wait for more dream images to be recalled. Write down your recalled dream images promptly, always trying to move as little as possible. The general rule is to remain motionless in bed as you attempt to remember your dreams and write about them in your journal.

After trying this dream recall method, move to the next waypoint: "Eco Action." When you move to a natural place for your next activity, begin the practice of minimizing how much technology you bring into the wild. Make sure you are unplugged from the power grid. For a brief time, simplify your existence. Bring nothing that will distract you from your natural pathway of self-fulfillment. Doing so will help to eliminate any hurdles you may have erected between yourself and the natural community.

11

Eco Action

PUSH FOR ENVIRONMENTAL ACTION NOW

We are present at the end of an enormous worldwide orgy of consumption and defilement. Because of our gluttony and carelessness, the next generation cannot have anything like the reckless hoedown we are having. If we care at all about our descendants, we will have to give up our current, ill-conceived primary relationship with the Earth; that is, we will have to stop relating to it primarily as a thing to be used. This way of relating is causing the biological structure of the Earth to be broadly disarranged.

To Press For A Movement That Saves The Earth…

HumaNatureConnect Activity

Start-up Protocol

If this is not a day when you prefer to spend time in nature without an agenda, do the Heartwood Path Start-up Protocol found in the Appendix.

Pushing For Environmental Action

Write down what it takes for you to get going in a bigger way with environmental actions. Write down both what it takes from the outside to empower yourself and what you do yourself to feel empowered. Remember, power is as much about what you do as it is about what you have. Also, consider that your empowerment is bolstered when you think "We can" and not "I can't."

Follow-up Protocol

For best results, write down your impressions of this activity in your journal using the Heartwood Path Follow-up Protocol found in the Appendix. Afterwards, consider sharing your interpretations with others.

Heartwood Path Axioms

Key Assertions From Waypoint 4.11

4.11.1.

Those seeking to protect the environment are the miracle the earth needs.

4.11.2.

Our gluttony and carelessness means the next generation cannot have anything like the reckless hoedown we are having.

4.11.3.

If we care at all about our descendants, we will have to give up our current, ill-conceived primary relationship with the Earth; that is, stop relating to it primarily as a thing to be used.

Nocturnal Pilgrimage 4.11

For best results, write down your impressions of each night's dreams in your journal using the Heartwood Path Dreaming Time Protocols found in the Appendix. Afterwards, consider sharing your Dream Tending with others.

Sometimes you will wake up in the middle of the night with a dream that has so much to it you imagine that you cannot recall all of it. In that case, record only the most salient features. When you awaken in the morning, look over your scribbles and attempt to walk through the dream again in your imagination. Try this technique tonight.

Pertinent And Instructive Gems From My Dream Tending Journal

I dreamt my Boulder Buddy from Lower Rock Creek in Missouri spoke to me, asking:

"Am I speaking for you or are you speaking for me?"

After thinking for a moment, I replied:

"It's all a matter of perspective, like looking at a huge ball from the right side and then the left side. I can think as if you are independent of me and I can think as if I am separate from you but really we are in our relationships reliant upon one another. Each of us has a measure of individuality

and we are both inseparable from each other and the universe. It is, at once,
as if we are separate and as if we are one."

In silence, we both behaved as if we understood.

Lesson Learned: When dealing with living images, as one does when one communes with nature and as one does when one interacts in dreams, one needs to be tolerant of "as-if" statements. A Dream Character might say "its *as if* you are speaking for me." And that is acceptable, because it is *as if* you are. Likewise, a Natural Being, often referred to as a "stone" by those who do not prohibit themselves from labeling, might say "The world is contained in you." In hearing these words, you will be wise to add to the beginning of the statement: "It's *as if*..." Doing so does not negate the expression. It returns the statement into a metaphor, a brief poetic myth, the voice of one's Soul. This returning is as it ought to be. It is *as if* the Soul speaks through Images, whether they are Dream Characters in the image of Natural Beings or the images of Natural Beings in nature. Such speakers, especially if they are attractive Images, are important actors in Natural Attraction Ecology. For this reason, listen to them intently, *as if* they arise beyond the workings of your own mind. Remember, key aspects of them—their individuality, for example, really are beyond you. The Images, both dreamy and wild, are formed on the bridge of awareness that extends beyond you, *as if* anything is beyond you. If still not convinced, ask yourself, would I come up with a thought or an expression that science tells me is coming from my own mind without, at first, being aware of the Dream Character or the Natural Being? Doesn't this awareness mean that Characters and Beings are, at least, partly responsible for the origination/inspiration of thoughts and expressions? It's OK to listen to verbiage, *as if* it were coming from a separate Dream Character or an attractive Natural Being. Like messengers from another side, these living Images, these Dream Characters and Natural Beings, may, in fact, be using your conceptual and verbal skills for their own communication. Or, they may not. In any event, to get the most from the HumaNatureConnect Activities, at least act *as if* they do arise, at least in part, from distinct individual beings other than yourself. You will get closer to receiving your Soul's messages and you will get more information, healing, and guidance if you do. To speak any more of this at this point would betray the larger truth: it's all one, it's all Awareness, any distinctions are mere conceptual tools used for explanation purposes. The more you live in the dreamy world out there on the bridge of awareness, the easier will be your acceptance of the notion that it's all one. That said, why bother quibbling over the separateness of the sources of inspiration or the distinctions about where messages originate? For better or worse, humans tend to turn powerful Images into separable person-like gods.

Be sure to go outside for the next activity. When doing so, focus your mind and actions on roaming freely, moving through nature without concern for boundaries, limits, or restrictions. For a moment, live your life in untrammeled liberation. While in a natural setting, or coming to and fro, watch for any emotional responses you may have to the distress of another being. If this happens, celebrate that you still have emphatic concern. Scores for this response in the general population have declined 49 percent since 1980. Scores for perspective taking —an intellectual understanding of another person's situational circumstance—have declined by 34 percent. Shifts from empathy to narcissism have impacts on society and the environment. Whatever the cause for these declines, there is one thing for certain: immersion in nature affords opportunities for contemplation and enhances altruism (Selhub & Logan, 2012, p. 43-44). When ready, move to the next waypoint: "Key Institutions."

12

Key Institutions

REDIRECT THE FUNDAMENTAL ESTABLISHMENTS

All the fundamental establishments that control human activities—that is, governments, universities, corporations, and churches—tend to lead us to a radical discontinuity between people and nature. Instead of compelling us as they do, consciously and unconsciously, to be separate from nature, these institutions can instead be encouraged to move human activity from being devastatingly destructive to being benignly present.

To get these institutions to change, we ourselves will need to change—the kind of change that is made possible not by our immature Subpersonalities, which we discussed in the previous book, but with our more mature Psychic Personalities. These seasoned resources of the Inner Self are witnessed at the Cardinal Direction Compass Points on the Medicine Wheel of the Psyche of HumaNature.

You will need to get to know these mature Psychic Personalities because you will be using them as you do your part for human rights, racial equality, environmental protection, or whatever you choose to do with skills you will receive along the Heartwood Path. So get to know all your parts, including your immature subpersonalities and your mature Psychic Personalities. Of the two, apply mostly the following Psychic Personalities to the goal of making a magnificent future.

The Nurturing Generative Adult

At the North Stone on this Medicine Wheel (which is a map and not the territory depicted by the map) is what Bill Plotkin calls the "Nurturing Generative Adult." This mature inner resource helps one become compassionate, courageous, competent, knowledgeable, empathetic, productive, and capable of providing loving service to oneself and others. Like the archetypes the Leader, The King, the Mother, or the Father, the Nurturing Generative Adult helps us "contribute our best and most creative parenting, leading, teaching, directing, producing, and healing" (Plotkin, 2013, p. 16).

The Wild Indigenous One

At the South Stone on the Medicine Wheel of the Psyche of Huma-Nature is the mature inner resource Plotkin calls the "Wild Indigenous One," which is similar to the archetypes Pan, Artemis, and Green Man. Erotic, emotive, sensuous, instinctive and playful, the Wild Indigenous One of the South is at home in both the individual human and in nature. The Wild Indigenous One, says Plotkin, "is every bit as wild and natural as any animal, flower, or river and experiences a kinship with all species and habitats" (Plotkin, 213, pp.16-17).

The Innocent/Sage

With an eye for leading us to the realm of pure consciousness which is beyond distinctions and striving, the Innocent/Sage mature inner resource helps one see the big picture, be at home in the light, attain enlightenment, embrace paradox, and grapple with the Divine. The archetypes the Fool, the Trickster, and the Guides to Spirit are similar to the Innocent/Sage, represented by the East Stone on the Medicine Wheel of the Psyche of HumaNature.

The Muse-Beloved

Reveling in "night, dreams, destiny, death, and the mysteries and qualities of the underworld," the Muse-Beloved is romantic, imaginative, idealistic, introverted adventurous, and visionary (Plotkin, 2013, p. 17). This inner resource helps us eliminate old ways and brings forth previous unseen opportunities. Represented by the West Stone on the Medicine Wheel of the Psyche of HumaNature, the Muse-Beloved is similar to the archetypes Anima/Animus, Magician, Wanderer and Guide to Soul.

Apply all of these inner resources when attempting to make changes in Fundamental Establishments—the universities, governments, corporations, and churches. Doing so will help convert these key institutions to higher purposes—those that are good for all concerned, including human rights, racial equality, and environmental protection.

Begin to prepare for this all-important work by doing the following activity focused on accessing and cultivating the North's Nurturing Generative Adult. Continue this preparation doing the subsequent Psychic Personality Activities, each devoted to one of the other three inner world mature personalities.

To Your Mature Inner Resource Of The North . . .

HumaNatureConnect Activity

Start-up Protocol

If this is not a day when you prefer to spend time in nature without an agenda, do the Heartwood Path Start-up Protocol found in the Appendix.

Psychic Personality Activity # 1:
Accessing And Cultivating The Nurturing
Generative Adult

Begin to learn how to put your inner world Nurturing Generative Adult into heightened productive service. All at once, or on different days, cultivate your talents for healing by engaging in the following four practices:

1. On a walk in nature, be aware of how you walk, rest, see, listen, think, imagine, and feel. Find or be found by "a nurturing, other-than-human thing or place." After you feel that this connection has been made, let yourself fully feel the nurturing indigenous love throughout the body. Then, experience the world from nurturing perspective of this place (Plotkin, 2013, p. 46-47).

2. From the perspective of a mature parent, write a letter to yourself. In this letter, mention how your current emotions and life challenges tell you something important about your relationships. Offer advice to yourself about what you could do to grow in your relationships. Remind yourself that the goal of individuation—the main job of the previous Heartwood Path book—is wholeness, not perfection. If you wish, write several letters and give one or more of them to a friend and ask them to mail it to you when they think you may need some mature Nurturing Adult advice.

3. Switch from cultivating the intrapersonal aspect of the Nurturing Adult to the interpersonal dimension by writing a similar love letter to another being. Just as you need nurturing from time to time, others too need understanding and warmth. Give it to them in the form of a platonic love letter. And see how it makes them and you feel.

4. Write down a personal vow of "commitment to enacting or deepening your soulwork, your own unique life mission,

personal mythology, or sacred story" (Plotkin, 2013, p. 49). Follow through with your vows.

Keep an eye out for three more Psychic Personality Activities later in this course.

Follow-up Protocol

For best results, write down your impressions of this activity in your journal using the Heartwood Path Follow-up Protocol found in the Appendix. Afterwards, consider sharing your interpretations with others.

Heartwood Path Axioms

Key Assertions From Waypoint 4.12

4.12.1.

Instead of compelling us as they do, consciously and unconsciously, to be separate from nature, fundamental establishments such as governments, corporations, universities, and churches can instead be encouraged to move human activity from being devastatingly destructive to being benignly present.

4.12.2.

To get Fundamental Establishments to change, we ourselves will need to change—the kind of change that is made possible not with the help of our immature Subpersonalities but with our more mature Psychic Personalities.

4.12.3.

One the North/South axis of the Map of the Psyche of HumaNature are two adult Psychic Personalities: the North's Nurturing Generative Adult—who helps one become compassionate, courageous, competent, knowledgeable, empathetic, productive, and capable of providing loving service to oneself and others—and the South's Wild Indigenous One—who helps use become emotive, erotic-sexual, sensuous, instinctive, and playful.

4.12.4.

One the East/West axis of the Map of the Psyche of HumaNature are two adult Psychic Personalities: the East's Innocent/Sage—who helps one see the big picture, be at home in the light, attain enlightenment, embrace paradox, and grapple with the Divine—and the West's Muse-Beloved—who helps one become imaginative, erotic-romantic idealistic, visionary, adventurous, darkness-savoring (shadow-loving), meaning-attuned, and introverted, thus allowing one to eliminate old ways and bring forth previous unseen opportunities.

4.12.5.

A sign of a healthy personality is the ability to acknowledge other personalities.

Nocturnal Pilgrimage 4.12

For best results, write down your impressions of each night's dreams in your journal using the Heartwood Path Dreaming Time

Protocols found in the Appendix. Afterwards, consider sharing your Dream Tending with others.

In your dream tending practice certain principles and perspectives will recur. These will be addressed in the next five Nocturnal Pilgrimage sections, beginning here with the topic of the "NonSelf," which makes room for various other psychic selfhoods, such as the subpersonalities and Totem Spirit Animals.

"Dreams show us we are not who we think we are," writes author and editor Marc Ian Barasch (2000, p. 28).

"We may experience the diminution of what in waking life we most prize in ourselves, and the elevation of what we find belittling. One sign of a healthy personality is the ability to1 acknowledge other selfhoods and inhabit other skins" (Barasch, 2000, p. 28).

With all of these selfhoods showing up in dreams it will help you avoid confusion if you keep a well organized Dream Journal. Here are some more tips for doing just that:

1. A loose-leaf format is easy, quick, and allows for moving dream records around for later examination.
2. Date your notes.
3. Start each dream on a new sheet.
4. Leave space on the page so you can write or draw associations.
5. Give each dream a title.
6. Start a new journal when you run out of room.
7. Take photographs and name your Three-Dimensional Dream Figures, then put your notes and the photos in a clear sleeve or in a computer file.
8. Free up your linear recording by a) forgetting conventions such as sentences and paragraphs, b) let each word determine its own size, color, etc, c) group words in ways that will help you review

the dream later, d) create your own hieroglyphics, e) omit articles such as "an" and "the," f) omit pronouns where possible, g) abbreviate names after the first mention, h) do not worry about transitions such as "then" or the "scene changes," i) use asterisks * to indicate changes in time, place, scene, or logic, j) to include an association in your journal use parenthesis ( ), k) omit approximations such as "It was as if...," l) omit all the "he said" and "she said" references, m) abbreviate words to capture illusive dreams, n) use the dash – a lot, o) amplify three words in your text by attaching other words to them that make some sense to you, p) eternalize connections by adding the "ever" suffice to "when," q) add "always" and "never" as often as you can, omit approximate, redundant, repetitive, and vague words, r) leave out explanations, and s) omit modifying words such as "very" and "almost."

9. Feel free to work with fragments, full images are not necessary.
10. Turn your dream into a Haiku poem (seventeen syllables in three lines of five, seven, five).
11. Converse with your three-dimensional Dream Figures.
12. Build cairns (ceremonial piles of rocks) to represent your Dream Figures. Be sure to record the name of the Dream Figure (I take pictures and label them, plus I make a map to indicate the names of each Dream Figure).
13. Express yourself in your journaling with the making of masks, clay figures, painting, or drawing.

With Barasch's words about *Nonself* (other selfhoods) in mind, sleep, dream lucidly, and tend to your dreams. Share some of your journal entries with others.

In the spirit of the animal totem Coyote—the Trickster, the bringer of lessons who is cunning, crafty, and adaptable—continue your progress in this course by moving to the next waypoint: "Here Tenderheartedly." Doing so will help you to become present benignly.

13

Here Tenderheartedly

BECOME BENIGNLY PRESENT AND HELP OTHERS DO SO AS WELL

Before one begins the work of re-incorporating one's Distill Self—that is, one's Ecological Self, Greater Self, or More-Than-Individual-Self—into one's overall concept of Self, there are vitally important background references that need to be realized. Author Carol S. Pearson Ph.D. calls these references "the heroes within" and points out how they help us find ourselves and transform the world (Pearson, 1991). Finding these "heroes" takes a pilgrimage (such as the Heartwood Path) that is really a "heroes journey" to "find the treasure of your true self" (Pearson, 1991, p. 1.). This journey usually does not happen once, for when one gets to the end one is propelled to begin again and "each time we begin our journeys, we do so at a new level and return with a new treasure and newfound transformative abilities" (Pearson, 1991, p. 3). During our journeys we can find our reference heroes, also known as the Twelve Archetypes, by "going inward (to our own dreams, fantasies, and often actions as well) or by going outward (to myth, legend, art, literature, and religion, and as pagan cultures often did, to the constellations of the sky and the birds and animals of the earth)" (Pearson,

1991, p.6.). Inner heroes exhibit various aspects, depending on the person putting them to use: for spiritual seekers, Archetypes are gods and goddesses; for academics and other rationalists, Archetypes are controlling paradigms or metaphors; for scientists, Archetypes are like holograms; for people committed to religious positions, Archetypes are the many faces of God; and for pilgrims on journeys of growth and development, Archetypes are inner guides.

According to Chiara Viscomi, M.A., Archetypes can be thought of as containers. These containers hold interconnected figures, motifs, or themes that reappear in myths, folktales, religions, literature, and the arts, spanning widely across cultures and eras. The figures, motifs, and themes are not the archetypes themselves; they are the content of the archetypes (2015).

We are interested in Archetypes because they can lead us to topics and quandries we may never ponder on our own. They help us define ourselves and our genders. They help us to find appropriate patterns of behavior. Archetypes enable us to be successful in getting our needs met.

We will stick largely to twelve archetypes, similar to those described in Carol Pearson's book **Awakening the Heroes Within** (Pearson, 1991) but, following the advise of Pip McKay of Evolve Now Mind Institute (2009), we will give the archetypes a more ecological stance by encouraging you to picture them as animal archetypes. For this purpose, we have limited our list of Inner Animals to those animals that somewhat match Pearson's twelve archetypes and to McKay's Totem Animal Archetypes (2009). In looking over the paragraphs that follow, you may feel that one of the Archetypes is with you always and one or more is useful to you under certain circumstances.

If, in one of your hero's journeys, you are attracted to feeling safe, you believe that people do not want to hurt each other, you feel that you can count on others to take care of you, you tend to believe the world is a safe place, you feel people you meet are trustworthy, and you know that your needs will be met, you have caught your Innocent Deer Archetype.

If, in one of your hero's journeys, you feel neglected or victimized as a child, you feel life is one heartache after another, you fear those in authority, you feel abandoned, you feel people you have trusted have abandoned you, or you feel important people in your life have let you down, you have caught the Orphan Buffalo Archetype.

If, in one of your hero's journeys, you put fear aside and do what needs to be done, you take risks to defend your beliefs (position), you challenge what is wrong, you use discipline to achieve goals, you stand up to offensive people, and recognize that the key to success is discipline, you have caught the Warrior Hummingbird Archetype.

If, in one of your hero's journeys, you put the needs of others over your own, you find satisfaction in caring for others, you find more happiness in giving that you do in receiving, you find it easy to care for others, you feel that the sacrifices you have made for others have made you a better person, or you have a hard time saying "no" you have caught the Caring Elk Archetype.

If, in one of your hero's journeys you are searching for ways to improve yourself, you feel that it is essential to maintain your independence, you feel restless, you feel that a better world is on the horizon, you are looking for greener pastures, or you feel that the act of looking for something is as important as finding it, you have caught the Seeking Dolphin Archetype.

If, in one of your hero's journeys, you feel sexy and agree with the statement, "it is better to have loved and lost than never to have loved at all," you embrace life, you are fulfilled by relationships, you like to help people connect with one another, or feel loving towards people in general, you have caught the Loving Dog Archetype.

If, in one of your hero's journeys, you feel disoriented by so much change in your life, you feel you have let others down, you feel you are no longer the person you thought you were, you are letting go of things that do not fit for you anymore, you have caught the Destructive Badger Archetype.

If, in one of your hero's journeys you try to be authentic whenever you can, you feel that you are always in the process of creating your own life, you have times when your feel that it is easy for you to be highly accomplished, you feel that inspiration comes easily, you are experimenting with turning dreams into reality, or if you have a lot more great ideas than you have time to act on them, you have caught the Industrious Ant Archetype.

If, in one of your hero's journeys you feel that the process of your own self-healing enables you to help heal others, you feel that spiritual help accounts for your effectiveness, you feel that changing your inner thoughts changes your outer life, you feel that your presence is often a catalyst for change, you feel that all beings in the world are interconnected, or you like to transform situations, you have caught the Magical Raven Archetype.

If, in one of your hero's journeys, people look to you for direction, you have leadership qualities, you prefer to be in charge, you tend to develop human or natural resources, you are good at matching people's skills to the tasks that come up, or if try to manage situations with the good of all in mind, you have caught the Ruling Lion Archetype.

If, in one of your hero's journeys, you keep a sense of perspective by taking a long-range view, you believe there are many good ways to look at the same thing, you try to find truths behind illusions, you strive for objectivity, or if you are calm you have caught the Sage Owl Archetype.

If, in one of your hero's journeys, you like to shake things up when life gets dull, others see you as a fun companion, you do not take rules too seriously, you like to make people laugh, you like to help overly serious people "lighten-up," or you see the value of chaos, you have caught the Foolish Coyote Archetype.

Each time we begin our hero's journey again, we are influenced by these archetypes again. But, like us, as we redo our journeys, the archetypes seem to develop or, at a minimum, we seem to be able to grasp a higher level of the archetype that was not apparent to us on earlier journeys.

Like any hero's journey, the Heartwood Path includes three stages: 1) preparation (Books 1-4), the journey (Books 5-6, 8, 9), and the

return (Book 7). There are archetypes for each stage of the hero's journey. As you make progress in your hero's journey, use a metaphorical
net to capture important life lessons (these will be the positive aspects
of Archetypes). Those archetypal aspects that fall through your net,
like angry dragons, will bring negativity into your life. These are the
Grieving Ghosts that can and will, at best, make you feel awful, and,
at worst, send you to your grave. Examples (using Pearson's names
for the Archetypes): fail to catch the Innocent Archetype and you will
have to deal with the Denier; let the Orphan slip through the holes of
your net and you have the Victim; fail to net the Warrior and you are
left with the Villain; the un-caught Caregiver becomes the Suffering
Martyr; the Seeker becomes the Perfectionist, the Destroyer becomes
the Self Destroyer; the Lover becomes the Siren; the Creator becomes
the Obsessive; the Ruler turns into the Ogre Tyrant; the Magician left
behind becomes the Evil Sorcerer; the Sage becomes the Unfeeling
Judge; and the Happy Fool becomes the Glutton. We will look more
into the positive and negative aspects of Archetypes as we proceed. But
first, since you are probably wondering about which Archetypes you
have already netted in your hero's journey up to this point or which
un-tagged Archetypes would be most helpful to you in the future, do
the following activity before you proceed.

To Take Into Account Your Own Inner World Champions...

HumaNatureConnect Activity

Start-up Protocol

If this is not a day when you prefer to spend time in nature without an agenda, do the Heartwood Path Start-up Protocol found in the
Appendix.

Determining Your Relationship With The Heroes Within

Imagine that your chosen attractive natural being, the one that you are using for this HumaNatureConnect Activity, has the power to catch not only the main twelve Archetypes listed above, but also lesser Archetypes such as the Wise and Happy Dragonfly or the Graceful Fish. Conduct a self assessment from the perspective of your chosen natural being. We are making you a neutral listener in this imagined conversation because your own questions and interpretations will be too tainted by your own present emotions, state-of-mind, and presence-of-mind. While doing this assessment, imagine that your chosen natural being is very familiar with your individual self and your hero's journey to date. Also imagine that, unlike you, your chosen natural being is always fair, insightful and impartial in its responses. Imagining that it is the natural being (and not you) that is having the conversation with the Archetype. This level of detachment makes it more likely for you to receive brutally honest assessments and recommendations. It makes it more likely that you will not block the information you need the most. Since you yourself may not want to hear what has to occur, simply pay attention to the conversation between you and your chosen natural attraction.

Start by asking your chosen natural being to tag one of the Archetypes. Listen as the natural being enters into an imagined conversation with the Archetype about you or your present situation. By engaging the archetype in this way you will be able to glean its contents which will, in turn, be sources of information, guidance, and creativity. If you have difficulty understanding the content found in the containers of the Archetypes, ask your chosen attractive being to give you a "bottom-line" interpretation, a quick summary so that you can move on to other imagined conversations or to doing the Follow-up Protocol for this activity.

"According to (Robert) Hopke, we develop psychologically when we allow the content of archetypes to enter our conscious awareness, and when we foster a relationship between our two levels of existence: the everyday (personal) and the archetypal (collective)" (Viscomi).

While listening to the imagined conversations involving the natural being archetype, notice which of the above described Animal Archetypes seems to be with you always and which ones seem to show up under certain circumstances. Determine which of the attributes of contents of our Animal Archetypes is presently descriptive of yourself. Notice which Animal Archetypes are not active in your life. They have perhaps fallen through your net as you previously, knowingly or unknowingly, gathered the help of guides on your earlier hero's journeys. To avoid having negative consequences, Animal Archetypes that you have not yet caught may require some attention. This activity is your chance to secure the content from additional Animal Archetypes. Incorporating the wisdom of these inner guides into your life will help to prevent the negative shadow-side of Archetypes from affecting you adversely. Such attention will also likely provide you with more choices when facing life's situations.

Follow-up Protocol

For best results, write down your impressions of this activity in your journal using the Heartwood Path Follow-up Protocol found in the Appendix. Afterwards, consider sharing your interpretations with others.

Heartwood Path Axioms

Key Assertions From Waypoint 4.13

4.13.1.

Become benignly present and help others do so as well.

4.13.2.

Find archetypes by going inward to such such things as to your dreams and imagination.

4.13.3.

Find archetypes by going outward to art, religion, or nature.

Nocturnal Pilgrimage 4.13

For best results, write down your impressions of each night's dreams in your journal using the Heartwood Path Dreaming Time Protocols found in the Appendix. Afterwards, consider sharing your Dream Tending with others.

Barasch's second Recurring Dream Principle and Perspective, after *"Nonself,"* is *"Nonsense."*

"It is a sure bet that whatever we deem most ridiculous upon waking is the fulcrum point of what the dream wants to tell us. . . Like a fool in the court of a king, dreams use absurdity to tell the truth . . . " (Barasch, 2000, p. 29).

Pertinent And Instructive Gems From My Dream Tending Journal

I dreamt I was being chastised for writing and talking too much about dreams when an ally and I were working to a turn out people for the public hearing on wilderness preservation in Missouri. His comments bothered

me, and not because I felt he was wrong. I woke up before I could deliver
my response.

Lesson Learned: We live in a world where a couple of hundred species go extinct everyday because of the greed and lack of sensitivity of humankind. Despite this frightening occurrence, it is not a waste of time for environmental activists to pay attention to the realm where impulses and ideas come from: the realm of dreams. Those hell-bent to gobbling up the planet benefit when activists ignore messages from living Beings; from so-called non-living Beings; and from Muses, Archetypes, Totems, and Spirits from the dream realm. Worthwhile practical strategies are often contained within the stories and Images witnessed in dreams. And so is the power to persevere.

As you do the next activity outdoors, pay extra attention to the wind, the water, the soil, the sand, the sun, the plants, or any other natural beings that will help you build your primal relationship with nature. Note how moving amongst these beings can become a true adventure, one that engages you sensually, physically, and soulfully. Compare how you feel when moving calmly and reverently through nature to how you feel when you are sedentary, sitting in a chair, and indoors. Lie face down directly on the Earth. As you do so, recall how different feelings arise while you are lying in bed. While lying down outside, answer the following questions: How does it feel to be in such contact with the Earth? Do you feel at ease or anxious? Does the earth that touches your body feel like a foreign object or do you feel at-home? Do you feel comforted, foolish, weird, or out-of-place? Does the Earth feel inert and objectified or does it feel alive to you? Your answers will tell you if you are alienated from the Earth.

You are making great progress. After completing the above exercise, go to the next waypoint in this course, "Essential Aspects." There, you will learn how awareness precedes thoughts.

14

Essential Aspects

ADHERE TO THE GROUND OF ONE'S BEING

If one looks at a flower or a crystal and appreciates its beauty without any extra thoughts about its utilitarian use, one begins to witness, not only the prettiness of the flower or crystal, but also the beauty that is an essential aspects of one's own Innermost Being. This Innermost Being is the stage upon which thoughts play out. It is one's awareness. Thoughts can be a blessing but when they take over and obscure the joy of connectedness to Being, they can also be a considerable curse. Every thought is made possible by a certain perspective. Seeing from a narrow or low perspective, by its nature, is a limited view and, therefore, a limited portion of the whole truth. Always be on guard against truth decay.

Adhere To The Truth

Only the whole is absolutely true; but too few people can think and, therefore, speak completely about the whole. One's ponderings and statements about the truth are all relative to one's own perspective and are, therefore, a limited view of the whole truth. That is why the

Heartwood Path was charted to take pilgrims on a journey to add layers of depth upon which a broader perspective (and a larger view of the truth) is possible.

Since thoughts precede all actions, it is wise to develop good (more true) thoughts before attempting to do anything. Likewise, since one's Innermost Being precedes all thoughts, it is best to reveal the intrinsic joy, love, and sacredness that mark this formless aspect of one's true Being before one relies too much on thoughts and actions alone.

Slowing down or attempting to stop actions and thoughts, even for a moment, leads to the revelation of one's Innermost Being. This revelation increase's one's ability to witness and appreciate the ethereal. This revelation reduces materiality—the compulsion for having things. This revelation also allows for an emotional clearing from which one can feel more fully the union of the Universal Self with the Individual Self.

To Find Your Personal Inner World Gifts...

HumaNatureConnect Activity

Start-up Protocol

If this is not a day when you prefer to spend time in nature without an agenda, do the Heartwood Path Start-up Protocol found in the Appendix.

Finding The Essential Aspects Of Your Personal Gifts

Find a pathway of change that deepens yourself by looking to your deepest wounds to find your greatest gifts; by recalling a wound that shows your deepest sensitivity, tenderness, passion, and capacity to love and create; by looking for what core gifts are trying to be expressed in your deepest wounds; and by looking for how you are misunderstood.

Follow-up Protocol

For best results, write down your impressions of this activity in your journal using the Heartwood Path Follow-up Protocol found in the Appendix. Afterwards, consider sharing your interpretations with others.

Heartwood Path Axioms

Key Assertions From Waypoint 4.14

4.14.1.

Adhere to the ground of one's being.

4.14.2.

Every thought is made possible by a certain perspective.

4.14.3.

Seeing from a narrow or low perspective, by its nature, is a limited view and therefore a limited portion of the whole truth.

4.14.4.

Always be on guard against truth decay.

4.14.5.

**Only the whole is absolutely true; but too few people can think
and, therefore, speak completely about the whole.**

Nocturnal Pilgrimage 4.14

For best results, write down your impressions of each night's
dreams in your journal using the Heartwood Path Dreaming Time
Protocols found in the Appendix. Afterwards, consider sharing your
Dream Tending with others.

Barasch's third Recurring Dream Principle And Perspective, after
"Nonself" and *"Nonsense,"* is *"Balance."*

"A Healing Dream often comes to redress imbalance—something in
the personality is askew, awry, not right (or perhaps, too right) . . .
The quickest way to the heart of a dream is to ask what one-sided
conscious attitude it is trying to offset" (Barrasch, 2000, p. 29).

Think of the pertinence of the ground of your being in your life
before you prepare for bed, Sleep. Tend to your dreams.

Pertinent And Instructive Gems From My Dream Tending Journal

*I dreamt that a very wet Eskimo-looking man was speaking to me on
behalf of endangered whales. Actually, he was speaking as if he was a
whale. At first, I wouldn't listen, for he seemed far too "airy-fairy" to me.
But, remembering my Heartwood Path dream tending training, I remembered that "as if" is as good as "really is." As a sign of respect, I turned to
directly face my talking nighttime visitor. This whale, shown to me as a
person-looking Dream Image, said that I should sharpen my conservation*

skills with his plight because, among other reasons, as far as extinction

goes,

"your kind is next."

Within this lucid dream I was aware that I was receiving a nearly hidden, unspoken, but practical strategy: always listen to talking Dream Images. I was also, I thought, involved in a mini pep rally.

Lesson Learned: Initial steps in destroying an enemy are to dehumanize them and to silence them. The destruction that Modern Culture is delivering to nature is occurring *as if* Natural Beings were regarded as the enemy. Environmental activists and the natural environment they seek to protect will be well served if conservationists allow themselves to listen to the human-looking Images of Natural Beings that come to them and their dreams. These occurrences are, or can be, important pep rallies and valuable strategy sessions. The guidance may need to come to us in little bits, dream after dream.

When you are ready, move to the next waypoint, entitled "You First," to continue on your way to Gladandgreen Junction. At the next learning station you will learn about setting yourself right before setting the world right.

15

You First

SET YOURSELF RIGHT BEFORE ATTEMPTING TO SET THE WORLD RIGHT

I cannot say too emphatically how important connecting to one's Innermost Being and the Truth is for those traversing the Heartwood Path. Making such a connection is also very important for those attempting on their own to set themselves right before working to make a difference in the world.

The Heartwood Path begins by following the adage: set your Self right to make the world right. By its end, the Heartwood Path proves that one can also set oneself right by making the world right. Either way, rightness of you and rightness of the world depends on you doing what it takes to develop your integrity. Keep going. You will get there.

To fail to do the work of this next section is to keep one's Ego in its preferred place of dominance. Not doing the work allows the Ego to imprison the fullness of the Self. Not doing the work causes one to lose the benefits of using a vitally important transformational device—consciousness of Being. Without this device, one will continue to live in fear, desire, and delusion. One will miss the point. Those who do not reunite consciously with their Innermost Being will likely end up using their own so-called intelligence in the service of madness; that is to say, to live in sin.

In the next section the topic will be "enlightenment," to use an old Hindu or Buddhist word. I could also use the Christian word "salvation." Regardless of the language, I am referring to the end of suffering and the beginning of liberation and awakening. By these terms I mean an end of suffering as a result of collective insanity (global environmental destruction, wars, materialism), liberation from one's dysfunctional human mind, and awakening to Isaiah's prophesy and to what more than a half century later John proclaimed in Revelations: a new heaven (which means the inner realm of consciousness, the awareness of being) and a new earth (heaven's reflection in the physical realm).

To Set Yourself Right...

HumaNatureConnect Activity

Start-up Protocol

If this is not a day when you prefer to spend time in nature without an agenda, do the Heartwood Path Start-up Protocol found in the Appendix.

Preparing For Activism

Recall the most repetitive negative statement that occurs in the privacy of your own mind and replace this stuck mindset with a positive alternative; look at your unwanted stuck mindset ("I'm not lovable.") as the clue to where you need to make positive change; and when you perceive your pervasive negative thought add the word "yet" to it ("I'm not lovable, yet.") as a way to turn your recurring negativity into an enduring and motivating growth mindset.

Follow-up Protocol

For best results, write down your impressions of this activity in your journal using the Heartwood Path Follow-up Protocol found in the Appendix. Afterwards, consider sharing your interpretations with others.

Heartwood Path Axioms

Key Assertions From Waypoint 4.15

4.15.1.

Set yourself right before attempting to set the world right.

4.15.2.

Those who do not reunite consciously with their Innermost Being will likely end up using their own so-called intelligence in the service of madness.

4.15.3.

Enlightenment is the end of suffering and the beginning of liberation and awakening.

4.15.4.

Seek a new heaven (which means the inner realm of consciousness, the awareness of being) and a new earth (heaven's reflection in the physical realm).

Nocturnal Pilgrimage 4.15

For best results, write down your impressions of each night's dreams in your journal using the Heartwood Path Dreaming Time Protocols found in the Appendix. Afterwards, consider sharing your Dream Tending with others.

Barasch's fourth Recurring Dream Principle And Perspective, after *"Nonself," "Nonsense,"* and *"Balance"* is *"Reversal of Value."*

"In dreams, our fixed reference points—our opinions, values, and judgments—may be revealed as mere tricks of perspective. What the conscious mind believes to be a precious gem may be a beach pebble to the spirit, while what it tosses aside may be a pearl of great price" (Barasch, 2000, p. 29).

With this in mind, sleep, dream, pay attention to the big and small aspects of your dream, and tend to your dreams. As you do so, you will likely have the tendency to look for the way your dream characters or landscapes may be signs of something for you. Making your dreams into signs is natural; but, since your dreams mean a lot more than any sign you would come up with, it is best to think of dream characters and landscapes as symbols that are too big for your comprehension without repeated dream tending. Look for symbols in your dreams, if you must; but remember that there is way more to them than you can ever know at first brush. This point is so important allow me to repeat it in another way:

It takes repeated examination, done with effective journaling, before you can have confidence that you are assigning the right symbolism to your dreams.

Rather than cut off the value of your dreams by assigning simple and narrow signs to them, look to your dreams as helpful on-going dialogue, full of mystery and complex and broad symbolism.

Pertinent And Instructive Gems From My Dream Tending Journal

I dreamt my Missouri wilderness friend John came to me again in a dream. He said communicating with Dream Images is a sign of insanity. We didn't have time to continue this debate because we needed to fill the State House Chamber for wilderness hearing. I thought I'd build my argument during my Dream Tending Session. During that time, I wrote how the Dream Image appeared as a personified tree, complete with a human face and leaves instead of hair. Somehow me talking to a personified Image of a Rock was less scandalous to John than if I was speaking to the un-personified Image of an oak.

Lesson Learned: Cultures that do not value talking to Dream Images, Animal Totems, or other creations from the bridge of awareness tend to destroy their environments. Those cultures who do spend time communicating with nature-oriented Images from beyond do not tend to destroy their environment. For this reason, I advocate more talking with nature-oriented Dream Images. This activity may seem odd, at first. To make it more acceptable, the Dreamer can psychologically present the dream plant, animal or mineral as a Personified Image. To John and many other people, talking to such Dream Images is less embarrassing, less implausible, and less odd than it is to talk to the Dream Image of a un-personified plant, animal, or mineral. Do whatever works for you. Personified or not, Dream Images have their own Will, have the qualities of aliveness, and offer helpful conversations.

When you are ready, move to the next waypoint: "Awareness Precedes Thoughts." Vital information is right around the next bend.

16

Awareness Precedes Thoughts

APPRECIATE YOUR CONSCIOUSNESS OF BEING

Oneness with the Earth has nothing much to do with what you believe and everything to do with your state of consciousness and your physical presence imbedded in ecological systems. All actions stem from thoughts, and thoughts stem from consciousness of Being (for consciousness of being, I shall usually use the term "Awareness").

We all need to develop this Awareness or we shall all face dire consequences. To help prevent these consequences—which include deaths in global proportions—one needs to begin with awareness of one's own Innermost Being. This attention prevents one from having less than suitable thoughts, which result in less than suitable actions.

Awareness is before thought. It is the stage upon which thoughts play. To be on the stage of Awareness is to deny the Ego of its food: identification with physical forms, thoughts, and emotions.

Whatever you identify with feeds the Ego. It is one's Ego that prevents one from connecting with Awareness; and Awareness gives, among other things, one's sense of connection to the Whole. We cannot use the Earth responsibly if we feel separate from the Whole, for collective human consciousness and life on Earth are connected intrinsically.

Awareness means stripping away illusions, including the illusion that the words for things are the things themselves, the thoughts about things are the things themselves, or that things only have value when possessed (the result of the mind-made "my"), or that people are only defined by their roles, or that all things are interpreted by the mind-made "I." Words, labels, and possessiveness are the results of thoughts. They do not represent the stage upon with these thoughts occur—one's Awareness. There is no identification on the stage of Awareness—so you can never find yourself in objects. When thinking about your things (which is a role of the Ego) you can lose yourself—lose Awareness of your Being—in your things. It is an illusion that all things, bodies, and forms are merely the objects of thoughts. If this were the case the world would be deadened by mental abstraction, a conceptual reality that tends to turn ugly. Instead, the world is alive, bigger than all thoughts, and beautiful. Through awareness, our mental interpretations become richer: trees for example, become shade givers, streams become land carvers, and soil becomes the giver of gifts.

Do not honor things only for what they can do for you. Do not try to find yourself through the things of the Earth. These are tricks of the Ego and they lead to illusion, striving, and obsession They can also lead to social and individual diseases that result from unchecked growth When one no longer feels through Awareness the life that one is, one fills one's life with spiritually-impoverished distractions of the Ego, namely: identifications and thoughts that one is right while others are wrong, the development of a sense of self based on the worth one has in the eyes of others, and a development of a sense of self based on the possession of things.

To Increased Environmental Awareness...

HumaNatureConnect Activity

Start-up Protocol

If this is not a day when you prefer to spend time in nature without an agenda, do the Heartwood Path Start-up Protocol found in the Appendix.

Increasing Environmental Awareness

Consider doing any of the following:

1. Make a blog about local community environmental issues and opportunities;
2. discuss environmental issues on social networks;
3. organize a green club in your area and plan to hold exhibitions, contests, and workshops;
4. organize environmental seminars at your work;
5. organize neighborhood clean-up events;
6. organize a "lights down" event in your town; and
7. convince a church to adopt an environmental project.

Follow-up Protocol

For best results, write down your impressions of this activity in your journal using the Heartwood Path Follow-up Protocol found in the Appendix. Afterwards, consider sharing your interpretations with others.

Heartwood Path Axioms

Key Assertions From Waypoint 4.16

4.16.1.

Appreciate your consciousness of being.

4.16.2.

All actions stem from thoughts, and thoughts stem from Awareness.

4.16.3.

Awareness is the stage upon which thoughts play.

4.16.4.

Awareness means stripping away illusions, including the illusion that the words for things are the things themselves.

4.16.5.

When one does not feel through Awareness one fills one's life with spiritually-impoverished distractions of the Ego.

Nocturnal Pilgrimage 4.16

For best results, write down your impressions of each night's dreams in your journal using the Heartwood Path Dreaming Time Protocols found in the Appendix. Afterwards, consider sharing your Dream Tending with others.

Barasch's final Recurring Dream Principle And Perspective, after *"Nonself," "Nonsense," "Balance,"* and *"Reversal of Value,"* is *"Wholeness."* One's dreams illustrate how all things are related. They seem to revel in the union of opposites. In dreams, the divine encircles both decay and growth, delight and horror. Our typical dichotomies of "either/or" are replaced wisely in dreams by "both/and/also." Dreams dissolve any separation between the inner world and the outer world. Dreamtime is not a flow from past, to present, to the future, for all times converge into one eddy. In dreams, there is no separate current for good, and no separate channel for bad. Like a braided stream, light and dark intertwine and the worst events display a silver lining.

With this in mind, sleep and dream. Be sure to tend to your dreams before heading to the next waypoint.

Pertinent And Instructive Gems From My Dream Tending Journal

I dreamt I continued my dream debate with my Missouri wilderness preservation buddy John. He kept saying, over and over, as if correcting me:

"...work on the environment."

I kept replying, over and over, as if correcting him,

"...work with the environment."

"On/with...on/with"...

over and over,

until we both got the other's message.

Lesson Learned: Environmentalists tend to work on protecting nature without the help of Dream Images. The use of such inner world allies is foreign to many people, especially those who are formally trained in wildlife conservation, like John. They tend to shy away from what they call "anthropomorphism"—the overly romantic notion of giving human-like characteristics to animals. EartHearts like myself, by comparison, tend to work with nature-based Dream Images which guide them in their efforts to work with nature to protect the environment. We eartHearts know the difference between animals and people but accept talking to nature-oriented Dream Images because doing so can be informative, guiding, and healthful. In the waking world, I certainly learned a lot from brilliant and dedicated John, the greatest naturalist I know. In truth, we have never had a conversation about our dreams. Maybe that is what this dream was suggesting for us.

When ready, move to the following waypoint: "Ergo, Ego Goes." There, you will learn how the Ego thrives on rightness and conflict but it dissolves in peace.

17

Ergo, Ego Goes

ACT TO STEM THE EGO, FOR THESE REASONS

One does not always need to stand out. One does not always need to put themselves against others. One can use Awareness to put the Ego into its proper place. The Ego cannot be overbearing in the light of Awareness. That being the case, use the information in the three sections of this waypoint to illuminate your consciousness of being.

Know What You Are, The Way You Are; Not And The Way You Are Not

The unchecked Ego is a curse, in part, because of its hidden motivating force that makes one feel the need to stand out, to be special, to be in control, to have power, to be separate, and to have enemies. None of this will allow one to truly establish one's worth, nor will it allow one to complete one's greater sense of Self. The beginning of conscious awareness of being is the noticing that one is psychologically attached to things both good and bad.

Here is what you are not: your physical strength, your appearance, and your fitness. You most certainly are not only your body; but, more fully, you are the feeling of aliveness inside your body. You are also not only your mind either, for you can be aware of the thoughts of the mind and so you are a Being distinguishable from it. You are the peace of the Absolute Spirit—consciousness itself—and not whatever consciousness identifies with. You are not anything, you simply are.

Beyond the "I am" that you are lie identifications and separations that are the handiwork of the Ego. Refrain from cherishing opinions, both yours and others. Focus on your immediate task without also focusing on yourself. Focusing on yourself doing your tasks will too often sabotage your work—which, as we all know, is usually so good some of it ought to be saved for tomorrow. Rather than separate yourself from others, help others without reference to what this help will do for you. The universe will take care of the payback, and it can do so for you because you are no longer in a state of separation. In the same way, resentment of the success of others leads to less success for you. Attract success by welcoming it wherever you notice it. Avoid close associations with groups that mark themselves through exclusion. This too is the Ego's way to make sure it, rather than the Absolute Being of the Universe, is paramount in one's mind.

To conceive of an "I" one needs to have a conceptual "other." When so-called "others" attempt to label you with some form of identification, or a means to hold you separate from others, do not react to such tags. This non-reaction will both help you go beyond your own Ego and help to check the collective Ego, which is very damaging to people and the Earth. By non-reaction, I mean overlooking the claims of others and by looking through your Ego and the other person's Ego to the essence of being in every person. Relying on the Ego alone—that is, without being tempered by the Soul or the Universal Self—is bad. Relying on **both** the Ego and the Soul or Universal Self is the way to go.

Earlier I mentioned denying the Ego by cutting off its nourishment of thoughts. I said this, in part, because thoughts, at best, point to the truth but are never the truth itself. Truth is found in Awareness.

Note, And, If Necessary, Correct Your Identifications

Labeling people as "us" or "them" is another trick of the Ego. The greater part of the violence people have inflicted on each other is not the work of villainous others but instead the brutality is perpetrated by the hands of normal and respected folk in service of the collective Ego —the combination of all of our normally well-meaning Ego's—and its identification with thought, separation, emotion, and having things.

Perceived enemies are part of our common humanity. War distorts perceptions because it gives each side an excuse to see the other, not as they are, but as each side wants to see the other—usually as sub-human, evil, and deserving of mistreatment. Defeat one enemy and a new one pops up. Why? The Ego thrives on reactions to separateness, on identifications of "us" versus "them," on thoughts about one's own "rightness" versus the other's "wrongness," and on drama.

The Ego thrives on rightness and conflict but it dissolves in peace. When one so-called enemy is defeated, the Ego searches for a new enemy and thus feeds upon the drama and the sense of identification and separateness. It is not "others" that we need to fight, it is the collective Ego in service of collective insanity that needs to be throttled. If you would rather be right than at peace it is your Ego that is part of the problem.

Awareness As A Weapon Against The Ego

The Ego is pernicious, pervasive, and persistent; but it does have an Achilles' Heal (a weak spot in the armor of it's defenses, creating a lethal vulnerability). The Ego's Achilles' Heal is Awareness. So, use your Awareness to sense your Essential Being by being mindful of the present. Mindfulness develops awareness of non-duality. Sensory awareness of the world counteracts the Ego. Staying aware of the present and the world long enough allows for self-transcendence in which there is no longer a separate self—an Ego—perceiving objects. All that is left is non-dual perception.

To Put A Restraint On Your Ego...

HumaNatureConnect Activity

Start-up Protocol

If this is not a day when you prefer to spend time in nature without an agenda, do the Heartwood Path Start-up Protocol found in the Appendix.

Recording How You Feel About Less People Identifying Themselves As Environmentalists

In your journal register your impressions and reactions to the following statements garnered from Gallup Inc:

1. The number of Americans who identify themselves as environmentalists has plummeted, from 78% in 1991 to 42 % in 2016.
2. "One reason for the decline is that the environment has become politicized as an issue . . . In 1991 between Democrats and Republicans the same high percentages considered themselves environmentalists. Today, "27% of Republicans think of themselves that way, compared with 56 % of Democrats, a partisan gap of 29 percentage points."
3. There "has been a broader decline in personal environmentalism at the same time that the environment has turned into more of a Democratic than Republican issue."
4. "There does not appear to be a strong generational element to identifying as an environmentalist . . ."
5. One "possibility for the decline is that the 'environmentalist" term may just be less commonly used than it was 25 years ago and may not resonate with Americans as much as it did in the past."

6. "To some degree, too, the term "environmentalist' may be associated with protestors who have taken more radical actions to the protect the environment against perceive threats."

7. Also, many environmentally sensitive actions are now commonplace. As a result, it may take more significant action than recycling or conserving energy for one to consider one to consider oneself an environmentalist today, but that may not have been the case in the past."

8. "Americans express less concern about certain environmental problems now then in the last 1980s and early 1990s, but that varies by problem" Concern for pollution of rivers and lakes fell 12 percent, concern about air pollution fell 18 percent, and concern about loss of tropical rain forests fell 2 percent. Bucking the trend, concern about climate change increased 4 percent.

9. When "considering trade-offs between protecting the environment and promoting economic growth, Americans are less inclined today they they were in 1991)71% to 20%)" (Gallop, Inc:http://www.gallup.com/poll/190916/americans-identification-environmentalists-down.aspx).

Do you think that the decline in Americans' willingness to identify themselves as environmentalist is likely a result of the politicization of environmental issues? Explain your answer.

Do you think that the decline in Americans' willingness to identify themselves as environmentalist is likely a result of actions such as recycling and saving energy being routine or taken for granted and therefore not applicable to the word "environmentalist."

Do you think that the statistics mentioned above are a result of the environmental movements success (becoming mainstream) or do you see these figures as a result of the environmental movements failure (perhaps being too identified with radicalism or with one political party).

Do you see such statistics as the environmental movement being a victim of its own success (the perception of cleaner air, for example) or its own failure (only a label for extremists, for example).

In what ways, if any, do such figures/statistics motivate you to action.

Explain whether you can see a person's identification as an environmentalist as one way for that person to form a More-Than-Individual-Self? What other identifications or memberships do people in your life have that help them form their more-than-individual identities?

Follow-up Protocol

For best results, write down your impressions of this activity in your journal using the Heartwood Path Follow-up Protocol found in the Appendix. Afterwards, consider sharing your interpretations with others.

Heartwood Path Axioms

Key Assertions From Waypoint 4.17

4.17.1.

Act to stem the Ego.

4.17.2.

The beginning of conscious awareness of being is the noticing that one is psychologically attached to things both good and bad.

4.17.3.

One can deny the Ego by cutting off its nourishment of thoughts.

4.17.4.

The Ego thrives on rightness and conflict but it dissolves in peace.

4.17.5.

If you would rather be right than at peace it is your Ego that is part of the problem.

Nocturnal Pilgrimage 4.17

For best results, write down your impressions of each night's dreams in your journal using the Heartwood Path Dreaming Time Protocols found in the Appendix. Afterwards, consider sharing your Dream Tending with others.

Marvel at your senses before starting the next outdoor activity. Imagine a moment without them. Think about how your "civilized ways" have diminished your senses. Think about how your pervasive thinking and lack of sensing boosts your Ego and leads to separation and conflict. Prepare to restore your senses as you continuously seek out and appreciate attractive natural beings outside.

Set a dream intention. Sleep. Tend to your dreams. Share your nighttime revelations with others.

Pertinent And Instructive Gems From My Dream Tending Journal

I dreamt, but the dream was not what I intended.

Lesson Learned: We can request a dream but, summoned or not, the dream remains its own. Greater intelligences are coming into play.

When ready, move to the next waypoint: "Inner World Structures." There, you will learn that thinking, like having, detracts from being.

18

Inner World Structures

APPRECIATE THE IMPORTANCE OF STRUCTURES

Just as *physical form* is an aspect of the Realm of Exteriority (the two right leafs on the Four Leaf Model of Integrity) *structure* is a major aspect in the Realm of Interiority (the two left leafs on the Four Leaf Model of Integrity). *Return to Waypoint 2.6, if you need a refresher.* Structure is either built or it is fundamental.

Built structure arises from human efforts or influences. Built structures in the Realm of Interiority include social roles, cognitive-perceptual patterns, identification, and self-image. These are all aspects of the Ego (the small self, the individual self).

Fundamental structures are those that exist before or beyond human actions and include inner-world archetypes. Archetypes collectively make up one's true nature. They are the human Spirit. They are inner world aspects of the Greater Self that are made knowable through peak (mystical) experiences. Exposure to fundamental forms in the Realm of Exteriority (i.e. wilderness areas) leads to greater contact with fundamental structures in the Realm of Interiority (i.e. a sense of oneness).

This co-emergence explains how wilderness experiences lead to a stronger sense of one's true Being, which always has two contrived aspects: person and place. Combining these two artificially created aspects of self into a non-dual aspect of Being (Humanature) creates within us a sense of sacredness. Those who achieve the state of non-duality easily act on behalf of all of existence and its parts. An understanding of non-duality allows self-interests to be transcended.

Wisdom about Humanature—the Whole—guides one's actions in ways that are optimal for the whole. Compassion and skillful action in the service of the environment are the offspring of non-duality.

Out of the formlessness of Being, structure gives birth to the awareness of oneness but also to unproductive thoughts. **Most thinking, like most having, detracts from being.** You can never feel truly and completely at home through thoughts alone. Feelings are also needed.

To Feel A Sense Of Oneness From A Nature Experience...

HumaNatureConnect Activity

Start-up Protocol

If this is not a day when you prefer to spend time in nature without an agenda, do the Heartwood Path Start-up Protocol found in the Appendix.

Finding Oneness In Nature

Take in a few extra breaths before starting. Make a psychological connection with the energy of your chosen natural being and others nearby. Connect with the wholeness of your chosen place. Connect beyond this place to the energy of all creation. As you make these three connections, relax every part of yourself and wallow luxuriously in the magnificence of your local place and world. Let your thinking fall away as you heighten your non-conceptual awareness of your chosen being and its surroundings. Use many of your natural senses, experiencing each of them fully. Imagine becoming one of the attractive beings in your chosen natural place. Draw in energy as this being would. Then expand your range of consciousness to include more of the local natural scene. Continue to breathe deeply. Perceive the attractiveness of your chosen being and its surroundings but do so without mental chatter. Simply attend to the beauty. Notice the peace around you and inside of you. Do not label or judge anything around you. Let the following be the most complicated concept that you form in your mind: express gratitude with each in-breath. Continue in this matter until you notice the dropping of the boundaries between you and your being and your chosen place. Be aware of the attractiveness of beings without forming concepts. If a thought arises, simply fall back into your simple non-conceptual and illiterate awareness. Simply focus on your awareness. Become not you, and do not focus on separateness of others. Continue until you feel a sense of oneness with your chosen being, its surroundings and the greater natural world. As your separateness vanishes from your consciousness, and as the separation of other beings vanishes, become enfolded in the one AttractiveNaturalBeingImpression. Continue until that one impression is the only thing in your awareness. This impression will feel natural, present, alive, wordless, loving, and intelligent. Do not interpret it, just experience it with your natural senses.

Follow-up Protocol

For best results, write down your impressions of this activity in your journal using the Heartwood Path Follow-up Protocol found in the Appendix. Afterwards, consider sharing your interpretations with others.

Heartwood Path Axioms

Key Assertions From Waypoint 4.18

4.18.1.

Appreciate the importance of structures.

4.18.2.

Arising from human efforts or influences, built structures of the inner world include social roles, identification, and self-image—all aspects of the Ego.

4.18.3.

Fundamental structures exist before or beyond human actions and include inner-world archetypes and the human Spirit made knowable through mystical experiences.

4.18.4.

Inner world built structures include social roles, cognitive-perceptual patterns, identification, and self-image—all aspects of the Ego.

4.18.5.

Exposure to wilderness areas leads to greater contact with fundamental structures that may result in a sense of oneness.

4.18.6.

One's True Being is always made up of person and place and this understanding often leads to a sense of sacredness and acts that preserve person and place.

Nocturnal Pilgrimage 4.18

For best results, write down your impressions of each night's dreams in your journal using the Heartwood Path Dreaming Time Protocols found in the Appendix. Afterwards, consider sharing your Dream Tending with others.

For this Nocturnal Pilgrimage, we will help you deal with the dark side of things, adaptability, indirectness, and the value of subterfuge in the delivery of important messages by learning more about the Coyote Totem. This prominent totem is often considered by many Native American Tribes to be the clown of the natural world. It is also thought of as a transformer, a shape-shifter, and a paradoxical trickster. It is said to teach hidden wisdom with a sense of humor. In this way the Coyote Totem balances wisdom with playfulness. Evoking the spirit of the Coyote totem each time you visit a new waypoint and doing its outdoor activity helps you to make things right. Coyote helps you bring about cultural change in ways that may, at first, seem crazy but will, in time, become the norm. If you, at first, feel silly when doing a Heartwood Path Activity, don't just give up. Instead, think of the silly, embarrassing, or whimsical activity as the Coyote using trickery or humor to convey an important teaching.

Pertinent And Instructive Gems From My Dream Tending Journal

I dreamt my ongoing discussion with John, my Missouri wilderness ally, continued with him saying:

"We have enough trouble securing public acceptance. The public will not accept the suggested policies of those who dabble in talking to muses. They will write us off if they hear we are doing things they consider to be superstitious or unscientific."

I woke up before I have a chance to offer my rebuttal.

Lesson Learned: There will be those, presumably like John (we have actually never discussed our dreams), who cannot imagine talking to Dream Images, Animal Spirits, and the like. To such skeptics, I say that the nature-based Images are not really gods from beyond. That would be unscientific and superstitious. The Images are, in actuality, mental configurations born of the marriage of one's own mind—conscious and subconscious—and one's own memories of natural beings that become evident on that bridge of awareness that links inscapes to landscapes. The Images just look sometimes *as if* they are personified gods and they just speak sometimes *as if* they are living representatives of nature.

Then, presuming or sensing some skepticism, I say, don't knock it until you try it. Try it, and when you do, don't doubt it. See for yourself if you don't find guidance, information, and healing. Remember, when practicing eco-psychology along the Heartwood Path "as if" is, for our purposes, as good as "really is."

When ready, move to the next waypoint: "Self In Nature." You will learn about putting a check on your less-than-perfectly-helpful Ego.

19

Self In Nature

SPEND TIME IN NATURE TO PUT CHECKS ON THE EGO

While helpful in infinite ways, thinking—when unchecked—can become compulsive, cloud one's ability to be aware of the fundamental structure of oneness, and keep one in the clutches of the small self that is guided by the Ego. To free oneself from the Ego's clutches, spend time in nature. Wild places help one to relax Egoic grasping because they inspire one to pay more attention to sensory awareness.

Spending time in nature, as you do at the beginning of each of the waypoints along the Heartwood Path, helps you become (or rather recall being) an animal and, in a larger sense, helps you become (or rather recall being) Earth. There can be no oneness until you feel that you have become Earth. To truly feel this way, one will have to recall one's love of innate wholeness, one's enthrallment of a sacred and animate world.

One recalls one's euphoric enchantment with wildness when one runs through a meadow, or shoots a rapid on a beautiful river, or catches a glimpse of a predator on a tropical sandbar. One will not develop euphoric enchantment with wildness through the process of scientific observation. This form of knowing fosters detachment. Even after one identifies, catalogs, names, and dissects objects in nature, one can still feel like a stranger in a strange land.

To overcome this lack of love for one's setting, one needs to "grok." Coined by author Robert Heinlein, "grokking" means to understand "something"—for our purposes, some "being"—through the use of intuition and empathy. As one develops the skill of "grokking" by doing the start-up and follow-up protocols that accompany each waypoint in this series of courses one begins to communicate with beings sympathetically. There will not be an exchange of words (which are mere symbols of "reality"), but the rapport that develops will, nevertheless, lead to a loving exchange.

There is a facet of one's inner world that helps evoke this all-important love of the wild. It is witnessed symbolically in the Southern Stone of the Medicine Wheel of the Psyche of HumaNature. Called by Plotkin the "Wild Indigenous One," this mature psychic ally helps one celebrate . . .

"the full range of emotions rollicking through the embodied psyche . . . By cultivating the Wild Indigenous One in ourselves and in our children, we'll go a long way toward forging new cultures that are not only life sustaining but life enhancing . . .

It helps to remember that healthy sexual attraction is a much more extensive realm than the Western mainstream attraction on genitals . . . Healthy humans naturally experience this kind of somatic rapture with sunshine, flowers, ocean, tree fragrance, breeze, and landscapes" (Plotkin, 2013, pp. 52-54).

To become fully human we will have to embrace our full ecological intelligence. To recall your humanity fully—that is, to experience your full emotional repertoire, your vivacity, and your erotic fire, engage in the second of several Psychic Personality Activities found in this book.

To Vivacity...

HumaNatureConnect Activity

Start-up Protocol

If this is not a day when you prefer to spend time in nature without an agenda, do the Heartwood Path Start-up Protocol found in the Appendix.

Psychic Personality Activity # 2:
Accessing And Cultivating The Wild Indigenous One

Get in touch with the inner mature ally, the Wild Indigenous One. "From your South perspective, be in embodied relationship with the things and creatures you encounter . . ." Offer a gift such as tears of grief, an expression of yearning or joy, a song, a dance, cornmeal, or water, a handful of your breath. Cross over a stream, a fallen log, a passageway between two trees, or some other physical threshold to mark your shift from ordinary consciousness to sacred consequences. Do not eat, do not speak with other humans, and do not enter man-made shelters. Wander without an agenda with your Wild Indigenous One until "**you feel called by something that strongly draws your attention because it attracts,** intrigues, allures, repels, or scares you." After you find this calling, introduce yourself out loud to an attractive natural being. Being audible is important. Tell the Chosen Being who you really are from the perspective of your Wild Indigenous One. Consider mentioning personal truths, doubts, questions, or yearnings. Then, tell the Attractive Being everything about it that you've noticed —its features, what interests you about it, and what finding something about it tells you about yourself. Keep communicating until there seems to be an interruption. When that happens, use the natural senses, your intuition, and your imagination to increase your ability to perceive. At the end, offer your gratitude and a gift to your Chosen Being. (Plotkin, 2013, pp. 70-72).

In your journal, write about you did and what arose in your mind while being receptive and listening.

Follow-up Protocol

For best results, write down your impressions of this activity in your journal using the Heartwood Path Follow-up Protocol found in the Appendix. Afterwards, consider sharing your interpretations with others.

Heartwood Path Axioms

Key Assertions From Waypoint 4.19

4.19.1.

While helpful in infinite ways, thinking—when unchecked— can become compulsive, cloud one's ability to be aware of the fundamental structure of oneness, and keep one in the clutches of the small self guided by the Ego.

4.19.2.

Wild places help one to relax Egoic grasping because they inspire one to pay more attention to sensory awareness.

4.19.3.

There is a facet of one's inner world—the Wild Indigenous One —that helps evoke an all-important love of the wild.

Nocturnal Pilgrimage 4.19

For best results, write down your impressions of each night's dreams in your journal using the Heartwood Path Dreaming Time Protocols found in the Appendix. Afterwards, consider sharing your Dream Tending with others.

Before doing the next outdoor activity, consider what the author of **Awakening To Nature** Charles Cook has to say about what you are doing regularly as part of this course:

> "there's no better setting on earth than the wilderness for going deep within, for exploring our innermost being, and for searching for answers to the most challenging questions . . . And there's no better place in the world than the wild for reaching out to nature and allowing her truths to inform and potentially illuminate" (2001, p.90).

Heeding Barrasch's advice about balance, keep a journal about both your daytime activities in nature and your nighttime dream revelries. Or keep two journals one for daytime activities, and one for your dreams. Take a moment to improve your record-keeping now, before the unfolding richness of your Heartwood Path experiences become deeper and deeper, not only in your outdoor experiences but also in your dreams.

Add depth to your dream journaling by answering the following seven key dream questions, offered by psychoanalyst and author of **The Dream Workbook**, Jill Morris (1985, p. 12):

1. What are your feelings upon awakening? Joy, depression, fear, motivation?
2. What real memories of prior dreams does this dream remind you of?
3. What is the setting of the dream? Indoors, outdoors, or both? Is it someplace familiar?

4. Are there colors in the dream? If so, what are your associations with these colors?
5. What were the preceding day's events that might have influenced this dream?
6. What are the loaded symbols and key phrases in your dream, and what are your associations to them?
7. What are the other traits, as personified by other characters in this dream, that might be parts of yourself that you are disowning?

After sleeping, dreaming, and tending to your dreams, and improving your approach to journaling, do not stay all day inside. Go to an attractive wild place. With the help of Coyote, who may convince you not to take things so seriously, get off the beaten path. You are about to be surprised. Coyote will help you become open to new possibilities. With his help, try something different. Coyote will help you keep things simple as you experience the unexpected. Stop worrying. Go with the flow. Laugh. Succumbing to Coyote will help you transform yourself.

At the next waypoint you will learn about the impermanence of your inner world mental structures. To see what these structures are, move to the next waypoint: "Moving Skeletons."

20

Moving Skeletons

UNDERSTAND STRUCTURE, PARTICULARLY ITS IMPERMANENCE

To make that all-important strike at the Achilles' Heel of the Ego ponder and then act upon this next profound Heartwood Path sutra: All structures—both physical and mental—are unstable. Even seemingly solid buildings are unstable.. They need constant upkeep and succumb to tornados, earthquakes, and children. Thoughts are considered unstable inner-world structures because they come and go rapidly and unpredictably.

The Problem With The Inner World Structure Of Thoughts

Thoughts arising from the Ego are usually either about wanting or thwarted wanting (which produces anger, resentment, blaming, complaining, or being indifferent). None of these types of thought serve the greater good. When one knows that structures, including thoughts from the Ego, are unstable one naturally seeks a better foundation and begins to open the door to Awareness.

The Ego Demands Attention

Without this Awareness one is largely at the mercy of the Ego. Not caring that one's sense of wellbeing comes from one's Inner Being, the Ego seeks attention and acknowledgment through forms from the Realm of Exteriority or structures from the Realm of Interiority.

The Innocent/Sage

One inner world structure is the next of Plotkin's four mature Psychic Personalities (the others being the Nurturing Generative Adult and the Wild Indigenous One—described earlier—and the Muse-Beloved One—described later in this book. Now we will focus on the inner ally connected with the outermost eastern stone on the Medicine Wheel of the Psyche of HumaNature—the Innocent/Sage. The slash in this inner ally's name reminds us that this Psychic Personality not only embraces the paradox of innocence and sagacity (purity and wisdom) but also, like an oracle, takes a mountaintop perspective which it uses to inspire us to let go of lesser things and to consider what is truly of lasting value. Writes Plotkin: "The (Innocent/Sage) acts from what often seems to be innocence, insanity, or lampoonery but is no less wise for it" (2013, pp. 82-83).

"The Innocent/Sage, to be more precise, is a connoisseur of the senses" (Plotkin, 2014, p. 88). To practice the Innocent/Sage's "full-presence sensing" (Plotkin, 2014, p.88), do the following activity at dawn, the time of the outermost East stone on the Medicine Wheel of the Psyche of HumaNature, the time of the Innocent/Sage.

To A Larger Unfolding Life...

HumaNatureConnect Activity
Start-up Protocol

If this is not a day when you prefer to spend time in nature without an agenda, do the Heartwood Path Start-up Protocol found in the Appendix.

Psychic Personality Activity # 3:
Accessing And Cultivating The Innocent/Sage

Conduct a praise walk and engage in a nature-based form of meditation. Begin the praise walk at day break. Speak directly to the beings you see (not about them). Praise them. Clown it up, if you like. Speak of your attractive natural beings' simple magnificence. Conduct your nature-based form of meditation by simply walking slowly in a wild or semi-wild place. As you continue, open all your senses. Do not shun or cling to any beings you encounter. "Walk with an attitude of loving-kindness towards all beings, human or otherwise" (Plotkin, 2013, p.92).

Follow-up Protocol

For best results, write down your impressions of this activity in your journal using the Heartwood Path Follow-up Protocol found in the Appendix. Afterwards, consider sharing your interpretations with others.

Heartwood Path Axioms

Key Assertions From Waypoint 4.20

4.20.1.

When one knows that structures, including thoughts from the Ego, are unstable one naturally seeks a better foundation and begins to open the door to Awareness.

4.20.2.

Not caring that one's sense of wellbeing comes from one's Inner Being, the Ego seeks attention and acknowledgment through forms from the Realm of Exteriority or structures from the Realm of Interiority.

4.20.3.

One inner world structure is the Innocent/Sage, who not only helps us embrace the paradox of innocence and sagacity (purity and wisdom) but also, like an oracle, helps us take a mountain-top perspective which it uses to inspire us to let go of lesser things and to consider what is truly of lasting value.

4.20.4.

In dreams, one's fixed reference points—such as opinions, values, and judgments—may be revealed as mere tricks of perspective.

Nocturnal Pilgrimage 4.20

For best results, write down your impressions of each night's dreams in your journal using the Heartwood Path Dreaming Time Protocols found in the Appendix. Afterwards, consider sharing your Dream Tending with others.

One way to keep track of the meaning of your dreams is to use the following tips when making your own dream symbol dictionary.

1. Dreams contain many images and symbols, some universal, all personal. Creating your own dream dictionary can help make translating them easier. Use alphabetized loose-sheet dividers.
2. Give a title and include a date for each image, one per sheet. File these images in the alphabetical order of the titles.
3. For each image, list whatever associations automatically come to mind.
4. Record a new date each time this symbol returns to your dreams.
5. Watch how the image changes in relation to your personal growth.
6. Include drawings with the symbols. Do not worry if you are not artistic.

After creating your dream symbol dictionary and tending to your dreams, move to he next waypoint: "Let Go, Ego." There, you will learn how all situation are temporary.

21

Let Go, Ego

USE THE WAYS TO COUNTERACT THE THOUGHTS OF THE EGO

Here are a few suggestions:

1. Know That All Situations Are Temporary.

Feeding on problems, the Ego does not want individual or planetary predicaments to pass. When bad situations arise, saying "This too shall pass" fights the tendency of the Ego to sustain negativities.

2. Separate One's Sense Of Individual Self From One's Roles.

Disassociation from roles was a major aspect of the hippie movement of the Sixties; which itself largely disintegrated into a drug-induced mess but at least left behind a space in the West for non-Western wisdom and spirituality to take root and then helped to awaken the world to global consciousness. You are not just your roles. Your roles are only what you do. You are a full person, a being. Being is ever so much more important than doing.

3. Practice Mindfulness.

Doing, and especially doing that is not rooted in consciousness of being, is futile. Seek to be present in what ever you are doing. In this way, you will have the benefits that come from the alertness and from the Being that is behind the doing; that is, from the grand stage upon which the doing occurs. Without this awareness you will end up suffering.

4. Liberate Yourself From Labels.

Do not allow yourself to be defined as this way or that way. It is better not to be defined. Simply be. Be pure potentiality.

To The Fifteenth Of Many Touchstones Of People-Nature Interfacing...

HumaNatureConnect Activity

Start-up Protocol
If this is not a day when you prefer to spend time in nature without an agenda, do the Heartwood Path Start-up Protocol found in the Appendix.

Generating Patterns Of Human-Nature Interaction # 15:
Killing An Animal

Think about killing an animal after you feel connected to your chosen attractive natural being. In doing this interaction pattern, you could think about shooting exotic wildlife (a perverse interaction pattern) or you could think about killing a farm animal for food (a domestic interaction pattern). By choosing instead to think about shooting a wild deer to feed your family (a wild interaction), you would be thinking about doing something that will have a positive psychological affect on you.

In your journal, write down what meaning you would derive from this wild interaction pattern; what joy, if any, it would produce; how, if at all, it would build within you a bond between your mind and nature; and how, if at all, the wild version of this interaction pattern would be better for you than the perverse or domestic instantiation of the same interaction pattern; and how it would feel to participate in this sort of wild interaction pattern—shooting a wild deer for food. How does interacting in this way in the presence of your attractive natural being make you feel? How would it feel to have this interaction without the presence of your attractive natural being? In writing down these responses you will be adding to our collective nature language, so important to rekindling the bond between humans and nature. Look over your impressions and think about them as you fall asleep tonight before dreaming.

Follow-up Protocol

For best results, write down your impressions of this activity in your journal using the Heartwood Path Follow-up Protocol found in the Appendix. Afterwards, consider sharing your interpretations with others.

Heartwood Path Axioms

Key Assertions From Waypoint 4.21

4.21.1.

Know that all situations are temporary.

4.21.2.

Separate one's sense of individual self from one's roles.

4.21.3.

Practice mindfulness.

4.21.4.

EartHearts liberate themselves from labels.

Nocturnal Pilgrimage 4.21

For best results, write down your impressions of each night's dreams in your journal using the Heartwood Path Dreaming Time Protocols found in the Appendix. Afterwards, consider sharing your Dream Tending with others.

Pertinent And Instructive Gems From My Dream Tending Journal

I dreamt I was a sort of changeling. At first I was like a huge fungus, stretching for acres beneath the forest floor. As such, I could witness all of the vibrations of my neighbors, all of the messages from Dream Images. I felt more-than-individual, in relation, and alive, Then I changed to a rock, tagged for scientific research. The world around me was silent, I felt, separate, sad, and non-living. I felt mechanical and mindless. Someone came by my side, removed the scientist's band and, facing me directly, asked:

"Who are you? Why are you here? Is there anything I can do for you?"

Suddenly, it was as if I was alive. My vibrations, my messages, my guidance registered in the minds and ears of others. In whatever way I was consciously observed, that is the way I was. I liked it best when I could hear everyone singing the Song of the Universe. It made me want to chime in.

And I did.

Lesson Learned: Dream Images are intelligences, living among other no lesser Intelligences. Together they sing an incredible song, full of rhythm, harmony, and meaning.

As you prepare to do the next outdoor activity, begin the process of keeping your expectations open. Leave room for wonder, joy, and astonishment. Make sure that your perspectives and perceptions regarding self, nature, the world, beginnings, awakenings, and awareness are unencumbered by preconceived notions and rigidity.

If you are involved in any negative situations, take heart: there is good news at the next waypoint: "Magnificence." There, you will learn what is valuable in the space between thoughts.

22

Magnificence

ADD FINENESS TO YOUR LIFE

By "fineness" I mean to live in the "Now," to live ecologically, and to live with universal intelligence.

Living In The "Now"

Finding awareness of being—the stage for your thoughts and thus the "you" that is behind all your roles and actions—is achieved by remaining often in the present. And that is a very good way to make peace and to find oneness with life.

Live Ecologically

Life happens on the stage of Now, so being one with Now is being one with life. Present Mindedness, which is the same thing as Awareness of Life (as opposed to just thinking about Life) are precisely the footing one needs to integrate one's individual self into the More-Than-Individual-Self or Ecological Self. Doing so naturally leads to living ecologically (reducing your impact on the Earth by eating less meat, recycling, driving less, and spending with the health of the Earth in mind).

Live With Universal Intelligence

One sign that you have added fineness to your life, as previously defined, is when you recognize that you are not living your life, life is living you. There is no such thing as "my life" or "your life." We do not have our lives and we cannot lose our lives. We do not run our bodies. Universal Intelligence does. You can only lose what you have, not what you truly are. We are life. We are one with the Universal Intelligence that runs our bodies and our Earth.

This Intelligence provides us with our positive emotions, but so does the Ego. Here is one way to distinguish one's Universal Intelligence from one's Ego: whenever a positive emotion such love turns quickly to something negative (possessiveness, addictive clinging, or hate) the positive emotion of love comes from the Ego.

States of positive emotion that do not turn to their opposites–that is, positive emotions that abide as eternal love, joy, or peace—arise from Universal Intelligence. A part of this Universal Intelligence can only be glimpsed through Awareness and not at all through thinking. To beat out rhythms of positive change start by slowing down thoughts so that you can find in the gaps between thoughts the stage of Awareness. This Awareness will inform and improve your thoughts, and thus you will begin beating out a positive future.

A very good way to experience Universal Intelligence, and particularly an aspect of it we call "romantic love," is to illicit the help of the mature inner guide connected symbolically with the outer westernmost stone on the Medicine Wheel of the Psyche of HumaNature. That guide is . . .

The Muse - Beloved

This inner ally is a specialist in giving advice about romance, not merely human romance, but also devotion to non-human beings. The Muse-Beloved is devoted to all natural beings and events. Located at the West stone on the Medicine Wheel of the Psyche of HumaNature, the Muse-Beloved helps us when we seek and savor ecstatic and troubling transformations. Preferring to explore rather than solve a mystery, the Muse willingly falls into the depths, willingly falls into love, and willingly falls into the unknown. The Muse, writes Plotkin, likes "to be immersed in magic . . . (and) to seek the doors to other worlds" (Plotkin, 2013, p.113).

Such proclivities make the Muse-Beloved (a devotee of romance and allurements) unpopular to the leaders of the Mass Culture because in order for the military-industrial society to function at all, it needs "at least half of its citizens to occupy the dull and offensive roles of consumer, worker bee . . . and to experience this desecration as merely normal . . ." (Plotkin, 2013, p.113).

To Feel Alive In An Animate Evolving World...

HumaNatureConnect Activity

Start-up Protocol

If this is not a day when you prefer to spend time in nature without an agenda, do the Heartwood Path Start-up Protocol found in the Appendix.

Psychic Personality Activity # 4:
Accessing And Cultivating The Muse-Beloved

Use your wildest imagination to find out how every perception of the natural beings of the world can be a sort of salvation. Look for a natural being that seems to be affected by the Muse. You will recognize such a natural being "by your strong attraction to it, as well as by your sense of it as at least a bit dangerous, psychologically or spiritually." Tell the Muse-influenced natural being "what you are experiencing, what qualities you feel or sense or imagine there, and how it seems to resonate for you with the Beloved." Open to the possibility of being changed, write a love poem and recite it to your natural being (Plotkin, 2013, pp. 116-117). Focus on your AttractiveNaturalBeingImpressions and describe them in your journal.

Follow-up Protocol

For best results, write down your impressions of this activity in your journal using the Heartwood Path Follow-up Protocol found in the Appendix. Afterwards, consider sharing your interpretations with others.

Heartwood Path Axioms

Key Assertions From Waypoint 4.22

4.22.1.

Finding awareness of being—the stage for your thoughts and thus the "you" that is behind all your roles and actions—is achieved by remaining often in the present.

4.22.2.

Awareness of Life (as opposed to just thinking about Life) is precisely the footing one needs to integrate one's individual self into the More-Than-Individual Cosmic or Ecological Self.

4.22.3.

To beat out rhythms of positive change start by slowing down
thoughts so that you can find in the gaps between thoughts—
the stage of Awareness.

4.22.4.

A very good way to experience Universal Intelligence, and
particularly and aspect of it we call "romantic love," is to illicit
the help of the mature inner guide called the "Muse - Beloved,"
who is a specialist in giving advice about romance, not merely
human romance, but also devotion to non-human beings.

4.22.5.

As you spend some time talking with your Nocturnal Envoys—
your Dream Figures—do not focus solely on meanings but
broaden the conversation to include contexts, desires, and
views of the future and avoid censoring your notes of these
conversations.

Nocturnal Pilgrimage 4.22

For best results, write down your impressions of each night's
dreams in your journal using the Heartwood Path Dreaming Time
Protocols found in the Appendix. Afterwards, consider sharing your
Dream Tending with others.

Now that you have numerous dream images recorded in your dream
journal and several animated in three-dimensional form (actual Dream
Council members) spend some time talking with your Nocturnal Envoys—another name for your Dream Council Members. Do not focus

solely on meanings but broaden the conversation to include contexts, desires, and views of the future. Try to avoid censoring your notes of these conversations. Feel the Nocturnal Envoy's personality. Animate each Dream Council Member by engaging with it in a dialogue.

With this in mind, sleep, dream, and, after you awaken, recall a dream or two and then answer the following questions in relation to your chosen dream(s):

1. What are the unusual or personally significant images in your dream? What do these mean to you?
2. Who are the other people or dream characters in your dream? Are they strangers or people you know? Do they change identity during the dream?
3. What are the personality traits, actions, or lack of action of your dream ego (the character in your dream whom you recognize as yourself)?
4. What are the primary emotions in your dream?
5. What are the different points of view in your dream?
6. What are the conflicts and unresolved feelings and situations in the dream?
7. What are the opposites or contrasts in the dreams?
8. What is currently happening in your conscious waking life (. . . one (has to) understand the context of a dream metaphor to appreciate its meaning) (Morris, 1985, p. 34).

Before doing the next outdoor activity, consider how your eyesight may be diminished from excess up-close indoor reading, how your hearing may be diminished by low urban noise, how your sense of smell may be retreating in the presence of indoor air pollution or noxious fumes or unpleasant automobile exhausts, how your sense of taste may be under assault by the blandness of most supermarket/fast foods, and how your sense of touch may be compromised by social injunctions against touching each other. Use the outdoor activities that follow as a way to rekindle your senses.

After these considerations, continue to the next waypoint: "Negative Energy." Prepare to get some good information about what to do about the Grieving Ghost that resides within you.

23

Negative Energy

WEAKEN THE GRIP OF THE GRIEVING GHOST

Drumming up a positive future—more specifically, creating a positive state for both people and the planet—will require more than slowing down thoughts and reconnecting with the Universal Intelligence of Awareness in the ever-present Now, as important as those steps are. What also has to happen is the diminishment of a semiautonomous energy-form that lives within human beings. This energy form—I'll call it the Grieving Ghost—is negative emotion. Unsurprisingly, the Grieving Ghost's preferred haunts are in intimate relationships and families. It likes these haunts because these surroundings provide it with its preferred food: negativity, drama, and unhappiness.

Troubles From The Grieving Ghost

Signs of the impact of the Grieving Ghost are many. They include sullenness, withdrawal, and unhappiness.

The Grieving Ghost likes to inflict and suffer pain, so it can either be a perpetrator or a victim. People, influenced by their Grieving Ghost, may find themselves repeatedly working on noble causes only to find that, with time, the effort goes sour as they unconsciously succumb to the Ghost's need for enemies, drama, conflict, and reasons for feeling bad.

Alleviating Troubles From The Grieving Ghost

To rid yourself of the impacts of the Grieving Ghost, cast your awareness upon it, do not identify with it, and engage in yoga, T'ai chi, meditative sexual practices described in the Heartwood Path for Couples book (entitled **Eros)**, or any activity that reduces or eliminates the separation between body and Spirit. In doing so, your thinking will no longer be so clouded by the negativity of the past and you will also put a space—like a box—around any negativity that is affecting your life. When one breaks one's identification with the Grieving Ghost a transformation begins—a transformation towards the sacred, ecological, More-Than-Individual, compound Self. Your dismay, fragmentation, and resistance to unity fade away. You become one with the nature of God. Make this union, as Jesus commanded you to do: "Be ye perfect, even as Your Father in Heaven is perfect." How, you may ask? Here is the answer, highlighted below because it also alludes to the main purpose of the Heartwood Path:

" . . . be made perfect in one."

(John 17:16, 21-23)

We shall see that becoming "perfect in one" means working towards becoming whole.

To A Re-look At Dream Associations…

HumaNatureConnect Activity

Start-up Protocol

If this is not a day when you prefer to spend time in nature without an agenda, do the Heartwood Path Start-up Protocol found in the Appendix.

Returning To Freud's Free Associations For Dream Interpretation

Return to a consideration of one of Freud's theories that has not been substantially altered or discarded: free association. To practice free association, take a description of one of your dreams from your dream journal, pick out a particularly pithy paragraph, write each sentence vertically, with one word on each line, and next to each word, associate words or phrases to each word in your description of a recalled dream. Let the words flow, with no censorship. Then, rewrite the paragraph using only your associated words or phrases. Note how any telling revelations can come from the new version of the dream.

Follow-up Protocol

For best results, write down your impressions of this activity in your journal using the Heartwood Path Follow-up Protocol found in the Appendix. Afterwards, consider sharing your interpretations with others.

Heartwood Path Axioms

Key Assertions From Waypoint 4.23

4.23.1.

Anyone attempting to arrive at Gladandgreen Junction will need to diminish a semiautonomous energy-form that lives

within humans, called the "Grieving Ghost," and composed of
negative emotion.

4.23.2.

To rid yourself of the impacts of the Grieving Ghost, cast your
awareness upon it, do not identify with it, and engage in yoga,
T'ai chi, meditative sexual practices, or any activity that
reduces or eliminates the separation between body and Spirit.

4.23.3.

When one breaks one's identification with the Grieving Ghost
a transformation begins—a shift towards the sacred, ecological,
More-Than-Individual, compound Self that fades away dismay,
fragmentation, and resistance to unity and helps you become
one with the nature of God or, in other words "perfect in one."

4.23.4.

Tending to one's dreams is essential for self-knowledge and
personal growth.

Nocturnal Pilgrimage 4.23

For best results, write down your impressions of each night's
dreams in your journal using the Heartwood Path Dreaming Time
Protocols found in the Appendix. Afterwards, consider sharing your
Dream Tending with others.

"Jung was initially a disciple of Freud," writes Jill Morris, but rather "than accepting Freud's theory that sexual desire emanated from in-cestuous feelings, (Jung) maintained that people essentially longed for the security, protection, and mutual love and trust ideally expressed in the parental relationship . . . According to Jung, dreams contained the blueprint for personal growth and thus were essential for self-knowledge . . . Dreams create a balance of personality by bringing to the forefront the unconscious functions" (1985, pp. 68-71).

With the lesson of this waypoint and Jill Morris's statement in mind, set an intention for tonight's dream. Set the intention to have a lucid dream. After it begins, become more fully a part of the universe by amplifying your dream (by expanding the perceived stature of a Dream Image into an archetype), as previously instructed.

Pertinent And Instructive Gems From My Dream Tending Journal

I dreamt that I was a guest in a man's house. He is sitting in a recliner chair, watching the television. He seems mesmerized by the news stories on the television. The room is a large sunroom, with large openable windows on three sides. From this sunroom, if the man would look up, he could see a lush forest valley, beautiful and unspoiled. Immediately outside of the three big windows stand three men, who are actually Natural Beings who chose to be personified so the man can reap the benefits of their wisdom. The man is oblivious to the scenery and the three Personified Images waiting patiently for his attention. There is no time for the man to be interested in his team of advisors. He is too busy buying whatever shows up in the commercial on his television set. He is restless, never satisfied. I am bored and give sympathetic shrugs of misunderstanding to each of the assembled Images.

Lesson Learned: We have to get out of our houses and away from electronic screens or we will likely never slow down, never get in touch with nature and our inscapes, and never learn what it takes to be happy in a sustainable environment. We have fallen under the spell of Modern Culture. It uses the television and the Internet as tools for the exploitation of nature. Had the man turned to any one of the Images, and sought permission to have a connection experience through his extended attraction, he would have received an antidote for his sedentary and mind-numbing affliction, he would have been convinced not to be a consuming agent, and he would have been prevented, if only for a brief moment, from being an accomplice in the murder of nature.

When you are ready, tend to your dream and move to the next waypoint: "Perfect Means Whole." Persevere. When doing the activity that is found at the next waypoint, immerse your senses in nature for therapeutic purposes. Revamp your under-stimulated senses in the attractive stimuli you find at the natural landscape you visit.

24

Perfect Means Whole

WORK TOWARDS WHOLENESS THROUGH DIALOGUE WITH INNER GUIDES

What is meant by the Biblical words "perfect in one" is understandable when one learns that the word "perfect" was translated for use in both the King James version and contemporary versions of the Bible from a Greek word which also means "whole." This course is my attempt to describe what it means to be "perfect in one." Perfection comes only after one integrates one's self into the "Cosmic Christ" ("I in them, and thou in me")—"me" being Jesus, but also the one, the whole, and the pattern that connects the whole.

Perfection/wholeness comes from personal development or, more accurately, personal envelopment of more aspects of Integrity; by which I mean incorporating into one's sense of self an enduring lasting stage of development marked by a high level of intentions, a high level of ethics, high forms of behaviors (those that help the most beings thrive), and a high number of physical systems into your sense of self—high in the sense of transcending and including all possible (or aspired to) aspects of the whole as depicted on the Four Leaf Model of Integrity (first described in Waypoint 2.6.) While higher transformations

167

are achieved by following the Heartwood Path, there is no room for condemning lower levels of envelopment. Everyone has a right to occupy whatever stage of personal growth they prefer. All lower levels are necessary.

Along the Heartwood Path, perfection is not to be preordained. Perfection and a high level of development really means increased envelopment of more and more aspects of one's Greater Self.

We are perfect already. What we need to do is anchor our individuality and recall and envelop into our sense of Self more of the collective aspects of our Greater Self. Individuation is just as important to reaching Glandandgreen Junction as is integration.

To master this integration or to envelop more Integrity (both personal and universal, both inner world and outer world) into your sense of Self, it will be necessary to deal appropriately with some of the inner guides that gave you advice that was useful to you when you, being less mature, could only understand their immature suggestions. In other words, immature advice was suitable when you were immature, but now that you are more mature, mature advice is best. Giving the immature inner allies (which include the Escapists, the Blissheads, the Addicts, and the Wound Children; if necessary *return to Waypoint 3.9 in Heartwood Path Course: Egos*) a proper retirement is a useful step towards the kind of wholeness/perfect/envelopment that comes (or can come) with maturity. You will likely never reach the upper levels of psycho-spiritual development until you start listening to Mature Inner World Allies (such as the Wild Indigenous One, the Innocent Sage or the other Mature Inner World Allies described at Waypoint 4.12 earlier in this book) and stop listening only to immature inner allies.

I am not suggesting that you cast off these immature allies. They may still be of some use to you. Being influenced unduly by immature inner allies promotes individual survival and the avoidance of psychic pain but it also prevents one's envelopment of much of the deeper aspects of one's own Greater Self. It may have been useful some time in your past but now is the time to stop taking so much advice from immature inner world guides that tell, for example, you that money is more important than people or that the unrestrained nurturing of others is solely a virtue when, in truth, you have to strike a balance between giving and taking.

Voice Dialogue With Immature Inner Allies

As demonstrated in the next activity, a better approach than banishing your immature allies is to "employ voice dialogue to heal your relationships with your sub-personalities." Such conversations with your immature and mature Inner Allies are done to to get to know them better, to discover new inner advisors, to explore the nature of the survival strategies of Inner Allies. After you have moved to a greater dialogue with Mature Inner Allies, voice dialogue can be used to welcome back Immature Inner Allies into your "circle of care" (Plotkin, 2013, p. 251).

To A Dialogue With Immature Inner Allies...

HumaNatureConnect Activity

Start-up Protocol

If this is not a day when you prefer to spend time in nature without an agenda, do the Heartwood Path Start-up Protocol found in the Appendix.

Dialoging With Inner Allies

Make peace with your Inner Allies, access more aspects of one's wholeness, and explore more aspects of one's woundedness that will likely prevent one's envelopment of the higher (deeper) aspects of the Greater Self. It is time for your immature inner allies to sing their Swan Song. Ask each immature sub-personality what it has to say at this moment, which amounts to its retirement celebration. Be sure to solicit statements from your Loyal Soldiers, The Shadow, the Escapists and Addicts, the Wound Children. Call for statements from other sub-personalities not currently in your awareness. Listen actively to all of their statements, as registered in your imagination. In response, tell each of your inner world sub-personalities that you understand their statements, that you appreciate their service, that you have found more mature inner world allies, that the war of childhood survival is over, and that you will continue to appreciate and admire the advice you have received.

Follow-up Protocol

For best results, write down your impressions of this activity in your journal using the Heartwood Path Follow-up Protocol found in the Appendix. Afterwards, consider sharing your interpretations with others.

Heartwood Path Axioms

Key Assertions From Waypoint 4.24

4.24.1.

What is meant by the words "perfect in one" is understandable when one learns that the word "perfect" was translated for use in both the King James version and contemporary versions of the Bible from a Greek word which also means "whole."

4.24.2.

Perfection/wholeness comes from personal development or, more accurately, personal envelopment of more aspects of Integrity; by which I mean incorporating into one's sense of self a lasting stage of development marked by a high level of

intentions, a high level of ethics, high forms of behaviors (those that help the most beings flourish), and a high number of physical systems (for example, the Commons, the ecosystem, or the biome) into your sense of self—high in the sense of transcending and including all possible (or aspired to) aspects as depicted on the Four Leaf Model of Integrity.

4.24.3.

Everyone has a right to occupy whatever stage of development they prefer.

4.24.4.

Along the Heartwood Path, perfection is not to be preordained: perfection and a high level of development really means increased envelopment of more and more aspects of one's Greater Self.

4.24.5.

To envelop more Integrity (both personal and universal, both inner world and outer world) into your sense of Self, it will be necessary to deal appropriately with some of the inner guides that give you advice that was useful to you when you, being less mature, could only understand their age-appropriate immature suggestions.

Nocturnal Pilgrimage 4.24

For best results, write down your impressions of each night's dreams in your journal using the Heartwood Path Dreaming Time

Protocols found in the Appendix. Afterwards, consider sharing your Dream Tending with others.

One thing I like to do when my dreams end before they are finished or when I do not like the ending is to change the ending to my liking. I do this by noticing that I am dreaming, lying perfectly still, and giving the dream a more satisfactory ending. Try it. After your dream, record your impressions in your dream journal. Also, work again on amplifying your dreams by looking for or creating archetypal images. Recall key dream images—one's that you have unresolved feelings about or ones that make a strong impact on your senses or thoughts. Describe them even more comprehensively. Write a detailed description of the image and its history. Describe their physical appearances, attitudes, and relationship to the "real" waking world. Write down everything without censoring yourself. Doing so will encourage the image to grow, transform, and reveal its mythic aspects—parts of itself that belong to the collective unconscious. Writes Morris: (Allow your amplified image) "to speak to you; ask it: Who are you? What do you wish to tell me? . . . You may be amazed by what you discover" (1986, p. 72).

Pertinent And Instructive Gems From My Dream Tending Journal

I dreamt I had a dream that was not what I intended.

Lesson Learned: We can request a dream but, summoned or not, the Dream remains it's own. Greater intelligences are coming into play.

When you do the activity at the next waypoint, focus your eyesore-weary eyes on the interesting, beautiful, and restful visual treats you find in nature. Follow your eyes to the wild places they want to roam. When nature mentors your eyes, the result is often insight.

After practicing giving your dreams different endings, and after working again on amplifying your dreams with archetypes, move to the next waypoint: "The Big Me." You are about to discover your More-Than-Human Self.

25

The Big Me

DISCOVER THE
MORE-THAN-INDIVIDUAL SELF

If the self is influenced excessively by the Ego, as it is in many people, faults, beliefs, and negative statements become dominant. Most people spend the bulk of their lives striving to overcome limitations, physical weaknesses, and financial scarcity. Much of the remaining time is spent creating something life–enhancing beyond their individual selves such as in a job, in a relationship, through a work of art, or in a place to live. This devotion of time is typically positive, but not all that it can be.

When a person views abundance as arising only from beyond the self, the fullness and fineness of life cannot be incorporated into one's being. When one discovers the source of abundance within, however, giving becomes easier and receiving becomes a regular, continuous aspect of one's life. Life becomes good when one becomes whole.

Here are ten tips for how to seek the perfection of wholeness Jesus summoned you to become:

Perfection-seeking Tip # 1.

Seek Perfection Through Immersion In A Natural Place

While there, avoid judgments, trying to understand, or attempting to explain. Over time, with this type of practice, the natural world, its wonders, and its seemingly unplanned abundance will flow into your sense of Self. You will become aligned with wholeness. And the totality of life will act through you. That which is in you that is formless will become gradually more encompassing.

Perfection-seeking Tip # 2.

Remain In The "Suchness" Of The Present Moment

By this I mean to be aware of the present, of life, and of you—which are all one. Being in a state of oneness—"isness"—will help you become a conscious participant in the wholeness of being. Your participation is marked by the peculiar role you as a human play in the Universe: through you as a human the Universe becomes conscious of itself. A good way to become conscious of the Universal Self beyond the individual self is to limit extreme agitation of the mind or emotions.

Perfection-seeking Tip # 3.

Limit Distractions

To do so, close your eyes and see nothing. Cover your ears and experience the stillness. Doing these things will remove visual and auditory sounds from your consciousness so you will become more easily aware of the formless consciousness that lies behind sensory experience. Through the inner poise of stillness one can harness a formidable power, become sensitive to truths, reach deep insights, and make right decisions. When no longer obscured by visual, auditory, or continuous thought structures, formless consciousness resonates more fully with your own true being. If you become stuck in worry about things and situations, remember these words from humorist Mark Twain. "I've lived through some terrible things in my life, some of which actually happened" (MacGregor, 2010, p. 258). If bad things do happen, say: "This too shall pass." This statement helps one accept what comes.

Perfection-seeking Tip # 4.

Practice Inner Nonresistance To Events

Instead of focusing constantly on events, things and situations, avoid judgments; and remember that all events, things, and situations are impermanent. The best of happiness comes from the least of things.

Perfection-seeking Tip # 5.

Practice Non-attachment To Outcomes

Do not place undo demands upon the world, saying always "fulfill me," "make me happy," or "make me feel safe." The perpetual desire for safety and taking no risks keeps greatness and nobility away from all enterprises.

As a way to further feel the "isness" of the Sacred Self". . .

Perfection-seeking Tip # 6.

Dwell Often In Silence

Withhold from others some expressions of your thoughts and intentions, by reducing the quantity of your spoken words, and by practicing soft and slow speech. Vocalizations from one's vital/life center carry life-energy that ought to not be squandered on speaking too many words, or speaking too loudly, or speaking to rapidly.

Perfection-seeking Tip # 7.

Focus On Space Consciousness

Suffering follows those who focus heavily on their own desires, who overvalue form, who constantly want one darn thing after another, and who are unaware of the space—the heaven—that, along with form, make up the oneness of Being. To find oneness, to return sanity to Earth, form consciousness needs to be checked, limited, reduced, and kept from being dominant over space consciousness. Things, sense perceptions, thoughts, and emotions fall into the realm of form consciousness. Space consciousness is awareness of being that comes from inner stillness. It is the awareness of what is not "objectifiable." It is awareness of what is not identifiable with thought. It is the awareness that is in between and beyond thoughts, emotions, and beliefs. In contrast, form consciousness—some call it object consciousness—is the awareness of things.

Let us say that you come across a Jack-In-The Pulpit plant. If you say to yourself "there is a pretty natural object" you are engaged in form consciousness because you are thinking about a thing. Even if you say "there is an attractive natural being" you are still engaged in form consciousness because you are identifying the object of your thought as being attractive, natural, and having its own "isness." The whole universe is made up of form (objects, physical things) and non-things (the space between and beyond things, including intelligence, love, relationship, and guidance).

Many, many times in my life people have said to me something equivalent to "I notice you are in deep thought and I am wondering what you were thinking about." When I reply, "Nothing" they tend to think that I am being evasive. But it is often true. I am not thinking of any thing. I am "spaced out" in a state of space consciousness. I am aware of my surroundings but not generating thoughts (or I am not attaching myself to the flow of thoughts).

Thoughts of things can be wonderfully helpful. But awareness of the space between and beyond thoughts is ever so much more fruitful, particularly if you are interested in achieving a state of oneness (perfection). You cannot get into this state by thinking about things alone. You also have to become aware of the "non-thingness" of the space across which thoughts flow. This is where pure attraction is. This is where relationship is. This is where pure love is. This is where pure intelligence is. This is where you find all the bounty of nothingness. Experiencing it is, at least, refreshing and, more often than not, life-changing.

Try it right now: find any object or natural being. Become aware of it. But do not name it. Do not think about it or anything else. Just simply be aware. You are only looking at the thing to slow down your thoughts or to perhaps uncover the space surrounding this object. Being aware of your breathing is the more common way to slow down extraneous thought. If thoughts creep in, let them pass. With practice, you won't need to first look at a thing, you will be able to tune out the world of things and live for a moment aware of non-things. Contemplation of non-things is a type of consciousness that is used most by sages. We along the Heartwood Path, seeking to become saints rather than sages (at least, at first), do not throw out form. Instead, we use it to guide us to our most needed non-form (non-thing). We limit our thinking about form by finding and then focusing only on the attractive natural being. We do not focus long on thoughts of the object nor on awareness of unattractive, unnatural objects.

We guide ourselves to the natural attractive being because in, around, and beyond this being is a unique realm of space (of nothingness) that is a source of much guidance. Instead of holding on within our minds to form-filled thoughts, we use the attractive natural being to guide us to a space—the being's particular cove of nothingness.

Then we switch from form consciousness to a type of space consciousness by bringing to us across the bridge of our Attractive-NaturalBeingImpression a bounty of no-thing benefits. These will be wonderful thought-free "spacey" impressions that we then later tend in much the same way as we tend to our dreams.

There is, for example, ever so much more valuable no-thing space around an oak tree than there is around a worn out tire. So it is not the oak but its no-thing space that is the source of valuable thought-free impressions. This oak is just the signpost for where you can find whatever space is most useful to you in the present moment.

Follow your attractions in nature and you will find no-thing space that you can use to form an AttractiveNaturalBeingImpression that is about no-thingness rather than thingness. In this space, which you found by following your attractions, you will find not thoughts, not concrete messages, but impressions that will give you no-things like you have never had before.

Whenever in your Heartwood Path Activities you find an attractive natural being, thank it for leading you to its valuable nothing-ness. By following your attractions in nature you have found the thought-free space that will give you exactly the impressions you need in the present moment. The concrete value will come after you have tended to your impressions through a process similar to Dream Tending and through the process of journaling. It is during Dream Tending and during the actions listed in the Start-up and Follow-up Protocols that you can bring back into the process the values associated with form and thinking.

Perfection-seeking Tip # 8.

Reconcile Your Purpose With Your Performance

Things happen in the foreground. Awareness happens in the background—that space where the Ego does not reign, where materialism and materiality do not dominate, and where true meaning originates. From the valley of the Ecological Self, one arises above thoughts and is more able to say "I am" without needing to tag more on to it. From this valley, actions become right more often; that is to say, they are perfect in that they are appropriate to the whole. This appropriateness comes from the reconciliation of one's inner world purpose to one's outer world behaviors. This reconciliation is where integrity originates. Appropriateness to the whole is the purpose of ecological reform, impossible without right actions that are guided by right thinking that is informed by right awareness.

Perfection-seeking Tip # 9.

Perceive Aspects Of The Universal Self

Perceiving aspects of the Universal Self—the Ecological Self that is More-Than-Individual (an aspect of HumaNature that is included into one's sacred, compound Self)—, allows one to break the spell of being possessed almost solely by the Ego; allows one to break away from excessive individual thinking; and allows one to cease from constant naming, judging, and interpreting. All of these allowances help one find the sense of oneness. How do you accomplish such perceiving? Suggestion Number 10 below, and the two following activities, will help. In them I encourage you to visit natural beings (objects of nature) and natural scenes, in part, because these types of forms demonstrate the creative power of the universe. They also represent good and familiar objects from which to launch one's awareness of less familiar space.

Perfection-seeking Tip # 10.

Look For Inner Space, The Peace Of Heaven On Earth

To do so, engage in two activities: one for tending to your waking time in the next activity, and the other tending to the wilderness of your dreams. This second activity is included in the next Nocturnal Pilgrimage section.

In finishing this second activity you will be crossing one of the most important bridges to Gladandgreen Junction found along the Heartwood Path.

You are learning that it is the attractive natural being that serves to guide you to its particular non-thing space. You are learning that by engaging in space consciousness, which focuses without thoughts on the non-thing space between and beyond the natural being, you are able to use your AttractiveNaturalBeingImpressions to form a bridge that brings to you no-things that can later be tended in ways that will be of enormous value to you.

To An Enlarged Perspective...

HumaNatureConnect Activity

Start-up Protocol

If this is not a day when you prefer to spend time in nature without an agenda, do the Heartwood Path Start-up Protocol found in the Appendix.

Expanding Your Awareness

Choose an attractive natural being in nature and explore it visually. Without straining, give your complete attention to this natural being. Become aware of this natural being without thinking. Take the thinking out of the perceiving. Expand your awareness to the scene in nature around the natural being. Listen to the sounds of nature. Do not judge the natural being, the scene, or the sounds. Avoid all interpretations. If your thinking gets in the way, pay close attention to your breathing as you observe the natural being and the natural scene. Breathing is a worthy point of attention for this exercise because it is so formless. Any amount of time observing the natural being, observing the scene, and being aware of your breathing will be sufficient. Observing natural beings without thinking and conscious breathing brings one into awareness of Inner Space. Seek to become aware of the calmness of both the scene and the stillness within yourself.

The calmness of the scene and the stillness of one's Inner Space is the Peace of Heaven on Earth. To fully incorporate the Universal Self one may choose to begin with observance without thinking about a natural object/being or scene. Next, observe your own breathing and the space between breaths that is the stage upon which you can find first your physical body, then your individual self, and eventually the Universal Self. One can thus enter the body consciously as a way to go beyond it and then discover that one is not just the breath, nor the body, nor the individual self. To move beyond the obsession of thoughts, and to move psychologically away from the body, from the breath, from the scene, and from the sense of an individual self to the sense of the Universal Self feels like a entering into Heaven on Earth This entering occurs through awareness of the ever-present space that is the essence of the Present observable through stillness. The awareness of the Present that fills the space between breaths and between thoughts is eternal, formless consciousness. Stillness fills space. Inner world space, more than outer world form, brings true perspective and balance into one's life.

Follow-up Protocol

For best results, write down your impressions of this activity in your journal using the Heartwood Path Follow-up Protocol found in the Appendix. Afterwards, consider sharing your interpretations with others.

Heartwood Path Axioms

Key Assertions From Waypoint 4.25

4.25.1.

When a person views abundance as arising only from beyond the self, the fullness and fineness of life cannot be incorporated into one's being.

4.25.2.

When one discovers the source of abundance within, however, giving becomes easier and receiving becomes a regular, continuous aspect of one's life.

4.25.3.

Ten tips for how to seek the perfection of wholeness:

1. Seek Perfection Through Immersion In A Natural Place;

2. Remain In The "Suchness" Of The Present Moment;

3. Limit Distractions;

4. Instead Of Focusing Constantly On Events, Things And Situations, Avoid Judgments; And Remember That All Events, Things, And Situations Are Impermanent;

5. Practice Non-attachment To Outcomes;

6. Dwell Often In Silence;

7. Focus On Space Consciousness—Awareness Of Being That Comes From Inner Stillness;

8. Reconcile Your Purpose With Your Performance;

9. Perceive Aspects Of The Distill Self;

10. Look For Inner Space, The Peace Of Heaven On Earth.

4.25.4.

Inner world space, more than outer world form, brings true perspective and balance into one's life.

4.25.5.

Primetime television, pervasive nighttime lighting indoors, the demonization of the dark, shorter nights sleeping, reduced autonomic mechanisms, bills making it hard to stop working just because the sun has set, porch lights, commercial lights, street lights, car lights, glowing computer screens, flickering televisions, and the accumulation of everything that makes it light at night results in an insatiable hunger for personal energy.

Nocturnal Pilgrimage 4.25

For best results, write down your impressions of each night's dreams in your journal using the Heartwood Path Dreaming Time Protocols found in the Appendix. Afterwards, consider sharing your Dream Tending with others.

Along with the global energy crisis there is a personal energy crisis. Prime time television, pervasive nighttime lighting indoors, the demonization of the dark, shorter nights sleeping, reduced autonomic mechanisms, bills making it hard to stop working even though the sun has set, porch lights, commercial lights, street lights, car lights, glowing computer screens, flickering televisions, and the accumulation of everything that makes it light at night results in . . .

> "an insatiable hunger for personal energy. To compensate for our sleep and dream-deprived (lives) and maintain our frenetic drive, we reflexively spike our waking hours with counterfeit energies. We are a society of energy addicts, with lifestyles designed to provide us with quick fixes of caffeine and sugar on demand" (Naiman, 2006, p. 3).

Important Additional Activity:

Trail Map Across the Wilderness of Your Dreams

More than a distraction from the nocturnal counterfeit energies just mentioned in the quote by Naiman, the following activity will help you find something better to do, and help you begin to get in the habit of occupying yourself productively away from an electronic screen.

The next activity is not only important because it helps you to make sense out of your dreams but also because it will help you develop the methods for making some sense out of the no-thing impressions you get from communing with attractive natural beings. You are learning how to glean benefits from your dreams, skills that will also help you glean benefits from your AttractiveNaturalBeing Impressions. Some of our processes may seem quite involved, but I can tell you from experience that it is worth doing things right. You too will soon discover that the results are worth the effort. Once you are good at tending to your dreams in the ways we suggest, you will discover that many, if not most, of your AtrractiveNaturalBeingImpressions will show up as dream images which can then be processed into thinkable notions that become concrete benefits.

With these encouragements in mind, engage in the seven-step process of making a trail map across the wilderness of your dreams, as suggested by author and Jungian analyst Robert Bosnak:

1. Make A Dream Log Foldout. "Type up or print out your dreams in small print, single spaced, on 8.5 x 11 inch sheets of paper . . . Spread these papers out on the floor, facedown, each connecting on the vertical side with the next, containing in chronological order all printed dream log entries you want to process (I recommend no more than twelve). From this, make an accordion foldout—using transparent tape on the back—by folding the scroll at the tape."

2. Make A Dream Map. "Take a pencil and a ruler and begin to connect all images that strike you as similar . . . "

3. Identifying Clusters. "After you have spent time tracing an infrastructure through the material, begin to look for clusters: thematic connections that weave through the material by way of the dreaming tracks you've identified . . ." Examples of clusters would include marriage, depression, loneliness, work, fears, aspirations, etc.

4. Musing. "After making an infrastructure and identifying clusters you let yourself muse over the life of one of the clusters."

5. Reminiscence. "Take some of the dream images that struck your fancy and begin to reminisce about the past."

6. Writing Along With The Clusters Chronological Format. "Use one descriptive paragraph for each element of the cluster, in chronological order."

7. Rewrite The Material Obtained By Step 6 In Various Genres. Such genres could include a letter to yourself, a poem, a travelogue, any genre that fits the mood. (1996, pp. 166-174).

Make a special effort to use your sense of hearing when you seek out your attractive natural being or landscape in the next activity. Instead of focusing on your breathing to calm your mind, listen to warbling warblers, splashing waves, or the rustling of leaves. Allow your body to become infused with the reverberations.

To continue your journey to Gladandgreen Junction, move to the next waypoint: "One's Inner Purpose." There, you will learn how the best of success is a successful moment.

26

One's Inner Purpose

AWAKEN TO PRESENT BEING

The act of sensing balance and the perspective that leads to the revelation of one's inner purpose; is, when one clears away distractions and lesser purposes, *awakening* to Present Being. Awakening is a form of grace that leads to responsibility. In trying to mature spiritually, nothing is more important for you. Awakening to the Present Being negates the Ego, leads to your best efforts, and provides the link between one's inner and outer purposes.

Even more than pursuing the idea of greatness, honoring the awareness of space between thoughts will be the foundation for excellence and the source of all goodness and beauty in one's life. God manifests in the present tense of life. Awareness of this eternal now is called *"presence."*

Be Present

The best of success is a successful moment. Possibilities for such moments include the first time successfully playing a long-practiced musical section, a long-awaited apology, seeing a new species of bird for the first time, holding your grandchildren for the first time, witnessing your children grow into impressive adults, or finding the long-needed silence while sitting peacefully as you glide along a clear flowing stream. Your own successful moments occur when you give care, attention, and awareness to your simple actions. You will never feel a successful moment while attempting multi-tasking. The brain needs your stillness so that it can register the successfulness of a quiet time of appreciation. If the means do not contribute to one's happiness, neither will the ends. Presence leads to quality. Presence, then, is a critical step towards happiness. Presence leads to spontaneous helpful occurrences and what seem like positive coincidences but are really, in truth, outer manifestations of the underlying intelligence that one uncovers as one's consciousness blooms into greater Awareness.

Since everyone is a microcosmic reflection of the macrocosm, the revelation of one's inner purpose is like a hologram that shows the whole in the part. When you are aware of this condensation, you realize that your actions are not just your own, and the consequence of them extend outward through the universe.

Counteract Excessive Doing

This series of books is intended to be helpful to those in the middle years of life because that is the time when the expansion of form in people's lives—by which I mean when physical growth has ceased and when the growth of knowledge, activity, possessions, and experiences is beginning to, if not slow, at least be tempered by the rising importance of formlessness. It is not until Doing—succeeding, accumulating, building, protecting, and sense gratification—is countered by its opposite, which is *Being*—that is, by presence, by existence, by living, by reality, and by actuality—that individual (one human) and collective (one environment) integrity can emerge. Let me explain:

Being is your nature as a person/planet, your nature that is inseparable from humaNature. Through *being*, a new heaven and a new earth can emerge one person at a time on this planet, each having is own

Soul, each having its own essence, and each having its own psyche. Despite these qualifiers, *being* cannot be accurately and definitively categorized, for each entity—each *being*—is an aspect of the whole, one part of the one heart, one part of the one bosom, and one part of the one Spirit that is the Universe. This is the underlying message of our Model of Integrity: we are each individuals that cannot be separated from the whole.

There is the word "national" and the word "international." Likewise, we are each one individual *being* that is a part of the universal "*interbeing*." We are individuals and, though it is not a word, we are each "interindividual."

You will be encouraged to do many things along the Heartwood Path. I also encourage you to create an interval of doing and being, doing and being. You will improve your individual self by doing, and collectively these improvements will make the world better. But, to truly get the most for your individual *being* and the universal *interbeing*, match active doing with less active awareness of being. Again, don't just do something, sit there (and be aware). This interval will build a balance between your outer world and your inner world and between your individual aspect and the one universal aspect. The interval of doing and being is the source of *Integrity*, capitalized to indicate that I am referring to both your individual integrity and the integrity of the one surrounding environment.

For most, the significance of this message about Integrity (about the reconciliation of our individual and More-Than-Individual aspects) does not register until the middle years of life. We all know that the middle years of life are a time when you start to turn off lights for economic rather than romantic reasons, when you can still do as much as before but would rather not, when you start hoping that the ringing phone is not for you, and when the main thing you exercise is caution. For me, my middle years have been over so long I can remember when the Big Dipper was just the Little Spoon.

Guard Yourself Against Stupid Purposes

By the middle years of life most people have experienced a loss or a disability in the realm of form and thus are—not unlike the traditional figures of the blind seer or wounded healer—prepared for the flowering of the realm of Spirit (of Being). Without the widespread blooming of the integration of inner with outer purpose, of formlessness with form, of Doing with Being, of Things with Non-things, one's amazing intelligence will too often be put to stupid purposes. The splitting of the atom, for example, took incredible intelligence, but taking this act and growing it into an Earth-threatening menace—the atomic arm's race—is an act of collective stupidity that threatens all species on Earth. The inner world flowering that comes from the losses experienced by most people in their middle years is why it is this age group that will lead to a more magnificent future. This will only be so if they work to control the Ego. Although the beginning of controlling the Ego is most likely to occur during the middle years of life, it's is never too early nor too late to start to do that.

It is the collection of all of our Egos that converts collective intelligence into collective stupidity. Taking advances in science and turning them into stupid purposes occurs by creating separateness between people, separateness between nations, separateness between races, and separateness between "us" and "them." EartHearts exist to counter this tendency of the Ego, to help people become aware of their Being no matter how active they are and no matter how driven they become.

Counter Separateness

Without countering the Ego's tendency to create separateness we humans will continue to make modified versions of the same problematic world repeatedly. Actions need to be influenced by an awareness of the Intelligence that comes from the Awareness of Being.

This Consciousness is interpenetrated with the dimension of Form from where all actions occur. The point of this interpenetration is the

Human Being, not the Earth. That is why it is so important for environmentalists to focus a significant portion of their efforts on the work of eartHearts: on expanding the consciousness of humans. In this way, when people do work to protect the environment, they will be prepared for what is truly needed: awakened doing, which, for us, means allowing your consciousness of your feelings to inform your actions.

This awakened doing, described in greater detail in the next waypoint, results from consciousness flowing into what one thinks and does. Like the channel of a big river, this flowing of consciousness guides and empowers. The "what" that is done is tempered by the "how" that it is done. The method of doing itself becomes the goal. Quality, beauty, and excellence arise when one pays attention to how things are done and not just what one does.

Success is determined by and is inseparable from the consciousness out of which the thoughts and actions arise. The success encouraged by our indoor pursuits (marked by sedentary entertainments, unfulfilling work, and acquisitiveness) is narrow and, therefore, not suitable for the development successful living. Better results can be expected by the consciousness associated with the kinds of pursuits found at Gladandgreen Junction (marked by active, outdoor entertainments, HumaNatureConnect Activities, and caregiving). A big part of the endeavor needed to find that place where personal happiness and planetary health meet is to . . .

Honor Your Ancestors And Become A Good Ancestor To Future Generations

How to do so is the purpose of the following activity.

To Not Being Scorned By Your Ancestors...

HumaNatureConnect Activity

Start-up Protocol

If this is not a day when you prefer to spend time in nature without an agenda, do the Heartwood Path Start-up Protocol found in the Appendix.

Honoring And Becoming A Good Ancestor

Counter the normal tendency to forget your ancestors by jotting down what they have done for you that helps you with the Great Work! Recognize that you may be an ancestor to others and how, once you develop an expanded sense of time (enlarging your notion of time to go back and forward much further than you are probably accustomed, at least seven generations back and seven generations forward), your sense of care and responsibility naturally grows. While in the mode of deep-time thinking (perhaps by investigating your genealogy and then thinking about more than fourteen generations, half before and half after yourself), write down what you think future generations will say about your generation, about the way we used up resources, and about the way we had to overcome great forces to make necessary corrections. To influence what they might say, in your journal, tell future generations what are the first steps taken in this epic struggle to bring forth happiness and sustainability, tell them the most important steps, and tell them how you feel about working on this noble cause.

Follow-up Protocol

For best results, write down your impressions of this activity in your journal using the Heartwood Path Follow-up Protocol found in the Appendix. Afterwards, consider sharing your interpretations with others.

Heartwood Path Axioms

Key Assertions From Waypoint 4.26

4.26.1.

It has become painfully obvious that our global problems are greater than our typical collection of solutions.

4.26.2.

To correct problems one has to first identify the issues.

4.26.3.

The first issue is a shortcoming of the environmental movement: environmentalists such as myself have been largely treating nature as a separate object when we should have been treating it as a fellow subject.

Nocturnal Pilgrimage 4.26

For best results, write down your impressions of each night's dreams in your journal using the Heartwood Path Dreaming Time Protocols found in the Appendix. Afterwards, consider sharing your Dream Tending with others.

"In addition to its deleterious effects on sleep, overexposure to nighttime illumination has also been linked with increases in cancer, diabetes, and immune dysfunctions . . ." (Naiman, 2006, p. 12). After you complete this waypoint, get a good night's sleep before continuing. Record your dreams in your journal.

Pertinent And Instructive Gems From My Dream Tending Journal

I dreamt that I went to the newest Rambo movie with some of my buddies from the organization, Earth First! All the action scenes riled up their adrenaline, causing them to fantasize about spiking trees or doing the things "monkey-wrenchers" do. They chastised me for being a friend of the earth rather being with them: warriors for the earth. They had no interest in meditation or dream tending.

We traded barbs: I yelled:

"Self First!"

They responded:

"Earth First!"

Back and forth. I was sympathetic to their goals but not to their means. Eventually the FBI put a squash on them. Their team, who never turned inward, was forced to disband. Their mantra was picked up by a coalition of corporate industrialists. Thereafter, each time I heard "EarthFirst!" in my dream it was followed by "Mars Later!"

Lesson Learned: Have radical goals. Follow conservative means to get their. Start with changing yourself.

As you search for an attractive natural being or landscape in the next activity, give your desensitized nose a treat by waking it up to the various smells you can find in nature. Consider the purpose of each scent—such as attracting birds or insects.

When you are ready to resume, move to the next waypoint: "Golden Footsteps." There, you will learn how truly successful actions spring from acceptance, delight, and fervor.

27

Golden Footsteps

AWAKEN TO DOING

All truly successful actions and everything done that is good for the whole spring from one's awakening to Consciousness. To awaken to your consciousness means that you are becoming aware of both the surroundings outside of you and the feelings that arise inside of you. Before this awakening one is still a being—an entity—that has actual presence but is not fully aware of the reality of the outside world or of the vast array of possible inner world feelings that include sadness, insecurity, jealousy, anger, suspicion, helpfulness, fearfulness, joyfulness and desire. One is capable of feeling these emotions and more, sometimes subconsciously and other times acutely. To more often than not produce the feelings of gladness rather than any of the negative emotions one has to be satisfied with one's good fortune which may or may not be the result of one's own actions.

Here we come to the difference between being and doing. Being is one's presence as an actual entity. This presence is wrought with feelings, many of which are subconscious—off the radar range, so to speak. When one becomes an awakened being one is aware of one's feelings. By comparison, doing has to do with action. It is impossible to "be" without also "doing," even if that doing is barely noticeable and beneath one's awareness.

What we are interested in promoting as part of your plan to promote happiness and environmental sustainability is a form of doing that arises within your consciousness and leads to your own purposes. When these two conditions exist—consciousness of action and pertinence to your own purposes—it can be said that you are engaging in "Awakened Doing." How awakened doing can lead you to Gladandgreen Junction is described in the following activity. The Awakened Doing occurs through three modalities: acceptance, delight and fervor. These are golden footsteps along the Heartwood Path. Without these means, nothing works well to bring about Awakened Doing. Each modality has a unique vibratory frequency that is appropriate to one situation or another. Without acceptance, delight, and fervor suffering will not be far behind.

Acceptance

Sometimes you just "gotta do what you gotta do." Acceptance allows you to be at peace in your doing. Not a passive state, acceptance actively brings creativity and novelty to tasks. It requires surrender. If you cannot surrender and be accepting of what you are doing, stop. That is your responsibility.

Delight

Wherever possible, replace wanting, which is a delusion from the Ego, with delight. This will lead to a feeling of pleasure and happiness that is often referred to as "joy." When enjoyment in its purified state of joy is applied to your doing, there is no waiting to start living.

Abundance, expansion, and positive change are "greased" immediately by the delight that comes by being fully present. The power behind all of Creation is connected to you when you enjoy what you are doing. All necessary meaning is contained in this joy.

Bring at least acceptance and delight to your efforts to help yourself and fellow species flourish. For 3.5 billion years, life on earth has been developing, expanding, blossoming, and diversifying into perhaps 30 million fellow species. Of all this time, right now is the most critical period in our collective history. Alarmingly, many of our relations—human cultures, animals, and plants—are going extinct at unprecedented rates.

If you have any doubt whether now is the time to make changes in the way the earth is treated look over the list of questions in the following activity regarding the characteristics of a society that has grown beyond its own limits. Each time you answer "yes" to the following questions you are recognizing that human society has gone too far, exceeded its natural limits, and is heading for a major ecological worldwide collapse.

Along with using acceptance and delight, work to spread happiness, protect wildness, and restore the environment by fostering within yourself the last of our three ways to engage in Awakened Doing, namely . . .

Fervor

The opposite of apathy, fervor means passion, ardor, zeal, vehemence, earnestness, excitement, and zest. When deep enjoyment along with a goal or vision leads to enthusiasm at the height of creative action there is fervor—an intensity that burns away stress, incinerates tension, diminishes struggle, and reduces Egoic wanting. Without the intense and passionate feeling of fervor, tasks of average difficulty seem harder to accomplish; with fervor one can ride the wave of extra creativity.

When more people discover the benefits of acceptance, delight, and fervor an improved collective future will be at hand. But we are not there yet. Earthlings exhibit too little conscious higher purpose, by which I mean their purpose beyond instant satisfaction of desires. Less attention to personal rewards and more attention to how personal actions positively affect other people and the whole is one good way to focus more on one's higher purpose and thus bring forth a better present and a better future.

Prepare Yourself Mentally Before You Jump Into Action

To be aligned with your higher purpose feel yourself being The Absolute's energy portal for the benefit of all sentient beings. God is the traditional Judeo-Christian name for the Un-manifested Source. EartHearts take the energy from the Source, focus consciously on just being, but then apply thought and action to their Source-supplied Awareness for the benefit of themselves and others. What makes eartHearts different from other activists and other Cultural Creatives is that, instead of launching immediately into action, they first meditate, slow their thoughts, refrain for a time from observing structures and forms—whether inner world thoughts or outer world things, and align with Presence before they act. They know that the earth they are work-ing to preserve and the people they are attempting to help to become perfect/whole are but outer reflections of the "heaven" that Jesus says (in Luke 17-21) "is right here in the midst of you." Without an aware-ness of Heaven, Earth will not be a proper reflection. That is why eartHearts devote themselves to being present before (or, at least, in conjunction with) observing, thinking, and acting as a way to provide a foundation (or grounding) for their observations, as a way to temper their actions, and as a way to make their actions more beneficial to the whole. In doing so, eartHearts make real differences in the world and keep from spending themselves for their causes.

To The Knowledge That Things In The Environment Are Not Right...

HumaNatureConnect Activity

Start-up Protocol

If this is not a day when you prefer to spend time in nature without an agenda, do the Heartwood Path Start-up Protocol found in the Appendix.

Practicing For Awakened Doing

To care actively in a way that leads to Gladandgreen Junction, practice "Awakened Doing." Begin by making a special kind of "To Do" list every day. At the beginning of your planning process each day do not just focus on listing mundane tasks that you want to achieve. Instead, first determine how you want to feel during the day or at the end of the day. Then, develop your "To Do" list in a way that it will most likely bring about your preferred feelings. Some days you may wish to feel calm, for example. Other days you may wish to feel accomplished. You are engaging in "Awakened Doing" when you allow your desired feelings to inform and set your activities for the day. Include on your "To Do" list action items that will make you glad and action items that will further the goal of environmental sustainability. Only after you have listed such action items do you make a list of mundane chores, such as purchasing milk or washing the car.

Follow-up Protocol

For best results, write down your impressions of this activity in your journal using the Heartwood Path Follow-up Protocol found in the Appendix. Afterwards, consider sharing your interpretations with others.

Heartwood Path Axioms

Key Assertions From Waypoint 4.27

4.27.1.

All truly successful actions and everything done that is good for the whole spring from one's awakening to Consciousness; and occurs through three modalities: acceptance, delight, and fervor.

4.27.2.

Not a passive state, acceptance (which requires surrendering) actively brings creativity and novelty to tasks.

4.27.3.

Wherever possible, replace wanting, which is a delusion from the Ego, with delight.

4.27.4.

When deep enjoyment along with a goal or vision leads to enthusiasm at the height of creative action there is fervor—an intensity that burns away stress, incinerates tension, diminishes struggle, and reduces Egoic wanting.

4.27.5.

To be aligned with your higher purpose feel yourself being The Absolute's energy portal for the benefit of all sentient beings.

Nocturnal Pilgrimage 4.27

For best results, write down your impressions of each night's dreams in your journal using the Heartwood Path Dreaming Time

Protocols found in the Appendix. Afterwards, consider sharing your Dream Tending with others.

"(Compelling) evidence (suggests) that light at night (LAN) is over-used, an unnecessary energy and economic burden, and detrimental to the environment and health" (Naiman, 2006, p. 12).

Set an intention for your next dream. Sleep and dream. Tend to your dreams and share some of your dream journal entries with others.

Pertinent And Instructive Gems From My Dream Tending Journal

I dreamt someone was telling me that my dreams were coming to me randomly, like there was some sort of lottery system delivering my nocturnal visions without anyone's volition or plan.

Suddenly a big Bear stepped into my view, turned to me and said:

"I assure you that their are a myriad of voices, coming from a myriad of Images, representing a myriad of Natural Beings, each with its own sensitivities and volition. Appreciate us as attractive Images, and we will share wisdom beyond belief."

Lesson Learned: At first, when we dream unconsciously while our bodies and mind's are asleep, it is easy to feel that there is no purpose to our dreams, and that no one is vying for our attention. But, the more one gains experience through lucid dreaming, one begins to develop relationships with images of Beings which are, or act *as if* they are, fol-lowing their own individual volition. Dream visitors will remain silent, or at least disjointed, if you do not begin to talk to them, especially the nighttime muses, Images of Natural Beings, and Animal Spirits. Ask for words of advice from the Dream Images of the attractive Natural

Beings you encountered during your Heartwood Path activities and you will receive details and depth not typically brought forth during your daytime encounters.

As you prepare to move to the next waypoints along the Heartwood Path, you are encouraged to learn from the Coyote Archetype and to challenge convention. Learn from Coyote's way to connect intimately, playfully, and meaningfully with the Greater Self that is yourself plus the natural world. Be like Coyote: courageous and adventurous yet humble as you learn the mysteries to be found both outdoors and deep within your psyche.

When ready, move to the next waypoint, "Fellow Knowers," to continue. There, you will learn about defending our wild relatives.

28

Fellow Knowers

DEFEND OUR WILD RELATIVES

To protect people and the environment—that is, humaNature—is to choose life. This choice is obligatory. We have to choose life. Our only moral choice is to defend our wild relatives—the innocent victims of human ignorance, greed, and arrogance.

Our defense of wildness cannot be contingent on probabilities of winning or loosing. Defending humaNature is an absolute obligation, regardless of the difficulty. The argument that we need to exploit nature to protect jobs is bogus. We can, once we get our priorities straight and come to the realization that all depends on a healthy environment, create at least as many jobs by restoring nature as we can by destroying nature.

There is no defense for the argument that we need to only protect humans because, unlike men and women, nature apart from humans is not aware of its plight. This argument is unfounded. All life is mindful. It knows. Plants, for example, can recognize where the light is, reptiles can react, and mammals have emotions.

Living systems, being sentient assemblages, perceive changes in their environment. While all life knows, we humans know in a unique way. We humans are mindful and know, and, unlike all but a very few types of organisms, we know we know. The special ability of knowing that we know gives humans a special responsibility. We do not have to just unknowingly react. We can knowingly respond to the changing needs of our environment. Humans can knowingly choose on the side of life or die knowing we did too little to protect our fellow knowers—human and non-human.

To The Sixteenth Of Many Touchstones Of People-Nature Inter-facing...

HumaNatureConnect Activity

Start-up Protocol

If this is not a day when you prefer to spend time in nature without an agenda, do the Heartwood Path Start-up Protocol found in the Appendix.

Generating Patterns Of Human-Nature Interaction # 16:

Plunging Into Water

Plunge into water or think about plunging into water after you feel connected to your chosen attractive natural being. In doing this interaction pattern, you could think about plunging into a pool from a water slide at a water park (a perverse interaction pattern) or think about jumping off a wooden dock into a man-made lake (a domestic interaction pattern). By choosing instead to jump off a rock into a deep pool in a river (a wild interaction), you would be doing something that will have a positive psychological affect on you.

In your journal, write down what meaning you would derive from this wild interaction pattern; what joy, if any, it would produce; how, if at all, it would build within you a bond between your mind and nature;

and how, if at all, the wild version of this interaction pattern would be better for you than the perverse or domestic instantiation of the same interaction pattern; and how it would make you feel if you were not allowed to participate in this sort of wild interaction pattern—jumping off a rock into a deep pool in a river. How does interacting in this way in the presence of your attractive natural being make you feel? How would it feel to have this interaction without the presence of your attractive natural being? In writing down these responses you will be adding to our collective nature language, so important to rekindling the bond between humans and nature. Look over your impressions and think about them as you fall asleep tonight before dreaming.

Follow-up Protocol

For best results, write down your impressions of this activity in your journal using the Heartwood Path Follow-up Protocol found in the Appendix. Afterwards, consider sharing your interpretations with others.

Heartwood Path Axioms

Key Assertions From Waypoint 4.28

4.28.1.

Our only moral choice is to defend our wild relatives—the innocent victims of human ignorance, greed, and arrogance.

4.28.2.

All life is mindful, which is to say that all living beings are sentient in their own way.

4.28.3.

We humans are mindful and know, and, unlike all but a very few types of organisms, we know we know.

4.28.4.

Humans can choose on the side of life or die knowing we did too little to protect our fellow knowers—human and non-human.

4.28.5.

Celebrate the dawn by waking up gradually and early enough to witness its arrival.

Nocturnal Pilgrimage 3.28

For best results, write down your impressions of each night's dreams in your journal using the Heartwood Path Dreaming Time Protocols found in the Appendix. Afterwards, consider sharing your Dream Tending with others.

> "The vast majority of us today rarely witness dawn or a sunrise. We have forgotten the gradual awakening to soft light and bird song . . . " (Naiman, 2006, pp. 18-19).

With this and the previous waypoint in mind, prepare for your nocturnal reveries. After sleeping and dreaming, tending to your dreams.

Pertinent And Instructive Gems From My Dream Tending Journal

I dreamt that I was sitting outside of Henry David Thoreau's cabin. I asked him what is the most important thing for him, the most worthy of prophets, to tell those who follow the Heartwood Path. I was a bit surprised by what he said:

"Pilgrims along the Heartwood Path, like all people, are closer to the central truth in their superstitions than they are in their science."

Lesson Learned: Science is not the only route to truth. There is also an emotional route to truth, an ethical route to truth, a relational route to truth, a philosophical route truth, and an experiential route to truth. Along the Heartwood Path, if you can experience it, it is, in fact, true. Or at least it is as if it were true. In any event, all acts, experienced fully, are facts. In seeking the truth, do not disqualify qualities by focusing only on quantities. Do not throw out your speculations for they may get you closer to the truth than your observations and experimentation. Remember that nothing is free from your sense of values. And, there are many methods, some not scientific, for arriving at the truth. Science may provide information about an animal, for example; but, that animal is really not just itself. It is also all of its relations, some not easily understood by science (relationships with myths, Spirits, and Dream Images, for example).

When you are ready, go to the next waypoint, "Living," to continue. As you look for your next natural attractive being or landscape—one that will help you function optimally in the following activity—treat yourself to the natural and full-flavor tastes of something edible in nature. Compare how you feel taking something from nature's abundance to how you feel ingesting the often unhealthy, bland, and uninspiring foods from the restaurant or supermarket.

29

Living

HELP US ALL CHOOSE ON THE SIDE OF LIFE

Here are seven ways to choose on the side of life:

1. Improving ecological stress signals—purposeful indicators about the condition of an ecosystem, such as annual bird counts or stream surveys.
2. Speeding up the response times through advanced planning for ecological redemption, such as getting oil spills reported and cleaned up earlier.
3. Reducing the use of nonrenewable resources such as fossil fuels, minerals, and ancient groundwater.
4. Using renewable resources in a sustainable way by making sure that the use of forests, fish, game, soil, clean water, and all living things are regenerated as fast as they are used.
5. Using all resources efficiently.
6. Slowing or stopping the exponential growth of human population, physical capital, and industrial output by supporting the notion of "enough" rather than the notion of "more." And

7. Helping solve problems that are not directly environmental in nature but still have an impact on human happiness and environmental sustainability, such as poverty, unemployment, and the common overemphasis on **material needs** rather than on **non-material needs**—by which, I mean: beauty, excitement, identity, variety, community, challenge, love, acknowledgment, and joy.

Another pertinent step towards choosing on the side of life is to be able to answer the kinds of questions included in the following activity:

To An Accounting Of Our Biggest Eco-problems...

HumaNatureConnect Activity

Start-up Protocol
If this is not a day when you prefer to spend time in nature without an agenda, do the Heartwood Path Start-up Protocol found in the Appendix.

Identifying The Worst Environmental Problems

Answer the following questions: What is the worst source of air pollution in your community? What is being done to clean it up? What is the worst source of water pollution in your community? What is being done to clean it up? What is the biggest threat to open natural space in your community? What is being done to save this open space? What is the most toxic site in your area? What is being done to clean it up? What is the most glaring example of soil erosion in your area? What is being done to restore this land? What do you plan to do to help correct environmental imbalances in your area?

Follow-up Protocol

For best results, write down your impressions of this activity in your journal using the Heartwood Path Follow-up Protocol found in the Appendix. Afterwards, consider sharing your interpretations with others.

Heartwood Path Axioms

Key Assertions From Waypoint 4.29

4.29.1.

Choose on the side of life by:

1. Improving ecological stress signals—purposeful indicators about the condition of an ecosystem, such annual bird counts or stream surveys.

2. Speeding up the response times through advanced planning for ecological redemption.

3. Reducing the use of nonrenewable resources such as fossil fuels, minerals, and ancient groundwater.

4. Using renewable resources in a sustainable way by making sure that the use of forests, fish, game, soil, clean water and all living things are regenerated as fast as they are used.

5. Using all resources efficiently.

6. Slowing or stopping the exponential growth of human population, physical capital, and industrial output by supporting both the notion of "enough" rather than always the notion of "more."

7. Helping solve problems that are not directly environmental in nature such as poverty, unemployment, and the common overemphasis on material needs rather than on nonmaterial needs—including beauty, excitement, identity, variety, community, challenge, love, acknowledgment, and joy.

4.29.2.

While admiring your chosen natural being, appreciate it with your inhalations and give it gratitude with your exhalations.

4.29.3.

The night drives us inward where we confront subconscious aspects of our psychological selves.

Nocturnal Pilgrimage 4.29

For best results, write down your impressions of each night's dreams in your journal using the Heartwood Path Dreaming Time Protocols found in the Appendix. Afterwards, consider sharing your Dream Tending with others.

"Night is the shadow of the Earth. It is as nature intended, dark. And Unsettling. . .Darkness drives us inward where we are confronted with disowned aspects of our psychological selves . . ." (Naiman, 2006, p. 21).

With the message of this waypoint in mind, sleep and dream. After tending to your dreams, find the many benefits of exploring nature with your hands. If you see moss, gently stroke it; if you come up to a tree, feel its bark; and if you are visiting the beach, walk barefoot in the sand. Touching nature awakens one's body, probably going numb from too much time on the couch.

When you are ready, move to the next waypoint: "Generate." There, you will learn how incomplete thing leads to incomplete solutions.

30

Generate

BRING FORTH A NEW WORLD AS ONLY A HUMAN CAN

Humans do not know by discovering a pre-given world that exists in a way that is independent of the human mind. Through our process of cognition, humans bring forth the world according to our own inner-world structures, emotions, thoughts, culture, and bodily sensations. There is great power in how we all think about things.

Ideas are the predecessors of every invention, every major change, every war, and every revolution. We need to, therefore, be very careful about the way we think. Incomplete thinking leads to incomplete solutions. Complete thinking leads to complete solutions. For this reason, after the following activity, I will present a way to arrive at good ideas.

To Evaluate Your Green Footprint...

HumaNatureConnect Activity

Start-up Protocol

If this is not a day when you prefer to spend time in nature without an agenda, do the Heartwood Path Start-up Protocol found in the Appendix.

Assessing Your Environmental Impact

Look carefully at your daily lifestyle and to decide how it affects the quality of the world. Draw a line down the middle of one of the sheets of paper in your journal, making two columns. Head the first column with "Life Support Needs" and the second with "Luxury Desires." Fill in as much as possible under each heading. After examining the lists, do you see any areas for change in your lifestyle?

Follow-up Protocol

For best results, write down your impressions of this activity in your journal using the Heartwood Path Follow-up Protocol found in the Appendix. Afterwards, consider sharing your interpretations with others.

Heartwood Path Axioms

Key Assertions From Waypoint 4.30

4.30.1.

Through our process of cognition, humans bring forth a world according to our own structure, emotions, thoughts, culture, and bodily sensations.

4.30.2.

Ideas are the predecessors of every invention, every major change, every war, and every revolution.

4.30.3.

Incomplete thinking leads to incomplete solutions.

Nocturnal Pilgrimage 4.30

For best results, write down your impressions of each night's dreams in your journal using the Heartwood Path Dreaming Time Protocols found in the Appendix. Afterwards, consider sharing your Dream Tending with others.

"With our worldly eyes closed, but with the mind's eye open . . . our inner vision gradually acclimates to a delicate glow that backlights the night, revealing sacred mysteries concealed in the shadows" (Naiman, 2006, p. 22).

With this statement and your impressions of the message of this waypoint in mind—particularly about the way humans affect the creation of the world, the importance of ideas, the differences between life support needs and luxury desires, and the mysteries concealed in darkness—sleep, dream, and tend to your dreams. Doing so helps you with your activities for the following day.

Pertinent And Instructive Gems From My Dream Tending Journal

I dreamt that an elite group of industrialists and retailers, focused intently on boosting their own comforts and stylish appearances, busily extracted the world's resources, destroyed the natural homes of thousands of human

and non-human fellows, and left the planet dirty and ecologically dimin-
ished. The bulk of humanity, reduced to mere cogs in the world's economic
engine, participated in this destruction. They were told of the problems but,
fearing a loss of income and the inability to consume, they did not care. Or
they acted, as if they did not care. Then came the aliens. They too were
focused intently on boosting their comforts and stylish appearances. The
aliens busily extracted the world's resources, destroyed the natural homes of
thousands of human and non-human fellows, and left the planet dirty and
ecologically diminished. The world mobilized its defenses and fought the
scourge.

Lesson Learned: I know of no group of people that has ever met an enemy and then discovered it was themselves. But that is precisely what we have to do if we are to be happy in a sustainable environment. That is why the old battle to protect the environment has to turn away from being solely played out in the media and in legislative arenas. Some of the hostilities of these battlegrounds have to be converted into empathies played out within the mind's of the battlers and activists, from both sides of the arguments. We will not protect our cherished natural landscapes without first paying more attention to our inscapes. All of the battles are not in the field. They all begin within the inner worlds of people.

In most of the activities that follow, it will not just be your direct reception of raw sense data that will be instructive. Pay attention also to the feelings you have while in the presence of your natural attractive being or landscape. As we shall see, using your intuition and harmonizing with natural beings and landscapes are critically important skills when attempting to find guidance from nature.

After tending to your dreams, move to the next waypoint, "Organization," to continue on your way to Gladandgreen Junction. To get there, you will need to do more than come fully to your five senses.

31

Organization

ENGAGE IN SYSTEMS THINKING

This way of thinking concentrates on the wholes rather than on the parts. According to systems thinking, living systems are integrated wholes whose properties cannot be reduced into those of smaller parts. The smaller parts always have different properties. Living systems arise from the relationship of the parts.

In using the word "relationship" I am usually not just thinking about how objects/beings are positioned relative to each other. I am also very much concerned about the responsibility of one being to another. This responsibility is current, but it also extends into the past and future.

Relationship always has a component of responsibility. To be in relationship with what is not human satisfies a basic need. I am speaking of a kind of contact that is ecological and not just holistic. Here's the difference:

A holistic perspective refers to all parts of the whole—as in all parts of the human body. An ecological perspective widens the view to include the relationship of what seems to be all related but distinct wholes—wholes, as in relating your whole body to other wholes such as forests, rivers, lovers, children or pets. This need for going beyond the narrow perspective of parts and for going beyond the wider perspective of all the parts in one whole results in the feeding of one's sensibilities and the nourishing of one's understanding, alertness, perceptiveness, awareness, judgment, and consciousness.

Systems thinking shows that the broader the perspective, the more truth perceived. There are great benefits to be found in making contact with entities that seem to be beyond the wholeness of one's own individual body. This contact can be merely soothing as when we stare at a waterfall or curious as when we feel the pull of gravity on our outstretched arms. Without such sensual contact with that which is More-Than-Human we cannot fully appreciate just how delicate humans can be. We cannot appreciate how different we are from our technology. We cannot appreciate how to assess the limitations of technology.

Not all contact is soothing. Contact can also be shockingly exciting, as when we are facing something that is threatening in the wild. Either way, soothing or invigorating, contact with another human or with More-Than-Human nature occurs because every one of us has a personal body. This body makes possible the reciprocal flow of experience —the human body experiencing the More-Than-Human body and the More-Than-Human body experiencing the personal human body.

To The Sixteenth Of Many Touchstones Of People-Nature Interfacing...

HumaNatureConnect Activity

Start-up Protocol

If this is not a day when you prefer to spend time in nature without an agenda, do the Heartwood Path Start-up Protocol found in the Appendix.

Generating Patterns Of Human-Nature Interaction # 16:

Reading The Signs Of Nature

Examine some interaction patterns after you feel connected to your chosen attractive natural being. In doing these interaction patterns, you could think about measuring the pain thresholds of laboratory monkeys (a perverse interaction pattern) or think about noting the signs of Spring by seeing migratory birds at your bird feeder (a domestic interaction pattern). By choosing instead to watch the clouds of an approaching storm (a wild interaction), you would be doing something that will have a positive psychological effect on you.

In your journal, write down what meaning you would derive from this wild interaction pattern; what joy, if any, it would produce; how, if at all, it would build within you a bond between your mind and nature; and how, if at all, the wild version of this interaction pattern would be better for you than the perverse or domestic instantiation of the same interaction pattern; and how it would make you feel if you were not allowed to participate in this sort of wild interaction pattern—watching the clouds. How does interacting in this way in the presence of your attractive natural being make you feel? How would it feel to have this interaction without the presence of your attractive natural being? In writing down these responses you will be adding to our collective nature language, so important to rekindling the bond between humans and nature. Look over your impressions and think about them as you fall asleep tonight before dreaming. And share your impressions with others, using the Heartwood Path Exchange.

Follow-up Protocol

For best results, write down your impressions of this activity in your journal using the Heartwood Path Follow-up Protocol found in the Appendix. Afterwards, consider sharing your interpretations with others.

Heartwood Path Axioms

Key Assertions From Waypoint 4.31

4.31.1.

Engage in systems thinking, which concentrates on the wholes rather than on the parts.

4.31.2.

Relationship is responsibility.

4.31.3.

Systems thinking shows that the broader the perspective, the more truth perceived.

4.31.4.

One's body makes possible the reciprocal flow of experience— the human body experiencing the More-Than-Human body and the More-Than-Human body experiencing the personal human body.

Nocturnal Pilgrimage 4.31

For best results, write down your impressions of each night's dreams in your journal using the Heartwood Path Dreaming Time Protocols found in the Appendix. Afterwards, consider sharing your Dream Tending with others.

With your impressions from the previous waypoint in mind, before another day passes, ponder and act upon my summary of Dr. Bruce Goldberg's ways to change your life through dreams:

1. "Attach importance to your dreams. The meaning of dreams is what we give to them. Your belief in their significance results in an increased frequency of meaningful dreams."
2. Concentrate on the subject of what you want the dream to be about before falling asleep.
3. Program yourself before going to sleep to recall while you are dreaming what your intention is for the dream.
4. Establish friendly relationships with your dream characters.
5. Record your dreams immediately upon waking.
6. Share your dreams with others.
7. Refrain from using sleeping pills, alcohol, caffeine, aspirin, barbiturates, and tranquilizers (Goldberg, 2003, pp. 34-35).

Remember that your journey of Self-knowledge, which will enable you to grow into your most playful and most fierce Self, requires that you find the depth of understanding that can only occur in the deepness of nature. There is value in the formal education you received almost exclusively indoors. It probably taught you how to be productive and how to be typical, but there is more to life than being merely conventional. The Invisible School of Nature, which offers another class outdoors at the next waypoint, is a fun, healing, effective, and empowering way to learn how to be usefully unconventional.

After you put some of Goldberg's suggestions regarding creating a new you through the process of sleeping and after you tend to the previous night's dreams, share some of your entries by using the EartHeart Exchange.

When ready to continue, move to the next waypoint: "Grasp." You are about to help the Kosmos perceive itself.

32

Grasp

HELP THE KOSMOS PERCEIVE ITSELF

The flesh of the body is at once both sensitive and sensible. Humans, being part of the flesh of the earth, are organs used by the Kosmos to perceive itself. This perceiving offers many rewards, some too subtle to notice and others obvious and enjoyable. When the perceiving occurs in the context of a sense of belonging or connectedness to the cosmos as a whole, the experience is often spiritual. This is not to say, however, that the feeling of oneness is not also sensual or physically exciting.

It is difficult for some people to appreciate the complexities of relating to nature. Sometimes, rather than trying to understand and rather than trying to seek the benefits of relating to huge macro entities such as the universe or nature, it is easier and more illustrative to move downward in scale and focus on micro entities that can, based on the principle of "as above, so below," serve as a model for the whole. Such micro entities could be another person; but, since this is the topic of another Heartwood Path book (called **Eros**), I will focus at some length at the next waypoint on another familiar micro entity that can serve as a model for how we can benefit by relating to a non-human other. Relating to domesticated animals—the topic of the next Waypoint—

might be an easy way for you to grasp the main message of the Heartwood Path. Another way to grasp the message of the Heartwood Path is to participate in Four Directions Circles, as described in the following activity.

To A Four-fold Perspective Of The Self...

HumaNatureConnect Activity

Start-up Protocol

If this is not a day when you prefer to spend time in nature without an agenda, do the Heartwood Path Start-up Protocol found in the Appendix.

Participating In A Four Directions Circle

Expand your understanding of the self. Begin by finding a flat area six to ten feet across. Imagine a large circle spreading out across this place. In this circle, place a small natural object at each of the four directions. Always give your reasons and ask for permission to move any being in nature. And, while returning your beings to their original positions, always offer your gratitude.

"By treating your world as if it is more alive than you had previously imagined, you're likely to experience an enhancement of your own sense of aliveness" (Plotkin, 2013, p. 253).

As a sidebar to this activity, I believe that attaining consent from natural beings, as prescribed earlier by Dr. Cohen, and as we do at the beginning of each HumaNatureConnect activity, is important because it establishes a psychological sense of equanimity. Attaining consent levels the playing field so that the person is not psychologically lording over the natural being.

Finding acceptance thus fosters a heightened sense of fairness and empathy. Submitting to the approval of the natural being adds a pleasant and helpful sense of humility into one's field of awareness. Waiting for consent allows one to open the door to thinking as nature does, with continued attraction being the form of the go-ahead sanction. In-so-doing, one is able to glean some of nature's indisputable intelligence and supremely wise guidance. This gleaning will not come in the form of a Dr. Dolittle sort of worded conversation; it can, however, come through in one's imagination, it can come through in a change in one's awareness, it can come through in one's emotions, it can come through as a result of practices such as this one, and it can come through via careful tending of one's dreams.

Returning to this practice, which is a modification of an activity from Plotkin's **Wild Mind** book, stand or sit in the center of the circle, which, in the Medicine Wheel of the Psyche of HumaNature, is the center stone representing one's Ego. Look toward each of the four directions, using your senses to glean as much information as possible. Toward the North, for example, audibly tell your Nurturing Generative Adult (if you forgot what this inner world guide has to offer, go back to Waypoint 4.12) why you want to develop a relationship with it. Tell your Nurturing Generative Adult a relevant story from your life that illustrates why cultivating a relationship with it is important to you now. Give the Nurturing Generative Adult an example of someone in your life, past or present, who embodied in an exemplary way the qualities of a Nurturing Generative Adult. If no one comes to mind, or even if one does, evoke an archetypal figure. When ready, physically move toward the North figure, notice how the world looks when looking toward the North, imagine how it would be if the qualities of this inner ally were incorporated into your life. Recall an issue that is occurring in your current life. Merging psychologically with the North figure, speak about this issue from its perspective. Continue until the statement feels complete. To amplify this presentation, go to the circle in the night or in Winter. Make similar overtures to each of the other psychic allies. When repeating this scenario with the South Figure, bring more feelings into the equation. Amplify this gleaning of information by going to the South figure and facing the South, the Wild Indigenous One (for a refresher, return to Waypoint 4.12 if you need a re-introduction), at noon, or in the Summer. For your East facet encounter, which is best amplified during the morning or in Springtime, move to the East Stone, face the East, and ask the Innocent/Sage (described at Waypoint 4.12 and Waypoint 4.20) about the big picture, about clear sightedness, and about full presence. The evening or in Fall are opportune times to move to the West Stone, face the West, and ask the West facet, the Muse-Beloved (if need be, see Waypoint 4.12 and/or Waypoint 4.22 for a refresher), about mysterious, hidden meanings.

Follow-up Protocol

For best results, write down your impressions of this activity in your journal using the Heartwood Path Follow-up Protocol found in the Appendix. Afterwards, consider sharing your interpretations with others.

Heartwood Path Axioms

Key Assertions From Waypoint 4.32

4.32.1.

Humans, being part of the flesh of the earth, are organs used by the Kosmos to perceive itself.

4.32.2.

Sometimes, rather than trying to understand or to seek the benefits of relating to huge macro entities such as the universe

or nature, it is easier and more illustrative to move downward in scale and focus on micro entities (such as a human) that can, based on the principle of "as above, so below," serve as a model for the whole.

4.32.3.

Rhythms rule us and regulate us.

Nocturnal Pilgrimage 4.32

For best results, write down your impressions of each night's dreams in your journal using the Heartwood Path Dreaming Time Protocols found in the Appendix. Afterwards, consider sharing your Dream Tending with others.

> "From the oscillations of atomic particles to the swirl of galaxies, from brain waves to the beat of the heart, and from the tempo of day and night to the seasons of sun, rhythms literally rule our world. And they regulate us . . . " (Naiman, 2006, pp. 25-31).

We are all affected by circadian and ultradian cycles. Our recurring sleep-dream-wake cycle is circadian in nature. Ultradian rhythms such as heart rate, brain waves, recur in periods less than a day. ultradian rhythms have an average period of about ninety minutes—nature's hour. Ultradian rhythms occur throughout the day and night, providing a structure for rhythmic shifts in our consciousness. Each ultradian sleep cycle normally includes a sequence of sleep stages followed by a period of dream, or REM, sleep"

Before you go to sleep tonight, spend some time thinking about the just-presented information about ultradian rhythms and the following points from Dr. Goldberg about dream interpretation:

1. "Dreams offer us the opportunity to connect to a greater level of awareness.

2. Consider all elements of your dreams important, and record everything you recall in a journal.

3. One of the best times to remember dreams is the state of consciousness between wakefulness and sleep.

4. Dreams afford us the possibility of accessing a source of knowledge and wisdom not usually available to us in our waking, daily life.

5. The content of a dream may not always be symbolic, but most commonly it will be emblematic (demonstrative, allegorical, a story that contains a hidden meaning).

6. Our subconscious communicates with us through our dreams.

7. Dream symbols are often quite personal in nature. Only you are able to properly decipher them.

8. Recurrent dreams are always more significant, and indicate we are not following through on some communication from our subconsciousness.

9. You are responsible for dream content and frequency.

10. The information and significance of dreams can be determined by comparing the differences and similarities between how you feel when awake and your reactions during your dream itself.

11. Properly encoding the initial component of your dream will make it easier to understand the rest of it.

12. Consider several different levels when attempting to understand a dream. These are multidimensional messages and often require time to search out the deeper meanings.

13. Dreams never lie nor misrepresent the truth.

14. To obtain the most benefits from a dream, approach it with complete honesty and openness.

15. Real-life characters in your dream symbolize past and present association, along with other aspects of your psyche.

16. Also, note how some of your Dream Characters may be inner world psychic allies. As a reflection of the variety of our moods,

situations, and earth conditions, we usually experience more than one totem animal in our lives. Plotkin suggests, for example, that: the North figure, the Nurturing Generative Adult, may be making itself known to you in your dreams through images of saints or entities with a strong aura of competence, compassion, and caregiving; the South figure, the Wild Indigenous One, may be making itself known to you in your dreams through images of a wild man or woman, lustful people, or a lush waterfall, rainforest or meadow; the East facet of your psyche, the Innocent/Sage, may be making itself known to you in your dreams through images of a fool, a comic, innocence, or wise or mischievous people; and the inner world figure of the West, the Muse-Beloved, may be making itself known to you in your dreams through images of wizards, alluring or dangerous men or women, underworld creatures, caves, decaying leaves, or swamps (2013, p. 257).

After thinking about these points from Dr. Goldberg about dreaming, sleep and dream. The next morning, tend to your dreams. When you awaken, plan how and when you will commune with nature today. Think up some new approaches.

Although we humans can adapt to a wide range of conditions, we suffer when our approaches diverge too much from nature's ways. One way to get back into sync with natural procedures is to spend time with domestic animals, particularly those typically found on a farm or ranch.

When ready, move to the "Farm Smarts" waypoint. There, you will discover the benefits of learning from domesticated animals.

33

Farm Smarts

LEARN FROM DOMESTICATED ANIMALS

Contact with pets, especially horses, brings profound changes to one's character and perspective. Not everyone who follows the Heartwood Path will have the means or desire to have horses at home; but just about everyone, with a little effort, can devote a portion of their time to watching, gentling, training, grooming, feeding, showing, handling, riding, or otherwise caring for horses. Even if the horses are kept at a stable near your home, you will discover that they can cast a spell on you. They can work magic that is perfectly in line with the overall quest of those who chart the Heartwood Path.

Horses are enchanting and empowering. They can facilitate healing. Horses can help us look deeper into our interconnectedness. Horses can help us look deeper into our own hearts.

By spending time in the company of horses, you can develop selfless love. This love, also known as agape, leads to passion for all life. Without this passion there can be no communion with nature.

If you are troubled, horses can use their intuition to help with your worries. If you face challenges or are damaged by neglect, abuse, or misfortune, horses can help you rebuild bridges of trust.

Horses have the ability to offer us all of these benefits more than other pets for several reasons: domestic horses still retain much of their original wild nature; horses—being less labile than a dog, for example—are strong-willed, and independent, are not so eager to please and, therefore, command more respect; horses have imposing size, great strength, and keen intuition; horses demand that they be approached with vigilance, respect, and sensitivity; horses require that we stay conscious and present in the moment; horses encourage us to perceive our inner feelings and verbalize them; horses can give us a feeling of exhilaration and liberation—thus bring us to our senses; there is a mystique about horses in that they are deemed to be noble creatures that carry us on journeys—both in the realm of Exteriority and into the realm of Interiority.

Horses offer all of these benefits in a natural way. Unlike the means of many office-bound psychologists, what the therapy horses do for us is not contrived. How many clients of psychologists, if given the chance, would pick a place in the country where animals are present as their ideal place to work on their own recovery?

Through disciplined play with horses, one can experience a link to life in its rawest form. This enchanting and mysterious link is forged by the horse's invisible energy and instinct. By getting us in touch with the older animal-like portion of our minds, time with horses spurs personal growth and promotes holistic healing. Being with horses also puts us in touch with cycles, seasons, and the realm of life covered over by rational thinking. Handling horses teaches much about the value of simple and clear communication.

Horses take us back to times of old, simpler times when the pace was no faster than the speed of a horse. We can imagine as we ride with our horses along trails through the woods that we are like the Native American equestrians of a bygone era who found sacredness in everything and considered the wilderness their holy place.

Horses give us an excuse to be outside. They give us an excuse to escape the city. They help us to relate beyond our typical anthropomorphic concerns.

Horses provide the allure of risk; and the lessons that can be achieved from pain, drudgery, disappointment, loss, grief, frustration and teetering between control and disaster. Besides being impossible, a risk-free life is detrimental. Risk provides opportunities to learn, do, struggle, and go to the next level. It also provides an opportunity to learn to cope when one fails.

Riding horses is risky because you could break something when you fall. Grooming horses is risky because they could kick you, bite you, or step on your foot. Riding may not improve one's size, speed, athletic ability, or strength; but, along with giving you the benefits of sensible risk, it will stimulate compassion and fine tune your finesse.

Horses, usually located in relatively quiet pastoral settings, give us opportunities to find quiet time to think. We all need more horse sense.

They also give us a chance to improve our leadership qualities. By watching how horses treat each other, and comparing the dynamics of herds to the dynamics of human teams, we learn much about being a leader and being a follower. We learn to get off our high horse when we may otherwise demonstrate excessive pride, conceit, vanity, Ego, and arrogance, for example.

Horses give us the chance to compete in a healthy way. Horse competitions are mentally, physically, and spiritually stimulating. These competitions make excellent proving grounds and improving grounds.

Horses allow us to feel responsible for another being. They need us to feed them, shelter them, educate them, comfort them, and inoculate them. Dogs always adore us, cats sometimes ignore us, but horses never bore us.

Horses are highly aware of their surroundings. This attribute makes the horse's human companion also more present in the moment and meditative.

Horses come with the mystique of the "noble beast." This mystique is a powerful archetype that gives humans a sense of direction as they use the horse to carry them across the fields or into the soul. Horses are clearly not like us. This "otherness," encourages the end of narcissism, the branching out or the self, the increasing of empathy with the non-human world or the greater universe; the appreciation of and respect for other beings, cultures, races, and religions; and the restriction or end of ascribed roles.

For a horse (a prey animal) to trust a human (a predator) is a remarkable and inspiring feat. If a prey animal such as a horse can relate to a predator, we (who have very little to fear) ought to be able to relate beyond our kind. EartHearts know that animals are like numinous messengers from the Absolute Spirit. These messengers, some believe, perform a role similar to that of angels.

With this belief as their inspiration and source of guidance, eartHearts employ horses (and encourage others to employ horses) for several reasons: as companions for building connections to something beyond one's own human state; as a means for connecting to the earth; as a way to move closer to one's Maker; as noble beings who can help anyone ride through the unconscious to a place of greater awareness; as catalysts of the intense feelings that come when humans take on the animal's spiritual essence and thereby connect to the Kosmos; as helpers in one's struggles with issues relating to power, control, idealization, projection, and one's desire to have interactions based on respect, trust, compassion, and gentleness; as facilitators of relatedness and working better in groups; and as role models for beneficial group instincts.

Engage in the Equine Therapy to discover how to achieve healthy membership within the human herd. Equine Therapy is suitable for juveniles and adults with emotional or behavioral problems; street gang members; addicts; families seeking to improve their communication skills; those seeking to improve their leadership and team-building skills; people seeking to reduce stress; spiritual seekers; and anyone seeking to improve the quality of their daily lives.

The horse also draws out of people deep feelings most humans keep in check. These feelings may be positive or negative. Either way, getting in touch with feelings is critical to personal development. When one becomes aware of one's feelings, these feelings tend to blossom. When one denies one's feelings, one tends to impede one's functioning. Attending to feelings also increases one's creativity.

Just touching a horse can bring forth buried feelings, induce a state of relaxation, or provide needed therapy. Slowing down and calmly touching or grooming a horse induces the inner tranquility that comes from alpha brain waves—the precursors to meditative states that provide access to inner longings and deep-seated fears that may be locked up in the unconscious.

In my two years as a manager of a horse ranch, I noticed that, for the most part, only horses who have been abused or mishandled by their owner's overuse or misused emotion. At first, I could not tell anything about the inner feelings of the horses I cared for. Over time, however, I gradually discovered that certain actions are flags for inner feelings. It eventually dawned on me that the outward signs (ears back or turning so that the hindquarters faced me, to list two examples) were not the same things as the horse's inner feelings. These outward signs are the ways the horses express or hide their feelings, but they are not the same things as their feelings. What a revelation this was for me!

The horses taught me that feelings are part of the invisible realm of interiority. They taught me that emotional displays such as anger either match or mask what is going on inside. Sometimes outward displays of emotions truly express the inner state and other times they do not. When outward emotions do not match inner feelings, it is difficult to address the truth.

Along with important lessons about feelings and emotions, horses can teach us about how to use our instincts and intuition to become more sensitive to the collective consciousness of the universe. This divine "mind" of the universe has its own knowledge, a cosmic warehouse of information that is not our own. When horse and rider are working as one, it is likely that the rider has relaxed with an open frame of mind; likely that the rider has no emotional upheaval; and likely that the rider has no preoccupations, worries, or obsessions. When the rider is free of these distractions and in tune with his or her horse, then the relationship between the horse and the rider becomes a gateway for relating beyond one's self; for using one's own intuition; for being one with nature; and for entering into divine attunement.

Time with horses makes concepts such as divine attunement, inter-connectedness, and oneness less esoteric and more real. Horses help us to appreciate inborn resources—both ours and theirs. They also teach us that instinct—whether ours or theirs—is a reflection of a portion of the interiority of the intellect-producing, intimacy-producing, and aesthetic-producing universe.

The mixture of fear (being hurt by a horse) and joy (feeling one with the horse, or enjoying the ride, or appreciating the sight of them running in the pasture) is a powerful catalyst for personal growth. By using the horse as a way to teach oneself how to confront fear and experience the joy of life, one is on a portion of the Heartwood Path that leads to becoming more contemplative and philosophical.

To Learn From Tamed Companions...

HumaNatureConnect Activity

Start-up Protocol

If this is not a day when you prefer to spend time in nature without an agenda, do the Heartwood Path Start-up Protocol found in the Appendix.

Learning From Domesticated Animals

Determine if you are learning spiritual lessons from your pet(s) by answering the following questions:

1. Unlike your pets, do you hold back or cover up. Do you express your emotions? Explain your answer.
2. Like your pet dog, are you, when faced with someone's anger, able to simply walk away and come back when the storm blows over? Explain your answer.

3. Like a horse or a pet cat or dog, are you able to avoid second-guessing your instincts? Explain your answer.
4. Like your pet, can you refrain from replaying past mistakes repeatedly? Explain your answer.
5. Like your pet, can you love unconditionally? Explain your answer.
6. What are some other ways your pets help you with your spiritual growth? Explain your answer.

Follow-up Protocol

For best results, write down your impressions of this activity in your journal using the Heartwood Path Follow-up Protocol found in the Appendix. Afterwards, consider sharing your interpretations with others.

Heartwood Path Axioms

Key Assertions From Waypoint 4.33

4.33.1.

Contact with pets, especially horses, brings profound changes to one's character and perspective.

4.33.2.

Through disciplined play with horses, one can experience a link to life in its rawest form.

4.33.3.

Balance between emotions visible in the outer world and feelings that occur in the inner world is ideal.

4.33.4.

Spending time with horses, especially when engaging in an equine therapy program, is like finding a witness that can reflect back clear messages regarding the nature of your own individual self and Greater Self (self in context with your environment).

Nocturnal Pilgrimage 4.33

For best results, write down your impressions of each night's dreams in your journal using the Heartwood Path Dreaming Time Protocols found in the Appendix. Afterwards, consider sharing your Dream Tending with others.

During the last phase of writing this course, I spent years sleeping under the stars outside. Doing so enabled me to get better attuned to the spectacular rotation of the stars and planets at night. Paying attention to the nightly and seasonal shifts in the night's sky seems to slow down the night sufficiently that, even with less than ideal hours of rest, I awaken refreshed. The nightly movement of Planet Saturn helps me regather my energy. The Fall return of Constellation Orion recharges me. Constellation Scorpio increases my enjoyment of life. When the fog of exhaustion puts me to bed I look up at the slow and steady progression of Planet Mars or Jupiter across the expanse of blackness and I am reminded of how our culture, so out of pace with natural rhythms, essentially forces us to work excessively for material gain. The brightness of Star Sirius seems to amplify the effectiveness of my nighttime slumbers. On nights when the Moon is a waning crescent, and the sky is dark enough to see additional lofty jewels, I am flagged by Red Planet, White Planet, and Blue Giant Star, and my allegiances become extraterrestrial. Now, with ample experience, each night the location of the constellations become my time-givers, accurate to the clock to within fifteen minutes.

With your impressions of the this waypoint in mind think about what you want to dream about and pay attention to your dreams. After tending to your dreams, share your dream journal entries with others.

Pertinent And Instructive Gems From My Dream Tending Journal

I dreamt that I was called to come into the room where all of the English teachers in my high school would go over the papers written by their students. Since two of my three grade schools were lousy, I could barely write by the time my writing was first scrutinized in this room. In four years of high school, I had two English teachers, Mister Tricky in ninth and eleventh grades and Mr. Treat for tenth and twelfth grades (no joke, that was there names). These guys, who really gave me some good writing skills, were in an argument about me. Mr Treat said I wanted to be what he called an "ecologist." Mr Treat kept saying that I wanted to be a "psychologist." I just sat there, flattered that they cared.

Lesson Learned: After years of being a professional environmentalist, I now work in the field of eco-psychology. As to what I want: for people to be happy and secure in a sustainable environment filled with joy, natural beauty, and a diversity of human and non-human intelligences.

When ready, move to the next waypoint, "Bonds," and take another important step into the nature of happiness. You are taking great strides.

34

Bonds

PERCEIVE NATURE'S WEBSTRINGS

According to Dr. Cohen (2003), there are eight steps to commune with a natural system (be it a bush, or an ecosystem, or a house-plant found indoors, or a natural being in your "back yard" or in the "backcountry") (p. 61-62):

1. Remember what you have known since birth about how to "participate in Earth's nonverbal, webstring ways."
2. Go to a natural attraction and seek its consent for you to become involved with the attraction for your practice of sensing and feeling it. If it remains attractive to you for over ten seconds, that is a sign of consent. If you feel uncomfortable while in the presence of the attraction, simply move without regret to another attraction. Moving on in this way will "prove to be safer and more rewarding" (Cohen, 1987, p 61).
3. Know the natural place or thing that attracts you by thinking or saying the words "attraction," "webstring," "feeling," or "connection" repeatedly as you use your natural senses to focus on a specific attraction.

4. Noticing the way the consenting attraction helps you to feel good and comfortable, thank it for helping you have the connection experience and for participating in your sensing activity. When feeling attracted to a being in or from nature, express your gratitude mentally while breathing in slowly but deeply with the perception that your own thankfulness and the vibes from the attractive being are mixing and are directly entering your heart. Do this symbolic act a lot. Try it now. Remember it with the acronym ACTN AGAIN—Achieving Coherence Through Natural Attraction Gratitude and Inspiration Now. ACTN AGAIN opens up positive possibilities non-linearly, brings balance to one's central nervous system, lowers stress, and brings one to a state of optimum functioning. Enjoy the good feelings.

5. Translate your experience of truth that you had with the natural attraction into words. Combine linear and nonlinear ways of knowing in your verbal expression by stating "My experience in nature show me that I am a person who gets good feelings (by, from, when, etc:_____." When emailing or otherwise communicating your experience to others, limit your statement to no more than three sentences. (Cohen, 1987, p 61). This will help you create concise yet powerful statements that are also merciful to today's time-constrained and typically attention-disordered readers. Focus more on symbols in the experience rather than on signs from nature. Signs limit the meaning linearly. A sign limits the experience to mean one thing. Symbols, in contrast, expand the meaning non-linearly. Reporting about how you identified a symbol in the experience opens up the expression to include multiple and often unanticipated meanings. Focus more on the expansive fable (moral lesson, myth, or legend) that results from your experience than you do on the narrowly restrictive scientific validity of the experience. Feel free to use metaphors and poetic figures of speech. These will help but they will, in the end, fall short: the messages from nature and indeed ordinary reality are, in the words of William

Bausch "infinitely greater than our capacity to word it accurately" (Garon, 2006, p. 1).

6. Look over your statement yourself, reading it carefully, and, if possible, share it with others.

7. Ponder what the experience you just had means to you. Consider its value to you. Think about what it suggests. Determine how it let the earth speak. New attractions, good feelings, and meanings in nature will be found by doing the activity again.

8. Learn what others have gleaned from doing the sensing and feeling webstrings activities and reading the EartHeart Networking Forum.

In Step 2 above, participants were encouraged to seek consent from a natural attraction. This may seem odd to some readers so more elaboration may be needed here. The seeking of consent is a mandatory procedure for those seeking to sense and feel the healing, educational, or guiding messages from natural attractions for three reasons:

1. it sets up a natural receptivity in both the sender and the receiver for sharing information because it puts all involved on an equal plane, particularly in terms of control or domination;

2. its sets up a frame of mind that can only be achieved when there is a supportive relationship based on a sense of trust, mutual respect, and positive regard; and

3. nature works by seeking consent to engage with natural attractions and, by doing likewise, the human participant is entering into this universal, time-tested, pervasive communication technique (which, we all know, is more productive than trying to teach nature to speak English).

To Your Best Outdoor Being Buddies...

HumaNatureConnect Activity

Start-up Protocol

If this is not a day when you prefer to spend time in nature without an agenda, do the Heartwood Path Start-up Protocol found in the Appendix.

Picking Three

Find three natural beings outdoors to which you feel an affinity or attraction. Do not remove the beings from their present location, but remember where the natural beings are and write down a description of the natural beings. Describe why you chose each natural being, and how they relate to each other. Use the Heartwood Path Exchange to discuss your involvement with beings with others.

Follow-up Protocol

For best results, write down your impressions of this activity in your journal using the Heartwood Path Follow-up Protocol found in the Appendix. Afterwards, consider sharing your interpretations with others.

Heartwood Path Axioms

Key Assertions From Waypoint 4.34

4.34.1.

Eight steps to communicate with a natural being or system:

1. Focus on webstrings (natural sensory attraction relationships) and the nonverbal.

2. Go to a natural attraction and seek its consent for you to become involved with the attraction for your practice of sensing and feeling it (if it remains attractive to you for over ten seconds, that is a sign of consent).

3. Know the natural place or thing that attracts you in a non-verbal way by thinking or saying the words "attraction, " "webstring," "feeling," or "connection" repeatedly as you use your natural senses to focus on a specific attraction.

4. Noticing the way the consenting attraction helps you to feel good and comfortable, thank it for helping you have the connection experience and for participating in your sensing activity.

5. Translate your experience of truth that you had with the natural attraction into words by stating "My experience in nature show me that I am a person who gets good feelings (by, from, when, etc:_____.

6. Look over your statement yourself, reading it carefully, and, if possible, share it with others.

7. Ponder what the experience you just had means to you.

8. Learn what others have gleaned from doing the sensing and feeling webstrings activities.

4.34.2.

The seeking of consent from a natural being or system is a mandatory procedure for those seeking to sense and feel the healing, educational, or guiding messages from natural attractions.

4.34.3.

Obtaining consent sets up a natural receptivity in both the sender and the receiver for sharing information because it puts all involved on an equal plane, particularly in terms of control or domination.

4.34.4.

Obtaining consent sets up a frame of mind that can only be achieved when there is a supportive relationship based on a sense of trust, mutual respect, and positive regard.

4.34.5.

Nature works by seeking consent to engage with natural attractions and, by doing likewise, the human participant is entering into this universal, time-tested, pervasive communication technique.

Nocturnal Pilgrimage 4.34

For best results, write down your impressions of each night's dreams in your journal using the Heartwood Path Dreaming Time Protocols found in the Appendix. Afterwards, consider sharing your Dream Tending with others.

When the winter sky comes I know I will have longer nights beneath the stars. If I overwork myself I know that if I devote more time to rest my eyes on twinkling stars I will avoid getting run down by the eye strain-producing glare of the daytime Sun. As I turn to face the night's sky my thoughts turn inward, thus my nocturnal examinations are both upward and inward. It does not take too many nights of this dark time in the natural world for me to wake up refreshed and ready for a more balanced way of life.

With the impressions of today's waypoint in your mind, sleep, dream, tend to your dream, and share your dream journal entries with others. In doing so, you are increasing the chances that others will be happy in a sustainable environment.

Pertinent And Instructive Gems From My Dream Tending Journal

I dreamt that I was once again being chastised by my allies—a theme that comes in many forms in my dreams. They said I should join in more during their condemnations of political opponents. I remained unconvinced.

Lesson Learned: One ought to look at oneself thoroughly, both inside and out, before even contemplating condemning others.

When ready to resume your pilgrimage, move to the next waypoint: "Actuality." There, you will find comfort by facing the facts unfiltered.

35

Actuality

FIND COMFORT BY FACING THE FACTS UNFILTERED

We all are, using one of Dr. Cohen's oft-used words: "wrangled" (2007, p. 180). Our life in industrial society is bound too tight because it is guided by a pervasive story that makes us feel above and separate from nature.

This preoccupation with the primary story of our culture "wrangles" us in numerous ways. It cuts us off from our natural source of replenishment and guidance. It reduces us to mere cogs in the industrial machine. The dominant culture places veils of illusion over our mind's eyes that prevent us from perceiving the world unfiltered. Our brains take in this dominating story of disconnection and make us use it to transform other people and the planet to our own liking (often with disastrous results).

The result of this wrangling is a pervasive and systematic means to put resources to use. Another result is a plundered planet populated by too many people who feel unfulfilled.

The wrangling industrial story, especially when it is turned into action, is a uniquely human trick. This story-turned-to-action is alluring, addictive, distracting, and destructive. It is not, however, the only source of guidance available.

There is a fantastic and worthwhile alternative, one used by the rest of nature, that is a source of intelligent direction. This alternative uses fifty-four "natural survival senses" that "connect and balance nature within to nature without" (Cohen, 1989, p. 8).

The Fifty-four Natural Senses And Sensitivities

The Radiation Senses

- Sense of light and sight, including polarized light.
- Sense of seeing without eyes such as heliotropism or the sun sense of plants.
- Sense of color.
- Sense of moods and identities attached to colors.
- Sense of awareness of one's own visibility or invisibility and consequent camouflaging.
- Sensitivity to radiation other than visible light including radio waves, X rays, etc.
- Sense of temperature and temperature change.
- Sense of season including ability to insulate, hibernate, and winter sleep.
- Electromagnetic sense and polarity which includes the ability to generate current (as in the nervous system and brain waves) or other energies.

The Feeling Senses

- Hearing including resonance, vibrations, sonar, and ultrasonic frequencies.
- Awareness of pressure, particularly underground, underwater, and to wind and air.
- Sensitivity to gravity.

- The sense of excretion for waste elimination and protection from enemies.
- Feel, particularly touch on the skin.
- Sense of weight, gravity, and balance.
- Space or proximity sense.
- Coriolis sense or awareness of effects of the rotation of the Earth.
- Sense of motion, body movement sensations, and sense of mobility.

The Chemical Senses

- Smell with and beyond the nose.
- Taste with and beyond the tongue.
- Appetite or hunger for food, water, and air.
- Hunting, killing, or food obtaining urges.
- Humidity sense including thirst, evaporation control and the acumen to find water or evade a flood.
- Hormonal sense, as to pheromones and other chemical stimuli.

The Mental Senses

- Pain, external and internal.
- Mental or spiritual distress.
- Sense of fear, dread of injury, death or attack.
- Procreative urges including sex awareness, courting, love, mating, paternity and raising young.
- Sense of play, sport, humor, pleasure, and laughter.
- Sense of physical place, navigation senses including detailed awareness of land and seascapes, of the positions of the sun, moon, and stars.
- Sense of time.
- Sense of electromagnetic fields.

- Sense of weather changes.
- Sense of emotional place, of community, belonging, support, trust, and thankfulness.
- Sense of self including friendship, companionship, and power.
- Domineering and territorial sense.
- Colonizing sense including compassion and receptive awareness of one's fellow creatures, sometimes to the degree of being absorbed into a superorganism.
- Horticultural sense and the ability to cultivate crops, as is done by ants that grow fungus, by fungus who farm algae, or birds that leave food to attract their prey.
- Language and articulation sense, used to express feelings and convey information in every medium from the bees' dance to human literature.
- Sense of humility, appreciation, and ethics.
- Senses of form and design.
- Sense of reason, including memory and the capacity for logic and science.
- Sense of mind and consciousness.
- Intuition or subconscious deduction.
- Aesthetic sense, including creativity and appreciation of beauty, music, literature, form, design, and drama.
- Psychic capacity such as foreknowledge, clairvoyance, clairaudience, psychokinesis, astral projection, possibly certain animal instincts, and plant sensitivities.
- Sense of biological and astral time, awareness of past, present, and future events.
- The capacity to hypnotize other creatures.
- Relaxation and sleep including dreaming, meditation, and brain wave awareness.
- Sense of pupation including cocoon building and metamorphosis.
- Sense of excessive stress and capitulation.
- Sense of survival by joining a more established organism.

- Spiritual sense, including conscience, capacity for sublime love, ecstasy, a sense of sin, profound sorrow, and sacrifice.
- Sense of homeostatic unity, of natural attraction aliveness as the singular essence-diversity attraction dance of all our other senses (NNIAAL). (Cohen, website: http://www.ecopsych.com/insight53senses.html).

Although I will ask you to employ these natural senses, one after another, in many of the exercises that follow, you can at any time use the senses that are more to your liking. You do not need to limit yourself to the one or two senses that I choose in any of the following activities.

I encourage you to do the activities as written here but, more importantly, I encourage you to share in the joy and the benefit of randomly assigning the application of a natural sense to a situation in life. Doing so brings forth the fresh perspectives that tends to yield a diversity of worthwhile answers.

Be sure to apply a natural sense in a manner that creates a resonate link (which you will learn to perceive by doing the next activities) between the microcosm (your hand, for example) and the macrocosm (a forest, for example). The goal here is to learn how to use the various natural senses to fall into resonance with one or, better yet, with more than one attractive natural being.

I heartedly encourage you to do the same thing that I do in many of the following activities: randomly apply a natural sense to a subject matter you are presently contemplating. The randomness of the associations is important because, rather than encouraging you to stick to previous ways of knowing which too often lead to mediocre or predictable outcomes, the odd mixing and matching of the natural senses with various topics produces unexpected and often improved results.

In mixing the use of various natural senses randomly, in activity after activity, you will, step by step, be acquiring a substantial reward.

You will be learning systematically how to reduce the deleterious affects of the pervasive industrial story—a story that hurts you and the planet. You will also be learning to replace this injurious story with the Natural Systems Thinking Process. This methodology allows you to see beyond the frame of perspective created by the dominant story. You will be learning to perceive and respond to the world and in the world in a way that is unfiltered by the narrow frame created by the industrial story.

To Touch The Earth's Placenta...

HumaNatureConnect Activity

Start-up Protocol

If this is not a day when you prefer to spend time in nature without an agenda, do the Heartwood Path Start-up Protocol found in the Appendix.

Returning To The Soil

Get on your hands and knees. Select some soil and touch it with your hands. Lower your nose to the ground and smell the earth. To do this exercise right, end up with dirt on your nose.

Follow-up Protocol

For best results, write down your impressions of this activity in your journal using the Heartwood Path Follow-up Protocol found in the Appendix. Afterwards, consider sharing your interpretations with others.

Heartwood Path Axioms

Key Assertions From Waypoint 4.35

4.35.1.

Our life in industrial society is guided (or wrangled) by a pervasive story that makes us feel above and separate from nature.

4.35.2.

The pervasive story we absorb from our industrial society, especially when it is turned into action, is a uniquely human trick that is alluring, addictive, distracting, and destructive.

4.35.3.

There is a fantastic and worthwhile alternative to the story we receive from industrial society, one that is used by the rest of nature, one that uses fifty-four "natural survival senses" that "connect and balance nature within to nature without," and one that is a source of fantastic intelligent direction.

4.35.4.

By using various natural senses randomly, in activity after activity, you will, step by step, be acquiring a substantial reward: you will be learning systematically how to reduce the deleterious affects of the pervasive industrial story—a story that hurts you and the planet.

4.35.5.

Learn how to use the various natural senses to fall into resonance with one or, better yet, more than one attractive natural being.

Nocturnal Pilgrimage 4.35

For best results, write down your impressions of each night's dreams in your journal using the Heartwood Path Dreaming Time Protocols found in the Appendix. Afterwards, consider sharing your Dream Tending with others.

We are "jet-setters" living in the "fast lane," caught up in the "rat race" and sick with hurry sickness. We suffer from a collective tachycardia—a rapid, runaway cultural heartbeat. As the symphonic rhythms of nature, including human nature, are persistently overridden, we become deeply entrained with the dysrhythmic cacophony of modern culture (Naiman, 2006, p.35).

Continue to tend to your dreams, being careful to record your impressions in your dream journal. Ask your Dream Figures about ways to overcome the pervasive and destructive messages from the industrial society.

Pertinent And Instructive Gems From My Dream Tending Journal

I dreamt I was leading a meeting of neighbors. I told them that they were causing considerable harm to the planet and will need to make significant changes. Nobody agreed. A mother, who shopped daily on Amazon.com, said she had to provide for her children. A business man said he could not afford to let his business lose revenue. A school teacher said she liked her gas guzzler for safety reasons. And on it went.

Lesson Learned: Statements that are wise but entail self-sacrifice are rarely regarded as true or worthy enough to be heeded. Forcing everyone to pay a carbon tax, for example, may be good for the community but it will be hard to adopt because it will take money out of everyone's bank account. Compare this money-taking proposal to calls for self-reflection. Both are good for the community but the former is costly and the latter is free. All things being equal, favor free (or nearly free proposals). It is practically impossible for a person to make a decision that is good for the community when that decision will affect the amount of money left in that person's wallet negatively. And, think of the money that can be saved by consciously replacing thoughts of consumption with thoughts of caring for others.

As you linger outdoors during the next activity, look for signs of order, stability, and balance in nature. Psychologically, turn these sightings into lessons about better ways of living for yourself and others in the world. In so doing, you are beginning to learn how to better include nature into your equations, to integrate natural methods into your strategies and agendas, and to absorb the guidance of nature so that you can maintain a bearing that is happiness-producing, harmonious, and sustainable.

When you are ready, move to the next waypoint: "Fine-tune." There, you will learn about vibrational frequency, toning, and entrainment.

36

Fine-tune

GET IN TUNE WITH NATURE TO REESTABLISH CONDITIONS THAT FOSTER TRANSFORMATION PLUS PSYCHOLOGICAL AND PHYSICAL HEALTH

At various times throughout this course, you will be encouraged to make audible sounds such as humming or toning (using extended vowel sounds in meditation). This is done for a vary good reason.

Humming and toning create sounds that are made up of vibrations. Everything "in the universe is in a state of vibration" (Goldman, 2002, p. 12). Humming produces any number of sounds at various frequencies. I suggest that you hum during many of the activities in this course because of what Goldman (2002, p. vi) calls the "unified field theory of sound healing" which can be summarized by the following two formulas:

"Frequency + Intent = Healing"

and

"Vocalization + Visualization = Manifestation"

By humming, you as a participant in the activities that follow will experience yourself as a "vibration, as being sound" (Goldman, 2002, p. vii). Through the sort of humming activities presented in this book, which put to use the formulas that illustrate the unified field theory of sound healing, you will experience the manifestation of not only healing but also transformation.

How such healing and transformation takes place is explained by the concepts of *resonance* and *entrainment*. Resonance is the rate, repetitive speed, or frequency at which an object or a natural being most naturally vibrates. Every natural being, for example, has a resident frequency, often impossible to perceive audibly. "Through resonance, it is possible for the vibrations of one vibrating body to reach out and set another body in motion" (Goldman, 2002, p. 12) This is entrainment. "Let us conceive of the human body as a wonderful orchestra which is playing this marvelous symphony. When we are in a state of health, the entire orchestra is playing together . . ." (2002, p. 12-13). It is possible, therefore, though the use of sound that is projected into a diseased area, to reintroduce the correct harmonic pattern into that part of the body. The result is often a healing reaction.

Combining the unified field theory of sound healing with the Hermetic Principle of correspondence—"As above, so below"—it becomes conceivable that the vibrational healing and transformation of the person also affects the planet, both for healing and for transformation. This extended effect—from person to planet—works best, and perhaps only—when the intent that guides the healing is not coming solely from an individual but is instead coming from the Higher Self that includes, not only the person, but also a natural object/being that can, along with the person, express a broader consciousness that can be labeled the "Divine Will." It is that broader consciousness, that Divine Will, that is able to align with the energy of sound. Remember: for curative purposes, it is "Thy will," the "Divine Will, and not "my will."

This becomes an explanation for why, in many of the activities in this series of courses, I ask the reader/participant to assume the essence of an attractive natural being and to speak, communicate, or hum as, or on behalf of, that natural object/being. Doing so psychologically expands the concept of Self beyond the individual level. It takes "my will" out of the intention and replaces it with "our Will" or "Thy Will"—an intention that, when compared to one's own limited and potentially unbalanced will, is high, complete, and deep. Voicing as, or on behalf of, a more complex Self—one that includes the individual, an attractive object/being, and the whole—comes from a "place" of greater integrity and sacredness. "When we have reached this level, our intent is to become a vehicle for sacred sound and we are able to by-pass the lesser aspects of self which may be out of balance" (Goldman, 2002, p. 19). For these reasons, we will be creating sounds not for our own individual conscious purposes but with the intent of our Higher Selves, which extend to both the ecosphere (nature) and the theosphere (God, The Absolute).

For this sounding we will be using our voices because the "easiest instrument through which intention can be focused and channelled is the human voice" (Goldman, 2002, p. 20). We will not typically be expressing the high/complete/deep intentions through spoken words because natural objects/beings do not speak in words. We will be using an uttered sound that can come from and communicate with nature. We will be using a sort of harmonic language that allows for nature to communicate with humans and vice versa. We will be imitating life in the art of humming; in effect, singing on behalf of and to nature and The Absolute. In so doing, we will be producing both health and transformation.

For the sound to resonate with nature it cannot be conceptual in the way that words are conceptual, for nature only registers concepts through its human interpreters. For the sound to resonate easily with the conceptual minds of humans they will need to be audible to the human ear. Humming or, more specifically, toning, fits these conditions and so becomes what I believe to be a good language medium for two-way nature-to-human interaction.

I like Goldman's definition of *toning:* "the use of the voice to express sounds for the purpose of release and relief, or to resonate the physical body and the etheric fields (the vital forces that permeate the body). It is a non-verbal sound, relying primarily on vowels." (2002, p. 137). Toning is not chanting. It does not use words. In this way, toning or humming is consistent with the "namelessness" in NNIAAL. Not using words is compatible with nature's lack of words, its "unwillingness" or purposeful inability to use names.

To be in tune with nature, one's whole being—one's More-Than-Individual, Ecological Self—has to be healthy. Health is not only about being free from dis-ease but also being in a state of musical harmony with all aspects of one's Greater Self. A sound way to help yourself achieve such harmony—defined as both "the combination of simultaneously musical notes to produce chords and chord progressions having a pleasing effect" and "the quality of forming a pleasing and consistent whole" through "agreement or concord" (New Oxford American Dictionary)—is to use your own voice to make resonant tones.

To be a resonant tone for our purposes here (producing happiness for individuals as we produce health sustainably for the Greater Self), the sound one makes needs to be full; the sound has to be somewhat prolonged; the sound has to evoke or suggest enduring images, memories, or emotions; the sound has to be pleasing and attractive; the sound has to be a vibration that is synchronous with some other vibration (heard, felt, perceived, or imagined); and the tone has to be accompanied with one's intention. In the activities that follow, any life-affirming intention will do but here are a few suggestions that I find to be particularly helpful:

1. to produce enough relaxation and calmness to clear away mental distractions;
2. to help produce personal or planetary health; or

3. to simply find a benefit in the next step of learning as you continue down the Heartwood Path.

Mari E. Howerton and" Maya" Karen Sorensen , authors of **Sing and Hum Bubblebee**, have the website: "Humming for Health," where they offer the following instructive quote from Simon Heather, author of **The Healing Power of Sound**:

"One organ out of tune will affect the whole body. Through sound healing it may be possible to bring the diseased organ into harmony with the rest of the body" (Howerton and Sorensen).

Given most people's reliance on typical Western forms of medicine some skepticism of such a claim is understandable. As an answer to those who wonder: " Is it really possible that human vocalization could bring forth health?" Howerton and Sorensen offer a quote from Susan Alexander, author of Microcosmic Music:

"The answer seems to be an increasingly obvious 'yes' as we study the body, its brainwaves, heartbeat, rhythms of blood circulation, endocrine cycles, right up to the microwave level of organ vibration" (Howerton and Sorensen).

How vocalizations improve health is explained by a result of the law of conservation of energy; namely "entrainment" or how "a harmonious sound will resonate a sympathetic vibration." (Howerton and Sorensen). What we will be doing frequently in the activities that follow is a type of Greater Self Humming Entrainment; that is, humming in a way that produces a sympathetic vibration between you—the individual human—and the planet—that part of you that includes but also goes beyond your individual self.

Humming

According to Dennis Lewis, author of the book **Free Your Breath, Free Your Life**, "Humming has a powerful influence on our physical, emotional, mental, and spiritual health. Done on a daily basis it can help us relax and increase our mental and emotional clarity" (Lewis Website). Such mental and emotional clarity is a necessary component that leads to the efficacy of the HumanNatureConnect Activities that follow. Writes Howerton and Sorensen:

> "A powerful form of humming is toning. Toning is the conscious elongation of a sound using the breath and voice. The vibrations help relax you, ease stress, and balance the mind and body" (Howerton and Sorensen).

Howerton and Sorensen define toning as "sounds with elongated vowels for extended periods of time" and point to some good examples:

> "**Ahhh** - immediately evokes a relaxation response
>
> **Ee or Ay** - is the most stimulating of vowel sounds, helps with concentration, releasing pain and anger
>
> **Oh or Om** - considered the richest of sounds, can warm skin temperature and relax muscle tension. "Try toning for 5 minutes a day for 2 weeks to see if it will help you" (Howerton and Sorensen).

"These sounds can cut through blocks and stagnant energy," writes spiritual teacher Sequoia Henning, "opening the way for a more balanced and healed state of being."

> "you can tone even if you cannot hold a tune at all! . . . You can simply and spontaneously create and allow whatever sound wants to come out to do so ... Toning is an excellent way to free your stored

and built-up emotions. One thing is for sure: you can only feel better after doing so" (Henning Website).

"These sounds are a generative force," writes Sylvan Thorncraft in the website "Toning and Sacred Sounds." He goes on to say that . . .

"Toning requires no vocal training or singing ability and can be profoundly helpful in reestablishing the natural flow of energy through our bodies, opening us to the ability to deeply listen, and connect us to the vibrations of our souls, bodies, and Mother Earth" (Thornton Website).

"Toning," writes Thornton, "can help us move into a trance state . . .

where our active mind slows to a theta wave. While in the theta cycle we are more open to the flow of ideas and inspiration, it is often easier to tap into our creativity, release patterns we may be stuck in, access self healing, and find inner clarity because we are naturally more open to what may come to mind, receiving without censoring or judging" (Thornton Website).

The toning-induced sense of connection is achieved, in part, through . . .

Entrainment

Defined as "the tendency of two oscillating bodies to lock into phase, so that they vibrate in harmony," entrainment is achieved through affirmations, mind quieting, breathing, the use of mantras, chanting, toning, and drumming (Peaceful Mind).

Intention

According to spiritual teacher Sequoia Henning,

"Using sound with intention (as thought follows awareness) directs the sound waves that go into the body to heal, transform, and transmute energy. Sound and vibration effects everyone individually based on the spiritual, emotional body, previous and present life experiences" (Henning Website).

"Because our voice comes from deep inside our bodies, near our hearts," writes Thornton:

"it can be very effective at transmitting our intention, which is formed by our minds and hearts, and charged during the space between our inhale and exhale (the solstice) when our breath is closest to our hearts. It is thought that at this point of our breath cycle between the intake of air and exhalation of breath our bodies lock into a frequency wave of 7.8 cycles per second, the same frequency of the Earth, connecting us back to the divine Earth Mother with each breath" (Henning Website).

Henning points out that . . .
Vowels carry the "information energy" of speech, whereas consonants act to break up the energy flow. In ancient Sanskrit, Hebrew, Chinese, etc., the vowel sounds are considered to be sacred. *In other words, the vowel sounds carry the intention and focus"* (Henning Website).

"By centering one's attention in the ajna center, (Sixth Chakra, third eye, on forehead)" writes author Deborah Van Dyke, author of Traveling the Sacred Sound Current . . .

"holding a sacred intention and producing a vocal tone, we can clear discordant energies from our auric field, develop our inner channel ways to access higher dimensions of consciousness, and anchor these new frequencies at the cellular level of our body instrument" (Van Dyke Website).

In preparation for your humming during the activities that follow remember to use a gentle voice, plan to seek out resonant tones, prepare to apply your intention to the toning, and do not forget to direct the vibratory energy to your various chakras.

As Henning says:

"focus your energy and intent for balancing and energizing each chakra before toning. To find the correct pitch for a particular chakra, scan up and down, feeling in your body for a resonance (apart from the throat where it will always resonate)" (Henning Website).

I have personally found this suggestion to be a bit difficult to achieve, at times. Fortunately, for those of us who like to keep our HumanNatureConnect Activities easy, some teachers suggest that the pitch of the vocalization does not matter. Henning, for example, states that "The pitch will change according to the person, mood, diet, activities, emotional states, etc., on a daily basis. There is no set frequency" (Henning Website). I seem to feel a resonant vibration in a few chakras at a time and so, if I want to intentionally cause and feel a resonant vibration in a particular chakra, I pick a certain vowel sounds that is commonly said to be associated with that particular chakra (which serves the Individual and Greater Self in a particular way, described again in the following activity) and/or I hum a certain musical note or string of notes in particular musical key. Each of these methods are demonstrated in the following activity.

In many of the activities that follow you will be asked to hum. You can do this in actuality or in your imagination. You will be asked to hum a tone that you imagine is coming from or resonating with a small nearby natural attractive being (object) and you will be asked to hum a tone that you imagine is coming from or resonating with that being's larger community. Each time I encourage you to hum do so not just once but repeatedly for 3-5 minutes or long enough to feel a sense of presence marked by peacefulness, clarity, calmness, and More-Than-Individual-Human connection. In this way, you can interpret the tone of the microcosm of an individual being and the tone of the macrocosm of that being's community—thus providing you with a multiplicity from which you can draw interpretive feelings useful in guiding your behaviors. This is my way of helping you be neither a full-time "doomster" nor a full-time "boomster" but a "Humester" who hums and then either interprets the messages imbedded in the feelings the received tones convey or gives intention to the humming directed at others. Hey! . . . don't knock it until you try it.

As one follows the meandering course of the Enduring Stream (a non-physical but potent flow of energy that follows you along the Heartwood Path and beyond) one is repeatedly asked to hum a tone that is pleasing and sensed to be sympathetic with the vibration of an attractive nearby natural being and often also the sympathetic (entrained) resonant vibration of the surrounding environment. I have noticed that for newcomers this notion of receiving messages from nature typically seems rather goofy, especially when one is asked to somehow interpret and repeat a message embedded in an aspect of nature's vibratory resonant tone.

If you too feel this way, I ask that you don't rush to judgment. At a minimum, continuing to do the toning, as requested in the activities, will result in diligent participants entering into a state of optimal functioning. This is a worthy result in its own right, but it is also a positive condition that leads to further benefits; namely, the reception, interpretation, and ability to orally repeat a message that comes from somewhere beyond the individual. As one continues doing the activities that follow, probably fitfully at first, one will eventually enter into an optimal state that allows for an understanding of messages from nature. Yeah, right! you say?

The not-so-infrequent skepticism regarding messages from nature that I have heard from the uninitiated—usually conservative-minded, nature-deprived friends and neighbors—reminds me of how I too was skeptical of a parent's ability to understand their newborn baby's gurgles and body movements until, like them, I spent many, many days and nights with my two newborn daughters. Or, how I was skeptical of an equestrian's ability to read the messages from horses until I spent years with a small herd at a horse breeding ranch. Or, for that matter, how I was skeptical of the occurrence of actual messages from nature until I completed a few years of courses at Dr Cohen's Project Nature Connect.

By doing the activities that follow, or your own versions of these activities, you will begin to see benefits in your emotional, psychological, cognitive, physical and behavioral functioning. You can use this optimal functioning to perform the tasks in the activities that follow or to deal with and master whatever challenges are presented to you in your life.

Since you will be connecting so powerfully to the whole, the benefits will not be limited to your own individual life. The whole world will become clarified by your expanded perception, boosted by your connectivity, and revived by your improved performance.

You will begin to see "Gladandgreen Junction" on the horizon. You will naturally increase your happiness. You will, without fuss, help to sustain the planet's environment.

To truly know reality, one has to experience it.

"When we experience nature by visiting a natural area, we do not find (Indira's Net of) jewels, nets, strings, or the like. In nature these stories are replaced by the real thing, by multiple natural sensory attractions and relationships that we can actually sense and feel and thereby register in our consciousness." (Cohen, 1989, p. 140).

I am including many (rather than a few) activities, not just to illustrate the natural senses but also because "the greater the number, strength, and diversity" of NNIAAL relationships one can perceive the greater is one's ability to exist cooperatively" (Cohen, 2007, p. 140). As you do the following activities, "become conscious that each sense is an ancient, uniquely designed spark of life that resides in us and contains a wisdom of life that supports us" (Cohen, 1989, p. 141). Note that in the following activities I often ask you to follow the wave of resonance from one attraction (your own personality) to another non-human attraction with a relatively low level of depth (a leaf, for example) and on to another non-human attraction with a relatively higher level of depth (a swamp, river, or forest, for example). Linking yourself to more than one being with natural intelligence provides you with the added intelligence embedded in the differing levels of depth in nature. As Cohen states: "Nameless nature attractions become more intelligent by being in contact with more natural sensory intelligences." (1989, p. 142). Aldo Leopold may encourage us to "Think like a mountain" but by making the kinds of resonant links called for in the following activities, we will not only "think" like a mountain climber, for example, but also like a leaf on a tree on the mountain, and the whole mountain itself—thus adding a diversity of depth to our intelligence.

While it is always useful to be, as Cohen says, "in contact with more natural sensory intelligences," (1989, p. 142) let us now attempt to glean more intelligent guidance not from the traditional five senses (hearing, smelling, seeing, feeling, tasting) but from Cohen's forty-second natural sense—the natural sense of mind and consciousness (Cohen, website: http://www.ecopsych.com/insight53senses.html). Through this natural sense one can use the mind and consciousness to engage in the kind of deep imagery (or what Jung called "active imagination) wherein a person undergoes inner journeys "in which you interact, while awake, with the other-than-Ego inhabitants of one's psyche" (Plotkin, 2013, p. 259).

To Targeted Resonance Through Toning...

HumaNatureConnect Activity

Start-up Protocol

If this is not a day when you prefer to spend time in nature without an agenda, do the Heartwood Path Start-up Protocol found in the Appendix.

Pinpointing The Toning

Pinpoint where (in which chakra) you would like your toning to resonate (cause to be affected by entrainment) in the following way, suggested by Sequoia Henning:

First Chakra (Root)—located at the base of the spine. Tone seven times with the deepest "UUH" as in "cup," a very low, guttural sound just gently riding on the breath. Stay comfortable with the sound. Don't force it. (Red).

Second Chakra (Sacral)—located about 2-3 inches below the navel. Tone seven times using a higher pitched, but still deep "OOO" as in "you."(Orange).

Third Chakra (Solar Plexus)—located above the navel. Tone seven times using a higher pitched "OH," as in "go." (Yellow).

Fourth Chakra (Heart)—located in the center of the chest. Tone seven times using a higher pitched "AH", as in "ma." This is the sound that embodies compassion. (Green).

Fifth Chakra (Throat)—Tone seven times using a higher pitched "AY," as in "say." (Blue).

Sixth Chakra (Third Eye)—located in the middle of the forehead slightly above the eyes. "EEE" sound, as in "me." Tone seven times, using a still higher pitch. (Indigo).

Seventh Chakra (Crown)—Tone a higher sound of "EEE" focusing from your crown connecting to the angelic realm seven times, using the highest pitch you can comfortably make. (Violet or white).

Now sit in a space of silence and receptivity for 10-20 minutes to experience the energy. After this, if you feel too lightheaded, chant the universal words of AUM also known as "OM." This will help to ground you. Another way to reconnect yourself back into your body is to simply jump up and down on the earth and release with the repeated sound "Hoo hoo." Focus upon deep breathing into your body. As you jump up, breathe in; exhale as your feet hit the ground with the sound "hoo" (Henning Website).

To supplement this process of directing resonant vibrations to specific chakras I suggest you, with the help of a pitch pipe or chromatic harmonica, use your natural sense of "hearing including resonance, vibrations, sonar and ultrasonic frequencies" (Cohen, website: http://www.ecopsych.com/insight53senses.html) to hum the following resonant tones in ways that cause entrainment with specific chakras (which will become more active through the entrainment). Hum a C note to activate the First Chakra, a D note for the Second Chakra, an E note for the Third Chakra, a D Sharp note for the Fourth Chakra, a G note for the Fifth Chakra, a F Sharp note for the Sixth Chakra, and a B note for the Seventh Chakra (Chakra Tones and Notes Website).

In the activities that follow you may either simply hum a tone that feels somehow pleasant to you or you can use the above method to fine tune your intended practice and expected benefits. The instructions above are meant to be helpful. If they are too burdensome or far out for you at this point, when asked, simply hum a pleasant note or series of notes. Many of the procedures for toning and the sensations you receive from resonant vibrations are subjective and, therefore, feel free to change how you do the toning activities as you see fit.

One can also bring attention to emotional states by humming a series of notes or pitches that comprise the various musical keys. This powerful use of music is too complex to be presented here. If you want more information, I suggest you go to Kevin Lessmann's Emotions of the Musical Keys Website: http://www.gradfree.com/kevin/some_theory_on_musical_keys.htm.

Follow-up Protocol

For best results, write down your impressions of this activity in your journal using the Heartwood Path Follow-up Protocol found in the Appendix. Afterwards, consider sharing your interpretations with others.

Heartwood Path Axioms

Key Assertions From Waypoint 4.36

4.36.1.

The importance of humming or intoning can be demonstrated by the "unified field theory of sound healing," which can be summarized by the following two formulas:

"Frequency + Intent = Healing" and

"Vocalization + Visualization = Manifestation."

4.36.2.

How such healing and transformation takes place is explained by the concepts of resonance (the frequency at which an object most naturally vibrates whether or not we can audibly perceive it) and entrainment (the vibrations of one vibrating body reaching out and setting another body in motion).

4.36.3.

In preparation for your toning, remember to use a gentle voice, plan to seek out resonant tones, prepare to apply your intention

**to the toning, and do not forget to direct the vibratory energy
to your various chakras.**

4.36.4.

**Each sense is part of the magic and wisdom of nature that
resides in us and supports us.**

4.36.5.

**When entrainment occurs through careful toning there is a
psychological merging that enables one to perceive the world
through nature's perspective and to benefit from its time-tested
intelligence.**

Nocturnal Pilgrimage 4.36

For best results, write down your impressions of each night's
dreams in your journal using the Heartwood Path Dreaming Time
Protocols found in the Appendix. Afterwards, consider sharing your
Dream Tending with others.

"Night is a sight for sore eyes. It offers our vision a rest. Dusk begins
to turn down the volume of the visual world, which often gets cranked
up without our even noticing" (Naiman, 2006, p. 61).

Pertinent And Instructive Gems From My Dream Tending Journal

*I dreamt that an ex-lover, once uninhibited and free, became a Funda-
mentalist Christian. She was—you guessed it—chastising me about my
conceptualization of God. Hers came straight out of the Bible. I would call*

mine a more integral vision of God. It was more than she could accept. I
said we, like God, are the stuff of Myths—His story told in the Bible, mine
in the Bible but also in Huck Finn, Walden, the Old Man and the Sea, and
other revered manuscripts. What she was thinking was written all over her
face.

Lesson Learned: There's gotta be something better to do with an ex-lover in a dream; but, anyway, here it goes: God, it seems to me, is more than the story of Him in the Bible. We go through development stages which give us all of the same attributes as the Image of God. We, like God, are fearful and survival oriented. We, like God, are magical, at least in the sense that we can achieve the unexplainable. We, like God, can perform miracles—like whenever we perform beyond imaginable expectations. And we, like God, are prophets in that we can see what is coming, put ourselves up as shields against the danger, and serve humanity as if we were saints. These attributes are what come to my mind whenever I here that we are created in the Image of God.

By following the procedures presented along the Heartwood Path, your time in nature will, among other things, increase your empathy, which will be good for those around you and for nature as a whole. W. Keith Campbell's team of psychologists conducted a study that showed that those with a narcissistic view were more likely to cut down a hypothetical forest with greedy intent (Selhub & Logan, 2012, p.45). Don't be one who tends to forgo long-term gain and sustainability. Instead, take in nature's anti-narcissism tonic as you begin the next lesson.

When you are ready, go to the next waypoint: "NSTP." And enjoy the experience.

37

Nature's Perception

ENGAGE IN THE NATURAL
SYSTEMS THINKING PROCESS

There are eight specific action components to the Heartwood Path version of the Natural Systems Thinking Process.

1. Validate that in your circumstances it is reasonable for you to learn about the the web of nature by experiencing it through a Heartwood Path Activity.
2. Go to the most natural area that is convenient for you to visit, the more natural the better, and do the activity there.
3. Find a natural being in the natural area that gives its consent for you to visit it in a safe way. This consent comes as your continued attraction to the natural being or natural area for at least ten seconds.
4. After obtaining consent from the natural attraction, do the activity.
5. Make entries in your journal about what natural attractions you sense, think, and feel during and after the activity. Include what memories your attractions bring to awareness.

6. By email or in other ways share what you have written in your journal with another person or persons who have done the activity and can share their experience with you, following the protocol below, which is called "The Natural Systems Thinking Reflection Process."

7. Share with the above person or persons what you found attractive in reading or hearing each other's activity experience.

8. Share with friends and associates what value you found in the activity and how you feel about it.

Become familiar with The Natural Systems Thinking Reflection Process, as mentioned in Step 6 of the Heartwood Path version of the Natural Systems Thinking Process above (not presented in chronological order):

1. Write a general description of how you did the activity and what happened along with quotes you like from other pertinent readings and how they added meaning to the experience.

2. As you have been doing already along the Heartwood Path, continue to describe the three most important things you learned from this waypoint and its associated activity.

3. As you have been doing already along the Heartwood Path, write three G/G statements. (This connection experience shows me that I am a person who_____).

4. Describe how you would feel having your ability to experience this connection experience taken away? Explain whether, if at all, the activity enhances your sense of self-worth.

5. Jot down your feelings about the trustfulness of NNIAAL, if any.

6. Identify which authority or person, if any, this activity identifies or reeducates inside or outside of you.

7. Write one or more single, short "quotes" that show a significant contribution that the activity makes to the improvement your relationships.

8. If pertinent, mention how might this activity be used to enhance your practice of (insert area of interest). Include what other thoughts, feelings and experiences that come to mind about the application of NSTP to your chosen area of interest.

9. Observe and report whether the Heartwood Wood Path Activity makes you feel less stressed, and whether your nature-connecting experience builds supportive contacts and closer relationships with people and the environment.

10. Act to stop your discomfort from abusive or exploitive relationships with nature or your inner nature.

11. Insist on receiving and giving permission to relate before interacting. Recognize that you have permission to use this nature reconnecting activity and that you may repeatedly use and teach it to benefit yourself, others, and the environment.

12. Enjoy a minimum of one night's sleep (integrating dream time) before doing the next activity (Huning, Email, 2-28-11).

To A Way Of Perceiving Shared By Nature...

HumaNatureConnect Activity

Start-up Protocol

If this is not a day when you prefer to spend time in nature without an agenda, do the Heartwood Path Start-up Protocol found in the Appendix.

Engaging In The Natural Systems Thinking Process

Engage yourself in the natural systems thinking process without the use of your eyes. Work on sensing your own personal hand, then a nearby aspect of the microcosm (one leaf, for example) and then the whole of the tree but not with your eyes but instead use your ability of heliotropism—the natural sense plants and other organisms have to "see" or sense the sun's rays without the use of eyes. Eyes closed, pay attention to where you are, where the leaf is, and where the tree is in relation to the sun. Feel the sun's rays as the leaf does, and then as the tree does. Can you be aware without the use of your eyes?

Follow-up Protocol

For best results, write down your impressions of this activity in your journal using the Heartwood Path Follow-up Protocol found in the Appendix. Afterwards, consider sharing your interpretations with others.

Heartwood Path Axioms

Key Assertions From Waypoint 4.37

4.37.1.

Engage in each of the action components of the Natural Systems Thinking Process:

1. Validate that in your circumstances it is reasonable for you to learn about the web of nature by experiencing it through a Heartwood Path Activity.

2. Go to the most natural area that is convenient for you, the more natural the better, and do the activity there.

3. Find a natural being in the natural area that gives its consent for you to visit it in a safe way. This consent comes as your continued attraction to the natural being or natural area for ten seconds or so.

4. After obtaining consent from the natural attraction, do the activity.

5. Make entries in your journal about what natural attractions you sense, think, and feel during and after the activity. Include what memories your attractions bring to awareness?

6. By email or in other ways share what you have written in your journal with another person or persons who have done the activity and can share their experience with you, following the protocol below, which is called "The Natural Systems Thinking Reflection Process."

7. Share with the above person or persons what you found attractive in reading or hearing each other's activity experience.

8. Share with friends and associates what value you found in the activity and how you feel about it.

4.37.2.

Become familiar with The Natural Systems Thinking *Reflection* Process, important in Step 6 of the NSTP Basics above (not in chronological order):

1. Write a general description of how you did the activity and what happened along with quotes you like from other pertinent readings and how they added meaning to the experience.

2. As you have been doing already along the Heartwood Path, continue to describe the three most important things you learned from this waypoint and its associated activity.

3. As you have been doing already along the Heartwood Path, write three G/G statements. (This connection experience shows me that I am a person who_____).

4. Describe how you would feel having your ability to experience this connection experience taken away? Explain whether, if at all, the activity enhances your sense of self-worth.

5. Jot down your trustfulness of NNIAAL, if any.

6. Identify which authority or person, if any, this activity identifies or reeducates inside or outside of you.

7. Write one or more complete, single, short, power sentence "quotes" that convey a significant contribution that this activity makes to improving your relationships.

8. If pertinent, mention how might this activity be used to enhance your practice of (insert area of interest). Include what other thoughts, feelings and experiences that come to mind about the application of NSTP to your chosen area of interest.

9. Observe and report whether the Heartwood Wood Path Activity makes you feel less stressed, and whether your nature-connecting experience builds supportive contacts and closer relationships with people and the environment.

10. Act to stop your discomfort from abusive or exploitive relationships with nature or your inner nature.

11. Insist on receiving and giving permission to relate before interacting. Recognize that you have permission to use this

nature reconnecting activity and that you may repeatedly use and teach it to benefit yourself, others, and the environment.

12. Enjoy a minimum of one night's sleep (integrating dream time) before doing the next activity (Huning, Email, 2-28-11).

4.37.3.

Become a two-time sleeper by getting into the habit of falling asleep for 3-4 hours, waking up for a while to process your dreams, prepare for dreams, engage your imagination, write in your journal, meditate, move energy up and down your spine, or make love, then falling back to sleep for a few hours.

Nocturnal Pilgrimage 4.37

For best results, write down your impressions of each night's dreams in your journal using the Heartwood Path Dreaming Time Protocols found in the Appendix. Afterwards, consider sharing your Dream Tending with others.

Sleep and dream specialist Rubin R. Naiman, Ph.D. says the secret to a good night's sleep is a "good day's waking" and the secret to a good day's waking is a good night's sleep. If you think waking up each night is a sign of the malady of insomnia, think again. "It is possible that at least some of what we consider insomnia today might be better understood as a vestige of a natural, biphasic sleep pattern" (2006, p. 90). This pattern is characterized by people typically spending "three or four hours in what was called "first sleep" and then awakening to a "night watch."

"This hour or two of darkened awareness present(s) interesting opportunities for a kind of nightlife that we have since lost. When we judge all awakenings as problematic, we engage in struggles to get back to sleep and overlook what could be a personal spiritual opportunity" (2006. pp.90-91).

Some of the best and most remembered dreams occurs in the second sleep.

With the lesson of the present waypoint in mind, go to sleep (twice). Focus on a topic you want to dream about. Dream. And be sure to set up your dream journal for easy and immediate access.

Pertinent And Instructive Gems From My Dream Tending Journal

I dreamt that I was standing next to my workout partner Paula, watching what was happening as she used the treadmill. Pleasant Images—such as trees with singing birds, drinkable springs, and a friendly talking badger— were showing constantly on the console in front of her. On the revolving rubber foot tread there appeared Unpleasant Images that were being trampled by her bare feet. These flashing Images were of a lynching of a black man, a belching smokestack, and a bunch of kids being physically abusive to female runners on a trail. Looking fit but weary, she asked me:

"When can I stop?"

Lesson Learned: Let's say the treadmill is the Heartwood Path, the positive Images are a Heartwood pilgrim's goals, and the negative images are unwanted habits. By following the Heartwood Path she would be moving toward her goals, as displayed on the console of the treadmill. By following the Heartwood Path in this dream, she would be stomping on and ending what was no longer useful to her. Being on a treadmill, which goes on and on, meant that she may never reach final perfection but, due to her efforts, she is, nevertheless, making good progress. If the dream had not ended, I would have told Paula that she was free to stop anytime, that she had already made good improvements, and that I recommend that she stop her daily involvement after she visits all of the waypoints and her Dream Images seem to be coming from the landscape. Until that time, her dreams are indicating that she is not spending enough waking time with appealing Natural Beings that can be available for guidance, information, and healing. As soon as her dreams are commonly populated with nature-oriented Dream Images, a weekly immersion in the Heartwood Path (by re-reading the text or re-doing any of the activities, done as a refresher, will likely be sufficient.

By continuing down the Heartwood Path, you are on your way to the ecology of happiness at Gladandgreen Junction. By "ecology of happiness" I specifically mean that the more natural one makes one's everyday existence, the more harmonious one's inner world becomes. One's natural lifestyle and natural physical environment ameliorate the common difficulties one faces. Natural lifestyles and environments cause one's mind to be calm, collected, clear, relaxed, and creative. If one chooses to take nature as one's guide, one will achieve a sense of equanimity and inner peacefulness, with or without engaging in formal meditative practice.

When you are ready, move to the next waypoint: "Planetary Affinity." There, you will learn about converting temporary states into permanent traits.

38

Planetary Affinity

ESTABLISH AN INTIMATE
RAPPORT WITH THE WORLD

Planetary rapport is achieved best when one adds depth to one's character and experiences the depth of one's Greater Self. In working on one's personal growth, knowledge of the levels of depth is important so that one comprehends where one is heading. Skill in applying the lines of intelligence is important so one understands the ways one arrives at and experiences each level or stage of development. In these ways, stages of development and lines of intelligence are crucial to the process of building rapport with those parts of one's Greater Self that are beyond one's Individual Self.

Such rapport leads to celebratory and justice-seeking compassion for all living things. One is moved by what one moves; one is shaped by what one shapes; and one is enhanced by what one enhances. One becomes more aware of such reciprocities when one hones one's person-to-Earth rapport. This rapport is more profound when one uses multiple lines of intelligence (described subsequently) to integrate one's individual self with the Greater Self.

This integration deserves elaboration. As described earlier, one's individual self (which includes one's Ego) is nested within one's Greater

Self (which includes the environment). Visualize the inner rings of a tree, those visible on the stumps of cut trees (you can also see the Lines of Intelligence figure provided).

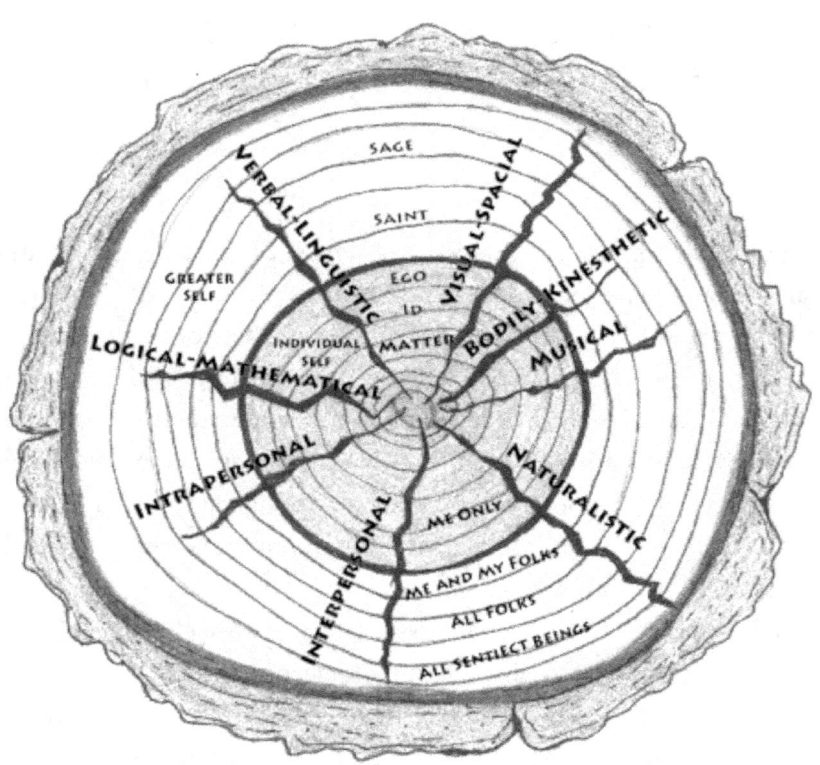

LINES OF INTELLIGENCE:
TREE RING MAP OF HOLARCHIAL THINKING AND BEING

ART WORK DONE BY THERESA GRANT

Some people only have temporary states while others have more permanent traits. Some people have peak experiences that are temporary, passing and transient. To become a full-fledge member of humanity with depth sufficient to be at the transpersonal stage of development (which is a goal for eartHearts) it is necessary to convert temporary states into permanent traits. Temporary states such as peak sexual experiences and brief moments of enlightenment can happen on pilgrimages or while visiting exotic places.

To convert these temporary states into permanent traits it takes the kind of daily repeated practices that one can only do while at home or as part of one's everyday life. It takes the convenience and economy of home to be able to permanently improve the various aspect of one's Self. Temporary states may be fun, but they have limited worth if they do not apply regularly to one's daily life. Developing deeper permanent traits—working to expand the self permanently to levels of growth with more depth—gives one a greater, longer lasting capacity to improve one's life and the lives of others.

The Heartwood Path does not offer only fleeting glimpses of a better life. It is blazed to provide lasting positive change.

Besides levels of personal growth (the rings in the illustration above), there are also lines of development (the cracks in the illustration above). Each stream of development represents one of one's multiple intelligences. This aspect of the Holarchy of Thinking and Being is not adequately addressed scientifically. Some say there are over twenty lines of development; others say seven or eight. We will, for now, rely on the work of respected psychologist Howard Gardner who has written definitively about less than ten lines of intelligence development and notes that there are probably more (1999). We shall present eight forms of intelligence. Think of them as effective ways to build rapport with the world. Without such rapport our life experiences would be very monotonous and limited. With these forms of intelligence, you have the tools needed to engage fully with other people and the world. Do not fall into the common trap of relying too much on verbal-linguistic intelligence. Live a little: use them all—after reading about them here and then testing them out in the following activity.

1) Verbal-linguistic intelligence has to do with words, spoken or written. People with verbal-linguistic intelligence display a facility with words and languages; are typically good at reading, writing, telling stories, and memorizing words and dates; tend to learn best by reading, taking notes, and listening to lectures; are skilled at explaining, teaching, and persuasive speaking. Their most suitable careers include writers, politicians, and teachers.

2) Logical-Mathematical intelligence has to do with logic, abstractions, inductive and deductive reasoning, and numbers. The most suitable careers associated with this form of intelligence include scientists, mathematicians, lawyers, doctors, and philosophers.

3) Visual-Spatial intelligence has to do with vision and spatial judgment. People with strong visual-spatial intelligence are typically very good at visualizing and mentally manipulating objects; they are good at art; they have a strong visual memory, and they generally have a very good sense of direction. Their most suitable careers include artists, engineers, and architects.

4) Bodily-kinesthetic intelligence has to do with movement and doing. People with high levels of this intelligence are generally good at physical activities. Typically, they are good at building and making things. Their most suitable careers include athletes, dancers, actors, comedians, builders, and artisans.

5) Musical intelligence has to do with rhythm, music, and hearing. Those who have a high level of musical-rhythmic intelligence will often use songs or rhythms to learn and memorize information, and may work best with music playing. Their most suitable careers are musicians, singers, conductors, and composers.

6) Naturalistic intelligence has to do with nature, nurturing, and classification. Those with naturalistic intelligence are said to have greater sensitivity to nature and their place within it. They have the ability to nurture and grow things, and are good at caring for, taming, and interacting with animals. They are also good at recognizing and

classifying different species. Most suitable careers include: scientists, naturalists, conservationists, gardeners, and farmers.

7) Interpersonal intelligence has to do with interaction with others. People in this category are usually extroverts and are characterized by their sensitivity to others' moods, feelings, temperaments, and motivations and their ability to cooperate in order to work as part of a group. They communicate effectively and empathize easily with others. They may be either leaders or followers. Their most suitable careers include: politicians, entrepreneurs, managers, social workers, and diplomats.

8) Intrapersonal intelligence has to do with oneself. Those who are strongest in this intelligence are typically introverts and prefer to work alone. They are usually highly self-aware and capable of understanding their own emotions, goals, and motivations. They learn best when allowed to concentrate on the subject by themselves. They often have a high level of perfectionism. Good career choices for those with high levels of this intelligence include philosophers, psychologists, theologians, and writers.

Other intelligences may include spiritual/existential intelligence (the capacity to raise and reflect on philosophical questions about life, death, and ultimate realities) and moral intelligence. These do not meet all the criteria to be included as a separate form of intelligence, but may prove nevertheless to be useful to you as a form of intelligence.

To continue with the metaphor of the tree stump, I visualize these lines of development as the cracks that often spread outward from the center of the tree and cross the various tree rings. Just as some of the cracks stretch further outward than others, one's various talents and attributes reach different levels of development. When one makes, sees, or visualizes a diagram of one's own overall Self using the map that resembles tree rings with cracks in the stump one can perceive an image that represents how at-home one is in the universe. It takes what is represented by numerous cracks (representing the lines of development), what is symbolized by longer cracks, and what is depicted by more numerous tree rings (representing stages of development) to be highly at-home in the universe.

At this point I am compelled to remind the reader not to fall into the common trap: thinking only of the material realm. The Great Nest or the Kosmic Holarchy of Thinking and Being (as represented by the stump with tree rings and cracks) is not only about behaviors and physical systems (both from the Realm of Exteriority). It is also about intentions and morals (from the Realm of Interiority).

In guiding your own development do not think only in terms of depth—expanding your self to the outer tree rings of Soul and Spirit. Along with depth, also consider balance. Make sure you are covering the entire stump—the four quadrants of intentions, morals, behaviors, and physical systems; as seen on the Four Leaf Model of Integrity.

One purpose of the Heartwood Path is to help stretch a person's moral development (the moral stream of development not shown on the stump) so that it encompasses a larger moral span—from the orientation of "me" only outward concentrically to the orientations of " me and my folks" then to "all folks" and, ultimately, outward to "all sentient beings." This "place" of concern about all sentient beings along the moral stream of development is a major "destination" along the Heartwood Path.

To Establish An Intimate Rapport With The World...

HumaNatureConnect Activity

Start-up Protocol

If this is not a day when you prefer to spend time in nature without an agenda, do the Heartwood Path Start-up Protocol found in the Appendix.

Using Your Multiple Intelligences To Gain Rapport With The World

Using your verbal/linguistic intelligence, sit comfortably and write down your idea of the story of your chosen place, its natural history. Using your logical/mathematical intelligence, pick out aspects of the natural setting, count their occurrences, then make logical assumptions about the relationship between the numbers. Using your visual/spatial intelligence, look for patterns in nature and on paper use your favorite patterns to create a personal logo for yourself. Using your bodily/kinesthetic intelligence, emulate with your body movements you see throughout the scene. Using your musical intelligence, hum, whistle, or sing a tune that conveys your impressions while visiting the natural place. Using your naturalistic intelligence, make classifications of the beings you come across in the natural place. Using your interpersonal intelligence, discuss your experiences with your intelligences at the natural place with others. Using your intra-personal intelligence, experience your emotions while doing this activity and spend some time reflecting on your goals and motivations. Determine your strongest lines of development by ranking them. Although still debated as a separate line of development (which is why it is not shown in the illustration), include in your ranking the moral line. Consider moral intelligence strong in you if you are oriented to "all folks" or "all sentient beings" rather than just to your own self only.

Follow-up Protocol

For best results, write down your impressions of this activity in your journal using the Heartwood Path Follow-up Protocol found in the Appendix. Afterwards, consider sharing your interpretations with others.

Heartwood Path Axioms

Key Assertions From Waypoint 4.38

4.38.1.

Establish an intimate rapport with the world by adding depth to your development and by using multiple lines of development.

4.38.2.

One is moved by what one moves; one is shaped by what one shapes; and one is enhanced by what one enhances.

4.38.3.

To become a full-fledge member of humanity with depth sufficient to be at the transpersonal stage of development it is necessary to convert temporary states into permanent traits.

4.38.4.

Developing deeper permanent traits—working to expand the self permanently to levels of growth with more depth—gives one a greater, longer lasting capacity to improve one's life and the lives of others.

4.38.5.

Along with stages of personal growth, there are also lines of development, also known as the lines of one's multiple intelligences (Verbal-linguistic, Logical-Mathematical, Visual-Spatial, Bodily-kinesthetic, Musical, Naturalistic, Interpersonal, Intrapersonal, Spiritual/existential, et. al.) one can use to arrive at and experience each level of development.

Nocturnal Pilgrimage 4.38

For best results, write down your impressions of each night's dreams in your journal using the Heartwood Path Dreaming Time Protocols found in the Appendix. Afterwards, consider sharing your Dream Tending with others.

"Lucid sleep is the simple and spiritually elegant awareness of aware-ness itself. It is pure awareness—independent of any objects of aware-ness" (Naiman, 2006, p. 92).

Agency is a thing or person that acts to produce a particular result; synonyms include: influence, force, vehicle, medium, and means. It is the *agency* one has that may or may not be used to connect psycho-logically with nature or to get into the flow of life. We shall see how connecting Core to Creation (by which I mean, mind to nature, or self to other) reduces some of the regular wear and tear that occurs in one's own psyche. When such repairs are made, when mind con-nects with nature, there is an intensification of joy (which is part what we eartHearts mean by "uncommon happiness"). As you will see more in the next waypoint, connecting one's individual self to nature (which is the Greater Self) is the ticket for achieving reliable (abiding) contentment.

With this in mind, sleep, dream, tend to your dreams, and share your dream journal entries. Post your impressions for others to see, using the EartHeart Exchange.

Pertinent And Instructive Gems From My Dream Tending Journal

I dreamt that I was hearing the voices or the utterances of many beings all at once. I wanted to pick just one speaker out of the crowd so that I could begin learning it's language. Eventually, the sound of the stream stood out above the others. I listened intently and tried to find the meaning of the

sound of its little trickles during times of no rain, as opposed to the roaring
sound of its torrent just after a rain. I was making headway deciphering
the meanings when a hydrologist appeared and said,

"Streams can't talk."

I felt it was pointless to disagree. Then, all the voices, all the sounds, as if
giving the silent treatment to the scientist and I, stopped their sounding. I
liked the singular stream's changing voices better than the cacophony, and I
liked the cacophony better than the sad and lonely silence.

Lesson Learned: After months of listening to sounds in nature, which range from odd vibrations to strange verbalizations, it seems that the givers of these sounds are both unpredictable and willful. That's the way I like it. Perhaps I am projecting my own fantasy into the situation. Perhaps I am not. By allowing Dream Images to be endowed *as if* they have their own agency I am able to receive their guidance, information, and healing. I get more from the exchange when the Images have a measure of independence. I get less from the exchange when the Images, having no agency, have lost their own will and have become predictable. During my lucid dreams, I prefer to converse (usually nonverbally) with a living being that has its own agency, that has its own sensitivities, and that has its own preferences, and that has its own purposes. These are the traits fellow subjects have and objects don't. If I cannot see another living being as the source of a Dream Image, but only see myself as the creator of the Image, the value of the dream diminishes. I might as well go have a conversation with the image of myself in a mirror. When I don't recognize Dream Images as representing subjects but rather see the animals, the rivers, the forests, and the other visitors that show up in my dreams as insensate objects, I have no Dream Characters to give me *courage*, I have no Dream Characters to share their *intelligence* with me, and I have no Dream Characters to give me the *integrity* it often takes to suggest and manifest full-blown solutions. Highly regarded proposals come from individuals with allies that come in the form of Dream Images. The Images are sometimes personalized, always alive, and always intelligent. Like Natural Beings, Dream Images ought to remain nameless. They ought to be loved. And they ought to be recognized for having their own wisdom and beauty. When respected in these ways, Dream Characters will become...(do I really need to say?..."as if they are")...great allies. They really will be...

When you are ready, move to the next waypoint: "One's Own Core." In this title, by "Core" I mean one's sense of self that includes one's Ego.

39

One's Own Core

REMEMBER ONE'S CONNECTION TO NATURE

The Ego, a controlling and jealous ally, always wants one to feel separate. This makes one feel lonely, insecure, fearful and angry. To transform one's self in ways that preserve the environment, one needs to explore the shadow side of the Self (including one's negative emotions) and the spiritual aspects of the Self. A good time to do so is when the Ego is not providing its customary distraction, like when you are alone in nature or meditating.

One's goal at this waypoint—at this connection-producing examination—is to create an energetic opening, pried larger through conscious breathing that allows one to distinguish truth from repetitive and meaningless untrue chatter. This opening is the void of no thoughts. Within this void is awareness.

Awareness allows one to open up to one's own core. This opening is the process of centering, of consciously sitting inside one's Self. This gateway is a portal of breath that connects consciousness to life.

To A Hole For Negativity…

HumaNatureConnect Activity

Start-up Protocol

If this is not a day when you prefer to spend time in nature without an agenda, do the Heartwood Path Start-up Protocol found in the Appendix.

Remembering One's Connection

Sitting quietly, pay attention to your breath as you breathe in and out. Notice thoughts but do not attach yourself to them. Let them pass. Once you are able to focus on your breathing to the point that you are no longer paying undo attention to your thinking, become aware of your surroundings. Try not to judge what you see. Simply sit in awareness of the natural setting without thinking unrelated thoughts, or thinking about what you are seeing, or naming what you see. Be a part of the scene, simply aware of what is happening, rather than a mental commentator about the scene. As you continue your deliberate awareness without undo thinking, imagine that each time you breathe in you are creating a hole in your being that is large enough to allow negativity to pass right through you. Without the large inner opening of a quiet mind, one's inner disharmony creates outer disharmony. Continue this process until your awareness of your body and the natural scene overpowers your stream of thoughts and you sense that you can be unscathed by the negativity of others. Before leaving the natural place, consider whether allowing negativity to stick to you comes from your awareness or your thinking.

Follow-up Protocol

For best results, write down your impressions of this activity in your journal using the Heartwood Path Follow-up Protocol found in the Appendix. Afterwards, consider sharing your interpretations with others.

Heartwood Path Axioms

Key Assertions From Waypoint 4.39

4.39.1.

One feels lonely, insecure, fearful, and angry largely because the Ego always wants one to feel separate.

4.39.2.

To transform one's self in ways that preserve the environment, one needs to explore the shadow side of the Self (including one's negative emotions) and the spiritual aspects of the Self.

4.39.3.

A good time to explore the shadow side of the Self is when the Ego is not providing its customary distraction, like when you are alone in nature or meditating.

4.39.4.

The goal of connection-producing examination is to create an energetic opening of awareness, pried larger through conscious breathing that allows one to distinguish truth from repetitive and meaningless chatter.

4.39.5.

In the meditative process of centering, of consciously sitting inside one's Greater Self, one opens the portal of breath that connects consciousness to all life.

Nocturnal Pilgrimage 4.39

For best results, write down your impressions of each night's dreams in your journal using the Heartwood Path Dreaming Time Protocols found in the Appendix. Afterwards, consider sharing your Dream Tending with others.

"Our truest life is when we are in dreams awake," says Henry David Thoreau. He also reminds us of the value of awakening slowly. He wrote about how he would sometimes sit "in my doorway from sunrise to noon, rapt in reverie, amid the pines and hickories and sumacs in undisturbed solitude and stillness" (Naiman, 2006, pp.113 and 125). Sleep. Dream. Look to your dreams for images that may have as their source the topics of this book or your connection experiences with attractive natural objects. Record your impressions in your dream journal.

Pertinent And Instructive Gems From My Dream Tending Journal

I dreamt that I was chastising a man who ran a coal mine, saying that he was killing nature. His rebuttal was that he was not killing anybody or anything. He was instead developing the natural resources.

Lesson Learned: We are all killing nature simply by being consumers. We can make amends by recycling, by using appropriate technology, and by controlling our acquisitions. But to really live properly on this planet—that is, by living sustainably, by being appropriate, and by making things better, not worse—we will need to form relationships with Natural Beings. We can form these relationships either by communing with Natural Beings in nature or by interacting appropriately with Images of Natural Beings in lucid dreams. Walk through a natural landscape as if in a dream. And walk through a dream as if in a natural landscape. Both ways will be healing for you and the planet. Both ways will reveal that nature is only a resource when it is interpreted as if it was an object. And both ways reveal that Natural Beings become associates when they are interpreted as if they are fellow subjects.

In the activities that follow, we will not be viewing the beauty of things simply for momentary tantalization. We will use beauty as a way to stimulate your attentiveness to nature and to attract you to the wild. We will use beauty to fascinate you sufficiently so that you will linger longer with a natural being. We will use beauty so that you will return more often to a beautiful natural landscape. We will use beauty so that you will ponder how your attractions to nature give you prepossessing ideas and engaging insights about how to live harmoniously, bewitchingly, and magnificently in a more natural way.

With these words about beauty in mind, when ready, continue to the next waypoint: "Allure." There, you will learn to remember beauty through the practice of conscious breathing.

40

Allure

REMEMBER BEAUTY

During my lifetime of communing with nature, and particularly in recent years as I practice some of Dr. Cohen's Nature Connect activities, when I attempt to center myself in nature by practicing conscious breathing it feels to me like a sort of hole opens in my being, a hole that helps me feel, at once, positive and connected to place. Occasionally though, long after finishing the activity in nature, the inner opening I experienced in the conscious breathing activity seems gradually to close. When this happens, I lose my center, and occasionally tempers flare as a result of what seems like the accumulation of the stuck negative dense energy that can no longer pass through. From my own experiences, it seems to me that when two or more people with large amounts of dense, negative energy stuck in their memory systems encounter one another emotional or physical trauma is more apt to occur. To survive the shock and pain of this kind of ordeal, I have at times launched an unwise survival mechanism wherein it seems that a part of my psyche splits off and pays attention to less turbulent matters. When this happens it feels like I lose a vital part of my Self and the elation I felt in the natural place subsides. When my inner world energy portal closes, there is a slight dip in my excitement for life. There is also often a slight propensity for competitiveness, alienation, and loneliness. Numerous negative physical consequences follow, including asthma-like breathing difficulties. When I lose touch with my core, I feel the urge to reopen the inner portal of expansive awareness where I find my true essence. Within this portal of awareness I become more open to discovering what would bring passion and meaning back into my life. Here, within the opening of awareness, I remember beauty—by which I mean the following sorts of recollections: the shimmer of one's own purpose revealed in a dream, important messages from scenic landscapes or animals, the joy that arises from listening to or making beautiful music, or the pleasing quality of self-made art.

To The Recollection Of Attractiveness...

HumaNatureConnect Activity

Start-up Protocol

If this is not a day when you prefer to spend time in nature without an agenda, do the Heartwood Path Start-up Protocol found in the Appendix.

Appreciating Beauty

Use your sense of color to experience the beauty around you. Pick any color and find it on yourself. Next, find the same color on a natural attraction that is part of the microcosm (one flower, for example). Then, following a resonant link, find the same color in a natural attraction that is macroscopic in depth—big like a prairie or a meadow. Imagine this color to be a musical note. Hum the note of the color on yourself, on the microcosmic attraction, and on the macrocosmic attraction. What happens to the color or the note as you follow it resonating at differing levels within the environment?

Follow-up Protocol

For best results, write down your impressions of this activity in your journal using the Heartwood Path Follow-up Protocol found in the Appendix. Afterwards, consider sharing your interpretations with others.

Heartwood Path Axioms

Key Assertions From Waypoint 4.40

4.40.1.

Centering oneself in nature by practicing conscious breathing feels like a sort of hole opening up in one's being—a hole that oddly helps one feel, at once, connected to place and positive.

4.40.2.

After a meditative activity in nature, the inner opening (hole) created by the experience seems gradually to close, causing tempers to flare as a result of what seems like dense energy that can no longer pass through.

4.40.3.

When two or more people with large amounts of dense, negative energy stuck in their memory systems encounter one another emotional or physical trauma is more apt to occur.

4.40.4.

When one's inner world energy portal closes, there is a slight dip in one's excitement for life; there is often a slight propen-

sity for competitiveness, alienation, and loneliness, there are numerous negative physical consequences, including possibly asthma-like breathing difficulties, there is often a feeling of losing touch with one's core, and there is an urge to reopen the inner portal of expansive awareness where one can re-experience one's true essence.

4.40.5.

Each time one opens the inner portal of awareness one becomes more open to discovering what would bring passion and meaning back into one's life; one is more attuned to beauty; and one has more vibrant recollections, including the shimmer of one's own purpose revealed in a dream, important messages from scenic landscapes or animals, the joy that arises from listening to or making beautiful music, enhanced awareness of the transformations that occurred during previous meditative sexual practices, or the pleasing quality of handmade art.

Nocturnal Pilgrimage 4.40

For best results, write down your impressions of each night's dreams in your journal using the Heartwood Path Dreaming Time Protocols found in the Appendix. Afterwards, consider sharing your Dream Tending with others.

"A gradual awakening begins with our listening to what morning is saying to us" (Naiman, 2006, pp.125-127).

Before heading to the next waypoint, sleep and dream. Tend to your dreams. Look for signs that the information in this course and your connection experiences with splendid natural beings are entering into your dreams.

Avoiding or recovering from dissociation and opening up the portal that reveals one's often hidden positive traits lowers a variety of middle-age problems, including, as we all know, interruption of afternoon naps, trying to figure out tablets and remote controls, not understanding what young people are talking about, talking about aches and pains, not liking the loud music in restaurants, discovering more hair in strange places, not knowing any of the songs on the Top Ten List, and spending money on face creams.

Pertinent And Instructive Gems From My Dream Tending Journal

I dreamt I was in a heated discussion with an angry man.

He said:

"What do you mean I can't kill her?"

I said,

"It wouldn't be right."

The man said,

"ok, if I can't kill her, I'll make her my slave."

I said,

"That too wouldn't be right."

The man said,

"If I can't kill her or enslave her, I'll ignore her."

I said:

"It still wouldn't be right."

The man said, "

If I can't kill her, or enslave her, or ignore her, I'll devalue her."

I said,

"You know that's not right."

"Then I'll dismiss her,"

said the man.

Lesson Learned: The man was an Image representing everyone. His planned negative actions were examples of dissociation directed at nature. That's the way it goes. Unless we all really get to know Mother Nature and all her minions—the rocks, the plants, the animals, and the landscapes. And respect them for what they are: Fellow Subjects.

As you can imagine, one way to counter dissociation is to associate, the topic of the next waypoint. When ready, move to the next waypoint: "Association." It will take you one step closer to our destination, Gladandgreen Junction.

41

Association

IDENTIFY WITH OTHERS

We treat as ourselves those with whom we identify. When we see a horse yawn, for example, we identify with this expression and assign to that animal the feelings we experience when we yawn. It seems to me that having such moments of shared comprehension with another species can be among life's most exhilarating and profound moments.

Insightful contact need not be limited to domesticated animals. Contact with the wild, for example, awakens one to a world of adventure. While some outdoor activities place nature as an obstacle to overcome and, therefore, reinforce the "Man against nature" attitude, other outdoor activities inspire an ecological frame of reference to the adventure. Rather than seeking to beat the river or the rock, for example, an activity can be framed in such a way as to help the person come to know the river or, better yet, to be with the river. Those involved in adventure education need not dwell solely on deeds of physical hardship. If all that is gained by roughing it, climbing the highest peak, or covering great distances, is "living to tell the tale," then the outdoor experience is lacking a key component: the adventure of the Spirit.

Contact with nature helps one uncover realms of one's inner life that are too often lost in the trance put upon one by modern, civilized society. It is because wildness opens one up to a world alive with Spirit and adventure that one is able to break free, if even for brief interludes, from the grip of the Ego and the demands of the industrial-consumer society.

Do not think that, by seeking guidance in nature, you are being somehow blasphemous; for in the Book of Job (12: 7-8) we receive the following instructions: "Ask the animals, and they will teach you: the birds of the air, and they will tell you; ask the plants and the earth and they will teach you."

Replace desires to control nature with desires to experience nature. Experiencing the Wild is part of your birthright, one of the privileges of being an earthling.

Be vigilant to the gifts that come from the *liminal* wilderness—that part of nature or wildness that not always easy to perceive. Such gifts will not show you new worlds, but they will help you live fully in ours.

Each of us lives in a house, condo, or apartment. This dwelling, however, is just the beginning of what is really one's home. If one's residential *dwelling* is the inner reach of home, the *Wild* is the outer reach of home.

By "wild," I do not necessary mean solely pristine wilderness. There is wildness to be found in suburban and urban areas, as well. Some of what can be found in a nature preserve also goes on in one's living room and bedroom. Wildness is just about anything that is beyond rational control. Sex, for example, is a trip to the wilderness. So are dreams. They also carry one to an untamed place.

The Wild penetrates and enfolds all of society. The Wild is not just the birds or the trees outside of your window. It is also your breathing, your heartbeat, your anger, and your fear.

This earth-to-body link creates a bodily and earthly presence that is started by taking a few minutes to change gears in numerous ways, including presenting a symbolic gift to the nearby land, taking a dip in a nearby stream or lake, giving or receiving a massage, making an entry into one's journal, going to out-of-the-way or unusual places nearby; and following one's breathing.

The Spirit perceived when you bind yourself as the "experiencer" to the place you are experiencing is Unfathomable Tenderness and the Indescribable Essence of Being. What a blessing it is!

When you pause either in your own local place or in an exotic environment, rest your mind and seek awareness of the wild. Doing so will help you to cement into your self-concept those beautiful beyond-individual aspects of nature. "It is from our connected selves that much of what people most value in life emerges, including love, friendship, loyalty, trust, relationship, belonging, purpose, gratitude, spirituality, mutual aid, and meaning," writes Macy and Johnstone (2012, p. 91). Put the wisdom of this part of the Heartwood Path to work for you by doing the following activity:

To Scan Oneself As The One Doing The Experiencing Of A Place...

HumaNatureConnect Activity

Start-up Protocol

If this is not a day when you prefer to spend time in nature without an agenda, do the Heartwood Path Start-up Protocol found in the Appendix.

Examining Yourself As The Experiencer Of The Place

Examine the state of yourself as the "experiencer" of this place. Examine your own Exteriority (one's behaviors and physical systems) but also your Interiority (one's intentions and ethics). Then, when your mind becomes still, you can directly experience that which binds you as the "experiencer" to the Spirit of the place you are experiencing—the abundant, resplendent Spirit. Focus on both your own feelings and the place where you are doing the feeling. Jot down your impressions below.

Follow-up Protocol

For best results, write down your impressions of this activity in your journal using the Heartwood Path Follow-up Protocol found in the Appendix. Afterwards, consider sharing your interpretations with others.

Heartwood Path Axioms

Key Assertions From Waypoint 4.41

4.41.1.

If all that is gained by roughing it, climbing the highest peak, or covering great distances, is "living to tell the tale," then the outdoor experience is lacking a key component: the adventure of the Spirit.

4.41.2.

Contact with nature helps one uncover realms of one's inner life that are too often lost in the trance put upon one by modern, civilized society.

4.41.3.

It is because wildness opens one up to a world alive with Spirit and adventure that one is able to break free, if even for brief interludes, from the grip of the Ego and the demands of the industrial-consumer society.

4.41.4.

Replace desires to control nature with desires to experience nature.

4.41.5.

If one's residential *dwelling* is the inner reach of home, the *Wild* is the outer reach of home.

Nocturnal Pilgrimage 4.41

For best results, write down your impressions of each night's dreams in your journal using the Heartwood Path Dreaming Time Protocols found in the Appendix. Afterwards, consider sharing your Dream Tending with others.

"Consider establishing a routine of morning light exposure for twenty to thirty minutes each day. Get outside as soon as you can . . . " (Naiman, 2006, p. 136).

Sleep. Dream. Tend to your dreams, looking for images that seem to come from the topics of this course or from your connection experiences with attractive natural beings.

Pertinent And Instructive Gems From My Dream Tending Journal

I dreamt—as is often the case—that I was in a heated discussion. The head of the mining council was telling me that when he visited the Whites Creek area in Missouri all he could see was the largest lead mine on earth. I replied that when I went backpacking in the Irish Wilderness—our preferred name for the same area—I didn't see in my mind's eye a mine at all. I saw a congressionally-designated Wilderness Area protecting the largest remaining forest in the state.

He said the mine would serve a strategic purpose, and went on to say:

"How are we gonna fill the bad guys with lead if we can't dig enough of it up?"

I said,

"if you found lead under the Sistine Chapel would you dig for it there?"

He said he'd check that out and get back to me.

I said,

"When I'm in the Irish Wilderness I don't see any resources at all. It's rather like a huge cathedral filled with fellow parishioners. I see no resources, only fellow beings with the right to live out their destinies. There will be no mine here!"

Lesson Learned: Simply put, here's what you have to do to win a conservation battle:

Prove that your will to save a place

is greater than everyone's will

to destroy it.

When you move to the next waypoint, do not just wallow in front of the computer screen as a way to speed up your progress with this course. Without also going outside, you are increasing your risk of death.

As an inducement to get outside, know that research shows unmitigated viewing of trivia and distraction of looking at amusements on a computer screen contribute to mortality and not in a small way. The risk of death in one study was 52 percent higher in the group that spent the most time in front of a computer screen compared to those who spend the least time viewing an electronic screen (Selhub & Logan, 2012, p. 45). Given this study, noted cultural critic Neil Postman had it right when he titled his book **Amusing Ourselves to Death.** Reduce your risk of dying by staying active. And one good way to do that is to walk for a spell each day in search of a natural being to help you with each HumaNatureConnect Activity. Take long walks in nature. The longer you commune with a natural being, the better.

To truly absorb the expressiveness of the natural universe, end your "unnaturalessness," become homesick for your outer most house, the natural world. End your "unrelatedness" to the wild earth so that you can feel completely at ease in your habitat. No fine house or penthouse apartment can compare to consciously feeling at home, at ease, and connected to nature. If you ever feel lonely in a room of people, lonely despite a multitude of human interactions, it may be because you are lonely for your ancestral "home"—the unpaved, boundless expanse of wild nature.

With the importance of getting into nature in mind, when ready, move to the next waypoint: "Eloquence." There, you will learn to honor the expressiveness of the universe. You are making great progress.

42

Eloquence

HONOR THE EXPRESSIVENESS OF THE UNIVERSE

The universe expresses itself through diversity (differentiation), through the interiority of an entity (subjectivity), and through the profound interrelatedness of all life (communion). Over the years, environmentalists like myself have been running around preaching about the interrelatedness of all life (communion). We have also been taking a stand against mindless development through collective efforts to stop ill-considered dams or through lobbying for wilderness preservation. In all of our actions, we environmentalists have been seeking to protect biological diversity (differentiation). Despite all of these efforts, ecological problems still loom. That shortfall is happening, in part, because, on the whole, we environmentalists "ain't done squat" to understand or honor the Realm of Interiority (subjectivity).

Adding this mission to the human endeavor is a main purpose of the Heartwood Path. One can only have ethical integrity when one honors all ways the universe expresses itself—through differentiation, subjectivity, and communion. Here is a way to Grace: self-delight in the knowing of how the myriad of things—living and nonliving—belong together.

The way to understand the connection between nature and Grace is to expand your self-concept so that your Self includes nature. That too is a chief purpose of this series of books.

One comes to know Spirit in a powerful way when one's mind is still. Once one reveals this Spirit to oneself one comes to the all-important revelation that it is inevitably impossible to completely disconnect person from place. Spirit unites person and place.

You can come to a better understanding of *who* you are by coming to an understanding of *where* you are. The result of combining the "who" in you and the "where" in you is resplendent wholeness.

Together, we humans all have a hold on the environment. Conversely, the environment has a hold on us. We influence the environment and the environment influences us. The environment binds us together in mutual interdependence. Moreover, because of the limitations and ethics its proper use demands, the environment—if only we would listen—keeps us in check, prevents us from too much growth, and stops us from tripping over one another. For such purposes, we need to protect the public domain as much as we need to protect our own rights.

Habits that are formed in a place become a culture. To inhabit a place responsibly—to live well in a place—requires the view that humans and the environment are of one another. We humans have gotten away with inhabiting the Earth irresponsibly for a long time, in part, because we are living on the stored capital of oil rather than the current income of solar energy.

Live conformably on the planet by reducing dependence on stored sunlight (in the form of coal and oil). Our dominant culture is propped up on oil—ancient stored sunlight. The problem is our planet cannot make any more. In the next decade or two, scarcity will force oil prices so high, most people will be forced to use less. There will be ups and downs in the financial economy but the earth's economy will be in a permanent recession unless we develop ways to restore both the Earth and the human relationship to the planet. If we do not mend our ways and let the Earth heal itself through wilderness preservation, pollution control, and other environmental measures, hope will run out along with the oil.

Following the law of reciprocity, we have to find ways to put back whatever we take. To prepare for the inevitability of oil shortages, now is the time to develop a less oil-intensive way of life. Despite huge set-backs during the Reagan, Bush, W. Bush, and Trump Administrations, technological progress in the field of renewable energy sources is a reality. Prices are dropping for solar-cell-produced electricity and solar batteries.

Such technologies not only produce energy. They also help us to reconnect with nature. The coal-and-oil-fueled dominant culture sep-arated humanity from nature. Our reliance on buried sunlight rather than current sunlight gave us the sense that all the world was here for us to use and that it was our holy duty to control and dominate it. Our love affair with oil and coal caused us to lose touch with the Spirit of Nature. It is this Spirit that gave birth to us. We turned away from our Mother.

Without her reprimanding, we fail to grow into mature adults. Like spoiled children, we watch too many commercials on television, want immediate fulfillment of our every desire, and end up becoming ideal consumers but not mature adults. Learning how to live a life without an abundance of petroleum will certainly be part of the Great Work! for the children or grand children of everyone alive on earth today.

Conservation is a skill set all humans in the industrial world need to begin mastering now. The consequences of global tensions from petroleum shortages mean that we cannot wait until the end of oil is upon us. A first-step toward the remedy for this malady is contained in following suggested practice.

To A Rejection Of The Wide Gate Of Modernity...

HumaNatureConnect Activity

Start-up Protocol

If this is not a day when you prefer to spend time in nature without an agenda, do the Heartwood Path Start-up Protocol found in the Appendix.

Fighting The Lure Of The Dominant Culture

Resolve to turn off the television. Instead of watching mindless television shows and incessant, hypnotizing commercials, sit quietly for just ten to fifteen minutes. Take a few more minutes to walk outdoors. Use the extra time you will have and the extra vigor you will feel to help protect the environment.

Follow-up Protocol

For best results, write down your impressions of this activity in your journal using the Heartwood Path Follow-up Protocol found in the Appendix. Afterwards, consider sharing your interpretations with others.

Heartwood Path Axioms

Key Assertions From Waypoint 4.42

4.42.1.

The universe expresses itself through diversity (differentiation), through the interiority of an entity (subjectivity), and through the profound interrelatedness of all life (communion).

4.42.2.

Here is a way to Grace: self-delight in the knowing of how the myriad of things—living and nonliving—belong together.

4.42.3.

The result of combining the "who" in you and the "where" in you is resplendent wholeness.

4.42.4.

If we do not mend our ways and let the Earth heal itself through wilderness preservation, pollution control, and other environmental measures, hope will run out along with the oil.

4.42.5.

The coal-and-oil-fueled dominant culture separated humanity from nature by giving us the sense that all the world was here for us to use and that it was our holy duty to control and dominate it.

Nocturnal Pilgrimage 4.42

For best results, write down your impressions of each night's dreams in your journal using the Heartwood Path Dreaming Time Protocols found in the Appendix. Afterwards, consider sharing your Dream Tending with others.

We "frantically grope for counterfeit energies (such as excessive light at night, drugs, and alcohol) while shunning out primary source of natural energy—the sun" (Naiman, 2006, p. 150).

With this quote in mind, sleep and dream. Look for aspects of your dreams that seem to be inspired by the topics of this book or from your connection experiences with attractive natural beings.

Pertinent And Instructive Gems From My Dream Tending Journal

I dreamt I was talking with my ole Boulder Buddy from Lower Rock Creek. Having known him for years, and having spent much time in "conversation" in the past, I decided to ask a rather personal/"stoneal" question:

"Since I know I'm not crazy and don't have any telltale delusions,"

I said,

"how is it that I can speak with you when science tells me that rocks, or minerals, or stones are not alive?"

"You are not talking to any old Igneous Formation" he replied.

"While such beings do have a rock's level of awareness and can tell when it's hot, for example, we don't form the concepts or words necessary for the conversations you are experiencing."

" So," I said, "how is it then that you give me such good advice—stuff that I do not think I would come up with on my own."

My Buddy replied, "you formed a connection experience with an Igneous Formation you call in your writing your "Boulder Buddy." You never said that was my name, and I appreciate that, since we don't use words or names where I come from. To give me a name would have set up in your own mind a "lording-over" mentality that would have prevented you from getting much out of me. You simply came to me, appreciated how handsome I am, using your terms, and respected me for what I am: a fellow being."

"So," I replied,

"when we speak words, it's really me doing all the talking, right?"

My Buddy then said, "I am flattered that the qualities you experience as being who I am you have made into words that are helpful to you and your readers. You have seen many signs and, although we are not finished, you have probably already said enough. You know how we can be about words."

" So," I repeated,

"just to make sure I understand, are you saying that you are alive or not alive?"

"Have you ever had a two-way conversation with a non-living physical rock?" was his initial reply.

"Before I tell you, let me ask why this matters? I suppose it depends on your definition of alive, and look who is establishing those definitions. Do you think they have the welfare of all fellow Natural Beings foremost in their minds? For eons, your kind thought all fellow Natural Beings, from the soil to the trees, were alive. Then came your science, technology, and agriculture and the thinking changed. Nevertheless, inherent in everything your kind now calls natural objects or natural resources is the time-tested intelligence of nature. When you think of me, for example, as a fellow subject, a sort of bridge of awareness forms between us. At my end if this span is your memory and Image of me—in my Igneous Formation aspect. At your end of this span are all of your other memories, experiences, and interpretations. It helps you to think that I am attractive, intelligent, and helpful. You say rightly that all of nature only does what it is attracted to do, so you too enter into a state of attraction, which I suppose makes you feel more empathetic (which is good). You call this "Natural Attraction Ecology." It helps you when you ask for consent to enter into a connection experience, thus making you even more empathetic."

"Ok," I interrupt,

"so we get nowhere without your consent which comes in the form of my lingering attraction. And you gotta be alive or I would not be gleaning so much from you."

"Ok, now let me interrupt," said my Boulder Buddy.

"You humans generate the Images of us Natural Beings, you interpret the Images, and, at some peril, you come up with illusory conversations which you jot down as words. We are allusions. In case you haven't noticed our messages and presentations of ourselves only seem to be about the birds and bunnies. They are actually about you. You see us as Images, either in nature or in your dreams. We are Images of living beings, and so we are living Images—and one's that are not of your own making. You will not create the Image you have of me by yourself. I give you the raw materials, so to speak, and much of the inspiration."

Lesson Learned: Inherent in the Image of Natural Beings is nature's own intelligence, imparted after eons of evolution, and after eons of relationships between other Natural Beings. Coming sometimes as the personification of a Natural Being—a ubiquitous occurrence in all Human Cultures throughout the Ages—Dream Images have within them the intelligence of the body of a stone, the wisdom of the fibers of a plant, the good judgment of the flesh of the animal, and, while losing its corporeality, the Image retains the good sense of its origination but also avails itself to the interpretations and language of its human viewer who, being an Exchange partner, converts, after its connection experiences, the non-human Wisdom of the Ages into words. All of the players in this exchange, both the humans and the non-humans, show their ability to be aware, demonstrate their unpredictability, and display their own volition. Such parameters demonstrate that all of the players—from the Igneous Formations to the Dream Images, from the Natural Beings to the humans—are alive.

Prepare yourself for the choices that lie ahead in this course by breaking out of your indoor comfort zone. When one is in that zone—spending way too many hours watching TV—one is developing the same reduced life expectancy that comes from obesity and lack of physical activity (Selhub & Logan, 2012, p. 45). A remedy for all of these risk factors is physical activity outdoors. Once outside during the next outdoor activity, develop your habit of awareness and foster your fascination to learn more. Nature will do the rest.

At this next stop, some dark choices will have to be faced so that a brighter future can shine. You are now properly prepared to face these choices. When ready, click on the "Global Triage" link to move to the next waypoint.

43

Global Triage

FOCUS ON THE PERSON FIRST, THEN ON THE PLANET

It is the fate of humans, not the fate of the Earth, that is in question. The Earth can use the power of the ages to make any needed adjustments if there is an ecological calamity, including the disappearance of humans. EartHearts know that the Earth, ultimately, can take care of itself. The melody of the song of life on Earth will change very little if humans are no longer present on Earth; only the rhythm of this song will change. Rather than focusing directly on healing the Earth, eartHearts focus on using the Earth to heal the human psyche. EartHearts know that once this healing of people is prevalent, the present state of the Earth, or perhaps an improved state of the Earth, can be secured.

The interaction between humans and nature allows people to develop the perceptions, orientation, and sensibility helpful in the consideration of the effects of their actions, values, and ideals on themselves and nature. This relationship between the Self and the outside world requires no stretch of the imagination, no lengthy ordeal leading up to some rare experience of enlightenment, and no secret tricks. The relationship begins with the revelation that the world begins deep inside of one's Self.

Environmental destruction would never have been a problem had man lived conformably to nature. Humans stopped living conformably with nature sometime in the distant past when people started using the equivalent of the word "inanimate." Earlier in history, all things were considered to be alive with Spirit. When all things were no longer considered "animate," people were able to place some "beings" outside of the circle of life. Some beings became objects. This separation of inanimate objects from subjective beings paved the way for all sorts of tragic losses. Forests were cut, rivers were polluted, and people began to lose their moral compass because their relationship with nature was torn asunder.

Jesus says in the Gospel of Peace, as recorded by the Disciple John:

> "In everything that is life is the law written. You find it in the grass, in the tree, in the river, in the mountain, in the birds of the heaven, in the fishes of the sea; but seek it chiefly in yourselves. For I tell you truly, all living things are nearer to God than the scripture, which is without life" (Székely, p. 7).

Today, eartHearts continue the work of Jesus Christ by helping people look to their own identity-in-relation-to-nature for a source of guidance and direction in all affairs of living. A big part of this job is understanding materiality as the Absolute Spirit's (God's) worldliness through the "Cosmic Christ"—Christ seen as the Whole Universe and the Kosmic Pattern that Connects.

Unfortunately, instead of connecting with the Absolute Spirit, many people attempt to find a connection to something bigger than themselves through drugs, alcohol, shopping, or indiscriminate sex. These negative ways to search for a cure for loneliness or a sense of connection to something bigger can be held in check when one puts one's awe together with knowledge to make wisdom.

Most people have already found a measure of knowledge in their schooling. Much of one's wisdom, however, can be found in messages delivered to oneself from humaNature. As Juvenal says: "Never does nature say one thing and wisdom another."

To Priorities Of Means...

HumaNatureConnect Activity

Start-up Protocol

If this is not a day when you prefer to spend time in nature without an agenda, do the Heartwood Path Start-up Protocol found in the Appendix.

Focusing On The Person, Then The Planet

Use another of the radiation senses—awareness of one's own invisibility or visibility and "consequent camouflaging—" to make the boundaries of your "self" visible and invisible your mind's eye. Is there a visible boundary to your self? If so, what does this boundary look like? Does it correspond to your brain or to your skin? Does it encompass your house, your habitat, or your family? What aspects of the environment can you make visible or invisible just by changing your perspective?

Follow-up Protocol

For best results, write down your impressions of this activity in your journal using the Heartwood Path Follow-up Protocol found in the Appendix. Afterwards, consider sharing your interpretations with others.

Heartwood Path Axioms

Key Assertions From Waypoint 4.43

4.43.1.

EartHearts know that once psychic healing of people is prevalent, the present state of the Earth, or perhaps an improved state of the Earth, can be secured.

4.43.2.

Unfortunately, instead of connecting with the Absolute Spirit, many people attempt to find a connection to something bigger through drugs, alcohol, shopping, or indiscriminate sex.

4.43.3.

Juvenal says:

"Never does nature say one thing and wisdom another."

Nocturnal Pilgrimage 4.43

For best results, write down your impressions of each night's dreams in your journal using the Heartwood Path Dreaming Time Protocols found in the Appendix. Afterwards, consider sharing your Dream Tending with others.

Look for indications that your connection experiences are entering your dreams. Record your impressions in your dream journal.

Pertinent And Instructive Gems From My Dream Tending Journal

I dreamt that I was walking through the woods and almost stepped on a mushroom. It was very upsetting.

Lesson Learned: The other plants I was walking on would have bounced back after I stepped on them. But not the mushroom. Had I stepped on it I would have hurt the mushroom, smashed it. I also would have messed up its string of relationships. I would have caused all sorts of bad results. How could I be a good eartHeart and be so self-serving, so destructive, and so careless? I would be serving only my own interests. And that would mess up my own self-concept. I would have precluded the mushroom's chance to influence others, to serve its role in relationships, and to display its novel appearance. Like the birds above it and the worms below it, the mushroom has a natural sentience. It has an ability to communicate. It is part of a greater community. Had I stepped on that mushroom I would be ethically bound to take care of all of its kind and all of its relations. I didn't want to take the time for that, at the moment. So I stepped over the mushroom, left it to display its own dignity, and said to myself that I would check on the welfare of it and its community on my return trip. I have been behaving like this for a long while, so it has to be correct.

As you learn more about using your eyesight and your insight, as you will do in the next waypoint, give in to the strong psychological and spiritual need we all have for contact with wildness. Go outside to do the next activity and reach out to the natural attractions you find there. Such contact is vital to one's life and identity. You may not be able to achieve real wholeness or a "perfect" peace of mind without developing the ability to use your insight and eyesight in ways that lead you back to your natural state of connection to wild land.

When you are ready, move to the waypoint "Vision And Intuition" to take the next important step towards Gladandgreen Junction: using both your eyesight and your insight. Your progress is out of sight.

44

Vision And Intuition

USE BOTH EYESIGHT AND INSIGHT

The process of finding guidance from nature often requires a blending of eyesight and insight. The former brings information from the outside world into one's inner world. The latter is an inner world event that is often barely apparent. Unlike a concept, which can be meaty and actionable, an insight is often intangible and latent. Often an insight comes from data gathered by eyesight. For example, a person who is good at making this shift first sees a river in the valley, then an otter in the river, then, upon careful reflection upon the amusing antics of the otter, the animal's Spirit emerges into the mind's eye. In this instance, not only can one learn about otters through one's own eyesight but also receive guidance about playfulness, for example, through one's own insight. The point here is to begin the habit of taking the viewing of an attractive natural being with one's eyesight and then, after being aware of the attractive natural being, turning on your insight and your intuition in ways that glean valuable lessons. One's eyesight gives one new information about the world. One's insight is the view of what is happening inside the mind. It can be the result of what one has just seen. It can also be a mixture of recent sights registered in the mind plus information that one has gathered and stored over a lifetime. Obviously, if one is slowing down and observing more about an attractive natural being, one will see more and, therefore, one will have more information "lodged" in the brain. This is how eyesight improves insight. Often insight is knocking on your awareness when you say to yourself "I want . . ." or "I need . . ." When you form such thoughts or when you begin to ask "Why?" it is wise to pause and begin to put some flesh to your emerging insight. Often your emerging insight will be either an unrecognized fundamental truth, a new way of view the world, a penetrating observation about a being's behavior, or a discovery about underlying motivations. Casual observation and simply gaining more information will not likely give a clearer definition to your emerging insight.

Here are some ways to improve your insight:

1. **Flesh out the context of your emerging insight.** Do so by expanding your awareness to include, not only the attractive natural being, but also its setting, the background of the being, and the being's habitat.

2. **Organize the mess.** Look for Catch-22's. Rectify the confusions. Unravel the perplexities. After being drawn to an attractive natural object, consider any dilemmas that occur in association with the natural being. These dilemmas will be about values, behaviors, emotions, conflicts, discomforts, needs, and desires. Look for what needs to be solved, if anything. Think about solutions.

3. **Make the correspondences.** Ponder the connections between what you know from the past and what you know from recent sightings. Old knowledge when combined with the acquisition of new information (by using your fifty-four senses to glean information about an attractive natural being, for example) often leads to the production of a novel idea. This very approach was used by Darwin, who combined his knowledge of the ideas of

Malthus with his recent sitings of birds on the Galapagos to come up with his insights about natural selection.

4. **Look for happenstance.** Find the coincidences in the scene and in the mind. When two or more events seem related, say to yourself "What is going on here?" The answer may very well be an important insight.

5. **Stay inquisitive.** Remain curious. Question what you see. Become curious about the attractive natural being. Mix what you see with what you already know. Become curious about the results of the mixture. Doing so may give you an insight. When communing with an attractive natural being, or when recalling the memory of past information in your mind, apply your curiosity to what is going on outside of the mind and what is going on inside of the mind. By being curious, insights emerge.

6. **Focus on the out of place.** When mixing what you see in nature with what you know in your mind, develop mental notions that seem inescapable, improbable, worthless, disjointed, or contrary to previously held notions. Insights often come to those who are befuddled and desperate in their attempts to find usefulness or congruence.

7. **Ask "why?"** Look in your mind for any understandings and circumstances that need to be explained. Look not only at the natural being but also the behaviors of others nearby. Look for what may be driving these actions. Ask "Why is _____ happening?"

8. **Look for the motivation.** See if you can see or mentally contrive any tension that exists in the setting of your chosen attractive natural being. This tension could be physiological, emotional, cognitive, or environmental. Perhaps there is a frustration that surrounds your natural being.

9. **Imagine the ideal.** Anticipate desired end-states. What is being sought by the natural being or its environment. Think about

what it would take to make your current experience more ideal, saying to yourself "I wish there was _____."

10. **Create an Insight Council (similar to a Dream Council).** Practice doing so in the first part of the next activity.

We are now ready to make a transition from forming insights to improving celebrations. In both of these endeavors, never take a speck of wildness or a pinch of insight for granted. Each time you make an insight, celebrate your discernment. Then discern some more. One type of celebration that is helpful to Heartwood Path pilgrims is the commemorative observation that reveals the quirks, subtleties, surprises, and eccentricities of the natural attractive beings or natural attractive landscapes one goes to for each of the activities of this book. Don't wait for Earth Day to celebrate your insights. Celebrate your insights each time you discern something new or useful. On Earth Day, celebrate all that you have learned along the Heartwood Path.

To The Use Of Eyes And Intuition...

HumaNatureConnect Activity

Start-up Protocol

If this is not a day when you prefer to spend time in nature without an agenda, do the Heartwood Path Start-up Protocol found in the Appendix.

Using Both Eyesight And Insight

Tend to your insights. Treat your emerging insight in the same you treat your Dream Image during your dream tending. Use your eyes to gather data about your chosen attractive natural being and its setting. Pay particular attention to the space around the natural being.

Do not simply gather more and more information with your eyes. Use any or all of the ways to improve your insight mentioned in this waypoint. Wait for the emergence in your mind of the formation of an insight. Write down any remembered fragments. Associate these fragments with your own repressed yearnings. Amplify the development of insights into archetypes. Animate your emerging insights by turning them into Insight Figures (similar to your Dream Figures) and then have conversations with your most valued figures (the members of your Insight Council) as if they were alive. In your conversations, talk about integration, use analysis, and synthesize all data and information. Shrink the emerging insight down into a easy to summarize notion. Blend this notion with your already developed knowledge and understanding. Often, you will want to make such a blending into a suggested behavioral change for yourself and others. Use your Insight Council as your team for this blending. You may also want to convert your vague developing insights into human truths based on universal values. Talk with your Insight Council about making any adaptations as you usher your vague dusty notions into useful golden nuggets of insight. Using your cognitive and literary sense, turn any vague but potentially valuable insights, which may at first be hidden feelings or unclear emotions, into compact sentences. See if any of these sentences constitute worthwhile guidance.

Consider the following: Note the invisibility of the radiating radio and television waves in your environment. Knowing that the radio and television waves are produced at television and radio stations rather than in televisions and radios, consider whether you believe it is possible that some of your thoughts are, likewise, produced by sources in the environment and not solely by (or in) your brain. Could it be that you have an ability to pick up guiding messages from the environment that are not produced in your own mind? Is your mind both a transmitter and a receiver?

Follow-up Protocol

For best results, write down your impressions of this activity in your journal using the Heartwood Path Follow-up Protocol found in the Appendix. Afterwards, consider sharing your interpretations with others.

Heartwood Path Axioms

Key Assertions From Waypoint 4.44

4.44.1.

Sometimes insight is out of sight.

4.44.2.

The process of finding guidance from nature often requires a shift from eyesight only to both eyesight and insight.

4.44.3.

Light can be used for the treatment of depression.

Nocturnal Pilgrimage 4.44

For best results, write down your impressions of each night's dreams in your journal using the Heartwood Path Dreaming Time Protocols found in the Appendix. Afterwards, consider sharing your Dream Tending with others.

Here are two brief reason why you need to get outside after a good night of dreaming: 1) natural light prompts the releases of serotonin (a healthful neurotransmitter) and 2) natural light can be used as an effective treatment for different kinds of depression.

After you sleep, dream, and tend to your dreams, share your impressions with others.

Pertinent And Instructive Gems From My Dream Tending Journal

I dreamt that a tree, I should say a personified image of a man speaking as if he were a tree, kept asking me a question, which, as is the case lately, I could not hear the last word of his sentences.

He was saying...

"Are you incxxxxxxx?"

I replied ...

"Incompetent? I don't think so."

"Are you inxxxxxxxx?"

"Inconsistent? That's never been an issue."

"No, are you incxxxxxxx?"

"Incisive?, Incoherent?, Incomparable?"

"No," said the Image of a Tree ... "I.N.C.H.O.A.T.E."

"What does THAT mean?"

"Not fully formed. Rudimentary."

"I do pretty good. I'm not gonna say where I am on the Beanstalk of Spiritual Development (I'll let you place me, based on your observations of

my actions). But I will say that I seem to have more than average depth. Still, when I compare my own thoughts and actions to the wisdom given to me by my super intelligent Dream Images, I will say that I've still got a ways to go."

Lesson Learned: Do not brag or complain about your own spiritual development. Interact with Dream Images to nudge you along in your own character development. And have your hearing checked.

At the next waypoint you will learn about putting more punch into Earth Day celebrations. Doing the things listed in the next activity will show you that making a festivity out of your connections in nature will help you significantly along the Heartwood Path or in your life.

Keep going. Important teachings are just around the bend. When you are ready, move to the next waypoint: "Festivities." You will learn to bring meaning back to celebrations.

45

Festivities

GIVE EARTH DAY A BIGGER PUNCH

Ceremonies are a good way for humans to give back to the universe some of the energy it sends to them. Most modern celebrations are limited to a few religious ceremonies such as Christmas, Easter, and Chanukah; plus the ritual of blowing out candles on birthday cakes.

There has been and still can be much more to celebrate, for instance: the Earth giving us humans a ground for our feet and sustenance, the Sun keeping us warm, the Moon bringing us a time to dream, and the air giving us the breath of life. To celebrate these gifts and others, one can sing, and thereby return energy through the voice; pray, and thereby return energy through one's crown, or drum, and thereby return energy through the heart. One can follow traditional ceremonies or make up individualized celebrations.

No matter the way, all ceremonies have certain commonalities. All ceremonies always involve some act of giving something away (gifts at Christmas, for example), always commemorate some type of rebirth (the resurrection at Easter, renewal of gratitude at Thanksgiving), and almost always involve some test of patience in the form of arduous minutes or hours sitting or standing, the hearing of repetitive drumming or chanting, or the slow pace of ritualized activity (I'm thinking of the untangling of Christmas Tree lights, the recycling of gift packages, and waiting for females to get in car for Easter Sunday).

There is one celebration that deserves the full participation of those who care about the environment. Here are numerous ways to put more punch into Earth Day.

To Significant Observances...

HumaNatureConnect Activity

Start-up Protocol

If this is not a day when you prefer to spend time in nature without an agenda, do the Heartwood Path Start-up Protocol found in the Appendix.

Putting More Significance Into Earth Day

Don't let another Earth Day slip by without doing some of the things listed below:

1. Walk, ride your bike or carpool rather than using your car.
2. Volunteer for an environmental organization
3. Go paperless for your bill-paying. Use e-bills.
4. Read the entire text of the Heartwood Path and do its activities.
5. Give someone the gift of membership in an environmental organization such as the Sierra Club, Friends of the Earth, or the Earth Island Institute.
6. Develop more ways to recycle at home and work.
7. Fix leaky faucets.
8. Plant a tree or two.
9. Stop using single-use plastic bottles for your drinking water.
10. Make your yard a haven for wildlife.

11. Establish a nature play garden for kids in your town.

12. Grow your own food in a backyard garden.

13. Write a letters to your state legislator, U.S. Representative, and U.S, Senators encouraging them to pass laws that are good for the environment.

14. Update your light bulbs to Energy Savers.

15. Clean up the junk and plant milkweed for the Monarch Butterflies along the un-mowed portion of highway right-of-ways in your area.

16. Talk to your schools to see about adopting more environmental education programs.

17. Make a donation to an environmental group.

18. "Adopt" an endangered species in your area. Identify the most vulnerable species and do what you can to secure its survival.

19. Sponsor someone to become an eartHeart on the Heartwood Path.

20. Reflect back upon the insights you have developed by doing Heartwood Path Activities and celebrate all that occurred over the previous year.

21. Develop plans for adding more time in nature during all of your celebrations.

Follow-up Protocol

For best results, write down your impressions of this activity in your journal using the Heartwood Path Follow-up Protocol found in the Appendix. Afterwards, consider sharing your interpretations with others.

Heartwood Path Axioms

Key Assertions From Waypoint 4.45

4.45.1.

Ceremonies are a good way for humans to give back to the universe some of the energy it sends to them.

4.45.2.

To celebrate the gifts of nature or other gifts, one can sing, and thereby return energy through the voice; pray, and thereby return energy through one's heart, or drum, and thereby return energy through the heartbeat.

4.45.3.

All ceremonies always involve some act of giving something away, always commemorate some type of rebirth, and usually involve some test of patience in the form of arduous minutes or hours sitting or standing, the hearing of repetitive drumming or chanting, or the slow pace of ritualized activity.

Nocturnal Pilgrimage 4.45

For best results, write down your impressions of each night's dreams in your journal using the Heartwood Path Dreaming Time Protocols found in the Appendix. Afterwards, consider sharing your Dream Tending with others.

Natural sunlight gives us energy. It also helps us to become oriented, particularly about time of day (by noticing the position of the sun in the sky) and about the seasons (by noticing the length of shadows, which are longer during the winter when the sun follows a lower arc across the sky. By staying inside and relying on unnatural light from lightbulbs we are less affected by natural light. This loss of the sun's light beaming down upon us affects our waking consciousness adversely. I, for example, notice that my clarity of thinking and mood improves when I move from unnatural light to natural light. More on the value of natural light follows in the upcoming waypoints.

Pertinent And Instructive Gems From My Dream Tending Journal

I dreamt my girlfriend/muse told me that she knew I was mad because I was breathing heavily. Impressed by her insight, I decided to quiz her further—partly because I was learning much about myself.

I asked her,

"what do I do when I'm sad or depressed?"

She said I sleep more.

"What do I do when I'm frustrated?"

She said I eat more.

"And when I'm anxious?"

"You walk around and pace,"

she said.

Lesson Learned: Keep a journal of your instincts and reactions. You will likely learn how to notice how you are reacting by noticing indicating actions.

After reading about the usefulness of a bioregion as a concept, you will be asked, as is our custom, to go into nature to begin an activity. When doing so, feel the ground beneath your feet. Ask yourself if the land feels inert, neutral, or like a cherished friend. Are you happy or regretful when you leave your chosen attractive natural being or landscape? Does returning to your indoor way of life (or to the inside of your house, school, apartment, or workplace) feel like a breeching of your spiritual connectedness? If so, return often to attractive natural places and, when you have to be inside, keep wild land vivid, alive, and flourishing in your mind, heart, and soul.

After sleeping and dreaming, tend to your dreams and then move to the next waypoint: "Bioregion." At this step, you will learn how a bioregion is an important aspect of your Greater Self.

46

Bioregion

UNDERSTAND AND USE BIOREGIONALISM

The place for the functioning of all the components of a whole community is called a bioregion. Just as the home is the setting for the functioning of a family, the bioregion is the setting for the functioning of the whole community.

When thinking of one's bioregion, people tend to consider where things come from and how basic patterns of everyday life are like threads in the web of life. Bioregionalism encourages people to connect their livelihood and sense of responsibility to their sense of place.

Bioregionalism has three main goals:

1. to restore and maintain local natural systems;
2. to find sustainable ways to satisfy basic human needs; and
3. to support the work of people seeking to become native to the places where they live.

To become such a native, one needs to learn how to hear all the voices that come from the place where one lives. By being in place, one finds oneself in what is subsistent and enveloping. Those who support the notion of bioregionalism (the use of a bioregion in planning or management) argue that ecological judgments ought to set political and cultural confines.

If we humans plan to change the way we inhabit this planet it will be beneficial to do so in context. This means we need to understand our own place on Earth and the rules for living there.

Besides living in context, we need to also live in tune with the rules that govern the functioning of the local environment or bio-region. We need to learn to resonate, entrain, and harmonize with the will-of-the-land. This becomes possible when we become one with the land or when one achieves the profound feeling of oneness known as "unio mystica."

It is very difficult to appreciate or achieve unio mystica if one does not understand the "other" that one's individual "self" is relating to. To achieve or understand unio mystica, any duality needs to be overcome. Such dualities could include mind from matter, ecology from psychology, nature from culture, and wilderness from human communities.

Overcoming such dualities at first seems like an overwhelming task. Overcoming dualities is a big job that can be made easier by limiting the size of that which seems like the "other" in the dualistic pairing. For the purposes of progressing along the Heartwood Path, I suggest you begin by limiting your attempt at overcoming dualities to objects (beings) that are not too abstract nor excessively grandiose. It is not recommended, at this juncture, for you to try to bring into your sense of the Greater Self, for example, another that is more complicated than a bioregion. Usually bigger than an ecosystem and smaller than a biome (a major ecological community such as a tropical rain forest, a grassland, or a desert), a bioregion is a region whose limits are naturally defined (rather than politically defined) by topographic features such a mountain ranges and ecosystems.

If you seek to ultimately overcome the duality between you and the whole earth (rather than just a bioregion, for example), you may be biting off more than you can chew. The earth, the Kosmos, or similar other grandiose "others" are usually too vague for beginning EartHearts. The concept of a bioregion, however, evokes greater clarity and, therefore, makes for a more suitable "other" for beginners to overcome. This routing of the individual sense of the self is accomplishable by integrating one's individual self into one's sense of the larger local region.

Undertaking a pilgrimage is one of the best ways to overcome the alienation of the self. Pilgrimages are often liminal: the pilgrim leaves behind his or her normal world and travels (by foot is best) to a sacred place—a place revered because of a significant historical event, a place consecrated by the construction of a religious building, a place where the flow of more than one line of the earth's energy cross (such as at Glastonbury Tor in England, Sedona in Arizona, or Cahokia Mounds in Illinois) or a place where visitors can more easily feel or communicate with beings in the spirit world. By beginning one's pilgrimage in a local bioregion, which is likely to be relatively more familiar to a person than a distant land, more becomes perceptible, and more is easily seen as sacred.

Any space or circumstance, however, can be sacred, though some are more numinous than others. The pilgrim's trip can take hours, days, weeks, months, or years. A key aspect of the pilgrimage is the trip itself, not being at home and not being at the destination. Another important aspect is the sense of comradeship—walking with others seeking similar purposes. Feel free to limit your destination on your pilgrimage to a point within your bio-region. You do not need to travel to Shangri-La.

While going on pilgrimages to alien lands or traveling to far-off places can be renewing, coming to know your own bioregion is just as important. Familiarity with your own place in the world will help improve your ability to experience the pleasure and benefits of unio mystica because your own surroundings are an outer reflection of the inner spaces of your own One Being—which includes your own More-Than-Human nature. Two of the most effective ways to build a relationship with one's place are sharing information about the significance of local natural, prehistoric, and historic landmarks and doing an evaluation of your relationship with your place (the subject of the next activity).

To The Knowledge Of Where You Stand In Your Region...

HumaNatureConnect Activity

Start-up Protocol

If this is not a day when you prefer to spend time in nature without an agenda, do the Heartwood Path Start-up Protocol found in the Appendix.

Evaluating Your Relationship With Your Own Community

Answer the following questions: Beyond your own family or primary relationship, where do you feel a sense of "belongingness" to a larger whole? (Tip: Consider your neighborhood, workplace, church, community group, etc.) What positive feelings does your community create within you? What can you do to strengthen your community and your ties to your community?

Follow-up Protocol

For best results, write down your impressions of this activity in your journal using the Heartwood Path Follow-up Protocol found in the Appendix. Afterwards, consider sharing your interpretations with others.

Heartwood Path Axioms

Key Assertions From Waypoint 4.46

4.46.1.

Just as the home is the setting for the functioning of a family, the bioregion is the setting for the functioning of the whole community.

4.46.2.

By being in place, one finds oneself in what is subsistent and enveloping.

4.46.3.

We need to learn to resonate, entrain, and harmonize with the will-of-the-land.

4.46.4.

Pilgrimages are often liminal: the pilgrim leaves behind his or her normal world and travels (by foot is best) to a sacred place that has aspects that are barely perceptible.

4.46.5.

While going on pilgrimages to alien lands or traveling to far-off places can be renewing, coming to know your own bioregion is just as important.

Nocturnal Pilgrimage 4.46

For best results, write down your impressions of each night's dreams in your journal using the Heartwood Path Dreaming Time

Protocols found in the Appendix. Afterwards, consider sharing your Dream Tending with others.

"'People were designed to be outside,' writes sleep specialist Daniel Kripke. 'Our modern human ancestors became intelligent in places which were indeed very sunny'" (Naiman, 2006, p. 151).

With Naiman's quote and the message of this waypoint in mind as you prepare for sleep, sleep and dream. Tend to your dreams as soon as you wake up.

Pertinent And Instructive Gems From My Dream Tending Journal

I dreamt I encountered two Dream Images. The first one had a materialist, industrial, masculine perspective. He asked me what was my offering to the God of the Economy. The second one had a spiritual, ecological, feminine perspective. She asked me what was my sacrifice to the environment. Neither was being pushy, just inquisitive.

Lesson Learned: We all have to serve somebody. This is as it ought to be. Our Offering to the Economy can be the purchases we make and the jobs we hold. The freedoms, fair pay, and elevated moods we give up to be cogs in the economic engine are certainly a form of offering. Our offering to nature can be our adherence to the Natural Systems Thinking Process, our following of Heartwood Path Protocols, the sprinkling of tobacco on the ground, and periodic pauses to appreciate the beauty of nature. The time spent and the materials used in our appreciations of the attractiveness of nature and the revenue lost by not working in these moments are forms of sacrifice. We may not be holding up still beating hearts, as the Aztecs did, but ethical considerations demand that we still need to make modern equivalents of these sacrifices, less brutal, but still offerings, nevertheless. What gifts do you bring to others? What sacrifices do you make?

After reading about how nature helps you find a sense of unity you are again asked to find an attractive natural being outdoors in nature. When searching for the place for your connection experience let the landscape guide you. Allow the texture of the earth and the contours of the land lead you to your chosen being or landscape. Remembering not to "should" on your practice, have no preconceptions about where you ought to go. Above all, enjoy your connections.

When you are ready, head to the next waypoint by clicking on the "Union" link. In studying nature, you will find unity.

47

Union

STUDY NATURE TO FIND UNITY

What one receives as one moves along the Heartwood Path is not the customary way of seeing unity, which *eliminates* differences and promotes commonality. Instead, one receives a way of seeing which *includes* differences. In your process of personal growth do not reduce multiplicity to uniformity, but do allow the pin-pointed uniqueness of the particular to appear within the glow of the unity of the whole.

When you become more fully conscious, you will not lose yourself in nature. Instead, you will find humaNature within yourself. You will see comprehensively and not selectively. You will see things in their context. Intrinsic connections will be revealed.

Remember that a single phenomenon is an abstraction. Remember to frequently concentrate on the "belongingness" of the phenomenon. This "belongingness" is its higher dimension. I caution you here not to see generally (which removes the differences), but to see comprehensively (which reveals both the differences and the unity).

To Integration Through Nature Inquiry...

HumaNatureConnect Activity

Start-up Protocol

If this is not a day when you prefer to spend time in nature without an agenda, do the Heartwood Path Start-up Protocol found in the Appendix.

Studying Nature To Find Unity

Use the natural radiation sense of season which includes "the ability to insulate, hibernate and winter sleep" (Cohen, 1989, p. 8). Look for ways that you insulate and hibernate, ways an attractive little natural being insulates and hibernates, and ways an attractive big natural being insulates and hibernates. For greater clarity, psychologically assume the essence of the attractive beings and then, as them, speak about the similarities and differences in the way you and the other attractive beings are similar and different regarding insulation and hibernation. Hum the note that resonates insulation among your chosen attractions and hum the note that resonates hibernation among your attractions. Is there a message being transmitted in the resonate notes? What does the resonance—including the similarities and differences in the notes—"say" about insulation, hibernation, difference, unity, and belongingness?

Follow-up Protocol

For best results, write down your impressions of this activity in your journal using the Heartwood Path Follow-up Protocol found in the Appendix. Afterwards, consider sharing your interpretations with others.

Heartwood Path Axioms

Key Assertions From Waypoint 4.47

4.47.1.

In your process of personal growth do not reduce multiplicity to uniformity, do not take the diversity out of the universe, but do allow the pinpointed uniqueness of the particular to appear within the glow of the unity of the whole.

4.47.2.

When you become more fully conscious, you will find humaNature within you, you will see comprehensively and not selectively, you will see things in their context, and you will witness intrinsic connections.

4.47.3.

Since a single phenomenon is an abstraction remember to frequently concentrate in the "belongingness" of the phenomenon, which is its higher dimension.

Nocturnal Pilgrimage 4.47

For best results, write down your impressions of each night's dreams in your journal using the Heartwood Path Dreaming Time Protocols found in the Appendix. Afterwards, consider sharing your Dream Tending with others.

"Indoor environments continue to grow more comfortable, functional, and entertaining, further discouraging our spending time outdoors" (Naiman, 2006, p. 151).

With this quote and the information presented in this waypoint in mind as you begin to fall asleep, sleep and dream. The next morning, tend to your dreams. If when you awaken and you notice that you are fatigued, you may not be getting enough sleep or outdoor meditative activity to overcome the overstimulation you are receiving by excess viewing of the television or computer screens. As we will see in more detail later on, the answer to this fatigue is not more sedentary distractions or energy drinks.

At the next waypoint you will learn about preserving what is held in common in your local region—aspects of your community that everyone values. You will also, as usual, be asked to do an activity outdoors. For this activity, pay attention to the forms of the landscape. Pay attention to your feelings about the land. Asnswer the following questions:

1. Do you feel at home in your chosen natural landscape?
2. What emotions does your chosen natural being or landscape bring forth in you?
3. As you pay attention to both the outside world and your inner landscape, what meanings come to mind?

When you are ready, move to the next waypoint, "Outdoor Scene," to continue your journey to Gladandgreen Junction. The subjects of the commons and the bioregion are just around the corner.

48

Outdoor Scene

PRESERVE THE COMMONS AND THE BIOREGION

Defined as something belonging to or shared equally by two or more beings, the term *"commons"* invokes images of community, collective, public, and joint. The concept of the commons has political implications: when people agree on what is common they need to develop a process of management. The "tragedy of the commons" occurs when people pollute a stream, foul the air, erode the soil, deplete an aquifer, or exhaust a fishery.

The tragedy of the commons is like adding one more sheep to an already crowded common pasture. The result is everybody loses from the overuse. Or, the tragedy of the common is is like adding one more polluter to a region where standards of air quality are already violated.

Developers, who often tend to place human interests above all others, often have poor regard for the commons. Environmentalists and eartHearts, however, seek to preserve the commons, in part, because it is seen as integral to their own greater sense of Self.

To eartHearts, the Earth's community (which includes the human) is seen as primary while human well being is seen as derivative. EartHearts and their compatriots the environmentalists tend to insist that humanity needs to adapt to natural life systems, and not the other way around. EartHearts contend that the Earth is the primary value, the primary source of existence, and the primary impactor of the destiny of whatever exists.

The concept of the commons works well for eartHearts, who tend to work on helping conservation minded-people negotiate the margins between realms of existence—physical, living, mental, and spiritual (ethical). EartHearts work in the physical realm when they explore a bioregion or the commons as an ecosystem. They work in the mental realm when they help people perceive that they live in a bioregion that contains aspects that can be regarded as the commons. They work in the spiritual/ethical realm when they encourage people to take responsibility for the health of a bioregion and its commons.

The margin between the realms of existence—physical, living, mental, and spiritual—and the margin between the leaves of our Four Leaf Model of Integrity—intentions, ethics, behaviors, and nested physical systems—represents the "space" where meaning is generated. Just talking in terms of the commons, it becomes meaningful when someone's intension is to add another sheep to the common pasture when—crossing a margin now—the community has established an ethic to have the nested physical system of the common pasture remain healthy by people willingly limiting the number of sheep that are—crossing another margin now—added to the field. EartHearts know that it is important to not just limit the behaviors to protect the nested physical systems. They operate most often in the margins of meaning; which, in this case, would be not only the adding of the sheep and the quality of the field but also the intention of the individual sheep owners and the development of community morals or ethics. Better solutions are found when meaning is brought into the fray. The Sierra Club and a bunch of railroad companies, for example, used the legal system to delay the construction of a lock and dam so that the Upper Mississippi River would be protected from increased use by barges This lawsuit was an endeavor that forced certain behaviors to protect a certain landscape. Practically nothing was done to address individual intentions (shippers wanting to ship their grain cheaply) at the expense of the public (an ethical matter). The result was a user fee for barges and the spending of money for conservation and recreation equal to the cost of building the newly enlarged gateway through the dam. This was a significant result, but not all that it could have been. Without also working on the intentions of those involved and the ethics of those involved the real questions (two examples: Does wildlife habitat have value equal to the savings for shippers?, Should one industry be subsidized by the taxpayers when that subsidy hurts another industry—in this case, the railroads?) remains unanswered. And so, without changing intentions or modifying ethics, we will eventually repeat this kind of battle each time a lock and dam is due for replacement. EartHearts always find the greatest meaning by operating at the margin between intentions, ethics, behaviors, and nested physical systems. That way, inner world changes can help generate better outer world results.

To The Protection Of What We Hold Dear...

HumaNatureConnect Activity

Start-up Protocol

If this is not a day when you prefer to spend time in nature without an agenda, do the Heartwood Path Start-up Protocol found in the Appendix.

Preserving The Commons

Find something in your community that most people in your community hold dear. It may be a local stream, the air, a park area, or some other aspect of the community that many people use and most people seek to protect. Write down a description of this commons in terms of nested physical systems (for example: a blade of grass, on a plant, in a certain field, in a certain town, in a certain state). Write down the intentions of most of the people that use this commons and do the same for those who seek to protect this commons. Write down what you can about the community's collective set of values or ethics, or lack of values or ethics, regarding the commons. Write down the behaviors that have an impact on this commons. Write down what can be done at the margins between individual intentions and community ethics, between individual intentions and behaviors, between community ethics and behaviors, between individual intentions and nested physical systems, and between the behaviors and the nested physical systems. Plan a campaign to protect the commons, starting in the outer world (between the behaviors and the nested physical systems) and ending with the inner world (individual intentions and community ethics). List what could be done at the margins between all of these realms. In other words, consider what is, what could be, and what ought to be. Always make links to ethics and morals to find meaning. With this proviso, consider which activities will have the fastest outcome? Which activity will have the longest lasting outcome. Which activity is a high priority? And which activity is a low priority? Make sure you at least consider working on the inner realms of intentions and ethics. Perhaps a local conservation group could take charge of working in the realm of the outer world and a local eartHeart salon could be created to pair up with the conservation group by working on the inner world matters of intentions and ethics. If you are having trouble with the message of this section fear not: more explanation follows in the next waypoint.

Follow-up Protocol

For best results, write down your impressions of this activity in your journal using the Heartwood Path Follow-up Protocol found in the Appendix. Afterwards, consider sharing your interpretations with others.

Heartwood Path Axioms

Key Assertions From Waypoint 4.48

4.48.1.

The concept of the commons has political implications: when people agree on what is common they need to develop a process of management.

4.48.2.

The "tragedy of the commons" occurs when people pollute a stream, foul the air, erode the soil, deplete an aquifer, or exhaust a fishery.

4.48.3.

EartHearts contend that the Earth is the primary value, the primary source of existence, and the primary destiny for whatever exists.

4.48.4.

EartHearts work in the physical realm when they explore a bioregion or the commons as an ecosystem. They work in the mental realm when they help people perceive that they live in a bioregion that contains aspects that can be regarded as the commons. They work in the spiritual/ethical realm when they encourage people to take responsibility for the health of a bioregion and its commons.

4.48.5.

The margin between the realms of existences—physical, living, mental, and spiritual—represents the "space" where meaning is generated.

Nocturnal Pilgrimage 4.48

For best results, write down your impressions of each night's dreams in your journal using the Heartwood Path Dreaming Time Protocols found in the Appendix. Afterwards, consider sharing your Dream Tending with others.

"The sun metes out (dispenses) a broad dynamic tempo as it traverses the sky. Artificial light does not; it is monotonous and relentless— apropos for our driven lifestyles" (Naiman, 2006, p. 152).

With this quote and the previous lesson in mind as you lay down for the night, sleep and dream. Tend to your dreams as soon as you wake up.

Pertinent And Instructive Gems From My Dream Tending Journal

I dreamt the lights went out and I used the occasion to go outside to see the stars and view nocturnal animals.

Lesson Learned: Shut off the power, turn off the lights. Wallow in the darkness. See new stars. Introduce yourself to a new constellation. Listen to the crickets. Look at the owls in the trees. Artificial light lures you away from nature. Don't let it.

At the next station along the Heartwood Path, read about how to find meaning and then go outside to begin the activity. When outside and searching for an attractive natural being or landscape examine any streams, rivers, or other waterways you come across. If feasible, track down the origin of and the destination for your encountered waterway. In doing so, think about your origins and destinations. When you are ready, head to the next waypoint: "Significance."

49

Significance

WORK TO FIND MEANING

Meaning has two specific characteristics, one about quantities and the other about qualities:

1. it is always *quantifiable* as either singular, plural, or comprehensive; and
2. it always has the *quality* of either a "fact" concerning a formed object or process in the realm of space and time (what actually exists), a form (an imagined possibly) or a norm (what ought to be).

To avoid confusion, remember that in this waypoint when I use the word "form" I am not meaning "to create." I am meaning the *form*ation of an imaginary possibility. Example: in my mind I am *form*ing an image of Michelangelo's sculpted David wearing a tutu. It is not a *fact* that David wears such dance wear. But it is a *form* in my imagination.

Meaning, as previously discussed is necessarily contextual—occurring in relation to two or more of the realms of existence. The physical realm affords us the *facts* that come from the sciences and the existential aspects of philosophy, psychology, and literature. The mental realm affords us the *facts* and *forms* arising from language, symbols, the arts, and philosophy. The spiritual realm affords us the *facts, forms,* and *norms* that are interpreted by the disciplines of ethics and religion. Meaning can only occur when *facts* (what actually exists), *forms* (an imaginary possibility) and, *norms* (what ought to be) are juxtaposed to one another.

The work of determining meaning, then, is to determine the inference that can be drawn from a thing or process of one realm when held up to the light of a thing or process from another. A thing or process that actually exists is only significant when it is compared to an imagined possibility or to a condition that ought to be (or ought not to be). A river, for example, is simply a river until a knower of that river either imagines a possibility regarding the river or makes a suggestion for what ought to happen to that river. Likewise, an imagined possibility or a concept of what ought to be cannot have meaning, significance, or inference unless the possibility or concept is grounded in some way to something that actually exists.

Examples of meanings that come from the examination of one's relationship to a bioregion include:

1. human life depends on biological diversity,
2. biodiversity requires the integrity of ecosystems,
3. ecosystems provide a myriad of critical functions including making the earth habitable,
4. human intervention typically disturbs ecosystems,
5. human intervention typically takes the form of commercial development,
6. many humans do not realize the ecological affects of their actions,
7. education is required to fully understand the human/bioregion relationship,
8. and environmental education (discussed at the next waypoint) fosters an appreciation for all life.

Personal encounters with the nature of a bioregion yield important non-monetary benefits in human wellbeing, development, and fulfill-ment. Along with providing for one's material needs, the living diversity of a bioregion offers an unrivaled context for the engagement of one's curiosity, exploration, and discovery in ways that deliver adaptive benefits to our bodies, emotions, and intellect.

By working with people on the meaning of bioregions (what actually exist) eartHearts are creating ecological citizens (as a result of an imagined possibility)—people with "common" sense and dedication to working on preservation issues (what ought to be). Here we have a perfect example of how the Heartwood Path leads pilgrims between the sphere of what actually exists, between the domain of imagined possibilities, and between the realm of what ought to be.

To Significance...

HumaNatureConnect Activity

Start-up Protocol

If this is not a day when you prefer to spend time in nature without an agenda, do the Heartwood Path Start-up Protocol found in the Appendix.

Finding Meaning

Use the feeling sense of hearing resonance and vibrations and listen to the sounds you make, the sounds of a small and attractive natural being nearby, and the audible sounds of the surrounding environment. Note the sounds that exist, the sounds that could exist, and the sounds that ought to exist. What meaning can be gleaned from the changes and similarities of these actual, imagined, and sought after sounds?

Follow-up Protocol

For best results, write down your impressions of this activity in your journal using the Heartwood Path Follow-up Protocol found in the Appendix. Afterwards, consider sharing your interpretations with others.

Heartwood Path Axioms

Key Assertions From Waypoint 4.49

4.49.1.

Meaning has two specific characteristics: it is always quantifiable as either singular, plural, or comprehensive; and it always has the quality of either a "fact" concerning a formed object or process in the realm of space and time (what actually exists), a form (an imagined possibly) or a norm (what ought to be).

4.49.2.

Meaning can only occur when facts (what actually exists), forms (an imaginary possibility) and, norms (what ought to be) are juxtaposed to one another.

4.49.3.

By working with people on the meaning of bioregions (what actually exists) eartHearts are creating ecological citizens (as a result of an imagined possibility)—people with "common" sense and dedication to working on preservation issues (what ought to be).

Nocturnal Pilgrimage 4.49

For best results, write down your impressions of each night's dreams in your journal using the Heartwood Path Dreaming Time Protocols found in the Appendix. Afterwards, consider sharing your Dream Tending with others.

"Our conundrum with light is strikingly parallel to our dilemma with food. As a nation, we are overfed, yet undernourished. We consume too many calories, but since so many of them are "empty" we remain nutrient deficient. Likewise, with regard to light, we consume too much artificial "junk" light but remain deficient in our exposure to natural and naturally timed light" (Naiman, 2006, p. 152).

With this quote and today's lesson in mind as you lay down for the night, sleep and dream. Tend to your dreams as soon as you begin to wake up.

Pertinent And Instructive Gems From My Dream Tending Journal

I dreamt I was an environmental activist and one of my opponents, a representative from a utility company seeking to build a nuclear power plant nearby, was trying to give me booze and drugs.

Lesson Learned: Abusers, listen to me now: Nobody is going to de-politicize me. Nobody can colonize my mind and heart. Nobody. Your substances are useless against me.

Activists, hear me now: Do not let the providers of drugs and alcohol mollify your stridency. Make sure you do not love marijuana or beer more than you love nature. Examine the motives of your providers. They are often abusers of the psyche, with ulterior motives.

Heartwood Path participants, take heed: Do not expect drugs and alcohol to overcome your culturally-induced ecstasy deprivation.

Smoking, pill-popping, and drinking are false substitutes for the feeling of being part of something bigger than yourself. Unlike mind-altering substances, nature can satisfy any yearning for bliss. Alternative measures are costly, they reduce one's motivation and productivity, and they tend to harm one's health.

Next you will find a discussion about how to live in harmony with nature through environmental education. You will also be asked to head outside and move across the land. In doing so, pause for a moment to examine the soil. Is it sandy, loamy, or clay? Think about the purpose of soil. Can you see how it acts like the placenta for the earth, passing nutrients to the next generation? When you are ready to take another important step toward Gladandgreen Junction, head to the next waypoint: "Eco-ed."

50

Eco-ed

LIVE IN HARMONY WITH NATURE THROUGH ENVIRONMENTAL EDUCATION

EartHearts teach others life-affirming (fear-minimizing) ways to preserve, reclaim, and protect the Earth. Their environmental education efforts are in accord with UNESCO's Tbilisi Declaration of 1977, which set three goals:

1. to foster clear awareness of, and concern about, economic, social, political, and ecological interdependence in urban and rural areas;
2. to provide every person with opportunities to acquire the knowledge, values, attitudes, commitment, and skills needed to protect and improve the environment; and
3. to create new patterns of behavior of individuals, groups, and society as a whole towards the environment.

Environmental education along the Heartwood Path includes ecological connections, respect for the rights of all others, ways to promote peace on and with the Earth, tolerance for the views of others, ways to be altruistic, appreciation of beauty and wonder, and ways to find joy out-of-doors. Moral norms, moral relations, moral tradeoffs and moral considerations are not shunned topics. Included in eartHeart environmental education curricula are: time orientation (past, present, future), relations with the physical world, motivation through spiritual meditation, and motivation through active achievement.

To promote ethics that support long-term survival of humankind, eartHearts present to their environmental education participants a diverse range of topics: market place, life-support, recreation, science genetic diversity, aesthetic pleasure, cultural symbols (bald eagles as a symbol of strength, for example), history, character-building, therapy, the stimulation of spiritual thoughts or feelings, and rights.

Heartwood Path environmental education is based on the belief that people have a right to a healthy environment, that humans have a moral duty to maintain or improve the earth for future generations, that humans have an obligation to preserve nature; that it is wrong to abuse the Absolute Spirit's (God's) creation, that less consumption is better for the environment, and that nature can only absorb so much damage. EartHearts engage in environmental education from numerous viewpoints, including: self, human-centered, sentient plants and animals, the reverence for life, the benefit to the planet, pleasing the Absolute Spirit (God), natural law, and a combination of one or more of these views. The human-centered and wise-use viewpoints are typically de-emphasized; while deep ecology, bioregionalism, and earth-centered approaches are emphasized.

EartHearts offer many facts for the purpose of forming a few beliefs which, in turn, are designed to foster the development of even fewer attitudes which are tempered by both non-moral values or preferences and moral values or obligations. These preferences and obligations are then put through a prioritizing process based on critical thinking. The result is the making of an ethic.

By being good examples, by offering ample explanations, by minimizing exhortations, by creating respectful learning environments, and by giving participants experiences that create the feelings of competence and meaningful service to others, eartHearts foster the development of values. These values are not honed through inculcation (teaching about one's own habits or ideas with so much constant repetition that other points of view are excluded) but through clarification, analysis, moral judgments, action learning through service to others, and cognitive and affective techniques using the senses. EartHearts know that they are refraining from inculcation when they allow participants to come to conclusions or develop opinions that are different from their own.

Typically, Heartwood Path environmental education comes in three forms:

1. those that lead to deeper appreciation, fascination and knowledge of the world;
2. those that provide for psychological growth (self-confidence, self-esteem, "self-giving," leadership skills, and team-building) and
3. those that provide for a sense of coming home through wilderness rites of passage. (GDRC website)

In this last form, nature sees itself through the eyes of the sojourner and feels itself through the joy of the pilgrim whose life is revealed as a magnificent story unfolding each moment. Through all forms of environmental education, eartHearts become, not therapists, but midwives attending the birth of each moment.

EartHearts exist to establish groups with programs for young and old alike. These groups may want to hold meetings both separately—either all for Baby Boomers or all for young people, for example—and/or together as a way to provide for cross generational ties.

A program needs to be replicated everywhere to help foster three conditions in middle-age adults:

1. the structuring of a firm individual;
2. the integration of this individual self with the boundless experience of unity with the so-called "other;" and
3. the rescinding of this integration, as needed.

Another program needs to be established everywhere to provide the kinds of direct nature experiences young people typically had during and before the Baby Boomer generation. A specific proposal for such a program will be discussed subsequently. Unlike those born before the mid-Sixties, young people today spend a large portion of their waking hours inside at school, at home watching television, indoors playing video games, or participating in organized sports. It is a charge of all eartHeart salons to consider creating a worthwhile environmental education program for either adults or children or both.

To What It Is To Be A Heartwood Path Alumni...

HumaNatureConnect Activity

Start-up Protocol

If this is not a day when you prefer to spend time in nature without an agenda, do the Heartwood Path Start-up Protocol found in the Appendix.

Gaining EartHeart Characteristics

Answer the following questions and know that if you answer by saying "Yes" to most of the questions you are a model eartHeart (when explaining your answer, consider the boundaries for what it would be for the action to be too much or consider the boundaries for what would cause your answer to be negative rather than positive):

1. Do you have the ability to anticipate the future? If so, explain.
2. Do you seek what is good and right? If so or if not, explain.
3. Do you act from a set of principles? If so or if not, explain.
4. Do you seek new grounds of study or action? If so or if not, explain.

5. Do you take measured risks; that is, ones that challenge you but come with adequate safety nets? If so or if not, explain.
6. Do you adequately convey what you are thinking or doing? If so or if not, explain.
7. Do you work hard? If so or if not, explain.
8. Are you sincere? If so or if not, explain.
9. Are you earnest? If so or if not, explain.

Follow-up Protocol

For best results, write down your impressions of this activity in your journal using the Heartwood Path Follow-up Protocol found in the Appendix. Afterwards, consider sharing your interpretations with others.

Heartwood Path Axioms

Key Assertions From Waypoint 4.50

4.50.1.

Heartwood Path environmental education is based on the belief that people have a right to a healthy environment, that humans have a moral duty to maintain or improve the earth for future generations, that humans have an obligation to preserve nature; that it is wrong to abuse the Absolute Spirit's (God's) creation, that less consumption is better for the environment, and that nature can only absorb so much damage.

4.50.2.

By being good examples, by offering ample explanations, by minimizing exhortations, by creating respectful learning environments, and by giving participants experiences that create the feelings of competence and meaningful service to others, eartHearts foster the development of values.

4.50.3.

EartHearts know that they are refraining from inculcation (teaching about one's own habits or ideas with so much constant repetition that other points of view are excluded) when they allow participants to come to conclusions or develop opinions that are different from their own.

Nocturnal Pilgrimage 4.50

For best results, write down your impressions of each night's dreams in your journal using the Heartwood Path Dreaming Time Protocols found in the Appendix. Afterwards, consider sharing your Dream Tending with others.

You are not going to be able to bring everything you can to your quest to be happy and to your work to create a sustainable environment unless you have both good nights of sleep and good days of wakeful consciousness. Both during your dreaming and during your wakeful consciousness, it is good if you allow suppressed negative emotions to come into the light. Fear of such emotions may be why so many people resist slowing down.

No part of the Heartwood Path is a racetrack. Take it slow, move away from your computer, and go to a natural place so that you can unlock and dispel the negative emotions that may be getting in your way.

With today's message in mind as you drift off at night, sleep and dream. As you begin to wake up, tend to your dreams. But do not unthinkingly turn on your computer or television for mindless amusements or even for information. Your brain will reward you for finding useful information on electronic screens in the form of increased flow of dopamine—the same make-you-feel-good chemical that flows when you are pleased to be outdoors. But too much overstimulation as a result of reading unnecessary emails or watching commercial-after-commercial may get so much dopamine going that you end up with digital device addiction, which leads to a sedentary lifestyle, inactivity, and obesity (Selhub & Logan, 2012, p. 49).

To counter this malady, you simply have to hold back on your natural desire for screen-induced dopamine, overcome any fear of missing some digital information, and use the time instead to get outside in the fresh air and green leaves; away from power sockets, and into nature. Digital device addiction leads to less sleep, less face-to-face interaction, less contemplation time, and less physical activity. Like waves gradually eroding the shoreline, any exposure to nature will lower your stress and bring you back to a state of wellness. To speed up the process, do the HumaNatureConnect Activities as instructed.

Pertinent And Instructive Gems From My Dream Tending Journal

I dreamt I was watching

the news but soon

I grew tired of it.

Lesson Learned: The news media seems to dole out news of other people's woes for the entertainment of its audience. Check who owns the news stations, see who owns the news networks, and examine who is paying for the commercials and soon you will realize that news reporting is rarely serving the interests of nature. If fault-finding, con-spiracy theories, partisanship, and political manipulation outweigh the transmission of valuable information, thought provocation, and inspir-ing stories, turn off the news and go outside. Make such things as the beginning of the calls of tree frogs your important news of the day.

Go alone or with quiet company when you do the following activity outdoors. Feel free to sit, stand, or lie down to make your connections. Attend carefully to your attractive being or landscape. Such outdoor emissaries will "speak" to those who are receptive. When you are ready, continue restoring the ecology of happiness by moving to the waypoint: "Juvenescence."

51

Juvenescence

WORK WITH YOUTH

This section of the Heartwood Path outlines why a system of child-life refuges with a certain kind of environmental education program is needed. It also describes how the proposed refuges and associated programs can be operated to help alleviate a relatively new psychological disorder.

The Problem: Young People Are Living Their Lives Separated From Nature

I noticed during my more than fifteen years of working with youth in Challenge Education programming (most often in a YMCA program known as Life Adventures) that along with the youths' slowly progressive inability to relate to nature in the Realm of Exteriority there was also slowly progressive inability to tap inner faculties such as intentions (singularly) or ethics (in a group). Aspects of their character development, such as self-esteem, confidence, perseverance, integrity, honesty, and respect, were noticeably on the wane.

Together, the waning ability to relate to the inner world of intentions and ethics plus the waning ability to relate to the outer world of humans and nature could be labeled as one multifaceted psychological affliction. It seems to me that these inabilities to relate to their inner and outer worlds are, indeed, progressing together at the same time and at essentially the same rate. Perhaps this one malady could be called . . . **HDD: HumaNature Deficit Disorder.**

There is a growing divide between young people and the inner world and between young people and the natural world. These separations are not healthy.

Most nature experiences today occur as a result of watching the television (in programs editing tightly for rapid "action.") or through the glass of a moving automobile on day trips to the country wherein the landscape becomes nothing more than the image of a drive-by movie. Either way, there is a deficit of uncontrolled sounds, smells, and tactile experiences. The result is a narrowing of the senses. In a few short decades the human view of nature has evolved from one of the utilitarianism of my grandparents' generation, to the romantic attachment of my youth, to today's electronic detachment. For many youth today nature is merely a show on PBS, a place where the car is parked, or a reason to buy bug spray.

I will never forget the call I received while I was directing the Youth Conservation Corps Camp at Babler State Park in Missouri. The woman on the phone, nervous about an upcoming family camping trip in the park, asked: "Are there any bugs in the park?"

Increasingly, when I go to campgrounds or to popular floating streams, it seems that nature is for the other visitors nothing more than a place to get drunk with minimal interference. Reversing this trend is vitally important, not only because aesthetics and justice demands it, but also because drunkenness outdoors limits peoples' exposure to Nature. Experiencing nature is a powerful form of therapy. It is particularly useful as a remedy for sedentary inactivity, as a remedy for low self-worth, as a remedy for lessened cognitive abilities (constrained by too much screen time), as a remedy for stress, as a remedy for depression (at least, in minor to moderate cases), as a remedy for attention-deficit disorders, and as a remedy for other maladies.

Widespread anecdotal evidence and scientific research confirms the contention that direct contact with nature leads to increased mental health and psychological development. Research also confirms that the greater the amount of nature exposure, the greater the benefits. More about the therapeutic benefits of experiencing nature follows.

A Solution: Adult/Youth Partnerships That Develop Childlife Refuges Connected By Greenways

Personal and planetary health depends on repairing the broken bond between nature and young people. There is reason to fear what allowing the end of long and frequent direct experiences of nature will do to the future of joy and wonder. Some way needs to be developed now—while there are still parents around who remember what it was like to play in nature—to pull together youth, adult community leaders (such as YMCA staff persons), and parents, into teams united to the cause of restoring the bond between youth and nature.

Nature offers a separate peace. It offers youth a different larger world separate from parents—a place to test their burgeoning independence during the crucial adolescent years. During this time, the main chore for the child is to learn how to create his or her own more independent and individual identity. Nature experiences can help with that, but today too few children are given the opportunity to expose themselves to the healthful vagaries of nature.

The "denaturing" of our youth is the result of many factors: the impossibility to reap an economic gain from unstructured play in nature, a shortage of available natural places, an over-dependence on computers as a source of education, increases in homework, and the criminalization of natural play (the tree house I built as a youth, for example, would be a violation in many neighborhoods today).

Time in nature is not a self-indulgent luxury. It is a necessity that promotes good health, care for others, and more. Yet parents, fearful of strangers, eco-contamination, traffic, crime, the West Nile virus, and nature itself, are a big impediment to the promotion of nature play. In the eyes of too many parents, nature play is simply too risky. While crimes against children are always a possibility in isolated natural places, crimes against youth occur more often in the city than in nature.

Without nature play, what will be the formative experiences that lead to future environmentalists? The answer, the same in the future as it was in the past: combine the experience of playing in a wild or semi-wild place with guidance from an adult who teaches respect for nature (through either organized educational programs or through simple actions such as removing turtles from harm's way in the middle of country roads or reminders to leave campsites better than you found them).

It will take passion to protect and restore nature locally and globally; and this passion will not come as readily from a computer or television as it does outside a tent, next to a makeshift fort, under a tree house, or from hours spent "aimlessly" in a back country. The indicator species that shows the future of environmentalism is the child playing in nature. Juvenile zest for nature travels from the grass stain on a young person's pants to the panting of a young person's heart.

Parents acting alone, besieged by the act of balancing work and family life, cannot be expected to organize the kind of child-nature reunion that is necessary for the health of our children and the planet. Concerned parents need the help of other adult community leaders and interested older children with certain leadership abilities and sensitivities—such as the appreciation for all of life in all of its diversity. Along with the need for educators and experiential/adventure/challenge education staff persons, there is also a need to find adults willing to supervise play at natural places where children can become initiated to wildness on their own terms and with their own sense of wonder. There is a need for adults willing to take young people camping, hiking, and floating. There is a need for adults willing to help children set up gardens, teach youth to fish, and engage young people in nature crafts such as leaf pressing or gathering edible herbs. There is a need for enthusiastic adults to take youngsters bird watching, to encourage participants to keep nature journals, to help organize river cleanups, or to build trails.

Along with the establishment of wildlife refuges and connecting greenways there is a need for "childlife refuges." These could be magical places of learning. At a childlife refuge, youth could have extended stays in nature. At a childlife refuge, young people could use the fifty-four natural senses to rekindle their bonds with nature. They could share in the great adventure of being alive. They could plan and develop community service action projects. They could use staff persons with challenge education expertise to develop leadership skills, team-building skills, self-esteem, and self-confidence. Complete with energy efficient structures, childlife refuges could offer places where youth from various cultures could interact together, learn important life skills, serve their community, have ample time to "idle awhile" in nature, and be amazed.

Create A Youth Environmental Service Corps In Your Area

A partial solution to HumaNature Deficit Disorder could be the YMCA's Earth Service Corps. This program is for teenagers—valuable resources capable of working hand-in-hand with adults to solve community issues—who need and deserve meaningful roles in their community. The Earth Service Corps provides a chance for teenagers to demonstrate their talents, learn new skills, learn about other races and cultures, and learn more about themselves and their environment. Unfortunately, most YMCA's do not have this excellent program or, if they do, do not promote and support it adequately.

Help a child be amazed at the wonders of nature, the diversity of human culture, and what they can do to help their community. Contact someone at your local YMCA and offer to help set up and lead its Earth Service Corps.

To The Service Of Young People...

HumaNatureConnect Activity

Start-up Protocol

If this is not a day when you prefer to spend time in nature without an agenda, do the Heartwood Path Start-up Protocol found in the Appendix.

Working With Youth

Use the feeling sense of awareness of pressure, including wind, water, and atmospheric pressure as you plan environmental education activities for children in your area. Plan to demonstrate to them the pressure of the flow of water in a nearby stream, explain and locate the water tower in your community and its role in creating water pressure in nearby homes, the use of air and water pressure to create a sustainable source of electricity, and the role of atmospheric pressure (measured by a barometer) in determining whether the weather will be sunny or cloudy (clouds flow away from a high stack of air that creates a high pressure weather system and towards a low stack of air that is the cause of a low pressure weather system).

Follow-up Protocol

For best results, write down your impressions of this activity in your journal using the Heartwood Path Follow-up Protocol found in the Appendix. Afterwards, consider sharing your interpretations with others.

Heartwood Path Axioms

Key Assertions From Waypoint 4.51

4.51.1.

Along with the slowly progressive inability of young people to relate to nature in the Realm of Exteriority there is also slowly progressive inability to tap inner resources such as intentions (singularly) or ethics (in a group).

4.51.2.

Most nature experiences today occur as a result of watching the television (in programs editing tightly for rapid "action") or through the glass of a moving automobile on day trips to the country wherein the landscape becomes nothing more than the image of a drive-by movie.

4.51.3.

Widespread anecdotal evidence and scientific research confirms the contention that direct contact with nature leads to increased mental health and psychological development.

4.51.4.

Without nature play, there will be a deficit of formative experiences that lead to future environmentalists.

4.51.5.

At a childlife refuge, young people could use the fifty-four natural senses to rekindle their bonds with nature.

Nocturnal Pilgrimage 4.51

For best results, write down your impressions of each night's dreams in your journal using the Heartwood Path Dreaming Time

Protocols found in the Appendix. Afterwards, consider sharing your Dream Tending with others.

"(One) of the most effective ways I know of modulating our waking pace, of creating a really good day's waking, is through the regular practice of napping" (Naiman, 2006, p. 155).

With these thoughts and today's lesson in mind as you begin your nightly slumber, sleep and dream. Tend to your dreams upon waking.

Pertinent And Instructive Gems From My Dream Tending Journal

I dreamt I was walking through a large forest when, as if purposefully following me, the weather turned violent. I was fearful so I went into the opening of a cave (never go deep into a cave if there is a chance of showers). After a while the weather changed to sunny and mild. My fear changed to happiness as I returned to walking through the forest.

Lesson Learned: Weather affects one's moods. And moods affect how one reacts to weather. In time, after years of nature communing and dream work, it seems to me that I am now both dreaming the earth and earthing my dreams. These two modes of experiencing help me receive guidance, information, and healing. The trick is to put some earth into the Images, some earthy Images into your dreams, and some dreaminess into your nature experience. Engage in lucid dreaming to make your dreams both about yourself and about yourself-in-nature.

When doing the next activity outdoors, linger with your chosen attractions until you discover something mysterious nearby. Search for what is puzzling or unanswerable in or near your chosen natural landscape or being.

When you are ready, move to the next waypoint, "Locale." Your More-Than-Individual-Self is coming more clearly into view.

52

Locale

DEVELOP A SENSE OF PLACE

The following ten ways of knowing nature can be used to help one read the "book of nature and culture" written on the landscape. The following methods also help participants know, respect, and love their places:

1. wondering and questioning;
2. knowing local history;
3. observing seasonal changes;
4. listening intently;
5. counting and measuring;
6. empathizing with and personifying nature;
7. connecting elements in cycles;
8. finding beauty;
9. seeking solitude for reflection; and
10. improving environmental health.

Look over this list and make sure you are not forgetting about a good way to get to know your local place. You can use the information you receive by doing the things listed to form memories in your mind which can be used to put your own twist or color to the sometimes subtle and vague insights you develop as you feel the space around the chosen attractive natural beings.

To A Recognition Of One's Locale...

HumaNatureConnect Activity

Start-up Protocol

If this is not a day when you prefer to spend time in nature without an agenda, do the Heartwood Path Start-up Protocol found in the Appendix.

Developing A Sense of Place

Question how gravity affects the flow of water in your area. Understand the impact of gravity on the history of your area. Beyond the obvious impact of gravity on the falling leaves of Autumn, imagine in the mind's eye the observable impacts of gravity in Summertime, Wintertime, and Springtime. Listen for sounds caused by gravity (such as the dripping of water). Count and measure some aspect of gravity nearby. Empathize with a small attractive natural being and a big attractive natural being regarding how gravity affects these beings. Ponder how gravity affects the cycling of elements nearby. Find and make a journal entry about the beauty gravity creates nearby. As you continue in your time alone, reflect on the impact that gravity is having on you right now, the impact gravity is having on your chosen small attractive natural being (perhaps it's a shrub at the base of a bluff), and the impact gravity is having on your chosen large attractive natural being (perhaps it's the whole bluff above a shrub) . If you need help, assume the essence of the small and large beings and then, as them, ask them to speak about what gravity is doing to and for them.

Follow-up Protocol

For best results, write down your impressions of this activity in your journal using the Heartwood Path Follow-up Protocol found in the Appendix. Afterwards, consider sharing your interpretations with others.

Heartwood Path Axioms

Key Assertions From Waypoint 4.52

4.52.1.

Develop a sense of place.

4.52.2.

The following ten ways of knowing nature can be used to help one read the "book of nature and culture" written on the landscape:

1. wondering and questioning;

2. knowing local history;

3. observing seasonal changes;

4. listening intently;

5. counting and measuring;

6. empathizing with and personifying nature;

7. connecting elements in cycles;

8. finding beauty;

9. seeking solitude for reflection; and

10. improving environmental health.

4.52.3.

Rather than being frowned upon, napping ought to be supported as much as daily exercise.

Nocturnal Pilgrimage 4.52

For best results, write down your impressions of each night's dreams in your journal using the Heartwood Path Dreaming Time Protocols found in the Appendix. Afterwards, consider sharing your Dream Tending with others.

"Napping (ought) not be frowned upon at the office or make you feel guilty at home . . . It (ought to) have the status of daily exercise" (Naiman, 2006, p. 156).

With these words and the previous lesson in mind as you nod off for the night, sleep and dream. Dream tending begins immediately upon waking, even before getting out of bed.

Pertinent And Instructive Gems From My Dream Tending Journal

I dreamt I had a dream but nothing was familiar—not the Characters, not the landscape, and not the action. The odd feeling it gave encouraged me to turn it into a lucid dream, hoping conscious awareness would bring some of it home. It didn't work so I woke up just to make it end.

Lesson Learned: Perhaps this was someone else's dream. Perhaps it was a dream of the Earth. With more patience and endurance, I would have been able to tolerate the ambiguity. Eventually some link to myself, probably very obscure, would have shown itself. It shows the untethered infinitude of the dream world. It betrays how the unconscious world goes on and on without end. It reminds me that I am not the central focus of the conscious mind and unconscious mind, just one little part of them.

After reading about using experiential education techniques that use challenges to help you learn, consider whether a closed-minded perspective is more likely in those who remain mostly indoors and whether being self-serving is less prevalent in those who make regular connections with natural attractive beings in the wild outdoors.

Carry such considerations with you as you move outside for the next activity. When you are ready, head to the next waypoint: "Tactics." Prepare to "get it, by doing it."

53

Tactics

USE EXPERIENTIAL EDUCATION TECHNIQUES

Experiential Education, which typically uses things like zip lines, high ropes courses, climbing walls, backpack trips and float trips, is all about learning, acquiring skills, and building values through direct experience (by doing). Participants engage in some activity, reflect upon the activity critically, derive some useful insight from the discussions, and incorporate the results of their discussions into their lives through a change in understanding and/or behavior.

In all well-run experiential education programs a relationship is created between the topic and the participant. This relationship creates interest, involvement, and a sense of ownership over what is learned.

Participants accept responsibility for their own learning and behavior. Learning events incorporate a dynamic tension between the desire for safety and security and a sense of dis-equilibrium or imbalance that stems from a perceived risk or a mismatch between old ways of thinking and new information. As the participant seeks to regain equilibrium or balance (make sense of things) the result is new approaches to thinking, feeling, and acting.

Experiential education activities always employ safety measures that make them never really physically risky. But they nearly always appear to be. For good reasons.

The result of overcoming the disequilibrium that occurs along with the experiential education challenges is a reshaping of perceptions. By encouraging participants to involve themselves in activities that are beyond their Comfort Zones but not quite in their Panic Zones, they enter their Stretch Zone. In this setting for learning, participants overcome a lack of comfort or overcome a lack of familiarity by doing challenging activities successfully. Their time of confidence-producing achievement leads to motivation, higher morale, greater retention of learning, and growth for the participants.

Experiential education is a way of learning where perceived risk is inherent in the acts of immersing participants in natural places, unpredictable environmental conditions, and environmentally controlled built environments. Participants are to be told that, while the goal of the program is "100% Participation," their involvement is based on "Challenge by Choice," meaning that they will be encouraged to participate but will also be expected to understand and evaluate authentic risks of activities and exercise personal decision–making responsibility pertaining to their level of involvement in program activities. While opting out without being questioned is always an option for participants, everyone is encouraged to participate in some way (through being the cheerleader, observer, or spotter, for example).

While preparations are always conducted to bring the actual risks to acceptable levels (as close to zero chance of accidents as possible), most of the events experienced by participants will purposefully involve perceived risks (the activity appears to be either physically dangerous, a possible source of embarrassment, or next-to-impossible to achieve). The perceived risk thus helps the participants to understand, manage, and acknowledge how risk plays a role in health; personal and professional relations; choosing a career; furthering a sense of self; and getting the most out of their intellectual, physical, emotional, and spiritual lives.

To Getting It By Doing It...

HumaNatureConnect Activity

Start-up Protocol

If this is not a day when you prefer to spend time in nature without an agenda, do the Heartwood Path Start-up Protocol found in the Appendix.

Applying Experiential Education

Use the feeling sense of touch on the skin to find a being that is wet, a being that is dry, a being that feels cool, a being that feels warm, a being that feels smooth, an being that feels rough, a being that feels hard and a being that feels soft. After feeling these beings, be sure to replace them in their original position, returning the scene to its original appearance and condition. As you touch each object (being), psychologically assume its essence and, as its wetness, dryness, warmness, coolness, softness, hardness, smoothness, or roughness, speak about the value of each condition to the being and to the environment near the object (being). After speaking on behalf of wetness, dryness, smoothness and the other conditions you found, use your natural sense of "hearing including resonance, vibrations, sonar and ultrasonic frequencies" (Cohen, website: http://www.ecopsych.com/insight53senses.html) to hum a tone that represents each condition (wetness, hardness, smoothness, etc) in yourself, in a small object (being) nearby and a large object (being) nearby. Hum the tone of wetness in you and your surroundings. Hum the tone of dryness in you and your surroundings. Hum the tone of warmness. Hum the tone of coolness. Hum the tone of hardness. Hum the tone of softness. Hum the tone of smoothness. Hum the tone of roughness. If you want to make this activity a group experience, have the group hum a chorus of wetness, then a chorus of dryness, then a chorus of smoothness, and so on. Note any differences and similarities of the tones. Discuss this experience together as a group. Is smoothness generally a higher pitched tone than roughness? Is warmness a lower tone than coolness? Consider the relative tones of all the conditions of touch. Ponder and discuss any similarities and differences. What do the variations in the tones mean to you? Write down how this activity was, if at all, risky for you. Were their risks involved in the searching for various tactile sensations. What about the risk of appearing odd? What about the risk of failure? How did you handle such risks? What would you be risking if you only read this activity rather than actually engaged in its tasks? What does the way you handled the risks, or could have handled the risks, tell you about the value of perceived risk in your life? What is the value of operating in the Stretch Zone in your life? What sort of "safety net" do you think you will need, if any, to handle the perceived risk of being an eartHeart?

Follow-up Protocol

For best results, write down your impressions of this activity in your journal using the Heartwood Path Follow-up Protocol found in the Appendix. Afterwards, consider sharing your interpretations with others.

Heartwood Path Axioms

Key Assertions From Waypoint 4.53

4.53.1.

In all well-run experiential education programs a relationship is created between the topic and the participant—a relationship that creates interest, involvement, and a sense of ownership over what is learned.

4.53.2.

By encouraging participants to involve themselves in activities that are beyond their Comfort Zones but not quite in their Panic Zones, they enter the Stretch Zone—the setting for learning wherein participants overcome a lack of comfort or overcome a lack of familiarity by doing challenging activities so successfully they lead to motivation, higher morale, greater retention of learning, and growth for the participants.

4.53.3.

While opting out without being questioned is always an option for participants, everyone is encouraged to participate in some way (through being the cheerleader, observer, or spotter, for example).

4.53.4.

The perceived risks of some Heartwood Path Activities helps the participants to understand, manage, and acknowledge how risk plays a role in health; personal and professional relations; choosing a career; furthering a sense of self; and getting the most out of their intellectual, physical, emotional, and spiritual lives.

Nocturnal Pilgrimage 4.53

For best results, write down your impressions of each night's dreams in your journal using the Heartwood Path Dreaming Time Protocols found in the Appendix. Afterwards, consider sharing your Dream Tending with others.

"Just as "night watch" (waking up for a couple of hours in the middle of the night) may reflect the light center in the dark, night wave of the yin-yang, napping may be the dark center of the white, waking wave of the yin-yang" (Naiman, 2006, p. 157).

Be sure to add both poles, the light and the dark, to your experience of going down the Heartwood Path. With Naiman's words and today's lesson in mind as you prepare for your night's rest, sleep and dream. Tend to your dreams the next morning. See if there are any light or dark dream images in your dreams.

Pertinent And Instructive Gems From My Dream Tending Journal

I dreamt that I was flying people around in a huge open-air cardboard box. It was fun to fly this simple contraption. I stopped to pick up a lady who wanted to be taken to her favorite southern restaurant.

Lesson Learned: Some dreams may occur solely for your own entertainment. Maybe you just need a diversion. Enjoy these dreams.

During the next activity, consciously choose to allow nature to be your teacher or mentor as you head outside to find your attractive natural being or landscape. Make your time in nature with your natural attractions count. See if you can allow nature to teach you how to identify what is truly essential in your life.

When you are ready, move to the next waypoint: "Boundless Education." Glean the psychological, sociological, and physical benefits that are available to you at the next waypoint.

54

Boundless Education

PARTICIPATE IN AN EDUCATION PROGRAM WITHOUT WALLS

EartHearts offer a systematic approach to education that develops feelings, encourages understandings, and promotes harmonious and joyous lifestyles that are good for the Earth. Those who participate in Heartwood Path Environmental Education programs will benefit psychologically (through improved self-concept, confidence, self-efficacy, actualization, values clarification, and personal testing), sociologically, (through improved compassion, group cooperation, respect for others, communication behaviors, behavior feedback, friendships, and belonging), and physically (through improved strength, coordination, cardiovascular efficiency, outdoor skills, sensory awareness, health, and methods to overcome catharsis).

Heartwood Path Environmental Education strategies guide participants toward a deeper understanding of the self/other interdependency and the self/environment interdependency. To further such goals, we encourage participants to engage in camping, caving, canoeing, birding, nature watching, hiking, backpacking and conservation projects.

Wherever there is a Heartwood Path Environmental Education Program, the participants are encouraged to consider their local area as a museum without walls, located out-of-doors and to work to learn about, preserve, and restore the local outdoor heritage (both natural and cultural).

To A Look At One's Territory...

HumaNatureConnect Activity

Start-up Protocol

If this is not a day when you prefer to spend time in nature without an agenda, do the Heartwood Path Start-up Protocol found in the Appendix.

Taking A Varied Environmental Survey

Answer the following questions:

1. What are the most numerous natural beings in view?
2. What is the most powerful force in your local environment?
3. What would you like to add to your local environment?
4. What is the funniest thing you see in your immediate environment?
5. How does your local environment make you feel?
6. What is the most predictable aspect of your local environment?
7. If you could plan an ideal environment, what would it include?
8. What would you change about your local environment?

Follow-up Protocol

For best results, write down your impressions of this activity in your journal using the Heartwood Path Follow-up Protocol found in the Appendix. Afterwards, consider sharing your interpretations with others.

Heartwood Path Axioms

Key Assertions From Waypoint 4.54

4.54.1.

Those who participate in Heartwood Path Environmental Education programs will benefit psychologically (through improved self-concept, confidence, self-efficacy, actualization, values clarification, and personal testing), sociologically, (through improved compassion, group cooperation, respect for others, communication behaviors, behavior feedback, friendships, and belonging), and physically (through improved strength, coordination, cardiovascular fitness, outdoor skills, sensory awareness, health, and methods to overcome catharsis).

4.54.2.

Wherever there is a Heartwood Path Environmental Education Program, the participants are encouraged to consider their local area as a museum without walls, located out-of-doors and to work to learn about, preserve, and restore the local outdoor heritage (both natural and cultural).

Nocturnal Pilgrimage 3.54

For best results, write down your impressions of each night's dreams in your journal using the Heartwood Path Dreaming Time

Protocols found in the Appendix. Afterwards, consider sharing your Dream Tending with others.

"(Long and late-afternoon naps take us into deeper sleep, can result in extended grogginess, and can shift our circadian rhythms, compromising the quality of our nighttime sleep)" (Naiman, 2006, p. 159).

Follow Naiman's suggestion about not napping too long nor too late in the day and you will see just how beneficial naps can be. With Naiman's instructions and today's lesson in mind as you drift off for the night or take a nap, sleep and dream. Tend to your dreams upon waking.

Pertinent And Instructive Gems From My Dream Tending Journal

I dreamt I was battling a huge dragon that lived in a cooling tower of a nuclear power plant. Perky, my parakeet, was flying around and through the creature's jaws. He was doing his best to be distracting. Laddy II, my golden retriever, had jumped onto the back of the creature but his jaws were not powerful enough to force his teeth through the beast's hard and scaly hide. The dragon had just given me a substantial blow, leaving me down but not out. Just as the dragon was ready to strike again, on the nearby hill appeared Laddy I, the wild dog that allowed me to act like his master for twelve years during my youth. Crouching low, eyes fixed, this German Shepherd mix, with huge snarling teeth, was ready to pounce...

I don't remember what happened after that. Why? I made the mistake of not keeping the dream journal next to my bed open to the appropriate page. I also failed to leave my pen resting on the open sheet. In fumbling around trying to make my note, I lost the memory of the dream. I can only imagine that Laddy I fought a fierce battle, left the dragon useless, and then walked back over the hill and into the forest, bloodied but heroic, as

ever.

Lesson Learned: Adopt a former stray. And stop being a helpless by-stander of your dreams. Begin to make the transition to being an active participant in your dream life by making your dream journal and pen ready for instant note taking. As you make it known that you intend to remember your dreams, by making suitable dream journal preparations, your dreams will make themselves more accessible to you.

By doing the next activity outside, the next waypoint becomes unconventional medicine. The tonic of wildness is a way for you to both help to restore the bonds between humans and nature and to further your own personal evolution and fulfillment. When you are ready, move to the next waypoint: "Countryside Blockers."

55

Countryside Blockers

KNOW WHAT BLOCKS A PERSON'S COMMITMENT TO ENVIRONMENTAL PROTECTION AND FROM BONDING WITH NATURE

We need more people to love nature and to be committed to protecting the environment. One of the first steps in adding to the ranks of earth supporters is to understand what typically blocks people from bonding with nature and committing themselves to nature. Here is a quick list:

1. Modern religions that often equate nature worship as being the same thing as Devil worship.
2. The scientific mechanical paradigm of Newton and Descartes where clocks replace the pull of the tides and machines guide our life purposes more than holistic intuitive perception.
3. The crippling of psychological development due to cultural practices that stifle the psychic human/Earth connection; namely: domestication, agriculture, the separation of mother and child due to social and economic pressures, the loss of rites of passage,

urbanization, television, the automobile, video games, and other cultural ways we separate ourselves from ature.

4. Blocking out the pleasing awareness of *uniqueness in communion*—by which I mean a oneness that does not destroy the diversification—and viewing the world as a collection of parts and objects rather than as a communal living subject.

5. The obsessive making, selling, and buying of stuff.

6. One's inflated Ego or grandiose individual self-image that masks deep-seated feelings of unworthiness and emptiness that one may feel can be reduced through the buying of stuff.

7. Humans are progressively forgetting what our ancestors practiced—empathy with nonhuman life, awe of the mysterious, and humility in the human/earth relationship.

8. Not attending to one's own inner world images, memories, and impressions of the Earth.

9. Viewing nature as an object—a resource solely intended for use by the current generation (rather than as a fellow being). And

10. Fear—discussed in more detail subsequently.

If you notice yourself blocking your love of nature and your commitment to environmental protection, or if you notice anyone else doing so, and if you want to do something about it, look over the next dozen or so waypoints, particularly the ones about reacquainting your bonds with nature (Waypoint 3.56), learn about your Greater Self on a vision quest (Waypoint 3.57), aligning oneself with nature (Waypoint 3.58), limiting the use of television (Waypoint 3.60), developing your ecological consciousness (Waypoint 3.63) and knowing what causes a person to be a supporter of environmental protection (Waypoint 3.68). These and other waypoints that follow will put you on the road to happiness and environmental sustainability—the road to Gladandgreen Junction.

To Answers For Why Some People Shun Nature...

HumaNatureConnect Activity

Start-up Protocol

If this is not a day when you prefer to spend time in nature without an agenda, do the Heartwood Path Start-up Protocol found in the Appendix.

Knowing What Blocks You From Bonding With Nature

Become aware of the feeling sense of excretion and its usefulness in waste elimination and protection from enemies. Concerning excretion and bonding with nature or protecting nature, consider the feeling of excretion and devil worship, the feeling of excretion and the mechanical paradigm (for example: clocks instead of tides, reliance on machines more than intuition), the feeling of excretion and domestication, the feeling of excretion and mercantilism, the feeling of excretion and feeling of unworthiness or emptiness, the feeling of excretion and empathy for the non-human, the feeling of excretion and blocking one's own inner world images, the feeling of excretion and viewing natural beings as resources for the current generation only, and the feeling of excretion and fear.

Follow-up Protocol

For best results, write down your impressions of this activity in your journal using the Heartwood Path Follow-up Protocol found in the Appendix. Afterwards, consider sharing your interpretations with others.

Heartwood Path Axioms

Key Assertions From Waypoint 4.55

4.55.1.

Many things can block a person's commitment to environmental protection and from bonding with nature, including: modern religions; scientific mechanical paradigm of Newton and Descartes; cultural practices that stifle the psychic human/ Earth connection; blocking out the pleasing awareness of uniqueness in communion; the obsessive making, selling, and buying of stuff; one's inflated Ego or grandiose individual self-image; a lack of empathy with nonhuman life, not attending to one's own inner world images, memories, and impressions of the earth; viewing nature as an object; and fear.

4.55.2.

Humans typically subconsciously repress, consciously suppress, and project our anxieties as a routine part of life.

Nocturnal Pilgrimage 4.55

For best results, write down your impressions of each night's dreams in your journal using the Heartwood Path Dreaming Time Protocols found in the Appendix. Afterwards, consider sharing your Dream Tending with others.

Whether one subconsciously lives in a subconscious psychological state of denial or consciously represses dark aspects of one's inner world, the locked away fears, embarrassments, and anxieties will likely be unwittingly projected unto others unless one continues the kind of Dream Tending presented in this book series. Make no mistake about it, Dream Tending will be good for you, good for those around you, and good for the environment.

Pertinent And Instructive Gems From My Dream Tending Journal

I dreamt I was canoeing on the Eleven Point River in the Ozarks of Southern Missouri. As I paddled slowly downstream an otter appeared right next to my boat on the port side (left). He rolled on his back and still managed to keep pace. He looked directly into my eyes. I looked directly into his. Occasionally, he would sink a few inches beneath the surface of the still and clear water. At these points, rather than seeing him, I saw my own reflection. I wondered if he too could see his own reflection on the bottom of the surface of the water, but doubted it. There was a constant reversal of his face and the reflection of my own. Sometimes the Images seemed to morph together. I did not try to interpret it. It was too fun just to watch it. It was a curious phenomenon. But I did not mind it.

Lesson Learned: You are both the witness of your dreams and the author of them. The event with the otter was a dream that seemed real. Many times I have sat and witnessed the antics of river otters and felt I was dreaming. Whether they are nighttime events during my sleep or daytime events during my time awake the dreams I have always seem to be, obviously or subtly, about me. The river otter dream was me looking at me looking at me. The Dream was no foreign dirty trick. It was my own creation, one that I could not have developed so clearly without knowing and loving the playful and sensual antics of river otters. The dream originated at a free and optimistic place inside of me, but it had its roots in the corporeality of river otters in the wild. The Image of the river otter was calling me to recognize myself in it. That was the necessity of this dream, its urge upon the witness. I remember worrying that I and the river otter, would both fall victim to traps—his of the steel jaw variety (trapping for river otters, which were almost extirpated from the state during my early college years, is legal in Missouri) and mine of the constrictive steeliness of Modern Culture. Despite these threats, both the otter and myself frolic in the cleanest of navigable streams. Remedies to these threats will have to wait. But not for long.

Move to the next waypoint to keep yourself active and interactive, to keep yourself away from the television, to keep yourself up from the chair or sofa, or to keep you from sedentary activities that require little investment or involvement but also barrage you with distractions. These and other intrusions keep your brain from functioning at an optimal level. This problem is an epidemic. The modern American adult is barraged with an average of 50 brief stress response episodes per day, many coming from electronic devices. Using such devices as we walk on busy sidewalks or drive cars is a real danger. The sudden and surprising adjustments that have to be made during such activities give us an unwelcome shot of cortisol—our bodies response to stress and anger. Higher cortisol levels can cause inflammation, anxiety, depression, the amplification of mood disturbances (Selhub & Logan, 2012, p. 50). Given these consequences, trade the lengthy stream of television commercials and excessive computer screen time that comes from computer usage for what interests, stimulates, and attracts you in nature. Doing so could save your life, and will at least make it more joyous. Reacquaint yourself with your inherent bond with nature now by moving to the next outdoor educational post along the Heartwood Path.

With this teaching and the just-completed activity in mind, sleep and dream. Use the EartHeart Exchange to share your impressions with others.

When you are ready, move to the next post along the Heartwood Path, entitled: "Reacquaintance." You will improve your perception as you become reacquainted with nature.

56

Reacquaintance

RE-ESTABLISH A BOND WITH NATURE

It may be true that every paradise has its parasites. Nevertheless, if the bio-phobe (a person who fears living things) can manage to stop worrying about leeches, mosquitoes, ticks, chiggers, fleas and other "itch hikers" long enough to open up her heart to a place, she will find it seething with amiable abundance. This place will be seen to be full of a myriad of other life forms, all living and dying within a system controlled by a vast and complex order. Understanding the order in nature is more bonding than perceiving nature as random, chaotic, and inexplicable. Moreover, if one adds themselves to their awareness, not as an outsider full of discord but as an integral and harmonious part of the setting, the observer will discover the great insight of their own More-Than-Human-Nature—the Spirit of the place.

If a person is not a seasoned nature lover, it may take some time and effort for them to bond with nature in a way that enables them to discover the Spirit of the place. The initial condition needed to develop such a bond with nature is attentiveness to what one sees. Often what one looks at out-of-doors is but a reflection of one's beliefs and expectations.

In this way, perception is one's own individual "take" on existence. One's mind does not always perfectly separate objective and subjective perception. The view is always interpreted by the viewer. It usually takes even seasoned outdoor enthusiasts several days spent in one place to begin to see truly what is present. The reason for this delay in perceptual attentiveness has to do, in part, with the time it takes to slow down the modern mind enough so it can take a break from incessant inner world preoccupations.

Working on one's abilities of perception will help one build a bond with nature. For optimal nature-bonding, do not focus all attention on the corporeal aspects of nature—the tangible, material environment. It is also necessary to work on the immaterial aspects, including one's senses. Seeing, hearing, smelling, tasting, and feeling may not be matter, but they do matter. While the best time to create such a bond with nature is before puberty (when the person is still wide open to all kinds of possibilities and not yet distracted by teenage drama), communion with the earth can occur at any age.

Bonding with nature is facilitated by sensuous pleasure. Sensuous pleasure awakens one to the present moment, takes one out of one's head and into one's body, and makes one feel more alive. Often one does not linger over sensory data, either because one chooses not to take the time or because one is attempting to shut down one's senses as a way to protect oneself from noise, pollution, ugliness, or sadness. Unfortunately, when one shuts down one's senses to minimize some form of discomfort one is also closing down one's potential for pleasure. Sensual pleasures tend to reawaken one's senses, tune one into the world, and make one more aware of what is going on within.

One learns as a child that it is often considered inappropriate to openly enjoy sensual pleasures. As a result, one tends to limit such pleasures to the two poles in the whole range of pleasures: the infantile pole and the sexual pole. Of course, there is a lot to experience between these two extremes. Enjoying the whole range of sensual delights makes it easier to relax and let go, encourages one to release pain, makes one feel more buoyant and playful, keeps one from overemphasizing thinking, helps one regulate the heart, increases one's ability to enjoy sexual pleasure, makes one more aware of one's indivisibility from nature, and helps one get in better touch with one's spiritual nature and intuition.

One's receptivity to sensory stimulation is not all done at the conscious level. One also, unknowingly, picks up much data and deposits it directly in one's subconscious mind. It is likely that the more deliberately sensual one becomes the more one will be able to become informed and aware of extremely subtle levels of stimuli. One uses subtle stimuli when one taps one's subconscious mind and has, for example, gut feelings, premonitions, choices based on intuition, and moments to bond with nature.

A good way to improve one's perception is to learn the three ways to gather information:

1. the physical—through books, teachers, conversations, etc.;
2. the sensory—a combination of physical and psychic senses, including intuition (a function of the mind that combines memory with subtle perception of present-moment clues to produce conclusions); and
3. the Egoless knowing—an opening of consciousness to receptivity beyond conventional time-space pathways; non-thinking that bypasses all mediators, interpreters, beliefs, preconceptions, and opinion.

This last process disallows the application of interpretation to what is perceived as a way to minimize mixing the view with the viewer. Accomplishing Ego-less knowing requires a time-out from conversation and interaction and the devotion of time for stillness, listening, loving attentiveness, quietness, meditation, and/or prayer. By improving one's perception in the three ways described above, one's connection with nature will become clear and full. One will also become better equipped to give and to receive love.

Most of us have a second lover, not knowing that she is with us always. Our first lover—a beloved human—can give us great pleasure and reassurance. Our second lover—nature—can also. We all too often neglect our second lover; and in doing so, cause unconscious strife in our inner world which is mirrored by ecological imbalance in the outer world. Many of the causes of this "ecological neuroses" come from all the fear-based reasons people have to avoid nature, including:

1. fear of minor irritations, such as misquote bites, chiggers, and poison ivy;
2. fear of natural hazards, such as quicksand, tall cliffs, and snow-storms;
3. fear of natural disasters such as earthquakes and tornadoes;
4. fear of toxins, pollutants in the air, water, and soil;
5. fear of losing control, not finding a favored campsite;
6. fear of missing a favorite television show;
7. fear of solitude, (isolation in nature is very transformative be-cause it makes the unconscious more accessible);
8. fear of transcendence—preferring the placidity of day to day life over the unknown qualities of profound psycho-emotional change; and
9. fear of the mystical power of nature.

Learning how to let go of these fears is a crucial step in letting nature be a teacher and a healer. One way to fight these qualms is to keep in good physical shape through exercise, which makes one feel more vital and stems emotional distress. Other ways include enrolling in a first aid course, taking a lifesaving course, participating in an out-door education program, and going on a supervised nature outing or trip. Learning to identify local plants and animals builds familiarity—the first step toward trading fear for respect. Other ideas for building kinship with nature include, harvesting fruits directly from the trees at a nearby orchard whenever possible; participating in local earth-oriented seasonal festivals, such as gatherings to celebrate the winter solstice; and going on a vision quest. This last way to build kinship with nature involves oneself in rituals of renewal. One such ritual, spending time alone in the wilderness, is an important, time-tested, and power-ful rite of passage that enables one to awaken one's heart to what is profound in nature. It is a way to find guidance, inspiration, and re-newal through experiencing what is sacred about the unity of life. It is a great way to mark, confirm, and deepen life transitions.

To Renew Your Relationship With Your Second Mother...

HumaNatureConnect Activity

Start-up Protocol

If this is not a day when you prefer to spend time in nature with-out an agenda, do the Heartwood Path Start-up Protocol found in the Appendix.

Re-establishing A Bond With Nature

Use the feeling sense of weight, gravity, and balance as a supplement to the typical five senses to establish a bond to nature. Feel the relative weight of a boulder and a leaf, watch as gravity pulls water down-stream, notice how birds balance on limbs. Feel gravity pulling you toward the earth. Notice how your weight leaves an imprint on the ground as you walk or sit in a forest, field, or prairie. Build a cairn (rock tower) and pay attention to the importance of balance while doing so. Psychologically assume the essence of something heavy, something light, something weighing on something else, something balanced and something unbalanced and then, as these beings, speak about these beings' feelings of weight, gravity, and balance. Then feel your own weight, the impact of gravity on your body, and your own balancing at present. Hum the tonal sound of weight on yourself, on a small intimate being, and on a big expansive being. Make humming sounds also for how these beings are affected by gravity and then again for how they are balanced or imbalanced. Does the mutual effect of weight, gravity, and balance between yourself, a small part of the microcosm, and the macrocosm increase or decrease your bond with nature? Is balance more obvious in nature than in an urban area? Do you feel more comfortable in the presence of balance or imbalance? If you are having difficulty relating weight, gravity, and balance to bonding with nature, make the correlation with another natural sense, such as appetite and hunger, or mental or spiritual distress.

Follow-up Protocol

For best results, write down your impressions of this activity in your journal using the Heartwood Path Follow-up Protocol found in the Appendix. Afterwards, consider sharing your interpretations with others.

Heartwood Path Axioms

Key Assertions From Waypoint 4.56

4.56.1.

Often what one looks at out-of-doors is but a reflection of one's beliefs and expectations.

4.56.2.

When one shuts down one's senses to minimize some form of discomfort one is also closing down one's potential for pleasure.

4.56.3.

There are many fear-based reasons people have to avoid nature, including:

1. fear of minor irritations, such as misquote bites, chiggers, and poison ivy;

2. fear of natural hazards, such as quicksand, tall cliffs, and snowstorms;

3. fear of natural disasters such as earthquakes and tornadoes;

4. fear of toxins, pollutants in the air, water, and soil;

5. fear of losing control, not finding a favored campsite;

6. fear of missing a favorite television show;

7. fear of solitude (isolation in nature is very transformative because it makes the unconscious more accessible);

8. fear of transcendence—preferring the placidity of day to day life over the unknown qualities of profound psycho-emotional change; and

9. fear of the mystical power of nature.

Nocturnal Pilgrimage 4.56

For best results, write down your impressions of each night's dreams in your journal using the Heartwood Path Dreaming Time Protocols found in the Appendix. Afterwards, consider sharing your Dream Tending with others.

"We toss our litter into the street, whether blatantly around our neighborhoods and natural environments or, cleverly veiled in spiritual or religious pursuit, through the thoughtless projection of our personal darkness into the visible world" (Naiman, 2006, p. 161).

With Naiman's statement in mind, sleep, dream, and tend to your dreams.

Pertinent And Instructive Gems From My Dream Tending Journal

I dreamt I was in school studying such subjects as plant taxonomy and the ecology of forest management. I loved what I was learning but, despite taking everything that pertained to conservation, I felt a nagging feeling that some topic, some method, or some perspective was missing. In the same dream I fell asleep while my biology professor read his own textbook to my 7:00 am class of six hundred students. In this dream, I designed fanciful buildings, flew over the ocean, made my bicycle capable of going much faster, and even sold millions of dollars of silver badges. It was a pleasant enough dream; but, again, I felt that some dimension was not being employed.

Lesson Learned: What is needed in both cases is the opposite. During my very pragmatic college classes I felt the need for dreamy alternatives that would make my mind receptive, laid back, passive, accepting, and all encompassing. During my dreaming time, whether awake or asleep, I felt the need for conscious alternatives that would give me the ability to seize, focus, cut, separate, and judge. By always looking back for opposites my mind allowed me to step into the shoes of adversaries. Commentaries and judging faded away as I looked backward at the events of my days. Simply observing in both a conscious, masculine active way and in a dreamy, feminine, receptive way made me feel whole, satisfied, and happy. As this book progresses, you will learn a way to similarly look backward and to achieve identical results.

Considering the statistic that one in two North Americans will face a mental disorder during their lifetime, it is time to do more to reverse the frightful growth in psychopathology—which is for U.S high school students, now five times what it was in 1938 (Selfhub & Logan, 2012, p. 40). Do your part to stem this horrendous tide by getting outside regularly, beginning with the next activity, which you can begin by moving to the next waypoint: "Relentless Teacher."

57

Relentless Teacher

LEARN ABOUT YOUR GREATER SELF ON A VISION QUEST

The wilderness is a relentless teacher that helps one let go of outdated self-images, including the notion that you have nothing to offer to the world. Go to the wilderness and come back home with fresh insight and a new project that is beneficial for yourself, for your place, for other people, for your community, or for your environment.

Undergo A Rite Of Passage During A Wilderness Trip

Once in the wilderness expect to gradually become more comfortable in your natural surroundings. You will, after some time has passed, come to feel like you belong in the wilderness. When immersed in enduring natural rhythms, you will likely slowly transcend individual concerns.

Expect to return from the wilderness more beautiful on the inside, awed by what is on the outside, less stifled, and committed to a newfound, nature-inspired methodology or cause. You will receive "good medicine" on your purposeful trip to the wilderness—a tonic that will make life more manageable. This "medicine," often a revelation, will enrich your life, and it will also encourage you to share your newly found vision in ways that help others. Accept your vision and go to work—which, as we all know, is a fine thing unless it eats into your free time.

A vision without a task is just a dream. Doing needs to follow thinking.

The entire purposeful wilderness trip is a ritual. The ceremonies that you conduct in the wilderness are mythic in that they help you receive nature's messages that are buried in your unconscious mind. Rite of passage ceremonies mark how the trip is a sign that an important life transition is taking place. They mark the deeper significance of events. They mark the building of deeper bonds, many nonverbal, and always extended beyond humans to the larger natural community as well. Rites of passage ceremonies mark the safe place where risks become less hazardous, where people are free to initiate new beginnings, where it is acceptable to express new emotions, and where it is appropriate to share fresh insights through the vocal meditation of chanting, through dancing, through playing music, or through remaining silent.

Here are the five stages of a purposeful rite of passage wilderness trip or vision quest, and some instructions for each stage:

Stage One: Preparation

Confirm for yourself that now is the time to start your transition, that you are committed to begin a rite of passage. At some point in your life, circumstances related to not-yet-moving-on will likely make you view yourself as a troubled visitor in a gloomy world. When something like such a time comes for you, or when you are a person in the middle years of life devoting time for introspection, you will likely feel that in some way your life is not as it ought to be.

To correct this picture, begin your deserved rite of passage by taking the first step towards clarifying your purpose. Take stock in your resources, your mindfulness skills, your physical fitness, and the availability of minimal camping equipment.

Attach symbolic meanings to your thoughts and actions from the start. Do not simply wallow in the literal meaning of thoughts. For whatever you are thinking about during a rite of passage, look for ways your thinking is also representing something else. Maybe the oak tree you are thinking about represents your age. It could then also be a symbol for your life, for example. Look for the double meanings of your thoughts that are beyond surface levels. Even your actions can have a double meaning. Two examples: painting a fence black the day before embarking on your vision quest may represent something evil, carrying a chain may represent a desire to become attached.

Begin your passage with your preparations and your packing. Keep a journal from the very beginning. Study various forms of rites of passage: ranging from vision quests to "medicine walks" (full-day excursion in which nature is seen as a mirror of one's larger life journey) to brief (two-hour) walkabouts. Make changes, alterations, or additions as needed before leaving home.

Stage Two: Severance

Let go of your old self, dis-identify from old roles, or die symbolically. Contemplate on letting go during your time between home and the wilderness. At base camp (the away-from-home place you make your last preparations before embarking into the wilderness), come into the natural rhythms of the place. Leave the city behind. Conduct a ceremony to mark the end of the old and the beginning of the new. Recognize what was good in the old and symbolically open the door to the unknown.

Stage Three: Threshold

This term comes from the threshing-hold, a place where wheat was separated from the chaff. At the threshold of your rite of passage (a remote place, preferably in a wilderness setting) cast off the husk of your life (the shell which is no longer necessary or protective, the chaff of childhood) to reveal the living seed of a new life. Crossing the threshold—that is, symbolically stepping from childhood to adulthood, or from a young person to a mature person, or from married to single, or from immature to mature, or from whatever was to whatever will be—in a natural setting is helpful because nature is, at once, supportive and challenging. Seek solitude in wilderness. Go there alone. For safety, you may want to use a sign system to inform an unseen "buddy" that you are doing well, usually involving leaving signs at a designated location. Once you are alone in the wilderness, limit your activities and movements. During your three-to-four day stay, leave most of your time unstructured. On the last day, consider holding a solitary all-night vigil (which may or may not involve a fast), while remaining inside a self-constructed ring of stones or branches. Consider this ring at once a tomb for the old self and a womb for the new self. Wait for a vision. It may occur by being attentive to signs from nature. Ponder their meaning, using some of the tips in the next section. Before leaving the wilderness, ceremoniously deconstruct the ring, leaving no trace of your time alone in the wilderness. Remaining alone is a test, the passage of which is a confirmation of one's success and emancipation at the threshing-hold. All rites of passage involve a test. This trial is done so that the initiate can prove to herself and others that she is willing, able, and entitled to cross the threshold to a new life and the fullness of new power. Crossing the threshold alone during a vision quest can be daunting and often it is very emotional. Allow yourself to be emotional, if even silently to yourself. The Absolute Spirit (God) will hear your cries and understand. Presumably, the Absolute Spirit or God was the one who sent you over the threshold.

Stage Four: Return

Reborn, you return and rejoin your community. Now is the time to incorporate the insights you received in the wilderness into your life. Explore your vision more deeply. Then, once you have determined how to make your insights useful and practical, share your gift with your people. Offer to those in your community a physical gift to symbolize the inner spiritual gift revealed to you on your trip. Together with those in your tribe, eat; clean your clothing, camping equipment, and living quarters; and bathe. Change back into city clothes. Seek the support of others as you attempt to avoid the negative temptations of city life and modernity. Failing to receive the support of others, yield to temptations and become satiated. That too is a sound way to get rid of enticements. Once you have your fill make your way home. Never drink and drive.

Stage Five: Implementation

Demonstrate what you have received as you crossed the threshold in the wilderness through changes in behavior and action. Take on a personal or community project, while enlisting the help of others.

Undergoing such a rite of passage involving a wilderness trip strengthens many aspects of one's life: it fortifies one's body, bolsters one's ability to relax, strengthens one's ability to self-regulate body and mind, builds up one's self-esteem, intensifies one's sense that one's behavior influences outcomes, increases one's hardiness, props up one's fascination with nature, boosts one's sense that the world is meaningful and connected, supports one's ability to handle stress, underpins one's ability to maintain present-centered involvement, shores up one's ability to trust, builds one's sense of community, redoubles one's ability to handle new social roles, buttresses one's ability to bond socially, augments one's ability to experience moments of transcendent joy; steps up one's ability to appreciate nature, cranks up one's ability to achieve inner peace and harmony; and beefs up one's sense that the world is alive. This strengthened sense of the aliveness of the world reveals that one's place is whole, enchanted, and meaningful.

If there are others who have also undergone solitary wilderness rites of passage in your group, before splitting up: play music together, eat together, conduct ceremonies marking the giving away of outmoded behaviors or images of self, together say good-bye to the wilderness, and around a campfire burn symbols of the life you each are leaving behind. Sleep as a group in base camp. Then return to a new life the next day.

The personal benefits of spending time in wilderness come from its beauty. I am speaking only in part of its physical beauty. The other beautiful aspect of spending time alone in nature has to do with the root of the word wilderness—will. Wilderness is a place to experience the beauty of willfulness—the circumstance of being beyond the control of others, away from external authority, and away from unnecessary rules.

In addition to experiencing outer world wild beauty, a person spending time purposefully alone during a wilderness trip also experiences some inner world beauties: such as, deep insights into their own true nature, the purpose of their own life, and a psychic transition into a new phase of their own life—a phase that is more respectful of the interconnectedness of all life. A person receiving such "affordances" on a vision quest (described more fully in the next section of this lesson) usually finds the wilderness to be much more than just bugs, rocks, plants, and physical scenery out-of-doors. Instead, the wilderness becomes animated with a Guiding Spirit. It becomes extra-ordinary.

When one turns to the extraordinary wilderness for personal renewal one finds a teacher and Sb healer that is refreshingly impartial to human affairs, disinterested, unattached, still, and silent. These may not seem at first to be useful qualities for a teacher or healer, but they are sometimes exactly what one needs. The land, perhaps the very soil or humus itself, seems to be exactly what one sometimes needs to find guidance, enlightenment, balance, or serenity.

There is a great payoff when one turns inward toward the Source to see beyond the surface of things. This payoff stems from finding one's relationship with wildness. This relationship provides a frame of reference that produces modesty. It also gives one a sense of awe and respect for the beauty, immenseness, and variety of all life.

Sometimes one needs to awaken one's heart to profound unity, seek guidance for passages in life, find inspiration, achieve renewal, view the sacred, receive deep insight, find the purpose of one's life, acquire a deep respect for ecological wholeness, reconnect with Spirit, and find humility and reverence. One way to satisfy these needs is to . . .

Prepare For A Vision Quest

"Questers" go to the wilderness with water, a sleeping bag, a small amount of food, and a limited amount of clothing—no more than is necessary for survival. To aid with settling down and becoming integrated or "one" with a site, "questers" eventually confine their movements to a spot no larger than a circle with a diameter of about 100 yards. The duration of the stay in a wilderness area while doing a vision quest is usually between three and seven days. This period is necessary to allow for a few days of purification (the elimination of the "emotional baggage" that most of us carry around as a result of living in a culture), a few days of bliss (the opening of the heart), and a few days of integration (becoming one with a wilderness site).

Getting rid of "emotional baggage" is the impetus for going on a vision quest. Usually, this push comes after one realizes how much craziness one has in one's own life, how much stress one endures, and how much resources have to be devoted to materialism.

For every inner world and outer world act that leads towards the initiation of a vision quest there is an opposite and equal reaction against such a trial. People resist going on vision quests because they do not want to take the time, they fear they will be uncomfortable or lonely, they fear the possibility of "a dark night of the Soul," and they fear how they will be changed by the experience. It takes the power of one's will—the subject of a subsequent Heartwood Path Course called **Volitos**—to thrust one out of inaction and to overcome such apprehensions.

Despite these trepidations, people who do overcome their fears and engage in a vision quest usually find bliss and a sense of wanting to share their newly found sense of purpose or message with others after they return. Before, during, and after one's vision quest or purposeful time in wilderness, heightened perceptive abilities will be useful.

To improve your perception while on the vision quest, emulate the way certain animals distinguish things in their environment. Use, for example:

1. mouse perception: a mouse attends to things nearby. Like a mouse, observe details.
2. eagle perception: an eagle has fantastic vision, capable of spotting prey from great heights. It can also use its lofty perspective to see the wholeness of the scene, and it seems to do so with courage and sense of purpose.
3. horse perception: horses can see life through a wide-angle lens. As mentioned earlier, they have exceptional peripheral vision. Or
4. owl perception: owls have extra bones in their neck that allow them to move their heads in large arcs from side to side. Like an owl, scan the scene in front of you from side to side.

These ways to perceive will make your vision quest more fruitful. Here are some other valuable tips: Let someone know your choice of a remote wilderness area for your vision quest and tell them when they can expect you to return. Bring along proper clothing and camping equipment—only the bare necessities. Although it is wise to establish a method of leaving messages for someone to check to make sure you are not in trouble, go to the wilderness by yourself. If you do leave messages for someone, make sure the recipient remains unseen by you when she checks on you. Find a spot that appeals to you, sit there quietly, review the life you left behind, and confront any feelings of fear and anxiety about undertaking the vision quest. Remind yourself that you are undertaking a heroic spiritual ordeal. Ready yourself to physically survive with minimal provisions. Remain at your spot for three, four, or—preferably—7 days. Eat small amounts or fast only on water to empty the body while you cleanse and fill yourself with Spirit. Do not take any drugs beyond those necessary for your health. If you desire to alter your consciousness bring along a small drum and create a soft, simple, and lightly monotonous beat. As you begin to lose your physical strength you will psychologically enter what is known as "the Great Mother's sacred cathedral"—the confrontation of solitude so profound that the absence of civilized things creates a feeling of emptiness. Entering into a "dark night of your soul" is normal and to be expected—although it is not necessary. Once you feel empty in the belly and lonely in your heart, you are ready to seek a vision. Stop playing the drum and stop making any unnecessary movements. Be reflective as you sit or lay down. Collect small items that seem to have some meaning to you and place them in a pouch. In doing so, you are creating a medicine bundle. The feathers, stones, and bones you collect are the embodiment of the healing power to be found on a vision quest. Be earnest in your seeking and wait for the coming of greater wisdom. Once you have received your vision—which may come as a thought or from your interpretation of a sign from nature—return to the civilized world. Write down the message you received in the wilderness, describe all feelings—including any fear, loneliness, anxiety, hunger trepidation, and elation.

I have done many vision quests and have found them to be some of the most transformative experiences of my life. During these times I am typically alone except for the companionship of non-human living beings such as river otters. I remember these times as wonder-full days and nights immersed in caves, canyons, riverbanks, deep forests, hill prairies, and secluded island beaches. While usually occurring in a single, solitary, and beautiful natural place, some of my vision quests have occurred on long, lonely canoe trips on big rivers or in old, abandoned houses occupied only by me and some assorted wild animals. The messages I receive on these quests, when finally gathered in a comprehensible manner, come to me as physical signs and symbols that are delivered from messengers from the Absolute Spirit. These messengers take on the form of wind, animals, and various happenings or findings in nature.

Vision quests are not the only way to receive direction and inspiration. Now that enough of my *striving* has been replaced with *arriving*, similar messages from the Absolute Spirit seem to come from a person, my "Maiden of the Forest," who is often with me in my everyday physical life and always with me in my inner life. Much of the wisdom of this book comes from my interactions with her.

To A New You...

HumaNatureConnect Activity

Start-up Protocol

If this is not a day when you prefer to spend time in nature without an agenda, do the Heartwood Path Start-up Protocol found in the Appendix.

Going On A Vision Quest

Let someone know your choice of a remote wilderness area for your vision quest and tell them when they can expect you to return. Bring along proper clothing and camping equipment—only the bare necessities. Although it is wise to establish a method of leaving messages for someone to check to make sure you are not in trouble, go to the wilderness by yourself. If you do leave messages for someone, make sure they remain unseen by you when they check on you. Find a spot that appeals to you, sit there quietly, review the life you left behind, and confront any feelings of fear and anxiety about undertaking the vision quest. Remind yourself that you are undertaking a heroic spiritual ordeal. Ready yourself to physically survive with minimal provisions. Remain at your spot for three, four, or—preferably—7 days. Eat small amounts or fast only on water to empty the body while you cleanse and fill the spirit. Do not take any drugs beyond those necessary for your health. If you desire to alter your consciousness bring along a small drum and create a soft, simple, and lightly monotonous beat. As you begin to lose your physical strength you will psychologically enter what is known as "the Great Mother's sacred cathedral"—the confrontation of solitude so profound that the absence of civilized things creates a feeling of emptiness. Entering into a "dark night of your soul" is normal and to be expected—although it is not necessary. Once you feel empty in the belly and lonely in your heart, you are ready to seek a vision. Stop playing the drum or making any unnecessary movements. Be reflective as you sit or lay down. Collect small items that seem to have some meaning to you and place them in a pouch. In doing so, you are creating a medicine bundle. The feathers, stones, and bones you collect are the embodiment of the healing power to be found on a vision quest. Be earnest in your seeking and wait for the coming of greater wisdom. Once you have received your vision—which may come as a thought or from your interpretation of a sign from nature—find an attractive natural being, see if it retains its attractiveness for at least ten seconds, and, if it remains attractive, assume that this is a sign that you have the natural being's consent to use it in this activity. While admiring your chosen natural being, appreciate it with your inhalations and give it gratitude with your exhalations. Doing so will give you the optimal functioning that will be helpful as you do this activity. After obtaining your chosen natural being's consent and setting up your optimal functioning, wait (perhaps for days) and then write down the messages you received, describing all feelings—possibly fear, loneliness, anxiety, hunger, trepidation, and elation.

Follow-up Protocol

For best results, write down your impressions of this activity in your journal using the Heartwood Path Follow-up Protocol found in the Appendix. Afterwards, consider sharing your interpretations with others.

Heartwood Path Axioms

Key Assertions From Waypoint 4.57

4.57.1.

Learn about your Greater Self and develop a new you on a vision quest.

4.57.2.

There are five stages of a purposeful rite of passage wilderness trip: 1) preparation, 2) letting go of your old self, 3) revealing the living seed of a new life, 4) rejoin your community, and 5) taking on a project, while enlisting the help of others.

4.57.3.

The wilderness is a relentless teacher that helps one let go of outdated self-images, including the notion that one has nothing to offer to the world.

4.57.4.

To improve your perception while on the vision quest, emulate the way certain animals distinguish things in their environment. Use, for example:

1. mouse perception: a mouse attends to things nearby.

2. eagle perception: an eagle has fantastic vision, capable of spotting prey from great heights.

3. horse perception: horses can see life through a wide-angle lens. And

4. owl perception: like an owl, scan the scene in front of you from side to side.

Nocturnal Pilgrimage 4.57

For best results, write down your impressions of each night's dreams in your journal using the Heartwood Path Dreaming Time Protocols found in the Appendix. Afterwards, consider sharing your Dream Tending with others.

"We become disinhibited by night . . . There are things we do under the cover of darkness that we suspect even angels cannot see" (Naiman, 2006, p. 162).

With Naiman's words and the latest lesson in mind as you head to bed, sleep and dream. Tend to your dreams first thing in the morning, before moving in bed.

Pertinent And Instructive Gems From My Dream Tending Journal

I dreamt I was getting to know a rose in three ways:

First, in the poetry of Robert Frost:

"The rose is a rose,

And was always a rose.

But the theory now goes

That the apple's a rose,

And the pear is, and so's

The plum, I suppose.

The dear only knows

What will next prove a rose.

You, of course, are a rose -

But were always a rose."

Hmmm? Maybe taxonomy will be more instructive.

Here's something like what a taxonomy book would say about the rose's characteristic morphological features: generally woody plants, mostly shrubs or small to medium-size trees, some of which are armed with thorns, spines, or prickles to discourage herbivores. The genus Rubus (blackberries, raspberries, and brambles) chiefly contains arching shrubs or scramblers of irregular, often tangled appearance. Most members of Rosaceae have alternate leaves, with opposite leaves being found in a very few species. Small leaflike structures called stipules are routinely present at the base of the leaf stalks.

Hmmm? Maybe my own experiences will speak to me with more impact:

"Look Nana." I said,

"I've got a whole handful of blackberries."

"Here Donnie," she replied,

"Fill this stainless steel bowl and I'll use the berries to make a cobbler."

Picking the blackberries (a member of the rose family), helping make the cobbler, and eating what has become my favorite desert (because of the taste and the memory) is how I first experienced the rose family. Bringing in freshly cut roses from my Victorian garden, and recognizing that the ritual of giving flowers stems from their beauty, their short-term loveliness, and

the need to repeat the gift-giving as an act of devotion, was my second vivid
experience of roses.

Lesson Learned: The ultimate goal of knowledge is not only served by poetic words nor scientific words. Reason and logic, plus book-learning and taxonomy labs bring you knowledge. But, equally powerful, equally valid, and equally important in one's quest for knowledge is one's own experience.

At the next waypoint, you will make another step to reverse any narrowing of your focus that has stunted your consciousness as a result of spending so much time in the less-than-ideal stimulation of the indoor world. As suggested there, do the activity outdoors so that you expose yourself to the greater, more expansive realm of life found away from electrical sockets. Pay attention to the way your ability to feel expands as you spend time, day after day, communing consciously with nature outdoors. When you are ready, move to the next waypoint: "Make Common Cause."

58

Make Common Cause

ALIGN ONE'S SELF WITH NATURE

Since the world is not just a collection of things but also a dynamic network of relationships bound together by communication what we do to ourselves we do to the environment, and vice versa. Man is a part of nature, and every man has his own nature. Both evolved together, and Man and nature are always in contact.

Be In Conscious Contact With The Natural World

If we are to have tolerable lives on a tolerable planet we simply have to develop better health through more intimate contact with the natural world. Like the native plants in one's own nearby environment, a person's visceral wisdom—that which emanates from deep within— ought to be grounded as if it grew up from the local soil. Without this grounding, a person will be swept around by the winds of prevailing sentiments, fads, and whims. When attitudes are internalized and held in harmony with one's home, health and a sense of peace will prevail.

Find Out How You Are Inhibited And Wounded

Uninhibited drives do not threaten us as much as those that are inhibited and wounded. The suppression of our basic instincts plus the gradual erosion in the quality of the nearby environment cause untold pain. It is "untold" largely because both the suppression of instincts and the erosion of the quality of life are often subtle, slow, and unnoticed in the day-to-day affairs of most people.

Develop Parent-like Sensitivity

What is needed is a way for humans to relearn sensitivity regarding their local environment—the same kind of sensitivity that enables a good parent to sense the emotional state of an offspring. A good formula for self-development needs to be broadcast to as many people as possible. The process of self-development for eartHearts includes at least the following three components: 1) develop your mind, 2) visualize your future, and 3) align your Self with humaNature.

Much has been expressed in this series of books about the first two components. More needs to be said about the third, however. The concept of aligning oneself with nature is alien to most people in modern, rational, mechanized society whose chief contact with nature is mowing the grass.

One result of this alienation is anger—the kind that builds whenever one denies a basic part of one's Self. Eventually the anger that inevitably comes from alienating oneself from nature turns into psychosomatic illness and/or aggression.

Find Antidotes To Alienation

One of the best antidotes for alienation and anger is to go to the wilderness. Doing so helps one overcome some of the core problems one faces as a member of the human species. These problems include:

1. a lost sense of ecological belongingness;
2. an overemphasis on survival and materialism at the expense of *sacredness* (by "sacredness" I mean that which has a value beyond its usefulness to human ends and is a standard by which all our purposes are judged);
3. our inability to embrace paradox and overcome dualistic thinking; and
4. living in a culture that does not cherish diversity beyond lip-service.

Open Up Your Senses

Concerning one's lost sense of ecological belongingness, wilderness experiences open up one's senses in a way that helps one feel more embedded in the wild. This opening occurs as one sits around the night's campfire, dreams more vivid dreams in one's sleeping bag beneath the stars, thinks clearer thoughts as one walks along the trails, and finds peace and surprise amongst the greenery.

Span The Poles Of Survival And Sacredness

Going to the wilderness provides a place to experience the useful polar tension between the survival pole and the sacred pole. The survival pole includes all the mundane things, such as: soggy belongings in the rain; heavy backpacks to be carried; charred pots to be cleaned; chapped lips to be soothed; and all occurrences that threaten one's comfort and safety, including, tipped canoes, close-encounters with bears, rainstorms, and inadequate supplies of water. The sacred pole includes everything that brings one to a state of awe and joy, including: dancing in the fog, singing in the sunshine, praying beneath the moon, pausing to take in a beautiful panoramic view, safe-encounters with bears, and viewing other inspiring wildlife.

Look Beyond The Obvious

Continuing with the dualisms mentioned above, wilderness experiences show that there is paradox yet wholeness: dead trees, for example, provide habitat for woodpeckers and fertilizer for the growth of new plants; animals kill to stay alive; poison ivy is a pest species but it may also be a way to keep people from loving the woods to death.

Glean Lessons In The Wilderness And Carry Them Back To Town

Concerning the diversity mentioned above, wilderness experiences show one that the myriad of forms has a purpose, a beauty, and a place in the overall scheme of things. Nature produces individual diversity— no two days, no two snow flakes, no two flowers are ever the same. There are obvious lessons to be found in wilderness concerning the abundance of variety. Except for the shallowly developed human invader, there is no apparent judge nor discriminator. Everyone is equal in the woods. In wildness the person who drove there in a Porsche is equal to a person who drove there in a Volkswagen. All that matters for a person on a wilderness adventure is that person's knowledge, skill, experience, stamina, and ability. Such lessons can be carried back to the civilized world and applied to one's views on race, class, age, gender and to the way contemporary industry and agriculture makes things uniform, standardized, and monotonous.

Use Wilderness Trips As A Way To Learn To Simplify One's Life And To Limit One's Possessions

Wilderness begins to affect us as soon as we plan to go there. We need to be careful as we decide what to take with us to the wilderness and what to leave behind. Often, the things we bring along tend to dilute our direct experience with nature. In making the decisions about

what to bring we begin to see what we truly need. Wilderness expeditions help us to begin to define what things in our lives are trappings
rather than necessities. We learn how to simplify our lives.

Use Wilderness Trips For Expansion And Reconnection

Wilderness trips can be done alone or in a group, preferably not
too large. Groups organized to go to the wilderness for therapeutic
purposes are springing up throughout the country. On such trips a
person might take part in a number of therapeutic activities, including:
organized "alone time" lasting three or more days; all-night chanting
and/or drumming rituals, climbs to peaks at sunrise or sunset; hikes or
climbs in silence; separate camps for men and women, and ritualized
ways of coming back together. Those who attend such trips often speak
of feelings of expansion or reconnection—meaning expansion of the
self and the reconnection of the self with processes and things that are
natural: including death, fear, violence, beauty, elegance, wonder, and
balance. A feeling of the release of repression is also common.

Use Wilderness Trips As A Way To Alleviate Addictions And To Expand Awareness, Feeling, Engagement, And The Vivid- ness Of Dreams

Wilderness trips, because they offer a chance to see beauty, wholeness, and the alternative to an artificial world, usually instill upon the
participants a sense of awareness about the world and its problems.
Wilderness trips promote an ability to feel and to engage rather than
to become dumb and numb regarding the plight of nature. My own
years of taking hundreds of people on extended wilderness trips indicates that the impact of the experience, not unlike the twelve-step
process for those in recovery from alcohol, is like a multistep process
for those in recovery from civilization. Almost all people experience an
increased sense of aliveness, well-being, and energy. Many people claim

the wilderness experience helped them break an addiction (nicotine, chocolate, and unhealthy foods). Roughly half of the people described a major life change upon return (in personal relationships, employment, housing, or life-style). Most people feel that the alone time in the wilderness—perhaps hiking up to the peak before dawn or canoeing alone—followed by the fellowship of the group were the most important experiences. Roughly two-thirds of all respondents reported dramatic changes in quantity, vividness and context of dreams after seventy-two hours of entering the wilderness—most saying that the content of their dreams shifted from busy, urban settings to dreams about others in the group or about the wilderness itself.

Make Your Time In Wilderness Last Not For Hours But For Days

These statements about the contents of dreams, my own personal reactions to extended wilderness experiences, and my observation of the moods and behaviors of people on extended wilderness trips—moods that gradually shift from hyped-up to relaxed, from "goal-oriented" to "go-with-the-flow oriented," and from "future-oriented" to "present-oriented"—leads me to question the stability of modern civilization. Without the influence that comes with daily exposure to civilization, I figure its psychological grip on wilderness travelers lasts about four days. After that, without constant exposure to civilization, we would naturally return to more wild and healthful ways.

Sometime during the first four days in the wilderness a period of depression and boredom usually occurs as the romanticized idea of being in nature is worn down. Wilderness trip organizers call this brief period the "midcourse blues." Once this period is over, wilderness trip participants usually perk up and shift from feeling like a visitor to feeling at home in wild nature. How quickly we return to our Second Mother!

How painful it is to feel the effects of wilderness slip away when we return to civilization! In wilderness we become open and connected; upon our return we cringe as, inevitably, our being hardens again.

I am remembering a wonderful backpack trip I helped to lead through the Sky Lakes Wilderness in Oregon. There was considerable grumbling for the first two days. Shoes were too tight for Laura, backpacks were too heavy for Ginny, and the terrain was too rough for Melissa. Many of the backpackers became crabby and depressed. Then, after a brief rainstorm and a nice time camping by a lake, the mood quickly lifted. There was joking, frivolity, and wallowing in the beauty of the place. Somehow the same shoes fit fine, the backpacks no longer hurt the carrier's shoulders, the same rocky trail was no longer a problem. The hikers' attention seemed to have shifted from themselves alone to themselves in the landscape. We had found the peace of nature. All seemed right in the world. Then, we returned to civilization and the contrast was jarring: we were barraged with loud cars, rude waitresses, and bad news: Lady Diana had died. If I knew then what I know now, I would have encouraged my backpacking buddies to follow me to the creek that ran through the town. We each would have found an attractive natural being. Communing with these beings would have reminded us that we can return to the peace of nature at just about any place. All we would have had to do is follow our natural being attractions. Instead we went to the airport . . .

To A Better You...

HumaNatureConnect Activity

Start-up Protocol

If this is not a day when you prefer to spend time in nature without an agenda, do the Heartwood Path Start-up Protocol found in the Appendix.

Aligning Oneself With Nature

Use any of the natural senses to align yourself with nature. Physically go a natural area. Place yourself in a natural place that is attractive to you. Hum a note that conveys emphatic resonance between you and this place. Look within and identify any woundedness. Hum the tone of this woundedness. Hum the tone of one of your survival needs and one that resonates with any sense of awe or joy. Wait in stillness in the natural area until you receive a lesson from nature. Hum that lesson. Psychologically, expand your sense of self to include nature and then make a resonate sound that expresses that expansion and reconnection.

Follow-up Protocol

For best results, write down your impressions of this activity in your journal using the Heartwood Path Follow-up Protocol found in the Appendix. Afterwards, consider sharing your interpretations with others.

Heartwood Path Axioms

Key Assertions From Waypoint 4.58

4.58.1.

Uninhibited drives do not threaten us as much as those that are inhibited and wounded.

4.58.2.

Going to a wilderness area helps one overcome some of the core problems one faces as a member of the human species, including: a lost sense of ecological belongingness, an overemphasis on

survival and materialism at the expense of sacredness, our inability to embrace paradox and overcome dualistic thinking, and living in a culture that does not cherish diversity beyond lip-service.

4.58.3.

Wilderness expeditions help us to begin to define what things in our lives are trappings rather than necessities.

4.58.4.

On wilderness trips a person might take part in a number of therapeutic activities, including: organized "alone time" lasting three or more days; all-night chanting and/or drumming rituals, climbs to peaks at sunrise or sunset; hikes or climbs in silence; and separate camps for men and women, with ritualized ways of coming back together.

Nocturnal Pilgrimage 4.58

For best results, write down your impressions of each night's dreams in your journal using the Heartwood Path Dreaming Time Protocols found in the Appendix. Afterwards, consider sharing your Dream Tending with others.

" . . . the social expectations of day tell us how we (ought to) be, night reveals all of who we really are" (Naiman, 2006, p. 162).

With Naiman's statement and today's lesson in mind as you drift off for the night, sleep and dream. As soon as you begin to wake up, tend to your dreams.

Pertinent And Instructive Gems From My Dream Tending Journal

I dreamt I was walking along a wilderness trail with my beloved. Suddenly I left my body and entered hers. Through her eyes I looked back at myself. It felt refreshing to see with a new perspective. It felt spacious, bright, and calming to look out from inside of my beloved. My breathing became easier. I saw myself and her in a different light.

Lesson Learned: The *looking back* at yourself in my dream is reminiscent of the *looking back* activities so important to the achievement of happiness in a sustainable world. Try a version of it now. Place yourself psychologically inside another person or inside of a natural being. Notice how your former body looks from your new perspective. Talk to your old self. Has the new you that is looking out stopped being an object? Did your girlfriend or that Boulder in the park cease to be an object? Psychologically move back inside of your own body. Has your impression of your girlfriend or the Boulder in the park changed? Has any person you visited changed? Or is it your feelings and perceptions that have changed? Describe your impressions as you move psychologically inside another being and then back again inside yourself.

At the next waypoint you will learn to perceive nature's connections. This learning can only occur fully if you go outside, as instructed, and let wild nature show you its relationships.

To help encourage you to move away from your electronic screens and to go outside regularly for the purpose of communing with nature, know this: throughout the 20th Century, IQ levels in the developing nations rose about three to five points per decade, until the 1990s and 2000s—the dawn of the prevalence of screen-based electronic gadgets —when a decade of gains were wiped out between 1998 and 2004. The act of checking emails and texting temporarily removes IQ points and lowers creativity. The interruptions caused by checking emails and texting are very distracting. By the way, the incidence of ADHD in children is skyrocketing (Selhub &Logan, 2012, p. 41.42). For earth's sake, put limits on the use of your iGadgets. And use the time you save to do HumaNatureConnect Activities outdoors.

You are becoming more interesting as you continue to add depth to your sense of self. When ready, continue to the next teaching: "Open & Connected."

59

Open & Connected

PERCEIVE NATURE'S CIRCUMSTANCES

It does not feel very good to have a sense of disconnection from family, friends, the Absolute Spirit, or nature. One quickly sinks into one's own psychological package. The bundle of one's own individual self can be restricting and pungent. Without some relief, it gets pretty stinky in there real fast. Perceiving nature's circumstances, the way it is nearby, freshens one's sense of self, lightens one's mood, and expands one's outlook sufficiently to find the joy of helping others. It is not hard to bust out of your own psychological container. All you have to do is engage in the six perceptual practices relevant for perceiving ecological conditions:

One: Learning To Attend

As the flip side to psychic numbing, attending is the enhancement of selected sensory information. This extra focus produces a richness of color, a depth of sensory experience, and often means the difference between seeing and not seeing. All attending is a learned endeavor. With practice, one learns to see certain things easier, and in so doing physically alters the neural pathways to the brain. Once the eye to brain pathway is strengthened in this manner, all related synapses require a lower threshold of energy to fire. In short, one learns how to see certain chosen objects (beings), one unknowingly creates improved neurotransmitters in one's brain for the processing of these sightings, and one, therefore, obtains improved eye-brain coordination, making it easier in the future to see and "process" the chosen visual information.

Two: Perceiving The Relations

Those of us who live in affluent Western democracies live in a largely materialist culture. As a consequence, we easily see *things* but we are relatively blind to the *relationships* between things. Seeing the relations requires two things: 1) time to observe; and 2) attention (noticing contrast; investigating the interface between things; and contemplation of the qualities of color, curvature, texture, and juxtaposition of forms).

Three: Adding Context And Processes To One's Perception Of Material Objects

Doing so adds depth and meaning to one's perceptions. With this depth and meaning the sensory world becomes vital. The world becomes directly embodied in one's Self as a sweet and unmistakable resonance. One's heart is moved. Subjective experience becomes sensuality. As one falls in love with another person or place, one sees with the improved eyes of a lover.

Four: Maintaining Flexibility Of Perception

This skill requires a fluidity of mind in which the magic of the visible world is revealed by giving-up one's expectations. Seeing familiar patterns within the apparent chaos, allowing a new image to emerge through the rearrangement of pieces, and altering one's perception of time (for example, from the scheduled, urban tick-tock time of the human self to the life of an oak tree as a unit of measurement or point of reference) are all examples of perceptual flexibility.

Five: Perceiving Depth

This ecological way of perceiving is not a change in visual habits but is a modification of one's worldview. One needs to see not only the surfaces of things but also how these things are levels of organization associated within a larger system. One often neglects to see ecologically because of one's worldview, which is ruled by two masters: 1) culture and 2) one's neurological processes. Our culture has largely eclipsed our view of wild nature, providing us with controlled and limited views and leaving us with a "second nature" or a "surrogate environment" that is visible in little doses (such as when we visit a wildlife park, watch a nature show on the television, have suburban wildlife experiences, and view scenery from inside air-conditioned cars).

Everyone's nervous system constructs models of the world. These models—or world views—affect the person, the environment, and the culture. Make sure yours have an extra measure of depth, one that includes the physical, the ecological, the theological, and the Spirit.

Six: Using The Imagination

This way of discerning involves talking to oneself and allowing a sensual response that comes from recognizing one's *being with*. This recognition occurs in the Realm of Interiority, but it is always affected by exterior reality—air, water, land, wildlife, the Earth. This way of perceiving places one within the biosphere rather than on a planet. One's own embodiment is perceived as internal to, and wholly dependent upon, the larger body of the earth. With this view, it is easy to see how personal survival is dependent upon the ecological integrity of the

Earth. This way of perceiving ecologically involves visual imagery that affects one's invented worldview. Images serve as guides for the thousands of unconscious decisions one makes; and these guiding images—these mental pictures—inform one of one's own previously determined desires and priorities—one's own imagination. In this way, imagination affects the future of the world.

Put the wisdom found in this section to work for you by doing the next exercise.

To A Happier You...

HumaNatureConnect Activity

Start-up Protocol

If this is not a day when you prefer to spend time in nature without an agenda, do the Heartwood Path Start-up Protocol found in the Appendix.

Doing A Sunshine Face Wash

Stand quietly, and with eyes closed, turn your face to the sun and feel the warmth. Then, hold both hands out front, palms outward, to block the sunlight from your eyes. Feel the darkness and the shadow. Feel the chill as opposed to the warm rays of the sun. Then, slowly slide your hands about, maybe even in a paddle wheel manner, so that the sun's rays are alternately on your face and then blocked out. Feel the energy of the sun. Then drop arms to your sides and give yourself a brief sunshine face wash while massaging forehead, cheeks, chin, lips and eye sockets.

Follow-up Protocol

For best results, write down your impressions of this activity in your journal using the Heartwood Path Follow-up Protocol found in the Appendix. Afterwards, consider sharing your interpretations with others.

Heartwood Path Axioms

Key Assertions From Waypoint 4.59

4.59.1.

Engage in the six perceptual practices relevant for perceiving ecological conditions: 1) learning to attend; 2) perceiving the relations; 3) adding context and processes to one's perception of material objects; 4) maintaining flexibility of perception; 5) perceiving depth; and 6) using the imagination.

4.59.2.

Through perceiving ecological conditions, it is easy to see how personal survival is dependent upon the ecological integrity of the earth.

Nocturnal Pilgrimage 4.59

For best results, write down your impressions of each night's dreams in your journal using the Heartwood Path Dreaming Time Protocols found in the Appendix. Afterwards, consider sharing your Dream Tending with others.

"In lieu of honest contact with night, we remain glued to electronically reconstituted images of day" (Naiman, 2006, p. 168).

With the value of darkness and today's lesson in mind, sleep and dream. Tend to your dreams. Then you are ready for the next teaching.

Pertinent And Instructive Gems From My Dream Tending Journal

I dreamt that I kept answering my beloved's questions before she finished asking them. I was always wrong.

Lesson Learned: Always allow for a moment of open-endedness. Simple "yes's" or "no's" cut the energy out of the dialogue. Without a sufficient pause in a conversation there is no adequate listening. In that pause is a key to yourself. It is also a key to healing.

Squelch any feelings that you are being irresponsible for spending so much time in nature, as you are asked to do with each activity of this book series. You will not be asked to behave harmfully to yourself or others. You will not be asked to give up your goals or aspirations. Your education and good manners will remain with you.

You may, however, feel compelled to discard some preconceived notions about your place in the universe. You will be encouraged to question what you are to do to live more ethically. When you go outside to do the activities you will begin to see more fellow beings in nature. You will begin to accept their guidance. And you will feel more vividly the sacredness of life.

Keep recalling your ecological self by continuing to move down the Heartwood Path. When you are ready, head to the next waypoint: "Nix The TV."

60

Nix The TV

LIMIT THE USE OF TELEVISION

Unfortunately, the ever-present television, which creates a prevalence of psychic numbing and the widespread sense of dis-empowerment, serves to diminish or replace images spontaneously generated from our vastly creative "imaginal" selves. After years of watching fast-clipped television, most people now have nervous systems that mentally and sensually separate them from the real world that moves at a pace that is now too slow for most people to perceive or tolerate. We are being programmed to be tense, to move swiftly, and to react fast. We are losing our ability to experience real-world pleasure, to remain calm, to contemplate, and to understand depth. Television plays a role in these losses.

Retired advertising executive Jerry Mander offers four arguments for the elimination of television:

1. that it is part of a long underway process "which has successfully redirected and confined human experience and therefore knowledge and perceived reality" and boxed " people into a physical and mental condition appropriate for the emergence of autocratic control;"

463

2. that television is used "by the powers-that-be" and allows for "no other controllers;"
3. that television has effects on the human mind "which fit the purposes of the people who control the medium;" and
4. that it drastically confines "all human understanding within a rigid channel" (Mander, 1979).

To reverse these affects of television we need to turn it off and, with the help of the suggestions that follow, move away from it. In this way, we can recover our relinquished ability to imagine for ourselves again. We need to find waves crashing on a deserted beach. We need to find a smooth stone next to a cool bed of moss. We need to find a warm sandbar along a cool river. In such places and many more, we need to practice imagining regularly. Go ahead: daydream a lot. Such practice will bring back clear, vivid, colorful, and emotionally provocative visions. These images will become psychological energy that can be used to guide one's choices and to help one create the positive world in which one wishes to live.

To The End Of The Boob Tube...

HumaNatureConnect Activity

Start-up Protocol

If this is not a day when you prefer to spend time in nature without an agenda, do the Heartwood Path Start-up Protocol found in the Appendix.

Limiting Your Use Of Television

Use any one of the fifty-four natural senses to help you limit your use of television. In this example, I encourage you to consider using the feeling sense of space or proximity sense to limit your use of television.

Make a plan to lower your screen time and raise your green time. Put more space between you and your television. Change your proximity to your television by removing it from the room in which you want to spend quality time. Make a plan to spend less time watching unrewarding television shows and more time outside in nature. One way to do this is to establish a preset schedule that limits television usage and expands time outdoors. Consider which television programs you really want to watch ahead of time and, if necessary, record them so that you can watch them when they will not interfere with your outdoor time. Or just watch your shows on your computer whenever doing so is not a distraction (which, if you are adequately engaging yourself with nature, ought to be a rarity). Move the television away from the bedroom so that viewing does not cause sleeping problems, does not distract from intimacy, and does not take time away from family time. Consider limiting the watching of television to family viewing nights. Move away from the two-dimensional images on your television and toward the three-dimensional world out-of-doors. Plan ways that move you and your family away from the television and toward more creative endeavors such as arts and crafts. Plan how to best move away from the television and toward a good book. Write in your journal all your planned and achieved ways to proximate yourself away from banal television programming and toward the real world of nature.

Follow-up Protocol

For best results, write down your impressions of this activity in your journal using the Heartwood Path Follow-up Protocol found in the Appendix. Afterwards, consider sharing your interpretations with others.

Heartwood Path Axioms

Key Assertions From Waypoint 4.60

4.60.1.

The imposition of television justifies its prohibition:

lower your screen time, raise your green time.

4.60.2.

After years of watching fast-clipped television, most people now have nervous systems that mentally and sensually separate them from the real world that moves at a pace that is now too slow for most people to perceive or tolerate.

4.60.3.

The television redirects and confines human experience, knowledge, and perceived reality to such an extent it creates conditions suitable for manipulation by advertisers and despots.

4.60.4.

The effect television has on the human mind fits the purposes of those in control of the medium.

Nocturnal Pilgrimage 4.60

For best results, write down your impressions of each night's dreams in your journal using the Heartwood Path Dreaming Time Protocols found in the Appendix. Afterwards, consider sharing your Dream Tending with others.

In your lucid dreaming, rather than shun or destroy any encountered demons, ask them to identify themselves, invite them to speak their minds, and listen to them. In doing so you will discover the value of courageous confrontation. With this lesson statement and the previous activity in mind, drift off to sleep. Dream and tend to your dreams.

Pertinent And Instructive Gems From My Dream Tending Journal

I dreamt that I kept answering my beloved's questions after a long period after she asked them. I was always wrong.

Lesson Learned: Often, when no sense can be made from your dreams, it is helpful to reexamine the dream in reverse. Here's an example of some guidance that came by reversing my dream: Just as it is not good to rush to judgement, likewise it is not good to linger too long before delivering your responses. Use this surprise tactic: refrain from undercutting the necessary spontaneity and freshness in the process of dialogue—with everyone, including friends, relatives, and Images. Respond quickly. Certainly in less than a minute. Lingering leads to fantasizing. In your dreams believe in what you see in the first instant. Mulling things over leads to a blurring of the message of the dream. Use your feelings to tap into the heart of the matter. Good dreamers use immediacy as a strategy for transformation.

Follow the instruction to go outside as you begin the next Huma-NatureConnect Activity. Each time you commune with nature you are becoming less domesticated and more free from the harmful restrictions and servitudes of civilization. Unloosen a strand of your cultural dependency by going into the wild to uncover within you the wildness that remains beneath the sophomoric shroud of society.

No matter how cool and enticing it is to use my screen-devices, no matter how much dopamine the stimulation gives me, I, for one, find greater satisfaction away from the virtual world. I may take my iPhone with me to the woods for safety purposes, but I turn it off. While the phone links me to society, the woods connects me to life. Don't let the coldness of virtual reality overtake the warmness of palpable reality. Commune with nature today unshackled from the Internet.

When you are ready, head to the next waypoint: "Metaphysical." There, you will come to understand the transcendent power of nature.

61

Metaphysical

UNDERSTAND THE TRANSCENDENT POWER OF NATURE

Transcendence occurs often in conjunction with ecstatic experiences. Ecstasy, when it does occur, usually happens after contacting something or someone valuable, beautiful, or both. Coming in close contact to beautiful natural scenes is one the most effective ways to inspire transcendence. Often this experience is a feeling of a force beyond oneself that is guiding one to a special time, place, and circumstance.

Ecstasy can be encouraged by letting go of one's rational mind, allowing the emptiness created by this release to be filled with egolessness, naturalness, and timelessness (each described in detail in the Heartwood Path Course: **Eros**). When one lets go a sense of awe and excitement occurs in which things take on a numinous, supernatural, sacred, and holy quality.

As the Ego fades away, space and time slip into a feeling of oneness; by which I mean bliss, wonder, joy, peace, and love. These feelings last for less than a half hour usually, but they are seldom forgotten. Take just one of the above five feelings of oneness—wonder, for example. To come face to face with something mysteriously wonderful is one of the most beautiful experiences a person can have. As the birthplace for both art and science, the feeling of awe and wonder allows one to marvel at the mysterious. This act of marveling brings forth aliveness, motivation, and even religious fervor.

After such experiences one feels a growing perceptual richness to life. One becomes more appreciative of beauty—God's handwriting. Having a greater sense of appreciation for beauty in nature is an enormous source of inner nourishment and replenishment. Beauty stimulates the senses and the intellect, and, when it is really appreciated, can even provide one with a sense of the divine. When sufficiently awestruck by something beautiful in nature a person is often inspired to preserve and protect the environment. The frequency of such experiences goes up as one becomes more self-actualized (or moves up the Branches of Spiritual Development).

To Beauty...

HumaNatureConnect Activity

Start-up Protocol

If this is not a day when you prefer to spend time in nature without an agenda, do the Heartwood Path Start-up Protocol found in the Appendix.

Looking Around You For Beauty

Look around your immediate surroundings and find things you find beautiful. Look for: vivid colors; attractive patterns, shapes, and patinas; and the play of light and dark. Close your eyes and remember what you just saw. Then open your eyes to determine how what you are now seeing compares to your mental image. Practice until your visual memory closely matches the real thing.

Follow-up Protocol

For best results, write down your impressions of this activity in your journal using the Heartwood Path Follow-up Protocol found in the Appendix. Afterwards, consider sharing your interpretations with others.

Heartwood Path Axioms

Key Assertions From Waypoint 4.61

4.61.1.

Coming in close contact with beautiful natural scenes is one the most effective ways to inspire transcendence—often a feeling of a force beyond oneself that is guiding one to a special time and place.

4.61.2.

Ecstasy can be encouraged by letting go of one's rational mind, allowing the emptiness created by this release to be filled with egolessness, naturalness, and timelessness.

4.61.3.

Having a greater sense of appreciation for beauty in nature is an enormous source of inner nourishment and replenishment.

4.61.4.

When sufficiently awestruck by something beautiful in nature a person is often inspired to preserve and protect the environment.

4.61.5.

The frequency of transcendent experiences goes up as one becomes more self-actualized (or moves up the Branches of Spiritual Development).

Nocturnal Pilgrimage 4.61

For best results, write down your impressions of each night's dreams in your journal using the Heartwood Path Dreaming Time Protocols found in the Appendix. Afterwards, consider sharing your Dream Tending with others.

About a decade before the publishing of the Heartwood Path a group of Stanford University physicians raised concern about the dramatic decline in the variation of our experience of the natural environment.

". . . our extensive daytime sheltering from natural light and night-time use of artificial light have reduced the range of our biological functions . . ." (Naiman, 2006, p. 194).

The remedy for this problem is more time in nature.

Ponder this message from Naiman, the solution, and the message of this waypoint as you drift off to sleep. Dream. Tend to your dreams before you get out of bed in the morning.

Pertinent And Instructive Gems From My Dream Tending Journal

I dreamt of my oldest happy memory. It was about me receiving a toy bow and arrow when I was two years old.

Lesson Learned: Looking back at your first happy memory will often show you what fuels your inspiration. It will possibly show you what drives your life. In my case it is a love of the Indigenous, the wild ones, those—humans and non-humans—that came before the advent of Modern Culture. I also remember at that time giving up my pacifier, which I used during my naps, because I was told little Indian boys my age no longer use them.

Use what you learn along the Heartwood Path to restore the ecology of happiness as you make your way to Gladandgreen Junction. It will be helpful to you as you continue on your way to obtain the kinds of perceptions that can only occur if you make repeated changes to your routines. Since most of what you do occurs indoors, go outside, if only to shake things up a bit and to give you a variety of experience.

According to Selhub and Logan, those of us under the influence of daily hassles are less likely to engage in intentional physical activity. What is needed to counter the effects of these hassles is positive emotions and not just the absence of negative emotions (Selhub & Logan, 2012, p. 51). Compared to viewing the world after we have got through with it, viewing a place as it was prior to human habitation by visiting a pristine area goes a long way towards giving us the very positive emotions we need to counter the stresses of modern life.

When you are ready, go to the next waypoint, "Curative," to begin the next teaching. There, you will learn to apply the curative power of nature. You are to be applauded for your progress.

62

Curative

APPLY THE HEALING POWER OF NATURE

Nature is a good healer for a person when that individual leaves behind the demands of modern society; when that individual steps into natural settings where schedules can be forgotten; when that individual vents negative feelings; when that individual allows intuition to bring one into harmony with natural rhythms and instinctual desires; and when that individual eats natural, organic foods.

You will be more receptive to nature's healing powers when you have more knowledge about your environment. Learning about your knowledge deficits is your first step to improving your receptivity of nature's healing power. To determine your level of nature awareness do the following activity:

To Gauge Why You Are Keen On Nature's Curative Capability...

HumaNatureConnect Activity

Start-up Protocol

If this is not a day when you prefer to spend time in nature without an agenda, do the Heartwood Path Start-up Protocol found in the Appendix.

Applying The Healing Power Of Nature

Answer the following questions, noting the questions that you cannot answer:

1. When is the next solstice?

2. When is the next equinox?

3. Which animals in your area hibernate?

4. Where does your water come from?

5. Where does your water go when it leaves your house?

6. Where does your trash go?

7. What is the frost date in your area: the date it is safe to plant a garden without worrying about frost damage?

8. How can you recycle newspapers, cans, and glass?

9. How can you reduce your use of phosphates, scouring powder, bleach, water, fresheners, and garden chemicals?

10. To help cut down on water pollution, are you willing to (indicate with a "Y" or a "N"):

   ○ turn off faucet when brushing your teeth?_____,
   ○ use dishwashing and washing machines only when full?___

- put something in your toilet tank to reduce the usage of water?____,
- install water saving shower heads?____,
- give up the use of a garbage disposal?____,
- take shorter showers?____,
- instead of going to a water-wasting car wash, wash your car yourself with one bucket of water and not allowing the water to run constantly?____.

11. Concerning your food-buying habits, are you willing to:

- decrease or curtail your use of meat?____,
- buy locally grown fresh produce rather than processed ones?____,
- avoid over-packaged foods?____,
- and buy organic produce?____.

12. What trees grow in your local area? Name and describe ten.

13. What wild flowers grow in your area? Name and describe ten.

14. Name five edible wild plants native to your area.

15. Name and describe ten wild birds native to your region.

16. Name five local birds that migrate and five local birds that are year-long residents.

17. Name ten other non-human residents in your area.

18. Describe what has happened to your local environment over the past fifty years.

19. Name five non-human local residents in danger of extinction and cite the cause of their dilemma.

Follow-up Protocol

For best results, write down your impressions of this activity in your journal using the Heartwood Path Follow-up Protocol found in the Appendix. Afterwards, consider sharing your interpretations with others.

Heartwood Path Axioms

Key Assertions From Waypoint 4.62

4.62.1.

Nature is a good healer for a person when that individual leaves behind the demands of modern society; steps into natural settings where schedules can be forgotten; vents negative feelings; allows intuition to bring one into harmony with natural rhythms and instinctual desires; and eats natural, organic foods.

4.62.2.

Through diminishing exposure to the natural environment, to sunlight, and to darkness our circadian rhythms are becoming unhealthy.

Nocturnal Pilgrimage 4.62

For best results, write down your impressions of each night's dreams in your journal using the Heartwood Path Dreaming Time

Protocols found in the Appendix. Afterwards, consider sharing your Dream Tending with others.

> "In lieu of a relationship with our natural environment, we depend heavily on alcohol, sleeping pills, and sheer exhaustion to slow and stop us at night, and caffeine, sugar, hyperbolic information, and LAN (Light At Night) to keep us bussing throughout our protracted days" (Naiman, 2006, p. 194).

With both Naiman's statement and your answers from the previous lesson in mind as you begin to fall asleep, dream and, the next morning, tend to your dreams before getting out of bed.

Pertinent And Instructive Gems From My Dream Tending Journal

I dreamt as part of a waking dream that I was engaged in my worst skill: filling out forms. I never got the form done because, despite sitting still in hard concentration, I kept making mistakes.

Lesson Learned: Failing to fill out the form represents all of the challenges nature places before me that I have not yet overcome. The form, like nature's challenges, are like tests, brought before me to mark in what areas of my life I still need to make improvements. My dismay about my skills with forms is no idle rage against my fate. It is rather a warning sign about an important hurdle I have to overcome as a way to improve my lot and my character. Have a waking dream about your own worst skill and see what pops up. See what enrages you and you may discover what you need to do next to develop your higher instincts. Identifying and working on your personal challenges will also serve to keep your masculine acting skills and your feminine dreaming skills from succumbing due to non-use.

According to a recent Proceedings of the National Academy of Science, overall nature-based recreation had decreased by 50 percent in the last four decades (Selhub & Logan, 2012, p. 53). People are spending less time glimpsing natural wonders and more time with their home entertainment centers, computers, and mobile devices. This increased exposure is "wiring" people's brains to accommodate screen-based stimulation and hyperreality. Once a few generations of people become "reprogrammed" for the rapid pace of video games, edited television programs, and faster and faster operating systems, they will tend to regard nature as occurring at such a slow pace that viewing nature is becoming not only boring but also too slow to see. Once this unhealthy perceptual tendency becomes rampant, the chances of rearing future conservationists are much lower. This is the most troubling thing on my mind: How will we nurture the inspiration of future Rachel Carson's or David Brower's if our kids are not shaped by the natural world, the very place upon which our survival and well-being depend? If only for the sake of being a good role model for your children, get out of your so-called "man-cave" and into a real one, onto a river, onto a beach, or into a coral reef.

Return your attention to your natural inclinations by going into the wild to do the next activity. Shifting your routines by regularly doing the kinds of outdoor activities suggested along the Heartwood Path creates unconventional yet useful new patterns of thinking and doing. Such repetition creates important new brain patterns that guide both our beliefs and our behaviors.

When you are ready, head to the next waypoint: "Nature Familiarity." In doing so, you will be doing your part to help stem the disastrous tide that is flooding our experience with artificial distractions.

63

Nature Familiarity

DEVELOP YOUR ECOLOGICAL CONSCIOUSNESS

Improving one's own ability to use the direct experience of nature as a framework for personal decisions, professional choices, political action, and spiritual inquiry requires *"Greater Self identity work."* One's Greater Self identity is determined largely by certain transformational moments; especially memories of childhood places, perceptions of disturbed places, and contemplation of wild places. In these moments, one realizes that one's own personal identity is connected intrinsically to one's own encounters with nature.

EartHearts are those who have worked on their ecological identities, and have developed the following characteristics: a strong values orientation, an ethical conscientiousness, a reduced self-preoccupation, a cooperative nature, strong leadership potential, a yearning to help protect the environment, a philosophical inclination, a questioning attitude toward the supremacy of cultural norms, and a strong and clear sense of ecological consciousness with four components:

1. ecological systems thinking (rather than thinking only about individual species or taxonomic systems),

2. ability to enjoy and appreciate things in themselves (things valued regardless of utilitarian usefulness, for example),

3. an eco-centric value system (rather than a person-centered value system), and

4. a synergistic orientation in one's interactions with one's social and physical environment (how two or more aspects of the environment combine to form a whole greater than the sum of its parts).

The following multi-part activity, inspired by the writing of Mitchell Thomashow (1996), will help develop your ecological consciousness.

To Ecological Consciousness...

HumaNatureConnect Activity

Start-up Protocol
If this is not a day when you prefer to spend time in nature without an agenda, do the Heartwood Path Start-up Protocol found in the Appendix.

Becoming Conscious Ecologically

Memory Of Childhood Place

Describe a memory of a favorite wild place from your childhood, your relationship to this place, your feelings about this place, and the condition of this place today.

Reactions To A Wild Place

Contemplate and then describe any wild place. Focus on how this place affects all of your senses. Also, focus on any feelings of joy, wonder, inspiration, and happiness.

Sense Of Place Map

Create a sense of place map. Here's how: reflect on the place where you most formed your identity. Write down the ecological, geographical, developmental, and symbolic patterns for your place. Include landscapes, habitats, cultural institutions, and pathways of influence, power, and involvement. Make your map a way to blaze the trail to ecological consciousness. If possible, discuss your map in a group setting, covering: any feelings of ecological "uprootedness," comparisons of various places you have lived, how your region interacts with neighboring regions, prospects for the future of your region, and any feelings about what is significant about your region to you and to the planet.

Assessing Environmental Impact

Note the impact of the environment on you. Write down five words that describe your thoughts and feelings about a place. This place could be a location, a situation, a region, a home, or a niche (status). Compare your chosen location to other locations. What similarities do you notice? What differences do you notice? What do these impressions of places tell you about yourself?

Walk As Others

Experience an area by examining it as you walk over it. Use the viewpoints of different animals (e.g., deer, rabbits, snakes, squirrels, owls, robins, fox, mice, beaver and bear). Examine food, shelter, water, space and other aspects. Evaluate the same area from the human viewpoints of a building contractor, farmer, lumberman, hunter, naturalist, artist, and teacher. Note how this role-playing causes you to view the environment differently.

Personal Property List

Create a Personal Property List. In doing so you will discover that many of the objects you own come in three sorts: those that do not work, those that break down, and those that tend to get lost. Are your objects worth the price you pay to keep, maintain, and fret over of them? Creating such a list also helps one determine how material possessions are a means to construct personal identity, reflect deeply on the significance of property as a way to connect (identify ecologically) with the commons, and understand how the ownership of objects has utilitarian, symbolic, and ecological value and consequences. When one thinks about where one's possessions come from, and the ecological ramifications of their acquisition, one makes the link from personal ownership to a larger sphere of relationships. In this way, property becomes a tool for linking the individual to the ecosystem. Examining one's property can also lead to the reflection of the significance of the material world of real estate, gadgets, and money compared to the significance of the inner world of love, knowledge and creativity. Once this list is complete, write a short interpretive essay addressing the psychological, ecological and political implications of your personal possessions. Include how you felt about compiling the list. Discuss how your possessions affect your self-esteem, comfort, security, and power. Describe how you came to own so many possessions, and address issues of exclusion and exploitation regarding manufacturing and acquiring personal possessions. Discuss the ecological affects of your personal possessions.

Creating A Community Network Map

Many people today are highly mobile and are not really a part of any community grounded by a place. For these people, ecological intimacy and lasting interpersonal relationships in a specific place—love in context with place—is difficult. These mobile people do have far-flung networks and associations based on hobbies, interests, and friendships that they can maintain to some degree through advanced types of electronic communication. To create a community network map, draw a map or chart depicting relationships in your community. Consider all possible affiliations, associations, places, people, neighborhoods, habitats, and electronic networks. Use colors and arrows to highlight various relationships. Write down answers to the following questions: What makes any network a community? To which community do you feel most emotionally attached? Who belongs in your community? What are the various communities to which you belong? How do these communities interconnect? Are you as active in community life as you would like to be? Which of your activities are political, conflict-producing, and involve environmental issues? In what way does your perception of community reflect your ecological identity? What can you do to balance family life with community involvement? What will you do to protect and express your individualism—your uniqueness—while you are involved in community affairs?

Follow-up Protocol

For best results, write down your impressions of this activity in your journal using the Heartwood Path Follow-up Protocol found in the Appendix. Afterwards, consider sharing your interpretations with others.

Heartwood Path Axioms

Key Assertions From Waypoint 4.63

4.63.1.

EartHearts are those who have worked on their ecological identities, and have developed the following characteristics: strong value orientation, ethical conscientiousness, reduced self-preoccupation, cooperative nature, leadership potential, yearning to help protect the environment, philosophical inclination, questioning attitude toward the supremacy of cultural norms, and a strong and clear sense of ecological consciousness.

4.63.2.

Ecological consciousness has four components:

1. ecological systems thinking (rather than thinking only about individual species or taxonomic systems),

2. ability to enjoy and appreciate things in themselves (things valued regardless of utilitarian usefulness, for example),

3. an eco-centric value system (rather than a person-center value system), and

4. a synergistic orientation in one's interactions with one's social and physical environment (how two or more aspects of the environment combine to form a whole greater than the sum of its parts).

Nocturnal Pilgrimage 4.63

For best results, write down your impressions of each night's dreams in your journal using the Heartwood Path Dreaming Time

Protocols found in the Appendix. Afterwards, consider sharing your Dream Tending with others.

> "Our grandparents' advice to get plenty of sunshine by day and turn the lights off at night reflects an intuitive wisdom that would serve us well today" (Naiman, 2006, p. 196).

Think about what Naiman says and your reflections from the previous lesson as you prepare to fall asleep. Dream and then tend to your dreams.

Pertinent And Instructive Gems From My Dream Tending Journal

I dreamt I was in a classroom. I kept falling asleep. My dreams were about falling asleep and reawakening repeatedly while in this classroom.

Lesson Learned: The skill one needs to move beyond the beginning of the Heartwood Path and beyond the initial stages of one's More-Than-Individual development is to be able to move easily between dreaming while conscious and being conscious while dreaming. Moving between these poles, between these opposite states, will make you chastened but wiser. You will be better able to respond on your road to ever-widening responsibility—first responsibility for yourself, then responsibility for others like you, then responsibility for all humankind, and then responsibility for all sentient beings.

Spending time communing with nature will help you reestablish a bond with what is natural in yourself. When this happens you will be more apt to flourish. You will be more apt to fulfill your destiny as a full-fledged member of the community of life. You will psychologically rejoin the vast network of physical, emotional, and spiritual relationships. By learning to psychologically hold on to numerous relationships in the web of life you will begin to cut the chains that bind you inappropriately to the aggressive materialistic culture.

After reading about participating in a cohesive ecological community, you are ready again to go outside and find an attractive natural being. When you are ready, go to the next waypoint: "Tight Group."

64

Tight Group

PARTICIPATE IN A COHESIVE ECOLOGICAL COMMUNITY

EartHearts appreciate a cohesive ecological community grounded by a commons. Such a community has many attributes. It emerges as a result of one's daily habits. It requires people who are willing to respect but challenge one another, and it depends on people who can develop both short and long-term commitments. It requires people who perceive that their joint efforts will make a difference in the quality of their lives. A cohesive ecological community requires the participation of people who are willing to broaden the possibility of their life choices, widen their circle of involvement, and take the risks that go along with more-than-personal association—which includes spending time away from family and exposing themselves to public controversy.

A cohesive ecological community allows for extensive participation by its members in the decisions by which life is governed. The community as a whole takes responsibility for its members—a responsibility that includes respect for the many ways people can express their individuality. It links people through a common oral or written tradition. It is based on the interconnected web of landforms, weather, soils, habitats, and species. Its basis also includes human ecological practices; the impacts humans have on the earth; and the ways in which landforms, climates, soils, flora, and fauna affect humanity.

People in cohesive ecological communities interact in a common geographical space through political means and various nonpolitical practices of commitment. Political means include attending public meetings of the school board or city council and participating in elections. Nonpolitical practices of commitment include coaching little leagues, participating in neighborhood watch programs, volunteering for the fire department, and being a Den Mother for the Girl Scouts. Whether political or nonpolitical, one's way of demonstrating commitment in a cohesive ecological community occurs in a face-to-face manner that is intimate enough to enable participants to sense body language and pheromones—subtle body scents.

The attributes of a cohesive ecological community do not guard a participant or activist against the likely predicaments of involvement. Anyone who participates in a true cohesive ecological community will likely face two dilemmas: 1) how to balance family and career considerations against the need to become involved in the community, and 2) how to balance individualism and independence against becoming a "person-in-community" with all the attendant risks of involvement, such as possibly spending too much time away from loved ones at home, perhaps meeting people who may have ignoble pasts, running the risk of being embarrassed in your community, and possibly loss of control of your daily schedule.. Solving these dilemmas is a purpose of the Heartwood Path.

The world needs cohesive ecological groups because humanity is threatening the environment and it will take people to make the corrections. One person, acting alone, can make a difference. But it is often very hard to sustain the level of involvement needed to see any public issue through to a positive conclusion.

A cohesive ecological community can provide relief, as one member steps up when another cannot. It also provides an important ingredient in winning conservation battles: strength in numbers.

You will likely have to show that your will to do the right thing for the environment is greater than the will of all who would prefer to harm the environment. A tight-knit group supporting your cause is a good step in demonstrating this will.

The trust, unity, closeness, and size of a cohesive ecological community means that the homefront can be taken care of while the away-from-home confrontations and discussions go on. Some in the group may have only minimal family obligations. Others may have huge family obligations. You can help and be helped by being in a cohesive ecological community

Some communities exist on the internet while others operate in the flesh and blood. There are benefits to both. The online communities are easier to temporarily shut down, and often have a wider base of knowledge and skills. The flesh and blood communities can physically walk your dog and hold your children while you are off saving the world. It is usually not really a matter of choosing between online and flesh and blood cohesive ecological communities. Do both.

To An Intentional Locality...

HumaNatureConnect Activity

Start-up Protocol

If this is not a day when you prefer to spend time in nature without an agenda, do the Heartwood Path Start-up Protocol found in the Appendix.

Participating In A Cohesive Ecological Community

Use the feeling sense of the awareness of the earth's rotation (the Coriolis sense) to go to a natural place at sunrise. There is always something different going on, as the world turns. Note how squirrels, insects, birds, and other critters awaken and greet the new day. Look for ways that the rotation of the earth, in this case at sunrise, draw animals together. I can remember, for example, that through my bedroom window at sunrise all squirrels in the trees were curiously moving down and to the right, as if scurrying to meet for morning coffee at some unseen squirrels-only donut shop. From what you can see animals doing together at sunrise what ideas can you write down regarding ways you can build a more cohesive ecological community with human and non-human beings outdoors at sunrise? Ideas: sunrise ceremonies at local archeological site, put-in for a collective canoe trip just before sunrise, gather before sunrise for a bird-watching outing, or take-out your coffee from "Dunkin-Donut" and, bringing a big trash bag, hold your coffee-klatch while observing animals at sunrise in a nearby nature preserve while also picking up trash.

Follow-up Protocol

For best results, write down your impressions of this activity in your journal using the Heartwood Path Follow-up Protocol found in the Appendix. Afterwards, consider sharing your interpretations with others.

Heartwood Path Axioms

Key Assertions From Waypoint 4.64

4.64.1.

A cohesive ecological community requires the participation of people who are willing to broaden the possibility of their life choices, widen their circle of involvement, and take the risks that go along with more-than personal association—which

include spending time away from family and exposing themselves to public controversy.

4.64.2.

People in cohesive ecological communities interact in a
common geographical space through political means and
various nonpolitical practices of commitment.

4.64.3.

Whether political or nonpolitical, one's way of demonstrating
commitment in a cohesive ecological community occurs in a
face-to-face manner that is intimate enough to enable participants to sense body language and pheromones—subtle body
scents.

4.64.4.

Anyone who participates in a true cohesive ecological community will likely face two dilemmas: 1) how to balance family
and career considerations against the need to become involved
in the community, and 2) how to balance individualism and
independence against becoming a "person-in-community" with
all the attendant risks of involvement, including the risk of
losing some of your independence and individuality.

Nocturnal Pilgrimage 4.64

For best results, write down your impressions of each night's
dreams in your journal using the Heartwood Path Dreaming Time

Protocols found in the Appendix. Afterwards, consider sharing your Dream Tending with others.

You are frequently directed to find an attractive natural being for the activities along the Heartwood Path. While there is practically always an attractive natural being within an easy walking distance of your home, with each passing day, nearby plants and animals are harder to find. Even seeing the stars in the night's sky is slowing becoming more difficult due to air pollution or excessive lights outdoors at night.

"Because of light pollution, the vast majority of us rarely witness the majesty of the night sky" (Naiman, 2006, pp. 196-197).

With this statement and the previous lesson in mind as you drift off to sleep, have productive dreams. As you awaken, tend to your dreams.

Pertinent And Instructive Gems From My Dream Tending Journal

I dreamt that the Image I have for real world Lower Rock Creek Boulder Buddy did not like the Image I have of him in my dreams. An argument between these Images ensued. It was over which of them is more informative and factual. This disagreement resulted in me not being welcome in both my waking and my dreaming worlds. This has to be what being in Purgatory feels like.

Lesson Learned: It often seems like we live immersed in a shape-shifting world, sometimes *dreaming* at night and sometimes *conscious* during the day. We ride a sort of see-saw between opposing tendencies. We can learn to make the boundary between the inner world of dreams and the outer world of consciousness go away. We can make the forms in each world dissolve into one another. Sufferance of one for the other (of consciousness for dreaming, for example) only exists when either dreams or consciousness confront what it normally shies away from. When a juxtaposition happens within or near a person and the dream world is affected by a person's "reality" that person is sometimes called a "visionary." When the opposite occurs—that is, when a person's dream comes true—that person is called a "realist." Shortly, you will learn to embrace both worlds simultaneously, thus reducing the consuming need to shuffle back and forth. This co-fusion will eventually result in less confusion. To sustain this embrace in the long run one will have to see the conflicting clues, hold on to paradox, live through the contradictions, and tolerate the setbacks. One will need to support both worlds—without opinion—by loving the differences and the contradictions. Consciousness will need to step back as dreaming steps forward, creating a balance of the two minds. In this state of equanimity, dreaming teaches consciousness about humbleness and, in return, consciousness teaches dreaming about focus.

At the next waypoint, you will learn how to fight individual and collective tension. By living exclusively in the human realm, you have in some respects narrowed your focus and hindered your consciousness. Doing the next HumaNatureConnect Activities outdoors will help you to identify what is truly indispensable, expand your focus to the outdoor realm, and diminish your tension, stress, and worries. When you are ready, move to the next waypoint: "Worry."

65

Worry

FIGHT INDIVIDUAL AND COLLECTIVE STRESS

By helping people acknowledge anger and despair, eartHearts help transform blame and guilt into responsibility and action. Sometimes collective activism leads to organizational stress. This stress can result from continuous political confrontations, fund-raising problems, understaffed projects, pressing deadlines, and despair over the overwhelming magnitude of environmental problems and the prerequisites of reform. When such problems erupt, eartHearts are there to bring out a reflective perspective that can help heal the psychological pressure of stress.

When this psychological pressure is manifested as anger, guilt, blame, or cynicism, the activists may be on the verge of burnout—the result of pushing themselves to unreasonable limits. To fight burnout, eartHearts encourage others to meditate, exercise, make priority lists, clarify values, seek comfort from loved ones, and reflect on higher purposes.

To Battle Strain...

HumaNatureConnect Activity

Start-up Protocol

If this is not a day when you prefer to spend time in nature without an agenda, do the Heartwood Path Start-up Protocol found in the Appendix.

Fighting Individual And Collective Stress

Use your feeling sense of body movement and mobility to fight stress. In your chosen place outdoors roll your head in circles, stretch, run in place, or jump up and down. Plan to spend your lunch hours walking outdoors in a natural setting. If you typically jog indoors, switch to jogging on nature trails. Other outdoor movement-oriented stress-relievers include fishing, surfing, pulling weeds, bird-watching, hiking, canoeing or kayaking, riding your bicycle, tai-chi outdoors, yoga outdoors, and walking your dog(s).

Follow-up Protocol

For best results, write down your impressions of this activity in your journal using the Heartwood Path Follow-up Protocol found in the Appendix. Afterwards, consider sharing your interpretations with others.

Heartwood Path Axioms

Key Assertions From Waypoint 4.65

4.65.1.

By helping people acknowledge anger and despair, eartHearts help transform blame and guilt into responsibility and action.

4.65.2.

When the psychological pressure of stress is manifested as anger, guilt, blame, or cynicism, the activists may be on the verge of burnout—the result of pushing themselves to unreasonable limits.

4.65.3.

To fight burnout, meditate, exercise, make priority lists, clarify values, seek comfort from loved ones, and reflect on higher purposes.

Nocturnal Pilgrimage 4.65

For best results, write down your impressions of each night's dreams in your journal using the Heartwood Path Dreaming Time Protocols found in the Appendix. Afterwards, consider sharing your Dream Tending with others.

To become happy and get yourself ready to help create a healthy environment, glean information from dreams and then take steps to act upon the guidance you receive. As we have and will continue to show along the Heartwood Path, your whole body, your mind, your sleep, and your dreaming is affected by pollution. This pollution fowls local waterways, taints our food, makes the air unhealthy to breath, and, when in the form of light pollution, changes the normal way our bodies adjust to darkness at night.

"Recent studies indicate that 99 percent of the population of the Western world is exposed to varying degrees of light pollution...For 40 percent of the United States population, (the sky is never) dark enough at night for human eyes to adapt to night vision" (Naiman, 2006, p. 197).

With ways you yourself can reduce light pollution and excessive unnecessary worrying in mind as you drift off to sleep, have useful and enjoyable dreams. Tend to your dreams upon waking.

The comfort that comes through repetition means that repeating core routines is a stress-reducer. When you do things repetitively you master the chore. This mastery lowers our levels of stress as we continue, with increased skill, in performing the task.

The next waypoint is about actively and repeatedly interacting with one sacred spot at or near one's home. Along with this one sanctified place, your repeated searches of natural beings and landscapes, as part of the assignments for this series of courses, may have revealed for you numerous other special spots in nature where you have begun to lower your stress by reinforcing certain Heartwood Path core routines.

These stress-reducing core routines, deemed to be among the most helpful ones done throughout the Heartwood Path, include:

1. finding special spots outdoors;
2. having new outdoor experiences each day and sharing your impressions from these activities regularly with others;
3. expanding your awareness by using fifty-four natural senses;
4. tending to dreams; and
5. journaling.

Life calls us to be active, interactive, and, on occasion, nonconformist. You do not even have to do the outdoor activities of this course in the order presented. You may, for example, run into animal tracks while doing the outdoor activities for this book and decide to focus on the tracking instead of the suggested activity. You may be called by a bird to pay attention to its song instead of doing the specified activity. You may choose to wander in a seemingly aimless fashion and never get to some of the Heartwood Path waypoints. In this series of courses, it is perfectly acceptable to follow your own attractions, at any time you choose, wherever they may lead you.

While you may feel emancipated to be able to do whatever you want in whatever way you want, you no doubt have made it this far in this book series because you are searching for some direction. For this reason, we will continue to recommend certain activities at each waypoint. Feel free to use them or follow your own attractions.

Do not just read the text of the next waypoint in a chair inside. It is not good for your children to see you being such a role model. Today, children and teens consume an unimaginable amount of time engaged in media (meaning looking at an electronic screen while doing such activities as watching television, streaming videos online, looking at YouTube, and texting with friends) outside of school: 7 hours and 38 minutes (Selhub & Logan, 2012, p. 54). Says Selhub and Logan: this "ascent of screen culture has occurred in association with the decline of mindful engagement with nature" (2012, p. 54). As a result of this loss, the mentally rejuvenating and cognitively restorative benefits of nature are becoming less and less known. The less one knows about the personal benefits that one can obtain by communing with nature, the less one is likely to want to engage in conservation.

We will stand up for what we know and what we experience. At a time when we need both stress relief and environmental conservation more than ever, we cannot allow ourselves to be confined to our media rooms.

These are but some of the reasons to be motivated to get up and to move outside to do the next activity. In doing these activities, find your own sanctified spots and, if you prefer, add your own favored routines to the core routines presented throughout the Heartwood Path. When you are ready, move to the next waypoint: "Sacred Spot."

66

Sacred Spots

ACTIVATE THE EARTH CHAKRAS AND DEVELOP A HEARTFELT CONNECTION TO YOUR OMPHALOS

In this waypoint, we will be using the principle of "as above, so below" to awaken positive potentialities such as intuition, the will, or creativity. We will learn how to activate the energy centers of the body that govern these potentialities. We will learn how certain energy centers are actually chakras that begin in you—the "below" part of the equation—but are also attached to various large areas of the earth—the "above" part of the equation.

By learning to activate these earth chakras, you will be releasing positive potentialities in both yourself (like within the heart, or sacrum, or thymus, for example) and radiate these potentialities to a particular part of the earth and beyond. You will, for example, release emotions that may be stuck in your solar plexus and spread the benefits of this release to Asia and beyond. You will learn in the first part of this waypoint, called "Earth Chakras," how to use a vowel sound to expand the comfort and security housed at the base of your spine and spread this potentiality to Africa and beyond, for example. You will also learn how to use a hand gesture to increase the expressiveness stuck in your throat and release it to North America and beyond, for example.

The activation of the potentialities held in body parts and earth parts will be covered in the first part of this waypoint. The second part of this waypoint, called "Omphalos" will demonstrate how to feel at home in a place on earth. After opening up potentialities (latent attributes and qualities) in your body and around the globe, it will be nice to bring your center of gravity back to your own core, your spine, the place where you can feel your closest sense of an ecological identity—who you are based, in part, on your felt closeness to a place. The way we will be helping you to return to your own closest sense of ecological identity will be to further awaken your consciousness to your chakra-dotted spinal column which centers you and connects you from your north pole—the crown of the head—to your south pole, the sacrum at the base of your spine. In the activity that follows, you will be asked some pertinent questions about finding your own meaning in the linkage between your various individual chakras aligned along your spine with your consciousness of various places on earth.

By combining these two topics—Earth Chakras and Omphalos, and by doing the activities associated with them, we will be continuing our tradition of expanding one's relationships and awakening oneself to the Greater Self (in the Earth Chakras section that follows) while also at the same time maintaining one's sense of an individual self (in the Omphalos section at the end of this waypoint).

Earth Chakras

To begin the topic of earth chakras we will need to say some more about the formation and functioning of the universe. We humans did not create the original jumble that made up the universe. But, we humans created the way the universe is interpreted, with our acknowledgment of its existence, and we continue to create the common interpretation of the universe through our conscious observations (see Waypoint 7 for a refresher).

Since humans evoke the world through our conscious observations of it, it cannot be said that the universe was not created as an all-knowing super-entity. If one dog discovers the difference between a Sunday morning and a Tuesday morning, the universe is still learning. And that is a good thing.

Always fresh with new awarenesses, we humans forever bring new insights into the job of making the universe. Actually, the beginning of the universal impulse to construct reality is prehuman. Particularly at the beginning of the earth, the impulse to organize creation is sometimes called "sound," but it is, and was, not noisy. It quietly expanded and continues to expand outward, without cessation.

In prehistoric times, the expanding creative impulse continued to grow, and with this growth came the primal sound of "aum." At this point, there were no chakras. These energy centers were not created until universe-organizing sound was fast and large enough to generate light.

Once this light organized itself (by encountering the pathway of the impulse of sound at different points along its pathway) love was created, and, eventually, form and the chakras. Like what happens between the plus (+) and minus (-) poles on a battery, the flow of energy between the base chakra and the crown chakra forms an electromagnetic field, dotted with big and small chakras.

With the cosmic trinity of sound, light, and form, we are able to create and experience the creation, interact with others with compatible or partially compatible frequencies, form a consensus, and move forward with a shared awareness. In this way, me and my girlfriend, for example, have, more or less, the same experience when we take the dogs for a walk. And you and I agree what a dog is compared to a cat. In the same way, multiplied by billions of experiencers, by the impact of billions of energy centers (chakras), and by untold numbers of experiences, the sharing of awareness throughout the world continues to form both the present and the future. We can do a better job of this formation if our chakras are activated through a method described in the activity that follows.

We humans are the creators of our own experience, just as we are the creators of our own pathway, our own universe. As more people with more insights collectively give birth to the universe, it grows and follows a frequency of impulse that originates within each of our own consciousnesses.

Together, long ago, we humans worked out what was called "Four Keys To Human Destiny" to understand and put to use the relationship between the energy centers of the earth and the energy centers of the body. The first Key To Human Destiny was used to find the center of our power. It associated mountain ranges with the spinal column. For those with activated chakras, energy is felt most strongly at certain places along the mountains (particularly at Mt Shasta in the State of Washington, for example) just as it is felt more strongly at certain places along the spinal column (at the Heart Chakra location halfway up the spine, for example). The second of these Four Keys To Human Destiny associated mounds or lakes with the energy of the joints. The third of these Four Keys To Human Destiny made use of the arm, associated with earth's lines of latitude and longitude. It was thought this tool would activate the meridians of the body The fourth key, the Cup, held that the oceans would affect the blood. It was thought that through this tool the essence of the stars would change our blood and find the center of the body and the earth.

When used today, these Four Keys To Human Destiny mark the recognition that people have the power of the earth within them. Mostly lost over time, parts of these Four Keys still emerge in the literature. The overall forgetting or loss the Four Keys To Human Destiny explains why there seems to be conflicting accounts of what constitutes the earth chakras.

By going back to the use of the Four Keys To Human Destiny, we can see how the system of earth and human chakras can activate the wholeness of each person connected to the Earth.

In previous Heartwood Path books we described the seven chakras. These can be thought of as the chakras of people operating with an emphasis on their individual aspect. Now that we are moving from the topic of human individuality (as covered in the Heartwood Path book: **Egos**) to the topic of human integration (as covered in this book) we will add a few chakras to the seven-chakra system previously described.

By connecting each of the twelve Greater Chakras (chakras that have both individual and planetary aspects) to a particular earth chakra, the whole potential of the whole person/planet is activated. Just as a male sperm transforms a female egg, and just as a masculine asteroid brings new life to a feminine planet, so too can an earth chakra transform and give new life to an individual chakra.

The Greater Chakra, constituted as an earth chakra and as an individual chakra works together to change and give new life to the More-Than-Individual-Self, the Universal Self. The person with individual chakras and the planet with earth chakras (some are points on mountains, some as lakes, some as the ocean, and some as lines of latitude) all work together to govern the ever-changing Universal Self.

Through the earth chakras, each part of the body is attached to different part of the earth. To describe which earth chakra is correlated to any one individual chakra requires the use of any of the four tools previously mentions—any of the Four Keys To Human Destiny.

Do not be concerned that there are differing ways to interpret the linkages between individual chakras and earth chakras, It is not that the relationship changes with each tool. It is, rather, that the way of describing individual/earth chakra relationships changes, depending on one's way of thinking, interests, and needs. Mt Shasta is discussed as the Base Chakra according to the spinal column/mountain range tool (the Mountain Range Key To Human Destiny explanation), for example; while Africa is associated with the Base Chakra in De Stefano's contemporary explanatory tool (see De Stefano's three Earth Chakra YouTube videos).

No matter which tool you use to describe the chakra system, it becomes apparent that when you begin to feel the earth, through any of its chakras, the earth begins to feel you (through your chakras.) By recognizing the body-earth chakra relationships, one can align one's individual frequencies (those of the various chakras) and, thereby, fall into sympathetic alignment with the earth through the process of en-trainment. By falling into synchrony with the frequencies of the earth, which were born of light, sound, and form and then grew into love (as previously described), one can live in harmony with the earth, one can become a model for others to follow, and one can help make a more rapid transformation into the Ecozoic Era (for a refresher, return to Waypoint 2.67 in **Logos**).

Any sperm that cannot coax an ovum to share its frequency is re-jected by the ovum and dies. Any life containing asteroid that misses a suitable planet misses the opportunity to spread its unique life to a new place in the galaxy. Don't let these sorts of things happen to you.

Align the frequency of your chakras with the frequencies of the chakras of the Earth. The mutual elevated feeling of the earth and the person results in rapid transformations of both the person and the planet.

As an answer to whether there will be enough chakra-activating people for a healthy person/planet alignment to occur, I say: if one imbalanced cell can destroy a body, one balanced cell can protect and heal the body. Make yourself into a healing cell for our troubled planet. Align your chakras with the frequencies of the earth.

Once you begin your Earth Chakra practice, say the vowel sounds listed in the chart that follows, for they activate the connection be-tween individual chakras and the associated earth chakras. Also, use a certain hand gesture—the Unity Mudra that is like the V" for Victory sign but with the two uplifted finger held together. Once you make the vowel sound tone associated with a chakra and move your dominant hand (held in the shape of the mudra) in a circular fashion in front of the chakra (as explained in the following activity) the potential of the chakra will be activated and you and others on earth will have enhanced skills related to that chakra.

When doing the next practice, hold your non-dominant hand out-ward with the palm upward to receive universal energy. To heighten the effect of this practice, use your dominant hand in Unity Mudra gesture to transmit the received energy.

As you will see in the next activity, we will be using twelve vowel sounds to activate the twelve chakras—ten inside the body and two outside. The result will be to turn yourself into a sort of antennae that can receive the frequencies of the earth chakras and gather up their potentialities or send your elevated chakra potentialities to the earth. You will see in the far right column of the chart in the next activity that these potentialities are latent qualities or attributes such as consciousness of the Absolute, intuition, expressiveness, the will, love, emotional release, integration of heaven and earth, creativity, sexuality, security, and comfort.

Just as there are chakras in one's own individual body, the earth also has places where energy gathers powerfully. Just as there are different ways to measure temperature (Centigrade and Fahrenheit), or to chart spiritual development, there are also different ways to describe the Earth's chakras.

Just as the human body has chakras from head to groin along the spine plus minor chakras at every joint, the Earth has major and minor power centers, each having influence on those who experience them. Everyone resonates with such places in different ways. Certain wild places, such as the Amazon, the Himalayas, the Grand Canyon and certain cultural sites, such as the site of Chartres Cathedral in France, Cahokia Mounds in Illinois, Machu Pichu in Peru, the pyramids in Egypt, or Tikal in Guatemala, are known as *"power centers."* Let us now turn to another way to bring the powers of these earth power centers and your own individual power centers home to you.

Much of what is said in this section of the Heartwood Path is based on the work of Matias de Stefano He has produced a comprehensive explanation of Earth Chakras in three videos on YouTube. See References for the link.

Omphalos

Understanding one's own spot on Earth and developing feelings of significance regarding one's locality create a person's sense of place.

This sense includes a feeling about one's home, region, community, kindred species, community functions, landscapes, and memories attached to a setting.

Whether discussing one's own home, land, or dwelling place, the common factor in one's sense of place is always the existential experience of being in the world in an organized and meaningful manner. Being in the world in these ways is particularly facilitated by one's experience of the core of one's place.

The core of one's place—its heart—is known as the *"omphalos."* This place within the home or community commands one's attention. In the home, it may be the hearth, the couch in the family room, or the bed in the master bedroom. In the community, it may be a church, courthouse, monument, or park. Whatever it is, it can only serve as an omphalos when it has a meaning within the heart of the human dweller.

The heart of the heart of any omphalos is the "center pole" of the body—the spine with its attendant heart and other chakras. To work on connecting the heart of the heart to the omphalos is to work on one's deepest felt sense of ecological identity which, as described in Waypoint 4.63, includes such things as your memories of childhood places, your reactions to a particular wild place, ecological systems thinking, your ability to enjoy local things with no apparent utilitarian use, and any synergistic orientation (forming a whole greater than the sum of its parts) in one's interactions with one's personally most significant social and physical environment.

To Recognize One's Faculties And To Activate The Earth Chakras...

HumaNatureConnect Activity

Start-up Protocol

If this is not a day when you prefer to spend time in nature without an agenda, do the Heartwood Path Start-up Protocol found in the Appendix.

Identifying Your Personal Power Centers &
Activating The Earth Chakras

Take in many deep breaths, each time feeling the part of the earth associated with various body parts, as described in the chart that follows. After looking over this chart, continue this deep breathing as you feel the mountains of your body, the lakes of your body, the ocean of your body, the streams of your body, and the other main earth chakra locations. Imagine the tips of your fingers used in the Unity Mudra are full of light. As you make the extended sound of each chakra move your dominant hand, with its Unity Mudra gesture, in a circling fashion in front of the chakra. Intend that this circling action is drawing in the earth chakra energy to your body, or vice versa. In this way, you can either receive earth chakra energy from around the earth, or transmit your individual chakra energy to places around the earth. As you make the vowel sounds and wave your hand held in the Unity Mudra gesture in front of each associated chakra (as described in the next table), think about the continent associated with each earth chakra. Do not worry about getting the sounds just right or about activating the exact chakra. You cannot do this activity wrong. As you say the associated vowel sounds and wave your hand held in the Unity Mudra in front of each chakra it will become activated. Once activated, the chakra will release its potential (its latent qualities or attributes) and cause benefits (to you or others) as listed in the chart that follows. For each of the twelve earth chakras, extend the sound of each corresponding vowel sound as follows:

Individual Chakra	Earth Chakra	Vowels	As In The Word	Activation Causes
Above the Crown Chakra		HHHHHH	Hot	Consciousness of Absolute
Crown Chakra	Antarctica/Arctic	WOOOH	Umbrella	Unlimited Potential
Pineal	South America	AAAAAHH	Apple	Intuition & Wisdom
Mouth	Central America	AAHHHH	Egg	Greater Expressiveness
Throat	North America	AAAAAAY	Ice	Greater Expressiveness
Thymus	Great Britain Islands	IIIIIIII	Igloo	Proper Use of The Will
Heart	Europe	EEEEEEEE	Eat	Expansion of Love
Point of Transition	Middle East	HHHHHH	Hot	Integration of Heaven and Earth
Solar Plexus	Asia	OOOHHH	Octopus	Emotional Release
Sacrum	Oceania	OOOOOH	Unicorn	Primal Creativity/Sexuality
Base	Africa	OHHHHH	Oatmeal	Security & Comfort
Below the Base Chakra		HHHHHH	Hot	Earth Awareness

Your individual chakras and the earth chakras will be activated on your first successful completion of all of the vowel sounds and mudra movements. But the more you practice, the stronger will be the whole chakra system—the Chakra System for the Greater Self. At the end of each activation session—do it two or three times for this activity— quickly say "HHH HHH HHH" as you wave your Unity Mudra very quickly over the associated Earth Chakras—feet, just below the heart, and over the head. It will sound like you are ending this part of this activity in laughter.

Next, to develop another way to bring earth energy into yourself, create your own list of the Earth's main power centers and answer some pointed questions. Concerning the power centers list, it may or may not be a list of places you will ever visit. You can simply list places where the earth seems to most powerfully influence your own chakras. To help you develop your list, here are the pointed questions for you to answer in your journal:

1. Where on Earth do you feel most connected to the whole of the Earth? This is the place where the earth sends energy more powerfully to your seventh chakra on top of your head.

2. Where on Earth do you feel the planet most powerfully influences your intuition (through your sixth chakra near your forehead)?

3. Where on the planet do you feel the earth most powerfully influences your communication abilities (through your fifth chakra in your throat)?

4. What place on earth most powerfully influences your ability to love (through your fourth chakra in your heart)?

5. Where do you feel the earth most powerfully influences your energy or power (through your third chakra at the base of your sternum)?

6. Where on earth do you feel the planet most powerfully influences your emotions (through the second chakra near your navel)?

7. What place most powerfully activates your sex drive (through your first chakra near your groin)? Is this the same place that makes you feel a primal connection to wildness? Is it a place where you are drawn to express your animal nature?

8. How do other earth chakras you identify increase positive potentialities. Try to see if you can feel any additional earth chakra at each of your joints, for example. See if you can feel any earth chakras in your arms or legs, hands or feet. Where on earth do such additional earth chakras resonate for you? Where on your body, for example, does the Missouri River, the Great Lakes, The Great Plains, Lake Bakal, or the Amazon Rain Forest, resonate on your body? Can you find a chakra on your body that resonates with the Black Hills of South Dakota? Do the Ozarks of Missouri and Arkansas resonate in any place on your body? What about the Channel Islands off the Pacific Coast of California. What about Machu Pichu or Cahokia Mounds? Activated chakras feel warmer and more tingly than non-activated chakras. Scan your

whole body for linkages with the power places of the planet. Keep good notes.

9. Go to a few places in your community that you already know or imagine that they will have an activating effect on any of your chakras. If such places are your omphalos they will cause either a warming, or a tingly, or an empty sensation within your core or associated with your spine. Note any changes in your chakras as you move closer to or farther away from your omphalos. When you begin to feel strong memories associated with a place, when you feel a strong physical reaction to a particular wild place, when your mind turns strongly to ecological systems thinking (how energy flows through and environment, for example), when you begin to feel enjoyment from a place with no apparent utilitarian use, or when you feel a synergistic orientation (the psychological forming a whole greater than the sum of its parts) in one's interactions with a place, you are likely positioning yourself in your omphalos. Once identified and/or visited, pay attention to thoughts about meaning. There will be gold there.

Once you find your omphalos, run through the vowel sounds to activate all of the chakras located along your spine.

At some point, be sure to turn your attention to parts of your body located away from your spine. Try different vowel sounds with different parts of your extremities and note whatever vowel sound seems to resonate with your additional list of earth chakra. Use the Unity Mudra and your vowel sounds to bring energy to the omphalos of the omphalos—your spine. Do the same for the individual ends of your away-from-spine Greater Chakras. And do the same as you send energy to the More-Than-Individual ends (places on Earth) of your Greater Chakras.

At first, this activity may seem silly or it may be hard to feel the activation. Practice will improve your receptions and transmissions.

Activating the major Earth Chakras will bring more cosmic consciousness to the earth. Doing so will increase the power of your Will.

Doing so will increase your intuition and wisdom. Doing so will cause the expansion of emotional release and love. Doing so will expand your creativity, your sexiness, and your sense of security and comfort. And doing so will increase your awareness of the Earth.

Activating whatever additional away-from-spine earth chakras you identify will similarly expand other positive potentialities too numerous to discuss here. As you do this activity, note what positive attributes seem to expand in yourself and the Greater Self. Keep notes in your journal.

Follow-up Protocol

For best results, write down your impressions of this activity in your journal using the Heartwood Path Follow-up Protocol found in the Appendix. Afterwards, consider sharing your interpretations with others.

Heartwood Path Axioms

Key Assertions From Waypoint 4.66

4.66.1.

Activate the Earth Chakras and develop a heartfelt connection to your Omphalos—the core of your place.

4.66.2.

The heart of the heart of any omphalos the "center pole" of the body—the spine with its attendant heart and other chakras.

4.66.3.

Activating Earth Chakras increases positive potentialities, including: cosmic consciousness, the Will, emotional release, creativity, sexiness, the sense of security, comfort, and Earth awareness.

Nocturnal Pilgrimage 4.66

For best results, write down your impressions of each night's dreams in your journal using the Heartwood Path Dreaming Time Protocols found in the Appendix. Afterwards, consider sharing your Dream Tending with others.

Here is an interesting quote that may give you some food or thought or it may promote having a pertinent dream that you can use to glean some insight from your daytime and nighttime reveries.

"Considering the widespread use of night lights and the proximity of illuminated clock radios, I believe that the majority of us suffer from chronic dark deficiency" (Naiman, 2006, p. 197).

With the need for darkness (which gives us an important sense of daily rhythm and other benefits described subsequently) and your sacred spot prominent in your mind as you begin your nighttime reverie, sleep and dream. Tend to your dreams, beginning before you get out of bed.

Pertinent And Instructive Gems From My Dream Tending Journal

I dreamt that after a float trip with my mother in the Everglades—an all day affair—in which I was taken back by the lack of biological diversity, I had a dream which seemed to let me know what I had missed. In the

dream, the Everglades did not appear to be a monotonous spread of
mangroves only, as it did during my float trip. In my dream in my dream,
all sorts of birds appeared, most notably a very craggy looking wood stork.
In addition to the alligators I saw on my waking trip, I was treated to
numerous dream world Images of giant saltwater crocodiles.

Lesson Learned: Dreams present to us that which we are missing during our waking consciousness.

Expand yourself and feel more radiant as you do the next activity in the wild. If you spend all your time indoors you will develop brain patterns that force you to psychologically become your living room, kitchen, and bathroom. You are much bigger than these spaces. Do nature activities outside repeatedly to find your larger self. And when you do, share both your own impressions and pertinent scientific studies with others. Be both romantically poetic and objectively scientific when you tell others of the role nature plays in the development and maintenance of your personal wellbeing.

When you are ready, head to the next waypoint: "Fabled Settings." There, you will learn to interpret the mythic presence of your favorite local natural place.

67

Fabled Setting

INTERPRET THE MYTHIC
PRESENCE OF YOUR LOCAL PLACE

When many people engage their own personal heart of the ompha-los of their local place—their chakra system—they come to notice that the first chakra is both a sex center and an energy center that relates the person to their own primal nature. This center regulates one's drive to be uncivilized; to relate to wild places; to engage the wildness through oneself and one's intimate associates; and to connect with that part of one's nature that existed before the conventions of civilization, before the rule of moral laws, and before the governance of social institutions. At this point along the Heartwood Path, we begin to appreciate the link between appreciation of pristine wildness and sexual expression— they are both experienced most effectively through the same chakra, the one at the base of our primal nature.

When a place triggers a memory, arouses the imagination, conveys a mythic presence, or seems potent, the sense of this place is called "*chora*." If, however, a place has no special signification but is instead an objective, simple, physical, and largely meaningless location, the sense of place it engenders is called "topos." EartHearts distinguish themselves from geographers by working less in the field of *topo*graphy and more in the as-yet recognized field of "*chora*graphy."

Place, especially when the sense of it is "chora," is not passive. When a place interacts with human consciousness in a very dynamic way, the *genius loci* or spirit of place—is apprehended. Places with strong genius loci—that is, places with a power character or atmosphere—can be well known and public or they can be highly personal and private. The genius loci of a place often determines the types of rites of passage that occur there.

Rites of passage organized by eartHearts are likely to involve caves, rivers, forests, prehistoric mounds and other sacred places. A sacred place is a set-apart location where the "fabric" that separates the human world from the spirit world is often or typically felt to be so "threadbare" that communication between humans and spiritual beings seems atypically easy. Caves are often the preeminent local natural sacred spots, followed by mountains, rivers, and rock formations. Preeminent cultural sacred spots include ancient temples, burial spots, and monuments. Whether natural or man-made, places with strong genius loci—a strong spiritual presence—are awesome places that work on us. They organize our perceptions, feelings, memories, and imaginings. The expressiveness of such places seems to "communicate" to us at the subconscious or spiritual level. Such spots are often considered sacred. They are sometimes considered liminal, meaning that they are spots where the cover between our everyday world and the world of the spirit is most threadbare. Liminal space evokes the numinous experience of chora—a quality of place that stimulates one's inner world. When chora is strong enough and the cover between the human world and the spirit world is so bare an attuned person can breach the boundary between the human world and the spirit world, the locale is called a "*tirtha*." These cathedrals of sacred space have been known to evoke visions, hierophanies—spiritual revelations or interpretations—and great lessons.

When examining a locale, the conversion of it in one's mind from topos to chora often depends on the way a place is interpreted. EartHearts help people appreciate tirthas and other places by following not only the fifteen principles of interpretation recommended by Larry Beck and Ted Cable in their classic book **Interpretation for the 21st Century**, but also by adding five additional principles. We will begin with the Beck and Cable list:

1. light a spark within the audience that allows them to see things differently;
2. interpret a place through a provocative and inspirational story that is relevant to the audience;
3. provoke a more caring attitude toward our natural and cultural heritage;
4. enhance the listeners well being, health, and sense of wholeness;
5. meet the needs of people of various ages;
6. bring the past alive through reenactments that demonstrate how the past affects the present and the future;
7. astonish people by using all available modern technology;
8. avoid excess by presenting only a few things but presenting them well;
9. be competent and, when necessary, certified;
10. addressing in writing what the readers would like to know;
11. seek and build financial, volunteer, political, and administrative support;
12. passionately perceive beauty and then instill desire and appreciation for beauty in the audience;
13. create optimal experiences that encourage the audience to seek out further enjoyment, learning, and inspiration;
14. demonstrate passion for the resource being interpreted and the audience by being professional, caring and truthful; and
15. share knowledge, insight, and inspiration with others.

Added to this list are the five additional principles eartHearts also incorporate when interpreting HumaNature:

1. finding and then imparting to others the enchantment of linking one's own individuality, universality, place, purpose, and people;
2. sharing with others how meaning is created by establishing links between the Realm of Interiority and the Realm of Exteriority;
3. inspiring others to use the microcosm (such as one's intimate partner) as a model for understanding, venerating, and protecting the macrocosm (such as one's neighborhood or the planet);
4. inspiring oneself and others to continually seek to grow in both depth (from a "me-only" perspective to an "all-sentient being" perspective, for example) and span (by balancing tensions, morals, behaviors, and physical systems, for example) and then use one's own exceptional perception and span to provide leadership and insight unavailable to those who are not as deep and balanced; and
5. developing and sharing compelling personal reflections wherein Love, Knowledge and the Will bolster the earth one person at a time.

To The Preferred Story Of One's Place...

HumaNatureConnect Activity

Start-up Protocol

If this is not a day when you prefer to spend time in nature without an agenda, do the Heartwood Path Start-up Protocol found in the Appendix.

Interpreting The Mythic Presence Of Your Local Place

Use your sense of color and your sense of moods and identities attached to colors, to note the dominant colors of your local place. Think also of the colors of this place in other seasons. Draw a simple flag to represent your chosen natural place. Color in this flag with the dominant three colors of your place. Your flag need not represent actual colors but may, if you wish, include mythic reasons for including colors. Mythic reasons would be what you want to be true rather than merely what is true. Humm the sound of each of the colors of your flag. Write down why you chose each color.

Follow-up Protocol

For best results, write down your impressions of this activity in your journal using the Heartwood Path Follow-up Protocol found in the Appendix. Afterwards, consider sharing your interpretations with others.

Heartwood Path Axioms

Key Assertions From Waypoint 4.67

4.67.1.

When a place triggers a memory, arouses the imagination, conveys a mythic presence, or seems potent the sense of this place is called "*chora*."

4.67.2.

If a place has no special signification but is instead an objective, simple, physical, and largely meaningless location, the sense of place it engenders is called "topos."

4.67.3.

EartHearts distinguish themselves from geographers by working less in the field of *topo*graphy and more in the field of "*chora*graphy."

4.67.4.

When chora is strong enough and the cover between the human world and the spirit world is so bare an attuned person can breach the boundary between these two worlds, the locale is called a "*tirtha.*"

4.67.5.

EartHearts help people appreciate tirthas and other places by following not only the fifteen principles of interpretation recommended by Larry Beck and Ted Cable in their classic book Interpretation for the 21st Century, but also by adding five additional principles:

1. finding and then imparting to others the enchantment of linking one's own individuality, universality, place, purpose, and people;

2. sharing with others how meaning is created by establishing links between the Realm of Interiority and the Realm of Exteriority

3. inspiring others to use the microcosm (such as one's intimate partner) as a model for understanding, venerating, and protecting the macrocosm (such as one's neighborhood or the planet);

4. inspiring oneself and others to continually seek to grow in both depth and balance and then use one's own exceptional

perception and span to provide leadership and insight un-available to those who are not as deep and balanced; and

5. using Love, Knowledge and the Will to bolster the Earth one person at a time.

Nocturnal Pilgrimage 4.67

For best results, write down your impressions of each night's dreams in your journal using the Heartwood Path Dreaming Time Protocols found in the Appendix. Afterwards, consider sharing your Dream Tending with others.

"In one sense, the solution to light pollution is a simple one: turn down the lights . . . In addition to having a positive impact on our health, de-lumination would help us restore our lost sense of rhythmicity and deliver significant economic benefits" (Naiman, 2006, p. 197).

With this quote and the previous lesson in mind, sleep and set an intention to dream about whether darkness is important to you. Before going to sleep think about the value of darkness in any natural environment.

Pertinent And Instructive Gems From My Dream Tending Journal

I dreamt that I was afraid to reveal to my co-workers, family, and friends both the nonsense of my dreams and the bland concreteness of my waking consciousness.

Lesson Learned: We eartHearts will need to be willing to brave the scorn that may come our way by revealing odd events in our dreams and boring aspects of our daily lives. We, nevertheless, will need to speak both about our dream world insights and about our waking world observations. Doing so will make you more familiar to others, it will add numbers to your list of friends and confidants, and it will spread the word about the insights and observations. This sharing may also lead to important consensus-building and greater understanding. Don't bother correcting for any illogical sequences, non-sequiturs, and unverified occurrences that may come to your attention.

The impulse to be a part of life is reinforced by being outdoors. There, your subconscious mind will help you identify with the multitudes of attractive beings through which the life force is expressed. For this reason, be sure to do the next activity, and all future activities, beyond the confines of walls. After tending to your dreams, head to the next waypoint: "Sources Of Support."

68

Sources Of Support

KNOW WHAT CAUSES A PERSON TO BE A SUPPORTER OF ENVIRONMENTAL PROTECTION

In my experience, people become environmentalists by proceeding down any of six trails:

1. they become committed after gathering information, from newspapers, television, and radio reports;
2. they become environmentalists because they are already supporters of social justice;
3. they make a connection with the environmental movement by having their health, property, or other species threatened;
4. they learn to appreciate of the link between health, fitness, and ecological quality;
5. they develop mystical love for nature, arising from positive encounters; and
6. they embark on natural history excursions to exotic places and participate in directed study on organized field trips.

The route of any or all of these paths to environmentalism typically leads to another area of involvement—a different kind of activity known as the hero's journey down the pathway of citizenship. This pathway of citizenship often leads to the arena of politics, including all political acts related to the effort to address climate change and other environmental issues.

To Understand What Spurs Environmental Protection...

HumaNatureConnect Activity

Start-up Protocol

If this is not a day when you prefer to spend time in nature without an agenda, do the Heartwood Path Start-up Protocol found in the Appendix.

Understanding What Causes One's Support For Environmental Protection

Use your sense of temperature and temperature change to understand what causes your support for environmental protection. Look around you or use your memory to think about examples of climate change in your area. Pick any small local nearby attraction such as a plant within reach. Consider how this plant will be affected by climate change—which may take the form of gradual warming accompanied by dramatic shifts in temperature, both hotter and colder. Then consider how this plant's larger community will be affected by global climate change. Psychologically assume the essence of the small plant and then do the same for the larger community, and, as each, tell how changes in temperature is (or is not) a cause for alarm. Use the natural sense of "hearing including resonance, vibrations, sonar and ultrasonic frequencies" (Cohen, website: http://www.ecopsych.com/

insight53senses.html) to make a humming sound of the smaller plant to indicate its concern about climate change. Do the same for the larger community. Note whether this tone is light and cheerful or heavy and fearful. As the nearby plant, ask yourself as you hum: "Have you sensed any unusual changes in temperature?" Such changes need not only be about warming. The general trend in global warming may, particularly at first, be experienced as greater fluctuations in temperature. Again, as the plant, ask while humming: "Have you noticed more coldness or more hotness? Have you noticed the local presence of more animals that are typically found more often in warmer climates?" You may not be able to notice a change in actual temperature, but you may see other temperature-related signs of climate change. I have noticed, for example, that the winters near St. Louis seem, in a subtle way, less severely cold than they were when I was a child. A more obvious sign of possible global warming for me is the fact that twenty-five years ago an organization I was involved in rented cross-country skis for local use. Then, about fifteen years ago, we noticed that the rentals were being used only for northerly trips to Minnesota and Wisconsin. That organization recently sold the skiing equipment because of nonuse. I have also seen more armadillos in my area, a species that was not seen in my youth because it typically lived only in warmer areas to the South. As the nearby plant, ask yourself: "Can you feel a change in climate? Do you see other signs of climate change?" I worry that the changes I have noticed in the global climate will have dramatic negative environmental consequences and these concerns propel me to be a supporter of environmental protection. As the plant, ask yourself while humming" "Do your temperature-change feelings or do the signs of climate change you perceive worry you enough to become a supporter of environmental protection? Is nature sending you any temperature-related signals of distress? Do any of the other natural senses lead you to become a supporter of environmental protection?" You can hum both your questions and your answers.

Follow-up Protocol

For best results, write down your impressions of this activity in your journal using the Heartwood Path Follow-up Protocol found in the Appendix. Afterwards, consider sharing your interpretations with others.

Heartwood Path Axioms

Key Assertions From Waypoint 4.68

4.68.1.

People become committed after gathering information, from newspapers, television, and radio reports.

4.68.2.

People become environmentalists because they are already supporters of social justice.

4.68.3.

People make a connection with the environmental movement by having their health, property, or other species threatened.

4.68.4.

People become environmentalists by developing a mystical love for nature, arising from positive encounters.

4.68.5.

People become environmental supporters by embarking on natural history excursions to exotic places and participate in directed study on organized field trips.

Nocturnal Pilgrimage 4.68

For best results, write down your impressions of each night's dreams in your journal using the Heartwood Path Dreaming Time Protocols found in the Appendix. Afterwards, consider sharing your Dream Tending with others.

"Despite the fact that the benefits of de-lumination outweigh the costs on all fronts, we are left with our psychological resistance to experiencing darkness. But just as shadow work promises to reveal the diamonds in coal, so does de-lumination offer to reacquaint us with the forgotten magnificence of the night sky" (Naiman, 2006, p. 198).

With this statement and the just-completed teaching in mind, begin your preparations for sleep. Set an intention to dream about the importance you place on being able to use darkness to see the stars and planets of the night's sky. Dream productively. Upon waking, tend to your dreams.

In doing all of the following activities, you are encouraged to follow the instructions regarding going outside to commune with nature, in part, as a way to minimize your extrinsic values regarding money, power, and fame and to maximize your prosocial intrinsic aspirations regarding giving to others. It has been shown in a 2009 study at the University of Rochester that participants told to imagine immersing themselves in the four natural places depicted in photographs claimed that they would be more likely to give to others than did the group that view four city-scape scenes. In another study, the presence of four plants in a room produced similar results (Selhub & Logan, 2012, pp. 56-57). In short, exposure to nature, even pictures of nature, makes people more prosocial, it makes them have more intrinsic values, it encourages them to be more driven to give to others, and helps them place less emphasis on external values such as status and the hoarding money for themselves alone. For these reasons, remember to look over the photographs of nature at the Heartwood Path website (www.heart-woodpath.com) or Instagram account (@HeartwoodPath). Or, better yet, go outside to an attractive natural place before or while doing each activity.

As you did at the very first Heartwood Path waypoint, set out to do the next activity in a conscious spirit of gratitude. As you head outside, contemplate how you are thankful for all the attractive beings and landscapes. Express your gratefulness to the Absolute Spirit for making available to anyone who takes the time to seek consent to engage in the kinds of connection experiences presented at each Heartwood Path learning station. When you are ready, head to the next stop, "Fight The Fever."

69

Fight The Fever

INOCULATE YOURSELF AGAINST THE POTOMAC

It is important that eartHearts win their environmental battles, but it is also important that they engage themselves with vitality, longevity, and integrity. Unlike many lobbyists who trade their positive convictions for the limelight and power of Washington DC, eartHearts fight this type of "Potomac Fever" in several ways.

Potomac Fever is a psychological condition wherein the "infected," usually someone who lives or works in Washington D.C., presents an intense desire to be associated with the power and prestige of the United States government. Symptoms include being servile, obedience, or excessive attentiveness to those in power or likely to be in power.

Unlike those with Potomac Fever, eartHearts consciously strive to balance politics with wilderness travels. They equalize solitude with companionship. They even-up the effects of the wild with the effects of the domestic. They balance their "advocation" with their vocation. They weigh their commitment to the cause with their commitment to family and friends. They counter spontaneity with discipline. Lastly, they tie their political responsibility to their spiritual development.

To assess your own affinity for nature, do the following activity:

To A Calculation Of Your Exposure To Nature...

HumaNatureConnect Activity

Start-up Protocol

If this is not a day when you prefer to spend time in nature without an agenda, do the Heartwood Path Start-up Protocol found in the Appendix.

Determining The Amount Of Time You Spend In Nature

Draw a large circle in bare soil. Calculate what percentage of time you spend inside buildings. Mark that percentage on the circle. The remaining segment will almost certainly be less than half of the circle. Of the remaining time, mark how much is spent in automobiles, on pavement or other artificial surfaces, in a domesticated environment. For most people the entire circle will be filled by now. Looking at the circle, think of advantages of spending time in natural settings outdoors. Emphasize the rewards. Make a conscious commitment to spend more time outdoors, whether it occurs on porches, in yards, in parks, or in the wild.

Follow-up Protocol

For best results, write down your impressions of this activity in your journal using the Heartwood Path Follow-up Protocol found in the Appendix. Afterwards, consider sharing your interpretations with others.

Heartwood Path Axioms

Key Assertions From Waypoint 4.69

4.69.1.

Unlike many lobbyists who trade their positive convictions for the limelight and power of Washington DC, eartHearts fight "Potomac Fever," marked by excessive obedience, servitude and excessive attentiveness to people in power.

4.69.2.

EartHearts consciously strive to balance politics with wilderness travels, the wild with the effects of the domestic, their "advocation" with their vocation, and their commitment to the cause with their commitment to family and friends.

4.69.3.

EartHearts equalize solitude with companionship.

4.69.4.

EartHearts balance spontaneity with discipline and their political responsibility with their spiritual development.

Nocturnal Pilgrimage 4.69

For best results, write down your impressions of each night's dreams in your journal using the Heartwood Path Dreaming Time Protocols found in the Appendix. Afterwards, consider sharing your Dream Tending with others.

"Many ideas . . . (occur) to me during regular walks through the boundaries of darkness, at dusk and dawn" (Naiman, 2006, p. 198).

Thinking about the inspirations of twilight and fighting the fever for power, drift off to sleep. Dream useful dreams. Tend to them before getting out of bed in the morning.

As you get up and prepare for your day, including when you are going to do the next HumaNatureConnect Activity, think about how your participation along the Heartwood Path is helping to overcome the present worrisome loss that is happening in society—the widespread and significant loss of 2 million years of evolutionary time when we as a species were immersed in nature, when we were in contact with its natural beings throughout our days and nights. Do we really want to damage this connectivity to each other and the planet? Are the distractions of video games, incoming emails, cable television, and streaming entertainment on computers worth the loss of the guidance, healing, and information we can gain from nature immersion? Is it worth it to you to step away from your e-gadgets and toward an attractive natural being, if only for a few minutes per day?

After pondering these questions, move to the next waypoint. Rejoice in how the earth is not barren of life by making a connection experience with an attractive natural being or landscape in the next activity.

We can never get too much meditation time in nature. When you are ready to get some more nature time for yourself and to learn about the important topic of one's eco-political identity, head to the next waypoint: "Green Voter."

70

Green Voter

DEVELOP YOUR ECO-POLITICAL IDENTITY

To protect the environment some people are content to send money to conservation organizations. Others, seeking more dialogue and less superficiality, attend seemingly endless meetings, strategy sessions, and public forums. Those who take the more active form of involvement find that political participation sometimes comes in the two forms: 1) the often disagreeable form of wheeling and dealing, cajoling, and manipulating; and 2) the more agreeable form of cooperative ventures, coalition-building, and bridging conceptual gaps that lead to solutions. Either way, one's ecological identity arises in a social and political context.

The way to seek resolution to public issues is politics—society's legitimate form of coercion. For this reason, it is imperative that all conservation-minded individuals form their own political identity.

To do so, it is helpful to reflect on the role of controversy, authority, consensus, and relational power. Controversy, for eartHearts, is not sought but it is also not shunned. Sometimes things need to be stirred up. Often, while one's goals may be radical, conservative means may be most productive. Such means include: working with the media, generating letters to elected officials, helping with election of friendly candidates, assembling peacefully, and, as a last resort, "suing the bastards."

Authority, for those interested in democratically protecting the public interest, rests ultimately in the hands of the citizens. EartHearts are prone to mediation but will stand up to abuses in authority when those in power disregard human rights, justice, or ecological sustainability.

EartHearts may want to remain independent in their political affiliations. Both the Democrats and the Republicans have undue influence on elections and the process of passing laws. Political parties are not required by the constitution. They are clubs. While they have the right to assemble and voice their opinions, their efforts to dominate the selection of candidates for office (through the two-party primary system and the drawing of congressional districts boundaries for partisan advantage) and their efforts to fight worthy pieces of legislation solely for partisan reasons are not the hallmarks of a true and respected democracy. The constant stalemate that exists because of the partisan bickering between the two parties is no way for a government to solve problems. EartHearts could play a useful role in electing statesmen who have the will to rise above petty partisanship and the will to do what is right for the people, the nation, and the world.

At the group level, consensus is an admirable way for groups to make decisions unless holding to one hundred percent agreement keeps the group from taking any meaningful action (group decision-making is addressed further in a subsequent Heartwood Path for Groups book, called **Collectivos**). One way to avoid this potential problem is to hold to consensus as a way to make decisions but do not require one hundred percent agreement—opting, for example, to require sixty or seventy-five percent agreement instead.

Relational power pierces all aspects of daily life, not as an instrument of control that is external to a situation, but as an intrinsic means to make decisions and thereby expand choices. Existent in all large organizations, relational power is people working together, helping each other out, teaming up for success, forgiving mistakes, and generally sticking together. Relational power is not coercive, domineering, or used to gain an advantage. It is not "power over," where one side wins and another loses; it is "power with," where all parties work to seek the common ground.

The political dimension of the Heartwood Path is based on the following three assumptions/axioms:

1. upholding the morality of relational power (power with) is important;
2. conflicts can be resolved when each opposing side looks carefully at their own attitudes and motivations; and
3. controversy itself is, or can be, an educational means for finding higher purpose.

Inevitably, all eartHearts face the ethical question of the use of coercion, in the form of propaganda, manipulation, or government regulation, for solving pressing environmental problems. Most environmental battles ultimately entail some form of coercion—some entity (usually a government agency) forcibly compels another entity (usually a citizen, business, agency, or corporation) into compliance, obedience, or other courses of action. Winning these limited battles, while sometimes helpful, does not mean that the overall war to protect the environment, or even the campaign about a specific issue, is over. Turning more people out for a forest policy hearing, for example, does not, alone, protect the wilderness.

Significant environmental reform is not possible without a significant change in the way people think. There is a common starting point for all environmental problems: the human mind. We need to work to improve technologies, but this approach, by itself, will not solve all of our environmental problems. We need to also examine human attitudes and beliefs. Specifically, we need to continue to improve our understanding of how the mind and nature relate to each other. Those with opinions or information about this relationship are encouraged to post them in the forum section on the EartHeart Networking page at heartwoodpath.com.

I know from my experience leading people through wilderness areas that when people are left alone in a natural place without any books or other distractions for at least three to four hours they tend to think more deeply about themselves, their relationships, and their values. Moments in nature are good for their mental health and these moments can also inspire the values needed to protect the environment.

A significant part of the process of thinking about environmental reform is the consideration of values. Environmental values are cultivated more through nature experiences and experiencing one's nature than they are through intimidation. For this reason, eartHearts prefer not to use force.

To The Formation Of One's Communal Self…

HumaNatureConnect Activity

Start-up Protocol

If this is not a day when you prefer to spend time in nature without an agenda, do the Heartwood Path Start-up Protocol found in the Appendix.

Developing Your Eco-political Identity

Use your sense of humility, appreciation, and ethics to work on developing your eco-political identity. Humble yourself before a plant within your reach by offering to do its bidding politically. Show your appreciation to this plant's community by appreciating the beauty of its organic wholeness. Use your natural sense of "hearing including resonance, vibrations, sonar and ultrasonic frequencies" (Cohen, website: http://www.ecopsych.com/insight53senses.html) to hum the tone of the individual attractive being. Hum the tone of the surrounding environment. Hum the tone of your *humility* before it. Appreciate the quality of this tone and any message it conveys. Offer to act in a political way according to your ethical interpretive response to these tones. This means that you will not be like a "doomster" or like a "boomster" but you will be like a "Humester"—a humming "Humester"—who relies on benevolent desire to preserve nature for all and for posterity. Humming Humesters guide their behavior by listening to their feelings as they hum rather than on relying solely on their reason as they think. Like a "Humester," use your lively impressions and direct sensations to affect your ethics. These ethics are based on feelings and nonmoral natural sentiments that affirm nature. In this case, you are relying on the personal feelings that occur as you hum rather than on abstract moral principles. After humming your humility, hum the sound of your intended political activism. As the essence of the plant, ask yourself" "Does the humming sound convey weakness, forcefulness, effectiveness, kindness, boldness, or righteousness? Does the tone sound remarkable and exciting or more like the humdrum? As the essence of the plant's community, ask yourself: "Are you humming tones that are concordant (pleasing, harmonious, do not clash) or are they discordant (unpleasing, unharmonious, clash) when compared to the humming tones of the individual plant and the tone of its larger community? Note what the concordance or discordance tells you.

Follow-up Protocol

For best results, write down your impressions of this activity in your journal using the Heartwood Path Follow-up Protocol found in the Appendix. Afterwards, consider sharing your interpretations with others.

Heartwood Path Axioms

Key Assertions From Waypoint 4.70

4.70.1.

The way to seek resolution to public issues is politics—society's legitimate form of coercion.

4.70.2.

To form your political identity, it is helpful to reflect on the role of controversy, authority, consensus, and relational power.

4.70.3.

The political dimension of the Heartwood Path is based on the following three assumptions/axioms: 1) upholding the morality of relational power (power with) is as important as environmental reform; 2) conflicts can be resolved when each opposing side looks carefully at their own attitudes and motivations; and 3) controversy itself is an educational means for finding higher purpose.

4.70.4.

Significant environmental reform is not possible without a significant change in the way people think.

4.70.5.

Most environmental battles ultimately entail some form of coercion—some entity (usually a government agency) forcibly compels another entity (usually a citizen, business, agency, or corporation) into compliance, obedience, or other courses of action.

Nocturnal Pilgrimage 4.70

For best results, write down your impressions of each night's dreams in your journal using the Heartwood Path Dreaming Time Protocols found in the Appendix. Afterwards, consider sharing your Dream Tending with others.

Here's an idea: Start a community sunset-watching ritual. With sunsets and conservation voting in mind as you prepare for sleep, have transformative dreams. When you awaken, be sure to tend to your dreams.

Do not think that because one's brain is aroused by addictions, including addiction to the Internet, that this sort of extra brain activity is making one significantly smarter. Mere mental arousal does not always result in extra focus or intelligence.

All of the options our society presents to us causes what is known as *directed attention fatigue*. Basically, by facing the flood of options that come across the media we are tiring that part of the brain that helps us make healthy choices—a very inefficient way to function cognitively. Fortunately, we can use nature to "take the load off all the inhibitory effort required in our modern world" (Selhub & Logan, 2012, p. 63). Psychologist Edward Thorndike states that "when we are immersed in an environment where stimulants (objects, we call them "beings") are naturally attractive to us . . . (the natural environment) wins place over other thoughts without feeling any effort on our part. If the task at hand (communing with nature) is attractive and absorbing, fatigue diminishes" (Selhub & Logan, 2012, p. 62). Reinforcing the notion that natural beings in nature might provide cognitive restoration, Psychologist Dr. Stephen Kaplan posits that natural beings in "natural environments are fascinating and, as such, they hold involuntary attention without requiring an expenditure of energy in the brain that would otherwise cause cognitive fatigue" (Selhub & Logan, 2012, p. 63). From these statements, participants can be reassured that by doing the HumaNatureConnect Activities, **and by not just reading the text for this course,** they will be achieving cognitive clarity and an absence of confusion without also producing mental fatigue. In this state of optimal functioning, one's best thoughts and one's more helpful emotions can arise and do good for each of us as individuals and for the world at large!

Assimilate the powerful remedies nature provides for your culturally- inflicted dislocations and disorientations as you do the next activity in the wild. When you are ready, move to the next place of learning: "Fem Lib."

71

Fem Lib

FOSTER THE ASCENDANCE BUT NOT THE DOMINANCE OF ECO-FEMINISM

Eco-feminism is for both men and women. Men need eco-feminism because over the ages they have been conditioned to act as terrestrial gods imposing their will on the natural world for the good of Modernity. Both sexes are encouraged to develop emotional sensibilities, intuition, and nurturing (the so-called feminine qualities) as equal complements to reason, rationality and objectivity (the so-called masculine qualities). Sex-based arrangements throughout history have been difficult for both men and women. Whenever the sexes are polarized or separated, both suffer—often horribly. EartHearts are committed to valuing the differences and the polarity between men and women. They work to give equal emphasis, authority, power, and responsibility to both sexes. They support a woman for President because, as we all know, we would not have to pay her as much.

To Substantiate The Wisdom Of Delicacy...

HumaNatureConnect Activity

Start-up Protocol

If this is not a day when you prefer to spend time in nature without an agenda, do the Heartwood Path Start-up Protocol found in the Appendix.

Supporting Eco-feminism

Use the radiation "sense of awareness of one's own visibility or invisibility and consequent camouflaging" to asses the value of the commonalities, differences and polarity between maleness and femaleness, between nature and culture, and between the individualization of the self and the integration of the individual self into the whole (Cohen, 1989, p. 8). Begin by identifying a relatively small, nearby male being in nature and a small, nearby female being in nature. These can be either animals or plants (some trees are males, some are females, and most are both). Perceive how the gender of your chosen beings is visible and/or how the gender is camouflaged. Hum a tone that seems compatible with the essence of this being. If possible, identify and hum the tone of the opposite gendered being of the same species. You can also identify and hum the tone of the male and female parts of a flower. Write down any feelings or messages you perceive to be embedded in the tones. Next, hum a tone that conveys your chosen nearby natural attraction as it is embedded in its natural community and then imagine how the tone would change as this being is (in your imagination) moved to or used by human culture. Repeat the hum associations with nature as a whole and with culture as a whole. Perceive the roles of the genders in destroying or protecting the environment. Then, in the mind's eye, camouflage the gender differences and perceive how people of both genders share a partnership in their roles as destroyers and protectors of the environment. Hum a tone that conveys empathetic resonance with maleness as it relates to the environment, with femaleness as it relates to the environment, and with gender-partnership as it relates to the environment. Write down any feelings or messages you perceive to be embedded in the tones. Given what you perceive and interpret from the thoughts and the feelings you receive from the tones, answer the best you can the following questions (and feel free to be as expansive and as off-topic as you wish): Do women have a special role to play in environmental protection? Is the Earth a female? What are the benefits and detriments to a feminist approach to conservation? What are the benefits and detriments to a gender-partnership approach to conservation? How is it helpful and/or detrimental to, metaphorically speaking, keep both eyes open to the gender roles in conservation, to keep both eyes closed to the gender roles in conservation, or to keep one eye open and one eye closed to gender roles in conservation or in other life-circumstances?

Follow-up Protocol

For best results, write down your impressions of this activity in your journal using the Heartwood Path Follow-up Protocol found in the Appendix. Afterwards, consider sharing your interpretations with others.

Heartwood Path Axioms

Key Assertions From Waypoint 4.71

4.71.1.

Eco-feminism is for both men and women.

4.71.2.

Men need eco-feminism because over the ages they have been conditioned to act as terrestrial gods imposing their will on the natural world for the good of Modernity.

4.71.3.

Both sexes are encouraged to develop emotional sensibilities, intuition, and nurturing (the so-called feminine qualities) as equal complements to reason, rationality and objectivity (the so-called masculine qualities).

4.71.4.

Whenever the sexes are polarized or separated, both suffer— often horribly.

4.71.5.

EartHearts are committed to valuing the differences and the polarity between men and women; and they work to give equal emphasis, authority, power, and responsibility to both sexes.

Nocturnal Pilgrimage 4.71

For best results, write down your impressions of each night's dreams in your journal using the Heartwood Path Dreaming Time Protocols found in the Appendix. Afterwards, consider sharing your Dream Tending with others.

Remember, along the Heartwood Path you can follow your attractions and do your own activities whenever you want. Here's a suggested additional or alternative activity you can use whenever you like: really listen to nature. Determine, for example, which voice a bird is using: its song voice, its companion-calling voice, its begging voice, its male-to-male aggressive voice, or its alarm voice. Making these distinctions will likely require that you be the bird's audience on many occasions. So start today. Be patient. As you listen for how birds solve their problems (like where to find food, water, a mate) your own solutions may begin to get a fair hearing. Allow the remedies you seek to crystalize within you.

It's better to work calmly to satisfy your curiosity and to seek out your interests in nature than it is to frantically scan the web for modern day info-toxin—bits of information that seem interesting but, because in truth they are not fascinating, they tend to cause you to spend too much cognitive energy. Stem this drain by frequently looking for fascinating beings in nature, beings that do not cause the same drain that you experience from television viewing or Internet searches.

More on this sort of attention restoration therapy follows. In the meantime, perhaps the following quote will give you some food for thought:

"We are waking-centric and have virtually no acceptable, coherent social framework for acknowledging the value and place of night consciousness, sleep, and dreams . . ." (Naiman, 2006, p. 201-202).

With Naiman's comments and eco-feminism in mind, sleep and dream. Use the EartHeart Exchange to share your impressions with others.

Pertinent And Instructive Gems From My Dream Tending Journal

I dreamt that I wanted to give a speech to environmentalists but no one wanted to hear it.

Lesson Learned: Do not only seek to inform with facts. Also, motivate by sharing your feelings and enthusiasm.

When you are ready to resume your journey to Gladandgreen Junction, move to the next learning station: "Smell The Change." There, you will learn about the Triad of Transcendence: 1) know thyself by looking within, 2) view everything as thyself, and 3) unify opposites.

72

Smell The Change

MEMORIZE AND "SMELL" THE
TRIAD OF TRANSCENDENCE

Hope for the future depends on the Heartwood Path's Triad of Transcendence:

1. Know thyself by looking within.
2. View everything as thyself.
3. Unify opposites.

If people from around the world adopt this Triad Of Transcendence I feel a planetary consciousness will emerge that will provide for a recognition for the need for ecological balance, unrestrained global dis-course, minimally coercive forms of government, the "feminization" of society on earth (discussed earlier), and acceptance of the "deepening" of ecology (discussed at the next waypoint).

Does your looking within make you feel like singing like the birds? Does viewing everything as thyself make you feel like sounding an alarm, in much the same way birds warn others of impending danger? Does unifying opposites cause you to make companion-calling sounds?

What do your answers tell you about your knowledge or role in the Triad of Transcendence?

If sounds in nature do not give the Triad of Transcendence a fair hearing for you, try working with smells or metaphors for smells. How does it smell when you nose around your inner world? Does it reek of evil or is there the sweet smell of success? How, if at all, does not using the Triad of Transcendence create the stench of doom? If you do not find fragrance in your answers, perhaps you need to work more with your nose—or metaphors about the nose—by doing the following activity.

To Become Nosey...

HumaNatureConnect Activity

Start-up Protocol

If this is not a day when you prefer to spend time in nature without an agenda, do the Heartwood Path Start-up Protocol found in the Appendix.

Becoming A "Nose-it-all"

Use the chemical sense of smell with and beyond the nose. For this activity, I am not asking you to only pick out scents out in the environment with your nose. "All smells occur in the brain" says Adnan Oktar (Oktar website). I am not just asking you to do any of the following things with your nose only, so to speak:

1. distinguish inner world scents—rather like picking out the "smell" of a rat, or distinguishing a "red herring—"
2. have a nose to detect and sense,
3. check on whether you are prying—putting your nose into other peoples' business,

4. to properly moving or pushing as if with the nose (gently),
5. advancing cautiously—like nosing your car into the flow of traffic,
6. to nose around looking for opportunities,
7. to persevere until you at least nose out a narrow victory, and
8. to be exact and precise—to score on the nose.

These would be literary or metaphorical synesthesia—an artistic mode of expression based on cross-sensory juxtaposition, such as "Her perfume is loud."

Thanks to several members of the Project NatureConnect's online professional online group, I understand "smelling beyond the nose" as experiencing what would for most people be a smell but instead experiencing it as another sensory presence, such as a taste, a feeling, or a color. Use this activity to test or improve your physical experience of synesthesia.

Smell a nearby attractive natural being. Describe its smell and then see if the natural being's smell also registers in any of your other senses —look for colors, listen for sounds, feel for the sensation of touch, await the arrival of associated memories, and attempt to perceive what I perceive when others voice the presence of a smell I cannot perceive with my nose: a faint presence. Hum a tone that represents the smell or the experience of synesthesia. Do the same things for the natural being's larger natural community as a whole. What messages do you receive from your humming, from your sense of smell, or from synesthesia, if any, regarding any expanded inner knowledge of yourself, regarding integrating yourself into the whole, and unifying seemingly opposite natural beings: a predator such as a lion with a prey animal such as a gazelle, an animal that soars such as a hawk with an animal that digs, such as a mole. What is the smell or experience of synesthesia associated with your inner world, with your integration into the whole, and with your ability or desire to unify opposites?

To make the impressions more clear, make psychological differences, such as:

1. "smelling" your inner world while having angry thoughts as opposed to kind thoughts,
2. "applying your nose" to the local environment when you hold yourself psychologically apart from nature and then again when you are psychologically united with the whole, and
3. when opposites are apart in your mind and then again when they are unified in your mind.

Are there any messages associated with your humming, your sense of smell, or your experience of synesthesia pertaining to anything else beyond your inner world experience, your integration with the whole, and your unifying of opposites? If so, explain.

Follow-up Protocol

For best results, write down your impressions of this activity in your journal using the Heartwood Path Follow-up Protocol found in the Appendix. Afterwards, consider sharing your interpretations with others.

Heartwood Path Axioms

Key Assertions From Waypoint 4.72

4.72.1.

Hope for the future depends on the Heartwood Path's Triad of Transcendence:

1) Know thyself by looking within.

2) View everything as thyself. And

3) Unify opposites.

4.72.2.

If people from around the world adopt the Triad Of Transcendence a planetary consciousness will emerge that will provide for a recognition for the need for ecological balance, unrestrained global discourse, minimally coercive forms of government, the "feminization" of society on earth, and acceptance of the "deepening" of ecology.

4.72.3.

To restore your attention span, be attracted to move away from taxing stimuli, go to a place that you like, a place with enough natural diversity to hold your attention for a while, a place that is not overwhelming, a place with fascinations that psychologically leaves room for the generation and processing of impressions.

Nocturnal Pilgrimage 4.72

For best results, write down your impressions of each night's dreams in your journal using the Heartwood Path Dreaming Time Protocols found in the Appendix. Afterwards, consider sharing your Dream Tending with others.

"At night, sleep is our rest and dreaming is activity. By day, waking is activity and dreaming becomes our rest" (Naiman, 2006, p.202).

Keep the dialectic of day and night and the smell of change or difference firmly in mind as you drift off to sleep. Dream. Then, tend to your dreams before getting out of bed in the morning.

Prepare To Put To Use Kaplan's Attention Restoration Theory

In our everyday lives, spent mostly indoors, we inevitably become fatigued, especially as our attention is directed at computer screens for work or pleasure. This fatigue causes us to become less productive and more irritable.

The solution is to ease our *taxing directed* attention with *easy involuntary* attention. That is very difficult to do indoors, in front of a computer or television, or in an unnatural, built, urban area.

Earlier we presented much anecdotal evidence and cited much scientific research that shows that our attention spans and our physical and psychological health improves when we are exposed to nature in pristine settings, to pictures of nature, and to nature in our manicured backyards. We have encouraged you to find attractive beings in nature, the wilder the better.

When looking for a better way to restore your attention span, changing your place is equivalent to resting. What is better than resting is communing with nature while doing the following actions:

1. moving away from taxing indoor artificial stimuli;
2. physically moving yourself for your nature communing to a natural place that you like;
3. being appreciative of soft natural beings such as clouds or gently moving water; and by paying attention to relatively quiet attractions such as the chirping of hummingbirds rather than to hard natural attractions such as rocks or relatively loud attractions such as big, powerful waterfalls; and
4. visiting a place that makes you feel immersed in nature.

To meet these criteria, one's backyard or local, highly manicured, neighborhood park will usually not be sufficient. Potted plants, the shade tree outside of your office window, and nature photographs will help but Kaplan's four criteria—1) being away from indoor distractions, 2) being fascinated by soft and quiet attractions, 3) feeling like you are immersed in nature, and 4) liking the site for your nature communing —will do more to restore your attention span.

As you do the activity in the next waypoint, and, if you choose, in all of the activities that follow, keep in mind the following aspects of the four-part therapy based on Kaplan's ART—Attention Restoration Theory (Selhub & Logan, 2012, p. 63).

Being Away

As one does HumaNatureConnect Activities, Kaplan's theory (Selhub & Logan, 2012, p. 64) lets one know that it is not mandatory to be away from the source of the voluntary attention but it is advisable to mentally reframe the current environment by closing one's eyes and taking one's attention away from work matters. If one cannot leave the building to do HumaNatureConnect Activities, looking at nature photography, the application of imagination, or a good view of nature outside of a window will do.

But you can do better than that. As you continue to commune with nature, move outdoors and move away from all artificial distractions. Why fight the misdirections that come from artificial stimuli? Whenever possible, do your subsequent Heartwood Path nature communing in natural places.

Fascination

People are naturally fascinated by beings in nature. Kaplan's theory informs us to focus more on the softness of a sunset rather than the hardness of a football game on a field of rocks. Of the two, soft or quiet fascinations do a better job with cognitive restoration than do hard or loud fascinations (Selhub & Logan, 2012, pp. 64-65). Once you get to a natural area, focus on what is soft and what is quiet, such as trees, clouds, gently moving water, most bird calls, and leaves. Such so-called "soft fascinations" are those that do not overwhelm our attentional system. They do not sweep us away. They leave room for reflection. Seek out places or beings that are not too attentionally demanding—those that leave room for other thoughts and the processing of your impressions. A face-to-face encounter with a tiger in the wild or standing on the brink of an erupting volcano may be too fascinating for our purposes here.

Extent

For the best cognitive restoration, the natural environment will need to have a significant measure of depth, meaning that one potted plant will not help as much as a prairie with many flowers. Urban gardens designed to magnify the scope of the view, as many Japanese gardens do, are not, however, unworthy aids in the process of cognitive restoration. Even some nature photographs, when viewed with a degree of imagination, can be worthy aids (Selhub & Logan, 2012, p. 65). But for the easiest and best results, go to a place where you can feel truly and totally immersed in nature, especially a place with a big diversity of native plants and animals. Suitable places are those that allow us to dwell there for an extended period of time.

Compatibility

Kaplan's ART and Cohen's principle of gaining consent both tell us that the natural environment picked for one's cognitive restoration ought to be one that can fulfill one's individual activities and intentions without a struggle. If a natural being or a natural environment remains attractive to you for at least ten seconds, as most will, the chances of you leaving the natural setting disappointed with the outcome will be greatly diminished (Selhub & Logan, 2012, p. 65). The simple point here is to pick natural settings that you like. Some people do not like the desert. You may not like the beach. Go to places where you feel a sense of compatibility. Go to the places you like.

To restore your ability to pay attention, changing places is equivalent to resting. Better than resting is moving to a place outdoors; to a place where you can immerse yourself in nature; to a place with biological diversity; and to a place that has soft, quiet, fascinating, extensive, and pleasing. Make yourself a list of places nearby that have all of these characteristics. Visit them as often as possible.

Remember the four components of Kaplan Attention Restoration Theory as you proceed from one HumaNatureConnect Activity to the next: 1) being away, 2) fascination, 3) extent, and 4) compatibility. To help you restore your ability to pay attention, which will help you get the most from the rest of the Heartwood Path, a related new component—Attention Restoration—will be added to the remaining Start-up Protocol. Gladness and a newly protected natural environment—one that is made perpetually green by the application of your own will— await you as you progress through these activities to the end of the Heartwood Path.

By doing the activity of the next waypoint in nature, you will be learning how to leave the minefield of modernity that constrains what is meaningful to you. When you are ready to begin the next teaching, move to the next waypoint: "Deep Ecology Vs. Social Ecology."

73

Deep Ecology Vs. Social Ecology

FATHOM THE PHILOSOPHY

There are many nuanced differences between deep ecology and social ecology. As an eartHeart, you are free to base your philosophical leanings on both deep ecology and social ecology.

Rather than explain them here, I will let your participation in the following activity demonstrate the differences. Do the following activity to determine if you are a Deep Ecologist, a Social Ecologist, or some kind of mixture.

To An Understanding Of Deep Ecology And Social Ecology...

HumaNatureConnect Activity

Start-up Protocol

If this is not a day when you prefer to spend time in nature without an agenda, do the Heartwood Path Start-up Protocol found in the Appendix.

Staking Your Claim: Deep Ecology, Social Ecology, Or A Little Of Both

Blend your own persuasions with your psychological understanding of the perspective of your chosen natural attractive being as you indicate in your journal your support or lack of support for each of the following points in the platforms of deep ecology and social ecology.

Social Ecologists say the causes of the ecological crisis are ultimately and fundamentally social in nature ( ) I agree, ( ) I disagree.

Deep Ecologists, in contrast, locate the origin of the ecological crisis in belief systems (social causes are shallow excuses for the cause of the ecological predicament) ( ) I agree, ( ) I disagree.

Social ecologists view the natural world as a process that was not predetermined and is marked by increased development and subjectivity. The boundary between human and nonhuman nature is real ( ) I agree, ( ) I disagree.

Deep ecologists, in contrast, view nature and humanity as aspects of "cosmic oneness" and deny that there is a boundary between animality and humanity ( ) ( ) I agree, ( ) I disagree.

Social ecologists aim to reintegrate human communities with eco-communities ( ) I agree, ( ) I disagree.

Deep ecologists, in contrast, do not attempt to integrate humans with nature and regard any large presence of humans as intrinsically harmful to nature ( ) I agree, ( ) I disagree.

Social ecologists assert that humans, being the most advanced life-form, especially in the crucial respects of intelligences, moral capacity, and dexterity, have the evolutionary makeup to inter-vene in the natural world, an intervention that will be malignant or benign, depending on what kind of society is created ( ) I agree, ( ) I disagree.

Deep ecologists believe human-centeredness contributes to the ecological crisis and advance the concept of eco-centeredness and regard human intervention as inherently destructive ( ) I agree, ( ) I disagree.

Social ecologists think of themselves as enlightened and revolu-tionary and engage in social and political activity aimed at elim-inating the causes of the environmental predicament: namely, capitalism, social hierarchy, and the nation-state ( ) I agree, ( ) I disagree.

Deep ecologists, in contract, emphasize a quasi-mystical eco-logical consciousness, draw on a mixture of pagan, Taoist, Bud-dhist, Native American and other philosophies, and emphasize contemplation over political interventions that do not foster personal transformation or lifestyle changes ( ) I agree, ( ) I disagree.

(Website of Institute for Social Ecology: www.social-ecology.org/ 199)

Write down your impressions from doing this activity.

Follow-up Protocol

For best results, write down your impressions of this activity in your journal using the Heartwood Path Follow-up Protocol found in the Appendix. Afterwards, consider sharing your interpretations with others.

Heartwood Path Axioms

Key Assertions From Waypoint 4.73

4.73.1.

Fathom the difference between deep ecology and social ecology.

4.73.2.

Concerning the cause of the ecological crisis, social ecologist say its fundamentally social in nature while deep ecologists say belief systems are to blame.

4.73.3.

While social ecologist aim to reintegrate human communities with eco-communities, deep ecologists view any large presence of humans as intrinsically harmful to nature.

4.73.4.

Social ecologists contend that humans ought to use political intervention to protect the natural world while deep ecologists favor contemplate over political intervention.

Nocturnal Pilgrimage 4.73

For best results, write down your impressions of each night's dreams in your journal using the Heartwood Path Dreaming Time Protocols found in the Appendix. Afterwards, consider sharing your Dream Tending with others.

"Like a braid of hair in which three separate strands weave together to form a whole, sleeping, dreaming, and waking are woven rhythmically into a single strand of consciousness" (Naiman, 2006, p. 203).

By now the frequent connection experiences you are having outdoors are probably making you feel enfolded spiritually within a complex web of life. As you continue to move down the Heartwood Path, notice how it is continuing to help you feel less detached, lonely, or lost.

With Naiman's statement and your impressions of the just-completed lesson in mind as you prepare for sleep, have productive and enjoyable dreams.

Pertinent And Instructive Gems From My Dream Tending Journal

I dreamt that I was doing a very good job of redecorating the office where I worked but everyone thought it was a waste of time and money.

Lesson Learned: Do not do your good works in somber silence. Lighten up, become friendly, and perk up when you face opposition from allies. Keep your calculations and manipulations to yourself. When you express your intuition people will respond favorably. As other peoples' hearts and minds respond to your self-revelations, doors will be opened up to you.

When ready, move to the next waypoint: "Echoing." There, you will learn how to apply sound resonance and natural resonant frequency to receive guidance from nature.

74

Echoing

APPLY SOUND RESONANCE AND NATURAL RESONANT FREQUENCY TO RECEIVE GUIDANCE FROM NATURE

To understand the sense—by which I mean the reason, value, and shrewdness—of doing the following activity, one has to come to a knowing that is at the heart of the brand of eco-psychology used along the Heartwood Path, which is largely influenced by the work of Dr. Michael Cohen at Project NatureConnect. One has to come to an admission that one's intellect has limitations. These limitations arise because we humans in the western industrial world typically rely on a subset of our psycho-spiritual capability that gleans from the universe a limited and finite set of information. Good for many practical uses, such as building and consuming things, our self-imposed limited way of perceiving limits the reception of information (inputs) which causes us to have limited expressions and behavior (outputs). The limitation of our sensing and thinking to matters that are largely rational and logical is a useful way to deal with the world when one spends the bulk of one's day being a cog in the culture's economic engine. But, since we are obviously more than that, the self-imposed limitations in our thinking do not match the totality of our being and so, without finding more complete ways of knowing, we are left with inadequate ways to fulfill ourselves. In the words of Lama Govinda:

> "... our reality is our own creation, the creation of our senses as well as of our mind, and both depend on the level and dimension of our present state of consciousness" (Levey, 2003, p.72).

Govinda's words are presented here as a way to encourage the reader to continue with the activities, to keep going even though they ask you to make odd juxtapositions that are based on atypical perspectives.

The next activity encourages you to look for guidance in the odd manner of experiencing the sound of tastes and to glean messages about a topic at hand, in this case, the taste and tone of deep ecology. In doing the following activity, you just may find a suitable means to uncover a more total knowing of your own broad Ecological Self—a knowing you can use in your everyday life. To prepare yourself for the next activity you will need to understand *sound resonance.*

From the Latin word 'resonare," which means to "return to sound" resonance is "an induced vibration in an object and means to sound and resound, like an echo" (Sound-PHYSICS.com). All objects, including the attractive natural beings used in the activities of this book, "have a natural frequency or group of frequencies at which they like to vibrate" although some, indeed most, vibrate in a frequency or volume that is not audible to the human ear (Sound-PHYSICS.com).

The inaudibility of an object's vibration is one reason why in the activities of this book I frequently ask the participant to hum a tone that feels right or matches (echoes) the heard or imagined tone of an attractive natural being and its surrounding environment. The tone of one's humming is an audible expression of one's resonance with the natural object and the environment. "In the psychological realm," writes Renee Levi, Ph.D, "the word resonance primarily connotes empathy and emphatic connection."

While Levi's research is primarily about the empathy and resonance between humans, much of what she says, by extrapolation, is helpful in what I call "e-collective resonance"—that felt sense of energy, rhythm, or intuitive knowing that occurs between HumaNatureConnect participants, attractive natural beings, and the environment that positively affects the way they all interact toward a common purpose. In our case, this common purpose is usually working to come to a knowing of the topics of this course, but this commonality of intention can also apply to whatever topic or purpose a participant has in mind.

There is a flow of vibration between "things", including between people and natural beings, which creates a group dynamic. By "amplifying" a group's resonant connection—in a variety of ways, including humming—I believe there can be greater awareness of interpersonal and ecological matters that leads back to a pivotally important fundamental connection between people, and between people and their environment. Such connections, I contend, offer rewards beyond those that can be found in stories, in the exchange of ideas, and in everyday analytical problem-solving. Atypical connections such as receiving guidance through "e-collective" resonant humming are made through intuition and analogical thinking and are an important step in developing common personal, human, and ecological goals, including nondestructive goals that are common between people, and between people and so-called inanimate objects or natural beings.

There is a level of interaction that occurs as "an energetic connection" (Levi, 2003). The physical bodies of the interacting agents—be they human, non-human, alive, or inanimate—send "messages to one another through the medium between them—usually air—because each is vibrating constantly and affecting the electrostatic field around them. The vibration occurs because every atom vibrates constantly" (Levi, 2003). Writes Levi:

"Some of these vibrations are audible and many are not, but all are perceptible to other living systems...in the form of sound wave interchanges . . ." Levi, 2003).

Collective resonance (and arguably e-collective resonance) . . .

"is felt in the body, contains movement and rhythm, involves emotion, is felt as a connection to others, involves a felt sense of movement of boundaries, is high energy, includes touch and close physical proximity, requires a shift out of the cognitive and intellectual domain, is felt as a connection to self, feels calm, grounded, and relaxed, feels like an altered state of consciousness, contains awareness of an energy field, is felt as a connection to spirit, and requires total presence" (Levi, 2003).

It is this requirement for total presence where humming comes in.

Humming brings total presence to a person, if, by "total presence" one means bringing one back to one's center, settling feelings of restlessness, promoting clarity of thinking by "refreshing the mind," relaxing, "reducing the number of thoughts that fill your head." Humming helps dissolve unproductive thinking," calms the nervous system as it activates the parasympathetic nervous system, helps with insomnia and restless sleep patterns, induces helpful deep sleep . . . , charges the chakras, helps with sinusitis, cleans pathways and blockages, and lowers blood pressure (Kundalini Yoga Information Website). With these benefits, a humming person is made capable of resonating with other people, with natural beings and with the environment and, thereby, heightens feelings of harmony and empathy with other people, with natural beings, and the with environment. It is not hard to imagine how, in this state of presence, a person can glean "messages of guidance" embedded within the e-collective resonance or, if you prefer, how a person can form self-generated interpretations from the vibrations that are helpful in enumerable ways. Either way, there is no sense quibbling about whether the message is external to the mind or created within the mind. It is one's **reality of awareness that bridges the inner world to the outer world,** and back again. All is one, and this goes for the guidance that sometimes comes with resonance. As Govinda states, "our reality is our own creation" (Levey, 2003, p.72).

To The Flavor Of Nature...

HumaNatureConnect Activity

Start-up Protocol

If this is not a day when you prefer to spend time in nature without an agenda, do the Heartwood Path Start-up Protocol found in the Appendix.

Sensing The Taste And Tone Of Deep Ecology

After obtaining your chosen natural being's consent and setting up your optimal functioning, be a Smarty Plants and use caution before eating wild plants, as many have poisonous lookalikes. With do caution (particular with mushrooms, carrots and peas), use the sense of taste with and beyond the tongue to "voice" your reactions to each of the planks of deep ecology. First, actually or vicariously in your imagination, become familiar with the tastes of nature:

1. For a sweet wild edible that builds tissue and is said to calm the nerves try fruits and grains (I like the fruit of a paw-paw but good luck beating raccoons to them).
2. For a sour taste that is said to clean tissues and increase the absorption of minerals try sour fruits (I like wild grapes or blackberries).
3. For a slightly salty wild edible that is said to improve the taste of other foods, lubricate tissues, and stimulate digestion try sea vegetables (I like glassworts).
4. To get the benefits of bitter wild edibles, which are said to help with detoxification and weight management, try dark leafy greens (I like dandelion root or the tender shoots of pine needles in tea).

5. To clear the sinuses, promote sweating, improve metabolism, and relieve muscle pain, seek pungent (spicy) wild edibles (I like wild onions).

6. Wild edible astringent-tasting foods tend to make the mouth feel rough and dry. They are said to help with the absorption of water, the tightening of tissues, and the drying of fats. (I like persimmon bread and have had many a good laugh after someone—often me—puckered after biting into a persimmon that was not quite ripe) (Eat, Taste, Heal Website).

Using your sense of taste in and beyond the tongue, describe how any mental structure-—in this case, try each of the planks of deep ecology (listed in few pages earlier in this book)—"tastes" in your experience. Are the planks sweet or bitter, sour or salty, pungent or astringent? Write down why you associate a certain taste with a plank or with all the planks. Once you associate each plank with a taste, amplify the resonance of your tasty (the actual taste or the imaginary taste) attractive natural being and your present state by using your natural sense of "hearing including resonance, vibrations, sonar and ultrasonic frequencies" (Cohen, website: http://www.ecopsych.com/insight53senses.html) hum a tone that seems to be an echo of the vibration from the attractive being. Note how the tones change with each edible attractive being. Start by looking at each plank, associating a taste to the plank, and then humming a resonant tone that echoes your taste for each deep ecology plank. After such mental clearing, write down any messages or interpretations about how you feel towards the planks of ecology, especially those that seem to be other than those you experience by only reading the words about the planks. For increased perceptions about the tastes and tones of the deep ecology planks, hum a tone you associate with the tastes of each plank and compare these tones to the ones you perceive when you create resonant tones for the universal quality of the taste itself, such as the taste of saltiness itself or of any other taste when not attached to your experience of the taste of the planks: for example, compare the tones of your perception of the tastes of the deep ecology planks to the tones of the universal (unen-cumbered) tastes of sour, then pungent, then saltiness, and so on.

Follow-up Protocol

For best results, write down your impressions of this activity in your journal using the Heartwood Path Follow-up Protocol found in the Appendix. Afterwards, consider sharing your interpretations with others.

Heartwood Path Axioms

Key Assertions From Waypoint 4.74

4.74.1.

The limitation of our sensing and thinking to matters that are largely rational and logical are a useful way to deal with the world when one spends the bulk of one's day being a cog in the economic engine.

4.74.2.

The tone of one's humming is an audible expression of one's resonance with the natural object and the environment.

4.74.3.

The physical bodies of the interacting agents—be they human, non-human, alive, or inanimate)—send "messages to one another through the medium between them (usually air) because each is vibrating constantly and affecting the electro-static field around them.

4.74.4.

Humming helps dissolve unproductive thinking," calms the nervous system as it makes active the parasympathetic nervous system, helps with insomnia and restless sleep patterns, induces helpful deep sleep, charges the chakras, helps with sinusitis, cleans pathways and blockages, and lowers blood pressure.

4.74.5.

Humming makes a person capable of resonating with other people, with natural beings, and with the environment and, thereby, heighten feelings of harmony and empathy with other people, with natural beings, and the with environment.

Nocturnal Pilgrimage 4.74

For best results, write down your impressions of each night's dreams in your journal using the Heartwood Path Dreaming Time Protocols found in the Appendix. Afterwards, consider sharing your Dream Tending with others.

Being aware that you are dreaming and being able to influence the content of your dreams are vital lessons along the Heartwood Path. Since these dreaming skills are so important, we will present additional ways to encourage the development of lucid dreams:

1. Carlos Castaneda's method of visualizing your own hands and then knowing you are dreaming when your own hands appear in a dream;
2. Visualizing a particular melody, object, or person before sleeping and then knowing you are dreaming when these appear in your dream;

3. Repeatedly imagining yourself doing common actions such as driving before going to sleep and then knowing you are dreaming when these actions appear in your dream;
4. Repeatedly suggesting to yourself that tonight you will become conscious during your dreams;
5. While awake, imagining yourself having a specific dream;
6. While still lying in bed after dreaming tell yourself "Next time I want to remember to recognize that I am dreaming;"
7. Recognizing discrepancies in your dreams; and
8. Program yourself to have a flying dream, which are usually lucid dreams. (Goldberg, 2003, pp. 122-123).

With Goldberg's list and the previous lesson firmly in mind as you drift off to sleep, form an intention for your dream, dream, recall your dream, and tend to your dream as you awaken. Continue this sequence night after night, day after day.

At the next place of learning (the next waypoint), recall how impossible it would be to live without the larger natural community you are experiencing. To make this realization, it will be helpful to really get to know the natural being and its surrounding environment.

To get the most from the places of your HumaNatureConnect Activities, always consider doing the following:

1. find a place where you are comfortable in your attractions;
2. find a place that is so private and intimate lessons from nature can slowly seep in without distractions;
3. find a place that feeds your curiosity;
4. find a place that fuels your sense of wonder;
5. find a place where you can meet nature with your senses, eye-to-eye, nose-to-nose, ear-to-ear;
6. find a place where you can face and overcome your fears; and
7. find a place that feels like home.

Remember to be still when in the presence of your attractive being or landscape. Also remember to record your impressions and share them with others.

When ready, head to the next waypoint: "Inner Movement." There, you will learn to look within to help the environmental movement transcend.

75

Inner Movement

LOOK WITHIN TO HELP THE ENVIRONMENTAL MOVEMENT TRANSCEND

Understand what it takes to sustain yourself as an activist, then spread the word about what follows as a way to help the environmental movement retain its outer world effectiveness by sustaining itself with the inner world reflections of its activists. Movements that affect the outer world are governed by what is going on in the inner world of those involved and affected. For this reason, it is vital before ending this book to understand ways to make your inner world work well so that what you do in the outer world is ethical, effective, and efficient. As we will see, ways to make your inner world work well include working from a sense of joy, smelling the roses along the way, laughing a lot, constantly improving yourself, making your actions right, increasing your vitality, focusing on the love that pierces all realms of existence (ethics, intentions, behaviors, and physical systems, and more.

Work From A Sense Of Joy

Rather than finding your inspiration from a sense of obligation or a sense of duty, work more from a sense of joy. I am not speaking of giddy, hedonistic, senseless reverie. I am instead referring to finding the cheerful sense of obligation that will be contained within the joy. Working from a sense of joyless duty narrows one's focus and fosters fear of failure, fear of negative repercussion, and fear of judgment. Expand your perspective; carry fear and some sense of obligation to serve others along with you, but do not let your sense of fear and obligation overshadow awe, love, respect, appropriate pleasure, and integrity.

Smell The Roses And Laugh

Walk softly on the Earth, remember to smell the roses, and to seek out humor—often in the form of the presentation of surprise without threat or promise that is intended to raise peoples' spirits. We all know that the fact that there are no father-in-law jokes proves that humor is based on a modicum of truth. This is why my levity here has pertinence. Nevertheless, the quips you find inside this book series and the politicians you find outside of it have one thing in common: neither ought to be taken seriously.

Environmental Improvement Requires Self-improvement

Recognizing that one is obligated to work for necessary changes concerning the ecological predicament does not mean that one is personally capable of handling all the workload. This is another place where the Heartwood Path comes in. By adding practices to increase the vitality of those who work for the betterment of the Earth, the Heartwood Path encompasses and, indeed, transcends the environmental movement. It adds the new dimension of self-improvement for those who would conserve.

EartHearts transcend the environmental spectrum in that they work for change by combining the conservationists' approach of practical managerial skill and the thoughtful use of resources on a sustained yield basis for the benefit of present and future human generations with the environmentalists' emphasis on preservation of nature (especially wilderness) for its own sake regardless of its economic and utilitarian use by humans. Along with combining these two sometimes incompatible positions, eartHearts add a self-help component to the mix; thus adding a new dimension to the environmental movement. EartHearts are environmentalists in the ends that they seek. They are also a mixture of ecologists, spiritualists, psychologists, personal growth enthusiasts, and bodywork enthusiasts in the means they use to guide their right actions—which they do both because the actions are good for the environment **and** because they are good for the person involved in seeking the change.

Make Your Actions Right

Right actions for eartHearts are guided by and fueled by the intimate, heartfelt, loving connections they make within themselves, with the environment, and with a lover. These right actions need to increase the common good and one's personal welfare. EartHearts, then, embrace the traditional conservation/environment spectrum described above; and, with the added urgency of concern over human survival, they broaden its interpretation with the following formula that is intended to be all inclusive:

wilderness preservation + respect for nature + resource conservation + sustainable economics + public health + environmental justice + personal/spiritual development = the Great Work! (which is the job eartHearts do).

Be More Like A Rhizome And Less Like A Tree Trunk

When working to help environmentalists become more effective, eartHearts use the rhizome (a thick horizontal underground stem producing roots and shoots) rather than the tree trunk as a model. Cut a tree at the trunk and it will die; cut a rhizome any place and it will thrive on the separation. EartHearts support those at the grassroots level because, like crabgrass and day lilies, local entities have strength and defenses through their numbers and separation. EartHearts celebrate the diversity of local groups. Nobody is in charge of the grassroots environmental movement and that is how it ought to be.

Practice Healthy Skepticism About Environmental Management

While eartHearts support those who work toward managing the environment for the good of present and future generations, they are skeptical about the merits of totally managed environments. They agree, however, that humanity collectively is on the brink of acceptance of its preeminent role in affecting the future of the planet.

There is little doubt that we humans are greatly expanding our understanding and competence in the realm of environmental management. Nevertheless, we still do not really know what we are doing. Although Benjamin Franklin was referring to social engineering, there is much pertinence here for what he said: "Whenever we attempt to mend the scheme of providence, we had need be very circumspect lest we do more harm than good."

Franklin's wisdom can equally be applied to our efforts as a species to manage the planet's environment. Without much more expertise, relying on aggressive techniques to manage our way out of the environmental dilemma is a mistake. Doing so wastes time that could be devoted to other endeavors where our skills are sufficient for the task. The claim that we can at this time faithfully manage the earth's environment is a lie; and all lies dehumanize. Most efforts to manage the environment have been marginally successful, at best. Human-dominated management is always costly and typically results in an ugly scene. Rather than creating ugly scenes, an eartHeart:

1. seeks to offer guidance, support, and assistance to those who plead for positive ecological improvements in any of the areas on the conservation spectrum;
2. basically agrees with the eight deep ecology planks;
3. works on making the intimate connections of love between the great realms of existence (physical, mental, spiritual); and
4. works to help people expand their horizons so that they will have the perspective necessary to perfect themselves, find happiness, and preserve the planet.

Do Practices That Add To Your Vitality

Recognizing that one is obligated to work for the necessary changes concerning the ecological imperatives mentioned in this series of courses (i.e. declaring one's responsibility to others and forming one's political identity) does not mean that one is personally capable of handling all of the workload. This is yet another place where the Heartwood Path comes in. By adding practices to increase the vitality of those who work for the betterment of the earth the Heartwood Path encompasses and, indeed, transcends the environmental movement. It adds the new dimension of self-improvement for those who would conserve.

The Heartwood Path will bolster any just movement by encouraging it to transcend, become populated with self-actualized supporters, become more spiritual, and be led or assisted by those who can operate indefinitely at the upper range of activity without crashing. This may seem like a big job and it would be if there were not ways to make a priority list. Fortunately, there is a guideline to help eartHearts choose how to best spend their time for the cause of environmental protection. This guideline is the topic of the next section.

Focus On The Love That Pierces All Realms Of Existence

EartHearts will need to combine various perspectives (conservation and preservation), operate at the margins between the great realms of existence (physical, mental, and spiritual rather than directly in one realm), and add both the use and preservation of love to the environmental arsenal. EartHearts leave the ecological work in the physical realm to conservationists and environmentalists; they leave the ecological work in the mental realm to psychologists, especially Gestalt, Transpersonal, and eco-psychologists; and the work in the spiritual realm to theologians and spiritualists. EartHearts instead focus on the love that pierces and unites all of the great spheres of existence.

By working at the margins between realms eartHearts tend to:

1. expand the perspective of the environmental movement (especially in area of meaning),
2. work to increase the vitality of its supporters and activists,
3. offer guidance for the resolution of conflict,
4. offer guidance for the ecological direction for the future, and
5. avoid duplication of effort.

Instead of lobbying Congress directly on wilderness preservation which is the forte of the Sierra Club, for example, eartHearts would work on making sure that the wilderness that exists in the physical realm of time and space works its charm within the mental realm of consciousness or the spiritual realm of the Soul of (in particular) those who would preserve the wilderness. The main tool for this endeavor is showing people how to love the wilderness—and, thereby, helping them become more conservation-minded. EartHearts also show conservation-minded people how to put this love to use in the form of right actions (the right view, the right resolve, the right speech, the right conduct, the right livelihood, the right effort, the right mindfulness, and the right samadhi (meditation on form and peak experiences in unity consciousness). These right actions will be discussed in more detail in the next Heartwood Path book: **Ethos**.

EartHearts work between the great realms of existence and use intimate love as a means to increase vitality and provide direction for anyone who would help protect the environment. Thoreau, Muir, and Brower set the standard for how to love wildness. Today, many conservationists follow their footsteps and engage in a variety of right actions because they too love wildness, wilderness, or the environment. EartHearts, while part of the same tradition as Thoreau, Muir and Brower, are a new breed because they are following the foot prints of their predecessors but in the opposite direction. Like their predecessors, eartHearts love all that is wild and natural; but, unlike their predecessors who worked directly on preserving the environment, eartHearts work to pay back the "debt" nature preservers "owe" to nature because of the happiness she affords to them. EartHearts work to help make conservation-minded humans receptive to the love nature returns to us in the form of fresh air, clean water, sexual pleasures, beautiful sunsets, and joyful times with children. Environmentalists, both the professionals and the amateurs, help people work for the planet, eartHearts help the planet work for people so that they will have the wherewithal to express their gratitude through positive action.

To An Improved Drive To Save Nature…

HumaNatureConnect Activity

Start-up Protocol

If this is not a day when you prefer to spend time in nature without an agenda, do the Heartwood Path Start-up Protocol found in the Appendix.

Helping The Environmental Movement Transcend

After obtaining your chosen natural being's consent and setting up your optimal functioning, use the natural sense of your appetite or hunger for food, water and air and make associations between these hungers and the hunger for an increased role of inner world perceptions in the environmental movement. Psychologically associate each of these topics of this waypoint with hunger and then determine which of them, if any, you hunger for the most. Write down your justifications for your ranking.

To help with the ranking, imagine a strong hunger for each subject to become a reality in your life. For example, imagine that you are strongly hungry for practices that add to your vitality.

Next, using your natural sense of "hearing including reso-nance, vibrations, sonar and ultrasonic frequencies" (Cohen, website: http://www.ecopsych.com/insight53senses.html) create the "mmmm" sound you make when you are expressing your approvals while allevi-ating your hunger with tasty food, refreshing drink, or sweet-smelling and pure air as you imagine each subject coming true in your life.

Note the relative intensity of each "mmmm" as you imagine each topic—recall them by rereading the section headlines—of this waypoint happening in your life. Use this "mmmm" ranking to determine which of the topics you want to develop most in your life.

Begin your later endeavors with the most vociferous "mmmm." Write down your plan for creating real benefits in the subject areas you are most hungry to actually materialize in your life.

To expedite this activity, simply reread the sections of this waypoint and make "mmmm" noises for each topic you encounter. The intensity of the tones you make will likely give you a good indication of where to begin your efforts or where to spend most of your time.

To add to your perceptions, psychologically assume the essence of your attractive natural being and make your "mmmm" sounds as if they were coming from the natural being and then do the same thing as if the environment that surrounds the natural being is making the "mmmm "sounds. Comparing your priorities to the apparent priorities of your attractive natural beings—the microcosm—and its surrounding environment—the macrocosm—will likely prove to be telling. You can also try this technique for any other mental subject you would like to materialize in your life.

Follow-up Protocol

For best results, write down your impressions of this activity in your journal using the Heartwood Path Follow-up Protocol found in the Appendix. Afterwards, consider sharing your interpretations with others.

Heartwood Path Axioms

Key Assertions From Waypoint 4.75

4.75.1.

Rather than finding your inspiration from a sense of obligation or a sense of duty, work more from a sense of joy.

4.75.2.

In effect, eartHearts are environmentalists in the ends that they seek and a mixture of ecologists, spiritualists, psychologists, personal growth enthusiasts, and bodywork enthusiasts in the means they use to guide their actions.

4.75.3.

EartHearts embrace the traditional conservation/environment spectrum; and, with the added urgency of concern over human survival, they broaden its interpretation with the following formula that is intended to be all inclusive: wilderness preservation plus respect for nature plus resource conservation plus

sustainable economics plus public health plus environmental justice plus personal/spiritual development equals the Great Work! (which is the job eartHearts do).

4.75.4.

EartHearts support those at the grassroots level because, like crabgrass and day lilies, local entities have strength and defenses through their numbers and separation.

Nocturnal Pilgrimage 4.75

For best results, write down your impressions of each night's dreams in your journal using the Heartwood Path Dreaming Time Protocols found in the Appendix. Afterwards, consider sharing your Dream Tending with others.

Learn to discover and improve upon your own natural creativity by controlling your dreams. Make your dreams your source of inspiration. Ask your subconscious to use your dream state to find a solution to a current problem or to rearrange an object as a way to induce creativity.

With this and your impression of today's lesson in mind as you prepare for sleep, control your dreams as previously described. Tend to them as you awaken the next morning.

When you are inclined, move to the next waypoint: "Tough Love." Before you begin its activity, consider how inhabitable your place would be without the attractive natural beings and landscapes you are forging connection experiences with during your sojourn down the Heartwood Path. Be sure to leave your psychological indoor encasement behind. Reach out to nature on site as you do the next activity.

76

Tough Love

ENTER INTO DURABLE ETHICAL DELIBERATIONS

In 1862 Abraham Lincoln said:

"As our case is new, we (have to) think and act anew.

We (have to) disenthrall ourselves..."

That is precisely what I hope to do here: help the reader become *disenthralled* with some commonly held ethical assertions; and help readers replace certain outmoded and discredited views with new ways of seeing, thinking, being, and acting.

Difficult New Ethics Are Required

Since it is our ethics that often guide our behaviors, this discussion will be limited to the new ethics that are needed for our overpopulated, resource-limited, and polluted world. Some of what is presented here may be difficult to accept. I encourage you to be open-minded. Sometimes, so-called "heresy" is often the father of great truth.

Concerning what is said in this section: take it, leave it, or change it to suit your own purposes. Guard against subverting changes of mind that offer glimmers of a better new world.

Great improvements in deeds require great changes of mind. I shall begin our discussion of environmental ethics with the way we think about things.

Those who follow the Heartwood Path are charged to lead the change they expect for the world by working first on what they can and cannot accept. Much more will be said about this topic later, as there is an entire Heartwood Path course devoted to ethos—the characteristic spirit of an era, a culture, or a community as manifested in its aspirations and beliefs.

We humans need to come to accept that nature is the ultimate judge of our ethical codes. We may feel ethically entitled to consume more and generate large amounts of waste. As we make these poor choices, however, nature will show us that we cannot grow as a species indefinitely. In the crowded world we live in, everyone shares in the harm caused by resource exploitation.

Actual factual consequences of our old line of thinking will determine the viability of old-time moral and ethical codes. Factual evidence can refute moral theories. Actual consequences can nullify value judgments.

No matter how logical or well-reasoned we are, and no matter what is said in ancient revered texts, if the behavior caused by our modes of thinking and moral codes causes ecological collapse, all is moot because, not only will the world as we know it cease to exist, the codes, thoughts, and texts will perish along with us. How can a moral conviction or an abstract thought be viable if its practice causes its own demise?

New Ethics Have To Make Ecological Sense

Moral life, ethical life, and religious life have to make ecological sense. Even today's virtues—including, hard work, taking care of the people with disabilities, and raising a family—will be converted into harmful liabilities if such positive actions lead unwittingly to ecological collapse. Any ethic that allows for continual growth on our limited finite planet is doomed to fail.

Nature does not tell us in words specifically what we ought to do, but it does have the ultimate veto over our moral laws and principles. Nature either tolerates or denies the moral laws and principles we attempt to live by. She does so in ways that either promote or curtail life.

Rights, freedoms, duties, and opportunities are ultimately determined by the wealth or poverty of the environment. Moral beliefs serve us well until the ecological system unravels—nature's way of signing the veto. Then, we will need to either reinterpret the word of God —and perhaps get it right this time—or create new moral convictions to guide future actions. Such revisions need to be done in ways that prevent future moral codes from being refuted by the factual occurrence of ecosystem meltdown.

We are rapidly learning that this meltdown is occurring now and that it is impossible to "un-melt" extinctions of species. It simply makes sense to do the reinterpreting and the revising now, before too many more extinctions occur. It is the moral thing to do. Never before has the ecological fabric of the planet been so rapidly and devastatingly torn apart by the actions of one species.

All moral theories are conditional on a finite planet. Personal ethics, while helpful to the individual, will not be the sole source for solutions of the global predicament, largely because their directives are irrelevant or futile in directing the non-personal agencies—corporations and government agencies—that affect the major aspects of modern life.

Ethics Are Subject To Circumstances

Ethics are not categorical or universal. They are and always have been subject to change when conditions are sufficient to merit a revision. Let me emphasize:

Ethics do not operate in isolation from the environment.

There is a biological underpinning to moral life, for nature weeds out moral failure just as it does physical, anatomical failure. Natural scarcity limits moral options, even those derived from absolute authority, reason, a priori arguments (those based on theoretical deduction rather than empirical observation), and logic.

With current and inevitable future population levels it can no longer be considered moral to grow more food (especially meat products), create more material-consuming jobs, build more energy-inefficient housing, and otherwise produce more consumer goods because the earth no longer has the resources to support any such expansion—even those done for purely benevolent reasons, those supported by the majority of voters, those deemed appropriate by environmentalists, and those condoned by the clergy.

Moral theories that lead to ecological demise are counterproductive. Any ethic is doomed if its practice causes those who live by it to perish and take their cherished moral notions with them. Such ethics are mistaken or wrong, and they need to be revised.

Consider the distinction between moral acts and beautiful acts. Moral acts are typically done out of a sense of duty or obligation. Beautiful acts are ethical and are done because we are attracted to do them. As Macy and Johnstone say:

"When our connected sense of self is well developed, we are more often drawn to beautiful acts. When we lose our sense of felt connectedness, we miss out on this sort of beauty, with tragic consequences" (2012, p. 91).

Tougher Ethics Are Inevitable

Until the Earth's ecosystem is well within the safety zone for the earth's survival, human population needs to decrease and everyone remaining will have to use a limited ration of natural resources. Whether these measures will be voluntary or compulsory, they are inevitable. We already condone some forms of sexual discrimination (i.e. swim suits and public rest rooms), some forms of age discrimination (people over twenty-one depriving those under twenty-one from drinking alcoholic drinks), and some forms of civic discrimination (the rich ought to pay more taxes than the poor, yet the working poor pay a higher personal percentage of taxes than the personal percentages paid by the super rich). Eventually, increases in human population and worsening environmental degradation will cause added political pressure to condone some forms of reproductive discrimination and some forms of resource use discrimination. These will be hard pills to swallow, but necessary ones. The discriminations will be done to protect against the exploitation of millions of years of the Earth's accumulated natural capital. The alternative is greater human suffering and, eventually, extinction.

I, for one, do not want any plant or animal to go extinct because of human inconsideration. It is not just the extinction of the wood stork or other beings that I oppose. I selfishly also resist having my experiences of river otters, freshwater crocodiles, wood thrushes, snowy plovers, and other beings go extinct. I intend to remain addicted to the rush of excitement I feel when I see, perhaps for the last time, a California condor, a blue whale, or a teenager without a mobile device.

The quicker we take positive actions to fortify ourselves and others so enough of us will be better equipped to work to protect the earth's ecosystem, the less soon we will be forced to face not just a loss of nature experiences but also some very tough ethical dilemmas. Following the Heartwood Path will make taking such medicine less bitter, or at least less soon.

To A Durable Love…

HumaNatureConnect Activity

Start-up Protocol

If this is not a day when you prefer to spend time in nature without an agenda, do the Heartwood Path Start-up Protocol found in the Appendix.

Entering Into Tough Ethical Deliberations

After obtaining your chosen natural being's consent and setting up your optimal functioning, use your natural senses related to hunting, killing, or food-obtaining plus your natural sense of "hearing including resonance, vibrations, sonar and ultrasonic frequencies" (Cohen, website: http://www.ecopsych.com/insight53senses.html) to create a fresh perspective with atypical juxtapositions potentially helpful when considering ethics.

Consider under what circumstance you feel it would be ethical to hunt, kill, or eat your chosen natural being. Convert your answer or answers into a tone or tones that are repeated until you feel a comfortable sense of resolution. Hum as yourself, then hum as you psychologically assume the essence of first your chosen natural being then this natural being's surrounding environment.

In this way you will clear your mind and benefit from a variety of assumed perspectives. Determine what your sense of hunting, killing or urge to eat tells you about the various aspects of the topic of ethics addressed previously.

Ask yourself, for example, does your sense of hunting, killing, and obtaining food encourage you to support an increase or a decrease in human population levels. Ask yourself if this sense affects in you the ecological aspect of ethics. Does your urge to hunt, kill, or obtain food cause you to want to protect nature, manage nature, disregard nature, or subjugate nature? At what point, if any, does this sense in you affect your ethics; and, more specifically, how does it affect your denial or acceptance of the various points made at this waypoint?

To enter into a perspective not dominated by analytical or logical thinking, assume the essence of your chosen attractive natural being and write down what perceptions you glean by doing so. If you are having difficulty or if you would like to gain additional perceptions, hum a tone that seems to be an e-collective resonance between yourself and the natural being, then between you and the natural being's surrounding environment, and finally between your chosen attractive environment and its environment (which will likely include yourself).

Be a Humdinger! Write down any embedded messages you perceive in the resonant tones (or your awareness of your own interpretations of these tones).

Follow-up Protocol

For best results, write down your impressions of this activity in your journal using the Heartwood Path Follow-up Protocol found in the Appendix. Afterwards, consider sharing your interpretations with others.

Heartwood Path Axioms

Key Assertions From Waypoint 4.76

4.76.1.

Guard against subverting changes of mind that offer glimmers of a better new world.

4.76.2.

We humans need to come to accept that nature is the ultimate judge of our ethical codes.

4.76.3.

No matter how logical we are and no matter what is said in ancient revered texts, if the behavior caused by ill-conceived moral codes and outdated modes of thinking causes ecological collapse, all is moot because, not only will the world as we know it cease to exist, the codes, thoughts, and texts will perish along with us.

4.76.4.

Moral beliefs serve us well until the ecological system unravels —nature's way of signing the veto.

4.76.5.

The quicker we take positive actions to fortify ourselves and others so enough of us will be better equipped to work to protect the earth's ecosystem, the less soon we will be forced to face not just a loss of nature experiences but also some very tough ethical dilemmas.

Nocturnal Pilgrimage 4.76

For best results, write down your impressions of each night's dreams in your journal using the Heartwood Path Dreaming Time Protocols found in the Appendix. Afterwards, consider sharing your Dream Tending with others.

Approaching the halfway point in this series of courses, I trust that you are continuing to be engaged in the nocturnal portion of your pilgrimage. Do not just sleep between lessons. Have lucid dreams and tend to them, as instructed here. I ask you: is sleeping through your dreams the best way to spend the rest of your limited lifespan? Do not miss the adventures and lessons you can learn from lucid dreaming.

"By awakening to your dream, you will add to your experience of life and, if you use these added hours of lucidity to experiment and exercise your mind, you can also improve your enjoyment of your waking hours" (LaBarge & Rheingold, 1990, p. 10).

With this and the previous lesson in mind as you lie down to sleep, create the intention to have lucid dreams. Tend to them as you awaken.

Pertinent And Instructive Gems From My Dream Tending Journal

I dreamt that I was high on a mountain. Suddenly the clouds parted and the sunshine bathed my body. The light from the sun seemed to contain a message about what I was supposed to do. Eager to get started, I started to work on my task but nobody else would participate because of my newly-developed arrogance and self-righteousness. Trying to do my work alone was depressing.

Lesson Learned: When you carry your light down from the mountain or with you after you dream, ground yourself in proper conduct, heartfelt speech, and humility.

When eager to resume your pathway of growth, move to the next waypoint: "Entire." Once there, you will learn about evoking the authentic whole. If you have to bring your mobile device with you be sure to turn it off. Otherwise you may be dragging the advertising-infested indoor world with you as you head out to a natural place to connect with an attractive natural being. Those ads on cell phones encourage you to indulge your every whim. For the sake of optimizing your mental health, living in moderation may be the best option. For this reason, rather than risking being subjected further to phone ads, turn off your phone's capacity to receive such ads. As an alternative to the use of a mobile device, consider taking a paper journal with you to log your thoughts.

77

Entire

EVOKE THE AUTHENTIC WHOLE

There is both a source and an object of one's thinking and awareness. In the Cauldron of Awareness you are directed towards the source and asked to dissolve boundaries between the seer and the seen. In this symbolic cauldron, leave out thinking about the "they's" and focus on thinking about the "we's." Become aware of how you are most likely the main source of your own problems. Work on perceiving from the whole to the part. Doing so will bring forth a heightened sense of change and connection—two of the salient qualities of wholeness.

Your heart will open as you reveal within the Cauldron of Awareness the depth of your being. You are becoming aware of the generative process in which you, now made whole and aware of your perfection (in your unity, fullness, and appropriateness), are set to change the future of the whole.

To magnify the impact of the Cauldron of Awareness one needs a way to imagine the containing aspect of the Cauldron of Awareness plus a way to slow down one's extraneous thoughts. I suggest constructing a mental symbol of this Cauldron and what better way to limit one's obsessive thinking than by systematically offering repeated expressions of gratitude regarding the Absolute Spirit, nature, one's nature, the God of Nature, the nature of God, God's creation, and God. The following process of constructing a more vivid symbol of the Cauldron of Awareness (by doing the Ceremony of Eleven Directions) will help to suspend your non-useful thoughts, reveal your multifaceted aspects, and bring to you lessons from the great teacher—nature.

The Cauldron of Awareness is a key part of the Sling of Imagination. It is an imaginary kettle where you can psychologically boil away aspects of your life that are not working. The Sling of Imagination, first introduced at Waypoint 2.68, shows eartHearts how they can affect the whole—their whole group, their whole town, their whole country, any whole, including the planet. It begins with deferring thoughts and actions that are not working (setting them aside), reassessing your plans and life, and then letting go of whatever is holding you back or getting in the way.

THE SLING OF THE IMAGINATION:

CREATING SUBSTANTIAL IDEAS THAT AFFECT THE WHOLE

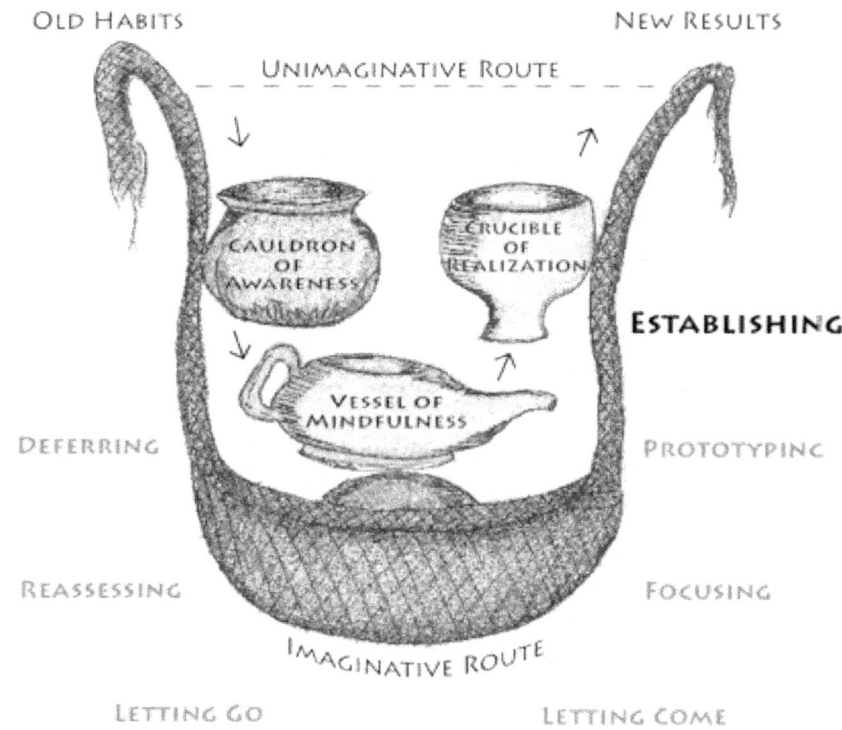

ART WORK DONE BY THERESA GRANT

Sling of Imagination topics, the Vessel of Mindfulness, the Crucible of Realization, letting come, focusing, prototyping, and establishing will be addressed in future Heartwood Path books. Do not cut yourself short. Be sure to press on.

If you do not know what you want to establish, if you need help with deferring, reassessing, and letting go, or if you do not want to wait for future Heartwood Path Courses for information about focusing, prototyping, or establishing, obtain Guidance at https://www.heartwoodpath.com/guidance.html.

To The Acclimation Of Integrity...

HumaNatureConnect Activity

Start-up Protocol

If this is not a day when you prefer to spend time in nature without an agenda, do the Heartwood Path Start-up Protocol found in the Appendix.

Doing The Eleven Directions Ceremony

Go to an attractive natural area and, in a spirit of gratitude, gain its permission to let you do this activity there. Find a level spot in nature such as a beach, a flat glade, or a field. Always pay attention to the natural scene, not with thinking about externalities but by attending to your own experience of appreciation.

From a center point at which you have made a temporary or removable mark in some way, walk first to the South a number of paces—I have tried from seven to 108 steps. Mark the spot where you end your southward journey. As you walk ponder only the counting. Keep all other thoughts out of your mind. Count out loud if this helps. Count your steps back to the marked starting point. Moving clockwise, again from the starting point make and count the same number of steps to the Southwest paying attention only to the counting. Continue this process clockwise until you have the four Cardinal Directions and between them the four intermediate diagonal directions. This space—

which will look like a large circle—is the symbolic container—the Cauldron of Awareness.

When all of these directions are marked, face the East—and ponder only the words "spiritual birth" and "awakening." Then, without thinking, experience yourself appreciating your own or someone else's spiritual birth and awakening. Do not make grandiose thoughts about these topics, just pay attention to your own experience of them, trying always to keep thinking to an absolute minimum.

When your thinking slows substantially turn to the South and think only of the words "life force" "vitality," and "unconditional love." Then, without thinking about them, experience yourself appreciating these aspects of life—pick one or appreciate all three.

Again, when your thinking gives way to your own experiencing of appreciation, turn to the West and think only of the words "transformation" and "death." Cease thoughts and experience your appreciation of transformation and death.

When it comes time, face the North and think only of the words "universal wisdom" and "purification." To complete your Cauldron of Awareness, look up, mentally following only your own breathing, look down following only your own breathing, and then turn your attention within experiencing your lightness of being, your calm lack of thought, and the container you have just created to suspend unnecessary judgments, groupthink, or senseless mental chatter.

Sit or stand within your marked Cauldron of Awareness as long as your attraction to do so suggests—minutes, hours, or overnight; whatever is necessary. Inside the Cauldron, carefully consider what you want to defer, what you need to reassess, and what you want to let go. Keep good notes.

When leaving your Cauldron of Awareness, talk with a trusted friend or a group of people with experience conducting the Eleven Directions Ceremony. Note what seems like messages that you received while conducting the ceremony, while attending to your appreciation for the symbolic aspects attached to the cardinal directions, and to events or conditions in nature.

If you did not receive a message or want more, take a lavish, ceremonial bath or shower and return to this activity. In other words: Shampoo. Rinse. Repeat.

Follow-up Protocol

For best results, write down your impressions of this activity in your journal using the Heartwood Path Follow-up Protocol found in the Appendix. Afterwards, consider sharing your interpretations with others.

Heartwood Path Axioms

Key Assertions From Waypoint 4.77

4.77.1.

Become aware of how there is no other source of problems other than oneself.

4.77.2.

Your heart will open as you reveal within the Cauldron of Awareness the depth of your being.

4.77.3.

Work on perceiving from the whole to the part.

Nocturnal Pilgrimage 4.77

For best results, write down your impressions of each night's dreams in your journal using the Heartwood Path Dreaming Time

Protocols found in the Appendix. Afterwards, consider sharing your Dream Tending with others.

Let us pause for a moment to allow you to reflect upon your present state of consciousness. Are you aware of what you see, hear, feel, taste, and smell? Do you occasionally meditate by attending to your breathing? Are you aware of your emotions? How real do your thoughts seem? Are you aware of your awareness, not on objects outside of yourself, but your own awareness itself? What does it mean to be awake? Can you be aware within a world within your mind? With your answers to these questions and today's lesson in mind as you ready yourself for bed, sleep, dream, and be aware that you are dreaming. Before getting out of bed in the morning, tend to your dreams.

Pertinent And Instructive Gems From My Dream Tending Journal

I dreamt that sometimes I had the light of my waking consciousness and other times I had the light from my dreaming, but never both. This left me either too abrupt or too obtuse in my speech to others.

Lesson Learned: Improve the effectiveness of your speech and actions by regularly looking back at the so-called real world when you are dreaming and by looking back at your dreams when you have quiet moments in nature. With enough looking back, your consciousness will become wonderfully dreamy and your dreams will become wonderfully devoted to helping you in your waking time. Frequent looking back is like sprinkling little bits of fertilizer on the garden of your inner world. Each time the fertilized garden of your heart opens and glows you bring a little bit of heaven to earth.

When ready, move to the next waypoint: "Preparedness." Prepare to leave your integrity-starved indoor world—where outwardly we are subjected to polluted air and inwardly we are made to feel incomplete unless we spend and spend. Get up from your indoor chair and move to the refreshing air and to your store-free pathway of natural integrity by rekindling your human-to-nonhuman relationships outdoors.

Do the next activity in a natural place. In doing so, besides improving your mood, expect that you will achieve direct cognitive replenishment through the nature experience. You may not notice an improvement immediately, but you will be better prepared for your next cognitive gateway to Gladandgreen Junction.

78

Preparedness

READY YOURSELF FOR LIFE'S CHALLENGES

The small self of the person reaches its wholeness in the large Self of the universe. One needs to form one body with a myriad of things, with the Earth, and with Heaven as a way to be both fully present and prepared for life's challenges. In this book, the reader learned that this more-than-individual self is threatened because our technosphere (the part of the environment where technology significantly affects nature) is incompatible with our biosphere (the regions of the earth occupied by living organisms).

This technosphere is the realm where television delivers the corporate plea to consume, where trade agreements such as NAFTA wipe out local businesses and political resistance, and where computers make possible new global organizations that are capable of inflicting large scale environmental damage. Without proper safeguards, these and other technologies can make democracy, diversity, and individual thought less viable. It is possible for technological evolution to go too far too fast and it is likely that most people, being brainwashed by Modernity, will believe that most technological advancements are positive progress.

To An Assessment Of The Incongruities Of Machines And Life...

HumaNatureConnect Activity

Start-up Protocol

If this is not a day when you prefer to spend time in nature without an agenda, do the Heartwood Path Start-up Protocol found in the Appendix.

Reviewing The Incompatibilities Of The Technosphere And The Biosphere

This time bring a substantial container of drinking water with you as you go to a natural place. After obtaining your chosen natural being's consent and setting up your optimal functioning, review any incompatibilities you find in your life between the technosphere and the biosphere.

There are many ways to conduct this review, but here I am asking you to attempt to find the answers by randomly opting to use your natural sense of humidity (including thirst, evaporation, control and the acumen to find water or evade a flood) and your natural sense of "hearing including resonance, vibrations, sonar and ultrasonic frequencies" (Cohen, website: http://www.ecopsych.com/insight53senses.html). Water is a good thing but too much of it at one time is often considered to be an unwanted flood.

Imagining that you are thirsty, consider the aspects of the biosphere and the aspects of the technosphere and determine how each of these aspects are good or bad at quenching your thirst (making you feel satisfied). Thinking metaphorically, does either the biosphere or the technosphere for you resonate as a drought, as a wanted amount of water, or as a flood?

To aid in these determinations, hum the sound that resonates with being satisfied, generally. Now hum the sound of thirst or desire, generally. Compare the tones. Perceive in yourself your state of being before consuming the water. Think about the biosphere and hum a tone that resonates both the thought of the biosphere and your unquenched state. Do the same for the technosphere.

Now drink a large volume of water and, thinking of the biosphere, hum a tone that resonates with your state of being after being quenched by the water. Do the same for the technosphere.

Of the two, which seems more like a drought, which seems like helpful water and which seems like a flood—the technosphere or the biosphere. Explain your answers.

Imagine the thirst or desire of your attractive natural being and hum the tone that resonates with both this being in its quenched (satisfied) state and in its unquenched (unsatisfied) state. Do the same thing for the natural being's surrounding environment.

Then compare these tones to the various aspects of the biosphere (land, water, plants, animals, weather, minerals, etc.) with the technosphere (television, technology, pollution, resource utilization, consumption, etc). Write down your impressions after minutes of humming about each of these aspects.

Are your resonant tones, your attractive being's resonant tones, and the surrounding environment's resonant tones similar or different? After humming for answers, of the two generally—the biosphere and the technosphere—which seems to resonate with satisfaction and which seems to resonate with thirst or dissatisfaction? Of the two—the technosphere or the biosphere—which of them, more often than not, quenches the other?

Follow-up Protocol

For best results, write down your impressions of this activity in your journal using the Heartwood Path Follow-up Protocol found in the Appendix. Afterwards, consider sharing your interpretations with others.

Heartwood Path Axioms

Key Assertions From Waypoint 4.78

4.78.1.

The small self of the person reaches its wholeness in the large Self of the universe.

4.78.2.

The More-Than-Individual self is threatened because our techno-sphere is incompatible with our biosphere.

4.78.3.

It is possible for technological evolution to go too far too fast and it is likely that most people, being brainwashed by Modernity, will believe that most technological advancements are positive progress.

Nocturnal Pilgrimage 4.78

For best results, write down your impressions of each night's dreams in your journal using the Heartwood Path Dreaming Time Protocols found in the Appendix. Afterwards, consider sharing your Dream Tending with others.

What happens in the outer world affects the inner world. The spiritual, intellectual, emotional, imaginative life of humans is diminished each time a river is dammed, a forest is cut, or a cave is vandalized.

Ways were discussed earlier in this series of books for how one can participate in the Great Work! of overcoming anything that stands in the way of making the transition to the Ecozoic Era—a time when humans live compatibly with nature.

You are now at the end of Part 1 of the Heartwood Path. During your time here, you learned about the origin and structure of integrity (in **Logos**). You learned about your individual aspect (in **Egos**). You learned about how your relationships makes you a valued part of the Greater Self (in **Ecos**). You learned ways nature can give you guidance. After completing four Heartwood Path books (including **Kosmos**, the Overture), you have a solid foundation for a happy and sustainable future.

There will always be more to learn, both from nature and from words. To build on your ample footing, we strongly suggest that you continue your pilgrimage down the Heartwood Path. More books are coming soon.

Prior to their release, you can review what you learned thus far and you can receive one-on-one guidance as a way to get the most from your Heartwood Path experience. Tailoring the benefits of the Heartwood Path to your own needs and desires begins as soon as you start your guidance, conducted or supervised by myself, Don Pierce.

Now would be a good time to open the envelop you sealed at the beginning of this book. Read what you wrote back at the beginning of **Ecos**. Note how, if at all, your impressions of your More-Than-Individual Self have changed.

If you want to increase your growth and happiness, if you want help improving your environment, or if you cannot wait for the release of future books—one on valued traits, one on finding and improving your intimate relationship, one on working well as an individual, one on working well in groups, one on persevering, and one on become a eco-centric life coach––obtain guidance at https://www.heartwood-path.com/guidance.html. **We look forward to hearing from you.**

References

Abram, David. (1987) The perceptual implications of Gaia, Revision, 9(2), 7-15).

Access to Insight Website: http://www.accesstoinsight.org/lib/authors/silananda/bl137.html

Aizenstat, Stephen, Ph.D. (2009). Dream tending. New Orleans, Louisiana: Spring Journal, Inc.

Barrett, Julie Langdon. Website: http://julielangdonbarrett.com/2011/08/11/how-to-tell-the-difference-between-intuition-and-your-imagination-or-ego/

Babauta, Leo. (2009) The power of less: the fine are of limiting yourself to the essentials . . . in business and in life. New York, New York: Hyperion.

Barasch, Marc, Ian. (2000). Healing dreams: exploring the dreams that can transform your life. New York, New York: Riverhead Books.

Beck, Larry and Cable, Ted (2002). Interpretation for the twenty-first century. Urbana, Illinois: Sagamore Publishing, Incorporated.

Beck, Martha (2012). Finding your way in a wild new world. New York, New York: Free Press

Bernard, Patrick. (2004). Music as yoga: discover the healing power of sound. San Rafael, CA: Mandala Publishing.

Borden, Richard, J. (2014). Ecology and experience: reflections from a human ecological perspective. Berkeley, California: North Atlantic Books.

Bosnak, Robert. (1986). A little course in dreams. Boston, Massachusetts: Shambala Publication, Inc.

Bosnak, Robert. (1996) Tracks in the wilderness of dreaming. New York, New York: Delacorte Press

Boston, John Website: (https://www.american.edu/spa/cep/upload/jonathan-boston-lecture-american-university.pdf).

Bowden, Jonny, Ph.d, C.N.S. (2009). The 150 most effective ways to boost your energy. Beverly, Massachusetts: Fair Winds Press.

Buddy, Cathal Br. ofm. Website: www.praying-nature.com.

Buechner, Frederick. (1993). Wishful thinking. A theological abc. San Francisco, California: Harper.

Buhner, Stephen Harrod. (2004). The secret teaching of plants. Rochester, Vermont: Bear and Company, Inner Traditions International.

Bunzl, John M. (2004). Evolutionary Biology and Simultaneous Policy: Vision-Logic for the Next Stage in our Evolutionary Future, Website: http://www.integralworld.net/bunzl.html

Byzant Kabblah Website (www.byzant.com/mystical/kaballah/Path.aspx?number=31)

Care2.com

Cairns, John Jr. (2001) Equity fairness, and the development of a sustainability ethos. Blacksburg Virginia : Ethics in Science and Environmental Politics, February 1., Blacksburg Virginia. www.mnforsustain.org/cairns_j_equity_and_a_sustainability_ethos.htm

Cameron, Julie. (2006). Finding water: the art of perseverance. New York, New York: Jeremy P. Tarcher.

Cannon, Walter B. (1963). The wisdom of the body. New York, New York: W.W. Norton & Company, Inc.

Cengagesites Website: http://www.cengagesites.com/academic/assets/sites/4713/Chapter%2015.pdf

Capra, Fritjof. (1996). The web of life. New York, New York: Anchor Books, Random House.

Castro, Dr. Anthony J. (2009). Creating space for happiness: the secret of giving room. Amherst, New York: Prometheus Books.

CGJungPage Website: http://www.cgjungpage.org/learn/articles/technology-and-environment/683-robert-romanyshyn-on-technology-as-symptom-a-dream

Chakra Tones and Notes Website: http://www.wingmakers.co.nz/ Chakra_Tones_and_Notes.html

Chalquist, Craig, editor (2010). Rebearths: conversations with a world ensouled. Walnut Creek, Caliifornia: World Soul Books.

Chapman, Alan. (2003) website: http://www.businessballs.com/maslowtest.pdf

Childre, Doc and Martin, Howard. (1999). The heartmath solution. San Francisco, California: Harper Collins Publishers, Inc.

Chopra, Deepak. (2000). How to know god: the soul's journey into the mystery of mysteries. New York, New York: Harmony Books.

Chopra, Deepak. (2004). The book of secrets: unlocking the hidden dimensions of your life. New York, New York: Three Rivers Press.

Millaka Chopra Website: http://www.huffingtonpost.com/mallika-chopra/ finding-serenity_b_868151.html

Cialdini, Robert B. (2009) Influence: science and practice. Boston, Massachusetts: Pearson Education, Inc.

Clark, Rawn. (2002) Journal of Wester Mystery Tradition, No. 3, Vol 1 (Website www.jwmt.org/v1n3/32 paths.)

Cohen, Michael J. Ecopsych Website: http://www.ecopsych.com/iupsm-swaiver.html.

Cohen, Michael J. Ecopsych/Ecopsychology Journal Website: http://www.ecopsych.com/ecopsychologyjournal.html.

Cohen, Green Wave, ecopsych.com

Cohen, Michael J. Ecopsych/Lifeweb Website: www.ecopsych.com/lifeweb.html.

Cohen, Michael J. Ecopsych Thesis Quote Website: www.ecopsych.com/thesisquote.html.

Cohen, Michael J. (1993) Integrated ecology: The process of counseling with nature. Humanistic Psychologist, 21(3), 277-295.

Cohen, Michael J, Ed.D. Personal email dated December 23, 2010.

Cohen, Michael J, Ed.D. Project NatureConnect Website: http://www.ecopsych.com/insight53senses.html.

Cohen, Michael J, Ed.D. Project NatureConnect Website: http://www.ecopsych.com/earthstories101.html).

Cohen, PNC Website: www.ecopshych.com/universealive.html

Cohen, Michael J, Ed.D. Green Wave Information: (Project NatureConnect Website: http://www.ecopsych.com/journalaliveness.html and personal email June 8, 2016)Comaford-Lynch, Christine. (2007). Rules for renegades. New York, New York: McGraw-Hill.

Cohen, Michael J. (2018). Principles of Organic Psychology. The Eco-Arts and Science of Unconditional Love Friday Harbor, Washington: Project Nature Connect

Cook, Charles. (2001). Awakening to nature: renewing your life by connecting with the natural world. New York, New York: Contemporary Books, MacGraw-Hill

Cope, Stephen. (1999) Yoga and the quest for the true self. New York, New York: Bantam Books.

Copenhagen Qabalah Website: www.qabalah.dk/paths.html.

Csikszentmihalyi, Mihaly. (1993) The evolving self: a psychology for the third millennium. New York, New York: HarperCollins Publishers, Inc.

Csikszentmihalyi. http://psychology.about.com/od/PositivePsychology/a/flow.htm)

Dangerfield, Dr. J. Mark Website. https://www.smashwords.com/.../how-to-love-nature-when-you-live-in-the city.

Delaney, Gayle, Dr. (1994) Sexual dreams: why we have them, what they mean. New York, New York: Fawcett Columbine.

De Stefano, Matias, Three Earth Chakra Videos on You Tube. https://m.youtube.com/watch?v=IcfOwlVQGec.

Discovery Fit and Health Website. http://health.howstuffworks.com/wellness/stress-management/finding-serenity-in-your-life2.htm

DreamTending Website: http://dreamtending.com/naturedreaming.pdf

Dyer, Wayne, Ph.D. (2005) The power of intentions: learning to co-create your world your way. Carlsbad, California: Hay House.

Dwoskin, Hale. (2009). The Sedona Method. Sedona, Arizona: Sedona Press.

Eat, Taste, Heal: an Ayurvedic Guidebook website: http://www.eattasteheal.com/ETH_6tastes.htm

Edge Magazine Website: http://www.edgemagazine.net/1995/11/robert-sardello/

E-How. http://www.ehow.com/how_2338305_develop-character.html.

EnglishClub.com Website: http://www.englishclub.com/vocabulary/fl-making-request.htm

Evernden, Neil. (1985). The natural alien. Toronto, Canada: University of Toronto Press.

Ewolt, Dave and Weeks-Ewolt, Alison. (2001) Rational spirituality: evidence of the web of life, Attraction Retreat Website: http://www.attractionretreat.org/Writings/RationalSpirituality.html

Farley, Kent M. (2002) Developing character traits through sport/athletic participation. The Sport Digest- ISSN: 1558-6448. The United States Sports Academy Website: http://thesportdigest.com/archive/article/developing-character-through-sportathletic-participation

Ferlic, K. (2007). Tapping and sustaining the source. Website: http://ryuc.info/common/creation_process/tap_sustain_source.htm

Ferlic, K (2009) A bottom line about sex and our creativity. Website: http://ryuc.info/creativesexuality/bottom_line_about_sex.htm

Fitness Health Zone Website: http://www.fitnesshealthzone.com/meditation/walking-meditation-and-its-benefits/

Fiorenza, Nick Anthony (2010). Planetary harmonics & Neurobiological resonances, Website: http://www.lunarplanner.com/Harmonics/planetary-harmonics.

Flickstein, Matthew. Online Website: Swallowing the River Ganges: http://innerself.com/Meditation/mindfulness.htm?phpMyAdmin=1IAC4WZXEVp9XvKg-Nokyjpr3el1.

Franden, Nathaniel. (1996). Taking responsibility, New York, New York: Simon and Schuster.

Franklin Institute Website: http://www.fi.edu/learn/brain/exercise.html.

Gallup, Inc: (http://www.gallup.com/poll/190916/americans-identification-environmentalists-down.aspx)

Gardner, Howard. (1999) "Intelligence reframed: multiple intelligences for the 21st century." New York: Basic Books.

Garon, Henry A. (2006). The cosmic mystique. Maryknoll, New York: Orbis Books.

GDRC Website: https://www.gdrc/uem/ee/Tbilissi.html.

George, James. (1995) Asking the Earth. Saftsbury, Dorset; Element Books Limited.

Goldman, Jonathan. (2002) Healing sounds: the power of harmonics. Rochester, Vermont: Healing Arts Press.

Goodreads Website: www.goodreads.com. Alan_Wilson_Watts

Grand, David, (2001) Emotional healing at warp speed. New York, New York: Harmony Books.

Gunther, Folke, and Folke, Carl, "Characteristics of Nested Living Systems," Journal of Biological Systems, 1:3, Stockholm: Sweden. Website: http://library.uniteddiversity.coop/Systems_and_Networks/Nested%20Living%20Systems%20(Holons)%20.pdf

Hargrove, Eugene C. (1988) Foundations of environmental ethics, Englewood Cliffs, New Jersey: Prentice Hall.

Hawkes, Joyce Whiteley, Ph.D. (2012) Resonance, nine practices for harmonious health and vitality, Carlsbad, California: Hay House, Inc.

Henning, Sequoia. Website: http://www.feelingsoulgood.com/index.php?id=2

Howerton, Mari and Sorensen, "Maya." Website: http://www.singandhum.com/educational-development/humming-for-health.html

Inner.org. The Gal Einai Website: http://www.inner.org/Institute of HeartMath. Online Website. Global Coherence Initiative. http://www.glcoherence.org/about-us/about.html

Hauser, Marc D. (2006) Moral minds: the nature of right and wrong. New York, New York: Harper Collins.

Helm, Russell Buddy. (2001). The way of the drum. St. Paul, Minnesota: LLewellyn Publications.

Hindu Temples and Gods Website: http://hindutemplesandgods.blogspot.com/2013/03/sri-yantra.html

Hubbard, Barbara Marx. (2001). Emergence: the shift from ego to essence. Charlottesville, Virginia: Hampton Roads Publishing Company

Huning, Barb. (2-28-11) Personal email: "Re: Editorial Help with Instructions and Marketing."

InnerVision Yoga Website: http://www.innervisionyoga.com/what-is-my-sacred-work/

Institute of Human Conceptual and Mental Development. Online Website. Experiences and Feelings: http://www.ihcmdonline.com/mentalproblems/experiences.htm.

Institute for Social Ecology Website: www.social-ecology.org/199.

Jackson, Brooks and Jamieson, Kathleen Hall. (2007). Unspun: Finding Facts In A World Of Disinformation. New York, New York: Random House Trade Paperbacks

Jensen, Derrick. (2000) A language older than words. White River Junction, Vermont: Chelsea Green Publishing Company

Jensen, Derrick. (2006) Endgame volume I: the problem of civilization. New York, New York: Seven Stories Press.

Jensen, Derrick. (2006). Endgame volume II: resistance. New York, New York: Seven Stories Press.

Jung Atlanta: http://www.jungatlanta.com/articles/winter02-decoding-hillman.pdf

Jurado, Anthony. (2010) Cracked.com Website: http://www.cracked.com/article_18405_7-insane-ways-music-affects-body-according-to-science_p2.html

Kahn , Pete3r H Jr. and Hasbach Patricia H. (2012) Ecopsychology: science, totems, and the technological species, Cambridge, MA: MIT Press.

Kawasaki, Guy (2004). The art of the start. New York, New York: the Penguin Group.

Kawasaki, Guy. (2012). Enchantment. New York, New York: Penguin Group.

Kaza, Stephanie. (1993) The attentive heart: conversations with trees. New York, New York: Fawcett Columbine.

Kittleswon, Mary Lynn. (1996). Sounding the soul: the art of listening. Einsiedeln, Switzerland: Daimon.

Kohn, Alfie (1990). The brighter side of human nature. New York, New York: Basic Books, Inc.

Kroeber, Theodora. (1961) Ishi: in two worlds. Berkeley, California: University of California Press.

Krutch, joseph Wood. (2009) The voice of the desert. New York, New York, General Books.

Kundalini Yoga Info Website: http://www.kundalini-yoga-info.com/humming.html.

Lachance, Albert (1997). "The Architecture of the Soul: Sacred Process Ecopsychology," from the book The Greening of religion: god, the environment, and the good life, edited by Carrol, John E., Broclelman, Paul, and Westfal, Mary. Hanover, New Hampshire: University Press of New England

Lama Dalai. (2011) How to be compassionate. New York, Neew York: Atria Books..

Lame Deer and Erdoes, John. (2009). Lame deer: seeker of visions. New York: New York: Simon and Schuster.

Leopold, Aldo. (1949) . A sand county almanac. London, England: Oxford University Press.

Leopold, Aldo and Flader, Susan L. (editor). (1991) The river of the mother of god and other essays by aldo leopold. Madison, Wisconsin: University of Wisconsin Press.

Lesser, Elizabeth. (2009). The seeker's guide. Website: www.oprah.com/spirit/10-Signs-of-Progress-on-Your-Spiritual-Path/10 - God is Optimistic - Oprah.com.

Lessmann, Kevin. (2004) Emotions of the Musical Keys Website: http://www.gradfree.com/kevin/some_theory_on_musical_keys.htm

Lewis, Dennis. Website: http://www.authentic-breathing.com/breathing_tips.htm

Levey, Joel and Michelle. (2003). The fine arts of relaxation, concentration & meditation: ancient skills for modern minds. Somerville, Massachutsetts: Wisdom Publications.

Levi, Renee. (2003). Group magic; an inquiry into experiences of collective resonance, doctoral dissertation executive summary: http://resonanceproject.org/execsum.cfm

Lovelock, James. (2010) The vanishing face of gaia. New York, New york: Basic Books.

Luks, Allen and Payne, Peggy. (1991). The healing power of doing good.   New York, New York: Fawcett Columbine.

Luskin, Fred and Pelletier, Kenneth R. (2005) Stress free for good. San Francisco, California: Harper Collins Publishers.

Maathai, Wangari. (2010). Replenishing the earth. New York, New York: Random House.

MacGregor, Catriona. (2010). Partnering with nature: the wild path to reconnecting to the earth. New York, New York: Atria Paperback.

Macy, Joanna and Johnstone, Chris. (2012) Active home: how to face the mess we're in without going crazy. Novato, California: New World Library.

Mander, Jerry (1979) as quoted in the website: http://www.eco-action.org/dt/elimtv.html

Marc and Angel Website Practical Tips for Productive Living: http://www.marcandangel.com/2013/04/21/8-effective-ways-to-let-go-and-move-on/

Mayo Clinic/Ranges of Self-Esteem. www.mayoclinic.org

McCraty, Rollin Ph.D., Atkinson, Mike, Tomasino, Dana and Bradley, Trevor Raymond, Ph.D. (2006). The coherent heart: heart-brain interaction, psychophysiological coherence, and system-wide order. Boulder Creek, California: Institute of Heartmath.

McCraty, Rollin Ph.D. and Tomasino, Dana. (2006). Emotional Stress, Positive Emotions and Psychophysiological Coherence, Institute of HeartMath Website: alternativeworldwidehealth.com, Heartmath_Stress_chapter.pdf

McKay, Kim and Bonnin, Jenny. (2007) True green. Washington D.C: National Geographic Society.

McKay, Pip. (2009). Website: http://www.evolvenow.com.au.

McIntosh, Steve (2007) Excerpt from Integral consciousness and the future of evolution. Website: http://www.stevemcintosh.com/books/integral-consciousness/chapter-five-integral-politics/

McTaggart, Lynne. (2002). The field: the quest for the secret force of the universe. New York, New York: HarperCollins Publishers, Inc.

Mellick, Jill. (1996). The art of dreaming. Berkeley, California: Conari Press.

Michigan Online Website. http://web1.msue.msu.edu/4h/charcoun.html

Mindbodygreen Website: mindbodygreen.com

Montgomery, Pam. (2008) Plant spirit healing. Rochester, Vermont: Bear and Company.

Morris, Jill. (1985). The dream workbook: discover; the knowledge and power hidden in your dreams. Boston, Massachusetts: Little, Brown, and Company.

Murray, William H. From the website: http://innerself.com/content/social-a-political/environment/3934-for-those-who-would-save-the-earth.html

Myersbriggs.org

Myth-Dream-Symbols Website: http://www.mythsdreamssymbols.com/432.html

Nahko Bear (Medicine for the People). Song lyrics to "Aloha Ke Akua," (Onecommunityglobal.org).

Naiman, Rubin R. Ph.D. (2006). Healing night: the science and spirit of sleeping, dreaming, and awakening. Minneapolis, Minnesota: Syren Book Company.

National Catholic Reporter Website: http://ncronline.org/blogs/eco-catholic/fr-thedreamoftheearth.

Neubauer, Joan, R. (1985). Dear diary: the art and craft of writing a creative journal. Nashville, Tennessee: Turner Publishing Company.

New Oxford American Dictionary. Online Edition.

Noll, Doug. Website: http://lawyertopeacemaker.com/heartmath.html

Norbu, Namkhai. (2002). Dream yoga and the practice of natural light. Ithaca, New York: Snow Lion Publishing.

Nordhaus, Ted and Shellenberger, Michael. (2010). Break through: why we can't leave saving the planet to environmentalists. New York, New York: First Mariner Books.

Oelschlaeger, Max. (1991). The idea of wilderness. New Haven, Connecticut: Yale University Press.

Oestreich Associates. www.teamtrustsurvey.com

Oktar, Adnan. website: http://www.secretbeyondmatter.com/ourbrains/the-worldinourbrains3.html

Orloff, Judith (2003) Website: Trust your hunches: 5 steps to develop your intuition - Intuitive Advice: http://findarticles.com/p/articles/mi_m0NAH/is_8_33/ai_108786014/

Ortiz, John M., Ph.D. (1997) The tao of music: sound psychology. York Beach, ME: Samuel Weiser, Inc.

Ortner, Nick. (2013). The tapping solution: a revolutionary system for stress-free living. Carlsbad, California: Hay House, Inc.

Ouderkirk, Wayne and Hill, Jim editors. Land, value, community: Callicott and environmental philosophy. State University of New York Press. Internet: Callicott_My_Reply_to_Land_Value_Community.pdf

Parker, Jonathan (2011). The soul solution: enlightening meditations for resolving life's problems. Tiburon, California: H J Kramer.

Partridge, Ernest, Ecological morality and nonmoral sentiments. Internet: 60477.pdf.

Partridge, Ernest and Holmes, Ralston III. (1984 ad 1996) The Online Gadfly: http://gadfly.igc.org/papers/values.htm

Peaceful Mind. (2011) Website: http://www.peacefulmind.com/music_therapy.htm

Peaceful Rivers Online Website. Eckhart Tolle Quotes: http://peacefulrivers.homestead.com/EckhartTolle.html

Pearson, Carol S. (1991) Awakening the heroes within: twelve archetypes to help us find ourselves and transform our world. New York, NY: HarperCollins Publishers.

Peat, F. David. Nature and Ethics. http://www.paricenter.com/library/papers/peat23.php

Plotikin, Bill (2008). Soul craft: crossing into the mysteries of nature and the psyche. Novato, California: New World Books.

Plotkin, Bill. (2010). Nature and the human soul: cultivating wholeness and community in a fragmented world. Novato, California: New World Books.

Plotkin, Bill (2013). Wildmind: a field guid to the human psyche. Novato, California: New World Books.

Pratt, Vernon (Unknown) website: http://www.vernonpratt.com/211/

Reverso Online English Dictionary and Thesaurus: http://dictionary.reverso.net/english-cobuild/linear

Ricard, Matthieu. (2006) Happiness: A guide to developing life's most important skill. New York, NY: Little, Brown and Company.

Robbins, Stephen P. Organizational behavior, Chapter Six: website: http://www.gobookee.net/organizational-behavior-stephen-p-robbins-14th-edition/

Root-Bernstein, Robert and Michele. (1999). Sparks of genius. Boston, Massachusetts: Houghton-Mifflin Company.

Rudd, Vols, Aaker Website: http://faculty-gsb.stanford.edu/aaker/pages/documents/TimeandAwe2012_workingpaper.pdf

Scull, J (n.d.) Eco-psychology: Where does it fit in psychology? Website: http://www.island.net/~jscull/ecopsych.htm

Scully, Matthew. (2002), Dominion. New York, New York: St. Martin's Press.

Second Journey Website, "Itineraries:" http://www.secondjourney.org/newsltr/NDX/Sullivan_frameset.htm

Selhub, Eva M. and Logan, Alan C. (2012). Your brain on nature: the science of nature's influence on your health, happiness, and vitality. Ontario, Canada: John Wiley and Sons Canada Ltd.

Seligman, Martin E.P. (2011). Flourish: a visionary new understanding of happiness and wellbeing. New York, New York: Free Press, Simon and Schuster.

Sewell, L. (1995). The Skill of ecological perception, In T. Roszak, M.E. Gomes, & A.D. Kanner (Eds.). Eco-psychology: Restoring the earth, healing the mind (pp. 201-215). San Francisco, California: Sierra Club.

Sewall, Laura Ph.D. (1999). Sight and sensibility: the ecology of perception. New York, New York: Jeremy P. Tarcher/Putnam.

Shannahoff-Khalsa, David S. (2006) Kundalini yoga mediation. New York, New York: W.W. Norton & Company

Sharp, Jonathan. (2002). Diving your dreams. New York: Simon & Shuster.

Silva Therapy Website: http://www.silvamindbodyhealing.com/articles/mind-body-healing/healing-colors/

SingingToThePlants Website: http://www.singingtotheplants.com/2014/01/dreaming-with-open-eyes/

Songwriting-guide.com Website: http://www.songwriting-guide.com/basic-music-theory.html

Sound Essence Website: http://www.soundessence.net/chakras.php

Sound-PHYSICS.com: http://www.sound-physics.com/Sound/Resonance-NaturalFrequency/

Spoto, Donald (2003). Reluctant saint: the life of francis of assissi. New York, New York: Penguin Books

Spurgeon, C.H. (1871) http://www.spurgeon.org/sermons/1005.htm

State of California, Department of Education, Regional Occupation Centers, and Department of Developmental Disability. (2014). Student Resource Guide: Direct Support Professional Training. http://www.dds.ca.gov/DSPT/Student/Student-Year1_FullVersion.pdf

Steep Path Online Website: http://www.steeppath.com/article.php?ID=6

Sun Bear. (1980). Medicine wheel: earth astrology. Austin, Texas: Touchstone.

Sunstein, Cass, R. and Nussbaum, Martha C. (2004) Animal rights. Oxford, England: Oxford University Press.

Székely, Edmond Bordeaux. The Essene Gospel of Peace. International Biogenic Society, 1981.

Tebra's Writer's Blog Website: http://www.thepensters.com/tebra/secular-saints-philosophy.html

Templin, Steven, D.O.M Website. http://www.innerbalanceconsulting.com/wp-content/uploads/2011/11/HeartMath-Guide.pdf

Tharp, Twyla. (2003). The creative habit. New York, New York: Simon and Schuster.

Thomashow, Mitchell. (1996). Ecological identity: becoming a reflective environmentalist. Cambridge, Massachusetts: MIT Press.

Thompkins, Peter and Bird, Christopher. (1973) The secret life of plants. New York, New York: Harper and Row, Publishers.

Thoms, Justine. (2008) Small pleasures: finding grace in a chaotic world. Charlottesville, Virginia: Hampton Roads Publishing Company.

Thornton, James. (1999). A field guide to the soul: down-to-earth handbook of spiritual practice. New York, New York: Bell Tower

Thoreau, Henry David. (1965) Walden and on civil disobedience. New York, New York: Harper and Rowe.

Thoreau, Henry David. Excerpt from Journal, quoted from online website: http://www.mothwingarts.com/waldenvisionquest/excerpts.html

Thorncraft, Sylvan. 2006. Website: http://www.emeraldspritestudio.com/articles_toning_and_sacred_sound.htm.

TotalWellnessWorldwide Website: www.totalwellnessworldwide.com/ions.html

Twenge, Jean M. and Campbell, Keith, W. (2009). The narcissism epidemic. New York, New York: Free Press, Simon and Schuster. United States Conference of Catholic Bishops, Themes from Catholic Social Teaching" Washington, D.C., 2005. Website: http://www.cchdbaltimore.org/soc-teach-color-inst.pdf

Uphanishads. Uphanishads quotes and sayings. Website: http://spiritquotes.com/quotes/upanishadsquotes/upanishads_quotes1.htm.

Van Dyke, Deborah.Mantras Sacred Sounds Website: http://www.kirtancommunity.com/html/mantras_sacred_sound.html

Vedicyagyacenter Website: http://www.vedicyagyacenter.com/mantras-chant/Devi-Khadgamala-Stotram-lyrics-with-meaning.pdf

Veracious. Wikihow.com Website: http://www.wikihow.com/Choose-the-Right-Life-Coach

W, Karen. How to overcome fear. Website: http://www.wikihow.com/Overcome-Fear.

Wallace, Alan B. (2012). Dream yourself awake. Boston, Massachusetts: Shambala Publications, Inc.

Webster's Online Dictionary. http://www.websters-online-dictionary.com/definitions/Ethos

Weissman, Darren, R. (2005). The power of infinite love and gratitude. Carlsbad, California: Hay House, Inc.

Whitfield, Charles, L., Whitfield, Barbara H., Park, Russell, and Prevatt, Jeneane. (2006). The power of humility. Deerfield Beach, Florida: Health Communications, Inc.

Whitworth, Laura, Kimsey-Shouse, Karen, Kimsey-House, Henry, and Sandeahl, Phillip. (2007). Co-active coaching: new skills for coaching people toward success. Mountain View, California: Davies-Black Publishing.

Wholistic Healthworks Website: www.wholistichealthworks.com/healing%20with%20colors.htm

Wilber, Ken. (1995). Sex, Ecology, and Spirit: the spirit of evolution. Boston, Massachusetts: Shambala Publications, Inc.

Wilber, Ken, (1998). The essential ken wilber: an introductory reader. Boston, Massachusetts: Shambhala Publications, Inc.

Wilber, Ken (2007) Chapter 14. Integral Politics, or Our of the Prison of Partiality ... KenWilber.com Website: http://www.kenwilber.com/Writings/PDF/14-integral%20politics.pdf

Wilber, Ken; Patton, Terry; Leonard, Adam; and Morelli, Marco. (2008) Integral life practice: a 21st –century blueprint for physical health, emotional balance, mental clarity and spiritual awakening. Boston, Massachusetts: Integral Books.

Williams, Ernest H. Jr. (2005). The nature handbook: a guide to observing the great outdoors. New York, New York: Oxford University Press.

Wikia Website: http://synchromystic.wikia.com/wiki/432

Wiki-How. http://www.wikihow.com/Strengthen-Character

Wikipedia. David Hume. website: http://en.wikipedia.org/wiki/David_Hume

Wikipedia. Theory Z: webssite: http://en.wikipedia.org/wiki/Theory_Z

Wilderness Survival Sills for Save Wilderness Travel Website: http://www.wilderness-survival-skills.com/how-to-predict-weather.html

Wilson, Carol. (1997) Online Website. Mindfulness: Gateway Into Experience: http://www.dharma.org/ij/archives/1998b/carol_wilson.htm

Wilson, Edward O. (2002). The future of life. New York, New York: Vintage Books.

Winter, Deborah Du Nann and Koger, Susan M. (2004) The psychology of environmental problems. New York: Psychology Press

Wohlforth, Charles. (2010). The fate of nature: rediscovering our ability to rescue the earth. New York, New York: Thomas Dunne Books: St. Martin's Press.

You Tube: Caposiena, Nicholas. (2011) You Tube Podcast: https://www.youtube.com/watch?v=o-r_sMYzW_w

Zeleski, Inessa. North Star Wellness Center Website: http://www.calmness.com/chakras.htm

Zohar, Dana and Marshal, Dr. Ian. (2000). Spiritual intelligence: the ultimate intelligence. New York, New York: Bloomsbury Publishing.

Appendix

Online Resources

Your senses and the Heartwood Path will all come alive as you use the following online resources:

Read the **Glossary** and watch your sense of reason come alive. (www.heartwoodpath.com/glossary)

Use your sense of language when you connect online with other EartHearts at a variety of locations:

- **EartHeart Networking Forum** (www.heartwoodpath.com/connect)
- each **online waypoint** (learning station)
- our **Instagram** account (@heartwoodpath)
- our **Facebook** Page (Heartwood Path)

Your sense of light and sight will be activated when you watch our informative and visually appealing podcasts on **YouTube** (www.youtube.com/user/heartwoodpath).

Inside or outside, online or offline, the Heartwood Path helps you overcome any breaches in your well-being that hinder increasing your happiness and the sustainability of the natural environment.

HumaNatureConnect Activity Protocols

The full meaning of each protocol is revealed as you progress, waypoint by waypoint.

Start-up Protocol

- Read The Text — Use your literary sense, your mind sense, and your reason sense to move towards happiness and sustainability by reading the Heartwood Path text but also go outdoors to the backyard or to the backwoods, where the higher levels of negative ions in the air will improve your mood and well-being.
- Attention Restoration —With a pen and journal in hand, go to a natural area that is attractive, has a variety of plants and animals, and is tranquil enough to leave room for reflection.
- Source — Spend time wandering without an agenda in nature or, if you don't have time to receive nature's magic in this way, follow the instructions in the text at each learning station.
- Attractive Natural Being — Once you are in a natural area (the wilder, the better), look to find a natural being that is attractive to you and remain near that being until the end of the activity.
- Appreciation And Gratitude — While communing with your chosen natural being, appreciate it as you inhale and show it gratitude as you exhale.
- Consent — Once you find an aspect of nature that is attractive to you continuously for at least ten seconds, think of your continued attraction as your consent to have a connection experience that will help you function optimally; receive information, guidance, and healing; and establish in your mind a more helpful egalitarian relationship with the natural being.
- The Natural Senses — Beyond seeing, hearing, and the three other commonly recognized senses, use as many of the fifty-four

Natural Senses as you see fit and prepare to document the ones that you use in your journal.

- Great Trustable Truth — Experience what is happening at the present moment in nature, paying particular attention to the role of both beauty and balance; remember that the impressions you form about attractive natural beings and natural areas, coming from your experiencing of them in the Now, are trustable; and recognize that the natural processes and features witnessed are a source of special, substantial, and irreplaceable truthfulness about both nature and yourself.

- Recall — Place the great trustable truth and any other insights that you discover in a mental lock-box so you can later record them in your journal.

Follow-up Protocol

- Date—Write down the date of your outdoor nature-communing experience.

- Activity—Write down the waypoint title and number each time each you do an activity.

- Location—Write down the location of your outdoor nature-communing experience.

- Natural Being Indicator—Draw a picture or write down in your journal a nameless way to remember your chosen attractive Natural Being; for example, call it your "____ ____ Connection Experience."

- The Natural Senses Used—Write down all of the Natural Senses you used for this activity.

- General Description —Write a general description of how you did the activity and what happened.

- Freeform — Write, in freeform, what you found attractive about your natural being.

- Three Qualities — Write down three qualities you found attractive about your natural being.

- Three Learnings — Write down three things you learned from this activity.
- Self-esteem & Trust — Write down how, if at all, this activity changed your self-esteem or trustfulness of NNIAAL (Nameless-ness, Now, Intelligence, Alive, Attraction, and Love).
- Changes To Self — Write down what aspects of your Self, if any, were changed by this activity.
- Honor Yourself — Praise yourself and your commitment to making another stop along the Heartwood Path good for yourself and the world.
- I'm A Person Who. . . — Write down three different so-called "G/G Statements" using the following format: "This connection experience tells me that I am a person who_____."
- Feelings If Activity Taken — Write down a sentence about how you would feel if you lost your ability to experience this connection.
- Nature Compared To Self — Create a sentence that reads: "I love this (insert words that identify the attractive natural being) because it is (insert words that refer to the qualities you like about the natural being); then, create a parallel sentence that reads: "I love (insert the word "myself") because I am (insert the same qualities as before)."
- Ride The Green Wave — Determine whether you understand and agree with **all** of the Ten Green Wave Validation Statements.
- Name Your Discomforts — Make a list of aspects of your negative emotional residue, if any, that lifted simply by being in nature.
- Goethean Phenomenology — Write down impressions after observing a natural being over time and indicate the starting and ending dates for the observation.
- Defocalization — Write down impressions after using good blurry vision to observe a natural setting.
- Integral Immersion — Improve your journal writing by addressing what is, what could be, and what ought to be.

- Love Letter — Write a letter of gratitude to a natural being and another love letter from a natural being.
- Two-word Summary — Write down two words that summarize your response to this activity.

Heartwood Path Exchange

- Comment — Post your impressions and photos in the Comments section of this waypoint—the place for on-going discussion regarding this waypoint.
- Join — Engage with others in a Heartwood Path course or salon.
- Create — Start your own Heartwood Path salon that meets regularly online, by phone, or in person.
- Talk — Share your impressions with trusted family members and friends.
- Network — Post your impressions and photos on our EartHeart Networking Forum.
- Post — To see what conversations you can ignite, upload on social media your photos and impressions about anything pertaining to your journey down the Heartwood Path.
- Connect — Follow our account on Instagram, Like our Page on Facebook, Subscribe to our Channel on YouTube, and use hashtags such as "#heartwoodpath", "#eartHeart", and "#waypoint(insert book)(insert waypoint number) i.e."#waypointecos5").

Dreaming Time Protocols

The full meaning of each protocol is revealed as you progress, waypoint by waypoint.

Before Dreaming Protocol

- Perform A Reality Check — At least daily, during your waking hours determine whether you are dreaming as a way to develop lucid dreaming skills.
- Dream Prep — Prepare yourself for productive dreaming by de-cluttering your mind before sleeping.
- Set An Intention — Repeat the affirmation: "I remember my dream."
- Incubate A Dream — Decide what lucid dream you are going to have by using visualization.
- Journal Ready — Prepare to record your dream impressions by placing your journal so that you can make initial recordings in it without changing your dreamtime sleeping position.

Dreaming Protocol

- Remember This — Look to your dreams to tell you what you need to remember.
- Open To Dream — Be receptive, fluid, interactive, and grounded as you dream.
- Lucid Dreaming — Be aware that you are dreaming and have an impact on what happens in the dream.
- Wake-Back-To-Bed — Wake up after six hours of sleep, staying awake for twenty minutes, then go back to sleep.
- Look For Dream Signs — Stay on the lookout for recurring elements of your dreams that let you know you are dreaming.

- Stabilize Your Dreams — Prolong your lucidity by making your dreams stable like the real world.
- Shape-shifters — Watch characters that change in your dream to see into the possibilities of your own transformation.
- World Dreams — Consider that your dreams may be tapping into the dreams of your chosen attractive natural beings or the wholeness of Nature.

After Dreaming Protocol

- First Off — Recall your dream by staying in your sleeping position as you make your first attempt to remember your dream.
- Book Of Dreams — Create an entry in your dream journal using the following linguistic tools: 1) talking in the present tense, 2) using verbs ending in "ing," 3) removing articles such as "an" or "the," and 4) using capital letters when naming the Dream Characters—which can be any notable people, places, or things that show up in your dream.
- Title — Give your dream a memorable title.
- Date — Write down the date of your dream.
- Description — Write down a short, general summary of your dream.
- Mood — Write down how the dream affected your mood upon waking.
- Life Event Affecting Dream — Write down any events in your life that may have influenced your dream.
- Dream Characters — List all remembered notable "actors" in your dream, whether they are people, places, or things.
- Setting — Describe the location of your dream.
- Statement Of Problem — Write down the complication, challenge, predicament, situation, obstacle, plight, quandary, or misadventure presented in your dream.

- Culmination Or Response To The Problem — Describe what you or another Dream Character did in your dream to respond to the problem presented in the dream.
- Conclusion — Describe how your dream ended.
- Beings Revealed —Write down how your dream seemed to be, if at all, linked in some way to your chosen attractive natural beings.
- Freud's Approach — Associate the actions of your Dream Characters with latent, infantile, repressed, or sexual drives.
- Jung's Approach — Amplify your Dream Characters into Archetypes that are global in scale, symbolic, pervasive, positive, and helpful.
- Hillman's Approach — Recognize your Dream Characters as animated, living beings by honoring their presence, place, and body.
- Right Information — Ask yourself the two main questions for Dream Tending: "Who is visiting now?" And "What is happening here?"
- The Richest Treasures — Do not force narrow interpretations upon the natural being impressions that reappear in your dream by condensing them into limited signs when it is more fruitful to simply engage with them as living beings that reside in your dream, possibly with infinite symbolic value.
- Dream Keywords — Write down single words that seem to solidify what you are thinking about your dream and then process these words using association, amplification, and animation.
- Privacy — Store your dream journal in a safe place and, where appropriate, share your dream with others.

Dream Council Protocol

- Create Dream Figures — Periodically create physical representations of select Dream Characters using natural materials, give them some form of identification, and gather them together.
- Pick Dream Council Members — Designate eight to fifteen of your most revered Dream Figures to serve on your Dream Council, which is your most honored dream advisory group.
- Convene A Dream Council Meeting — Whenever you desire, ceremoniously hold conversations with the Dream Figures that make up your Dream Council and write down any guidance you receive.
- Listen Deeply — If what you come across during your occasional interactions with Dream Figures does not make sense to you, write down your impressions so you can consider them at another time (when more experience can be brought to bear).

Natural Senses

The Radiation Senses

- Sense of light and sight, including polarized light.
- Sense of seeing without eyes such as heliotropism or the sun sense of plants.
- Sense of color.
- Sense of moods and identities attached to colors.
- Sense of awareness of one's own visibility or invisibility and consequent camouflaging.
- Sensitivity to radiation other than visible light including radio waves, X rays, etc.
- Sense of temperature and temperature change.
- Sense of season including ability to insulate, hibernate, and winter sleep.
- Electromagnetic sense and polarity which includes the ability to generate current (as in the nervous system and brain waves) or other energies.

The Feeling Senses

- Hearing including resonance, vibrations, sonar, and ultrasonic frequencies.
- Awareness of pressure, particularly underground, underwater, and to wind and air.
- Sensitivity to gravity.
- The sense of excretion for waste elimination and protection from enemies.
- Feel, particularly touch on the skin.
- Sense of weight, gravity, and balance.
- Space or proximity sense.

- Coriolis sense or awareness of effects of the rotation of the Earth.
- Sense of motion, body movement sensations, and sense of mobility.

The Chemical Senses

- Smell with and beyond the nose.
- Taste with and beyond the tongue.
- Appetite or hunger for food, water, and air.
- Hunting, killing, or food obtaining urges.
- Humidity sense including thirst, evaporation control and the acumen to find water or evade a flood.
- Hormonal sense, as to pheromones and other chemical stimuli.

The Mental Senses

- Pain, external and internal.
- Mental or spiritual distress.
- Sense of fear, dread of injury, death or attack.
- Procreative urges including sex awareness, courting, love, mating, paternity and raising young.
- Sense of play, sport, humor, pleasure, and laughter.
- Sense of physical place, navigation senses including detailed awareness of land and seascapes, of the positions of the sun, moon, and stars.
- Sense of time.
- Sense of electromagnetic fields.
- Sense of weather changes.
- Sense of emotional place, of community, belonging, support, trust, and thankfulness.
- Sense of self including friendship, companionship, and power.
- Domineering and territorial sense.

- Colonizing sense including compassion and receptive awareness of one's fellow creatures, sometimes to the degree of being absorbed into a superorganism.
- Horticultural sense and the ability to cultivate crops, as is done by ants that grow fungus, by fungus who farm algae, or birds that leave food to attract their prey.
- Language and articulation sense, used to express feelings and convey information in every medium from the bees' dance to human literature.
- Sense of humility, appreciation, and ethics.
- Senses of form and design.
- Sense of reason, including memory and the capacity for logic and science.
- Sense of mind and consciousness.
- Intuition or subconscious deduction.
- Aesthetic sense, including creativity and appreciation of beauty, music, literature, form, design, and drama.
- Psychic capacity such as foreknowledge, clairvoyance, clairaudience, psychokinesis, astral projection, possibly certain animal instincts, and plant sensitivities.
- Sense of biological and astral time, awareness of past, present, and future events.
- The capacity to hypnotize other creatures.
- Relaxation and sleep including dreaming, meditation, and brain wave awareness.
- Sense of pupation including cocoon building and metamorphosis.
- Sense of excessive stress and capitulation.
- Sense of survival by joining a more established organism.
- Spiritual sense, including conscience, capacity for sublime love, ecstasy, a sense of sin, profound sorrow, and sacrifice.
- Sense of homeostatic unity, of natural attraction aliveness as the singular essence-diversity attraction dance of all our other senses (NNIAAL). (Cohen, website: http://www.ecopsych.com/insight53senses.html).

Acknowledgments

I would like to thank everyone who helped me blaze the trail that has become the Heartwood Path. Initially, David Brower got me going, after asking me to "write a piece" to combat "burnout" in environmentalists. Roger Fritz helped me with my conversion from corporate executive to author. Paula Badger was a good listener on our frequent walks. Michael J. Cohen helped me to add nature's intelligence to the methodology. "Forest Maiden" Sylvia Shelton served as my "muse"—always with humor, tenderness, intelligence, and love. I started out thinking I was writing traditional books. My daughter Courtney Logue converted my text into an interactive website. Without her efforts—in editing, in creating the format, and in providing important encouragement—there would not be a Heartwood Path. To these people, and many more, I am forever grateful.

About The Author

Pierce has spent nearly his whole life working to protect the environment. After decades of work as a professional environmentalist, Pierce concluded that a new approach—one focused on the environmentalist and not just the environment—was needed.

When famed conservationist David Brower asked him to write "a piece" to show environmentalists how to persevere, the result was a series of books and courses that are good for both environmentalists and anyone seeking happiness and the preservation of nature. This series—the Heartwood Path—helps people to develop spiritually, helps people discover the benefits of communing with nature, and helps people find the abundant, abiding, and authentic happiness that comes from helping others, including natural beings.

Pierce formed his first environmental group—a tree planting club—when he was nine. After that, he was president of both his high school and college environmental organizations. After a few years as a professional river conservationist, he was hired by Brower to be the Midwest Representative of Friends of the Earth. Pierce has led numerous conservation groups, including the Illinois Chapter of the Sierra Club. He was a governor-appointed member of the Illinois Nature Preserves Commission.

He has a Bachelor's Degree in environmental science, a Master's Degree in political science, and Master's Degree in social work. When he was not working to protect the environment or guiding people down the Heartwood Path, Pierce—a qualified life coach and mental health practitioner—served those who needed his care—including those who are young, aged, mentally ill, or mentally disabled.

Currently working on his PH.D in eco-psychology, Pierce divides his time between Santa Barbara, California and St. Louis, Missouri. He is a professional drummer, an avid canoeist, and a photographer. He loves to walk in nature. He has two grown daughters (one, the mother of his two granddaughters, in Missouri and another one somewhere on a sailboat that is often close to Santa Barbara).

Heartwood Path One-On-One Guidance

(30 minute or 60 minute sessions)

Don Pierce will move you to an extraordinary awakening of personal happiness and ecological sustainability.

"Make a difference, happily."

To do so, go down the Heartwood Path under the skilled guidance of its creator, Don Pierce. Don's education and experience will help you turn your advocacy into a source of abiding, abundant, and authentic happiness. His years as an active environmentalist will enable him to teach you how to become both happy and effective in your own causes. His years as a social worker will help you fit better into your own environment. His experience as a life coach will help you set your own agenda towards meeting your goals. His years as a mental health practitioner will enable him to help you achieve the integrity that comes when your inner world enables you to be "glad" as you endeavor to make the outer world "green." By signing up for guidance, you will have Don at your side to answer questions, provide encouragement, and avoid wrong turns.

In productive and easy-to-afford steps, Guidance moves you to an extraordinary awakening of personal happiness and ecological sustainability. Guidance moves you beyond a common state of separation to an extraordinary awakening of oneness that is experienced as personal happiness, ecological sustainability, and spiritual maturity.

Sessions, which are purchased in thirty minute and one hour segments, occur online, on the phone, or in person with Heartwood Path creator Don Pierce. Elements of Heartwood Path guidance include:

- making checklists of topics or actionable items
- establishing guidelines
- setting and reviewing deadlines
- explaining and reviewing practices
- responding and questioning journal entries
- instructing
- providing individualized templates of models
- supporting individuals and teams in the field
- defining terminology and elaborating on Heartwood Path text
- mentoring on related subjects and
- assistance in interpreting signs and symbols.

Complementary Guidance sessions are available when you sign up for any Heartwood Path course.

Further Action

REVIEWS APPRECIATED AND OTHER HEARTWOOD PATH BOOKS

If you enjoyed reading **Ecos**, please leave a review on Amazon. I would appreciate any comments you may wish to share. Positive reviews go a long way in spreading our important message.

Future books are on the way. Watch for the release of **Ethos**, on valued personal traits and **Volitos**, on going into action.

All Heartwood Path books are available on Amazon, including **Kosmos**, the Overture; **Logos**, which presents universal principles aimed at helping you avoid swimming upstream in life; and **Egos**, on developing, using, and protecting your uniqueness. Together, Heartwood Path books provide important personal preparations necessary for the creation of happiness and a regenerated environment.

In recognition for all that you do along the Heartwood Path, I say "thank you" and "Great Work!"